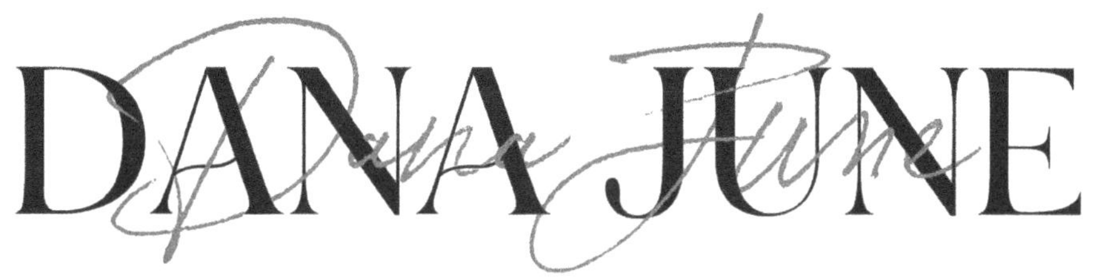

A LEAP INTO THE UNKNOWN

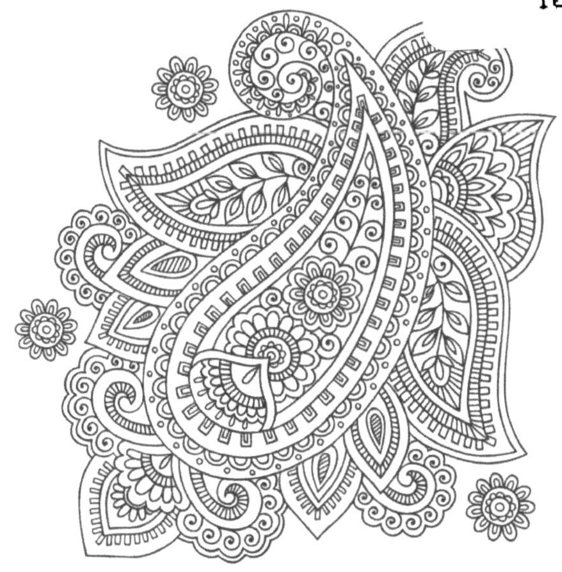

DANA MCCOWN

ISBN 978-0-6486579-4-1

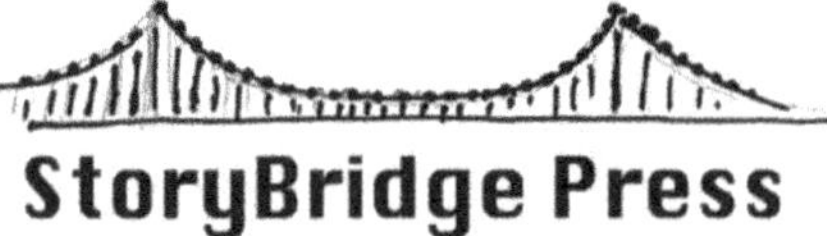

Brisbane, Queensland, Australia
2021

Historic photos from family collections unless otherwise credited.

Cover design by Samuel J McCown

Table of Contents

Table of Contents continued

01

My Story

IN THE BEGINNING...

Life began for me as the only child of June and John Spicer. The couple waited to start a family until they were 36 and 40 years of age due to the Great Depression. However they both already had a late start into marriage. June was the youngest of a big Scandinavian family of seven children with four bossy and protective brothers. Her parents died when June was in her twenties and the boys took over. Whenever she brought a prospective boyfriend home, they quickly found fault and discouraged the relationship.

When June was 31 years old she went to a party one night with the current boyfriend, but met John there and accepted his offer to take her home. That was the start of a whirlwind courtship that lasted for five weeks. June took John around to meet all the relatives in the evenings. Dad told me that he would be offered coffee everywhere, having had so many cups he was awake most of the nights. After June's past experience with her over-protective brothers, they decided to elope. They drove south from Milwaukee, finding a church minister to conduct

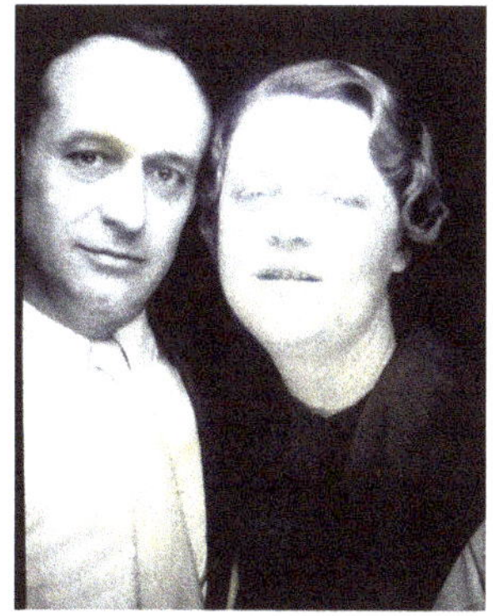

Photobooth pix

an official ceremony in Waukegan, then going on to honeymoon in Chicago, Illinois. June came home with a beautiful diamond ring. She had told her two sisters beforehand of their plans and the brothers soon accepted the *fait accompli*, sending out an official engraved wedding announcement. June told me in later years that she never would have eloped if her dear Norwegian mother had still been alive.

Despite the fact that John had his own business, he had boarded at a private home, which was not unusual in those days. But that helped him save a nice little nest egg to setup housekeeping with June. So they looked around and found an apartment in Milwaukee. June got busy finding furniture, Wedgewood china, and an elaborate sterling silver cutlery set, finally indulging in a baby grand piano. She had great taste and many of her purchases are still in the family today. Well, not the Wedgewood which met a sticky end. Several years later they were having a dinner party and mother liked to be organised having everything set up well ahead. The set of Wedgewood was on a drop-leaf table. Dad was doing something at the fireplace and happened to bump the drop-leaf in a way that dislodged it and the china fell into the brick hearth of the fireplace and smashed. Somehow it was not possible to replace the broken dinner plates; perhaps those designs were destroyed with the bombing in England. All that was left were some demi-tasse cups and saucers.

Sometime during the next year or two there was a visitor from Sweden. It was Aunt Sigrid Linde, a sister of June's father, Per Wilhelm Lillydahl, who had left his family homeland nearly 50 years before. Sigrid had travelled to the USA initially to visit her son who was a landscape architect living in New England, and she wanted for the first time to meet her brother's family as well. She also had friends who had migrated to America. One morning she got up dressed to go out, saying she wanted to visit her old friend now living in Minnesota. She planned to be home for lunch. However she had no idea of distances and had to re-evaluate the situation. Sigrid had brought gifts for the family of large tablecloths she had woven herself. There was one for John and June, the recently married couple and

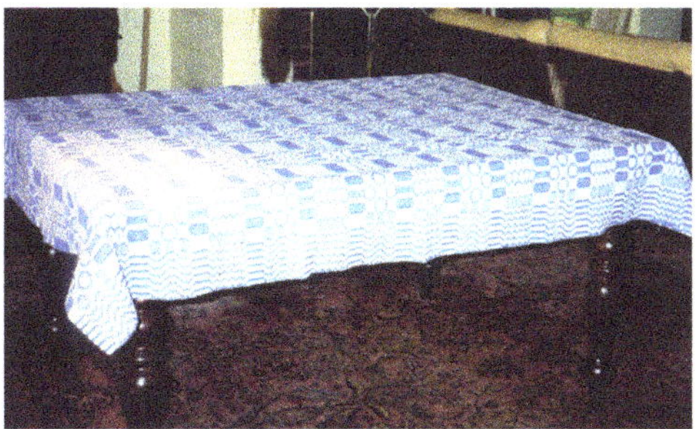

Sigrid's handwoven tablecloth

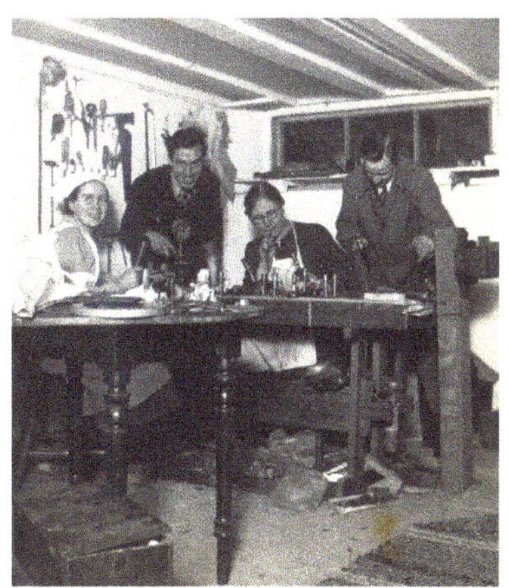

Sigrid third from left

one for the family home where the bachelor brothers still lived together. The cloths were woven in a traditional Swedish design out of fine blue cotton and white linen that Sigrid had spun herself from flax grown in her garden. From that day on, June used that tablecloth for very special family events.

Sigrid also brought metal candlesticks and coasters she had fashioned herself in her home studio. She sent letters to June upon returning to Sweden, telling of filigree jewellery classes she was attending and wishing that June were there to go with her and experience the fun. She was a talented artisan in numerous areas. Her sister Emma was an oil painter and my mother acquired one of her canvases painted of a scene along the Baltic Sea where they lived. Generations of the family had been full of various artisans.

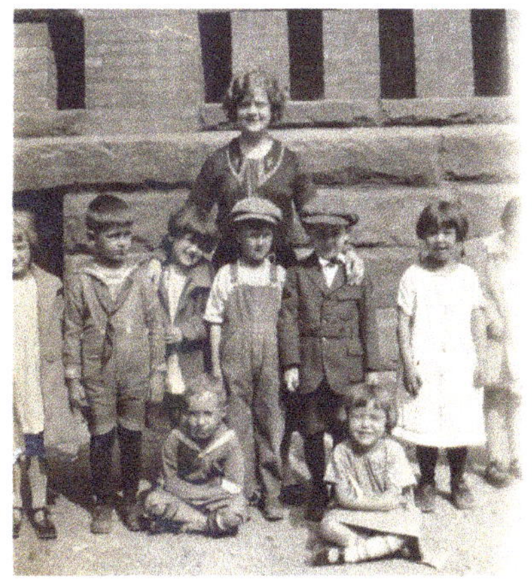

June with her Kindergarten class

June had trained as a pre-school teacher and taught kindergarten. John had attended technical college in Arkansas where the family had moved from Illinois, taking up and dabbling in various things before joining the Air Force in 1919. After being discharged, he joined the Merchant Marines and travelled the world. When settling down in Milwaukee, he started several different businesses. One was a printery that June helped him run. Then he set up a trade school offering courses in bricklaying as well as building homes. He liked to be self-employed.

As the Great Depression ended and the economy was recovering, it finally seemed a good time to start a family and I was born in 1936. My christening was planned as a family affair as Mom's cousin Hal Haug was an Anglican priest and performed the ceremony. As Godmother, an old friend, Dodo Shepherd had been chosen along with young Suzanne Pasteur, my first cousin. Although when asked about it in recent years, Sue has no recollection of taking the responsibility as she was only a teenager.

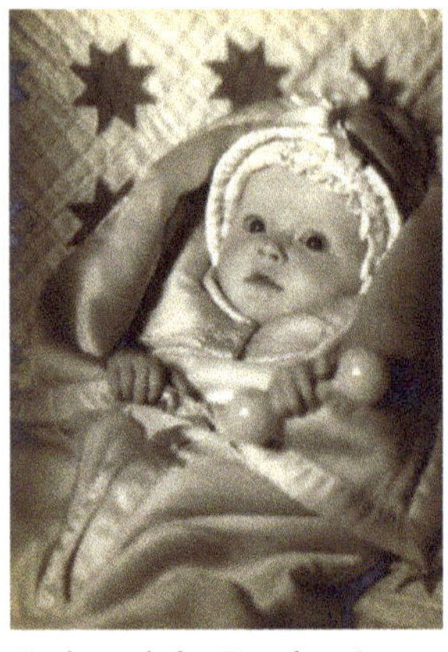

Quilt made by Grandma Spicer

Sometime after I was born, Dad decided to take a job with a greater opportunity. But it involved travelling through the eastern states setting up distributorships for a scaffolding company. He had gone on a reconnaissance trip back east, and wired June to say they should take the opportunity, and asked her to sell all the printing equipment. June liked the idea of adventure and so they put furniture in storage, packed the car with clothes and me as an 18-month-old. I have lots of photographs and movies of those days in Boston, Philadelphia, Atlantic City, and New Jersey and various New York cities. They would set up in each place for about three months and then start the circuit again. Eventually they worked their way to Pittsburgh, Pennsylvania where Dad was offered a job that was tempting, as I was getting to the age of starting school. It was wartime and all salaries were frozen without room to move ahead. So he subsequently took a government job as a building appraiser, and on the job he learned many skills and took advanced courses. Meanwhile June went back to teaching kindergarten where she used her artistic and musical skill.

SETTLING IN PITTSBURGH

Our first home was a rental in Mt. Lebanon. I was four years old and met the next-door neighbour, Mary Gail McConnell who was also four years old. Our first encounter was memorable to me because she and a friend had been playing small cubbies with cardboard cartons, which they encouraged me to crawl inside. But then, they sat on the box, barring the exits and entrapping me, with much giggling on their part. It left quite an impression on me, as I still remember it vividly after nearly 80 years.

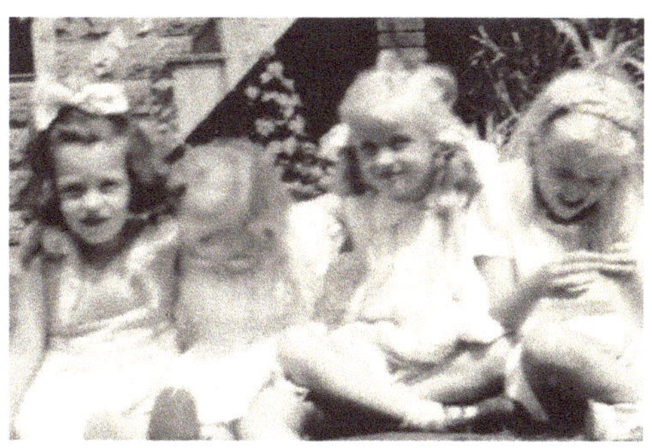

Mary Gail left and Dana third from left

Then there were the O'Brien kids on the same street. I was out playing when Peter O'Brien came chasing me with a toy gun. I ran home, but tripped on the curb and cut open my chin. My mother was not impressed. Well, Mary Gail and I walked to Lincoln school where we attended four year-old kindy. The incident with the cardboard box didn't seem to end our friendship as 19 years later she was maid of honour at my wedding.

My parents then went looking for a house to buy. As they liked the neighbourhood around Lincoln School and the frequent buses that ran into the city for Dad to go to work, they found something close by. The house we bought had numerous levels, as it was built on the side of a hill. On the street level, were the front yard, porch and normal ground floor rooms, where Mom immediately added her artistic flair of colour. The lounge she painted emerald green with the brick fireplace painted white. The dining room was painted a warm glowing rose. These were colours no one else that I knew used. Other parents had beige decor.

The basement was the full width of the house, divided into the furnace room and then the rest, which held the laundry and a back porch. This level was still above ground at the back, so there was another room underneath. It was dark and scary. Perhaps it was basic space with only an earth floor. But my friends and I thought there could be hidden bodies back in the dark recesses if we would only be brave enough to look. Outside our house was a school crossing and the retired policeman, Mr Davidson, was there twice a day, sometimes using our porch if it was a rainy day. My friends and I tried to get him to look under the house for any sinister-looking possibilities.

In the backyard was a great apple tree, from which my Mom made the world's best apple pies. She actually could make any kind of wonderful pie. And under the tree grew Lily of the Valley. This was like a special sign for us, as my mother's maiden name was Lillydahl. The name had been Americanised when my grandfather came from Solvesborg, Sweden in about 1882. It had been changed from Lilljedahl and when translated to English meant valley of lilies. His brother Carl, who migrated separately and settled in Texas, didn't change the spelling of his name but changed his first name to Charles. Their father owned the tannery and a ship building concern in Sweden. However their vessel, sailing to Argentina to pick up a shipload of hides for the factory, sank in a storm, and was not insured. So the young men decided to seek their fortune in the new world.

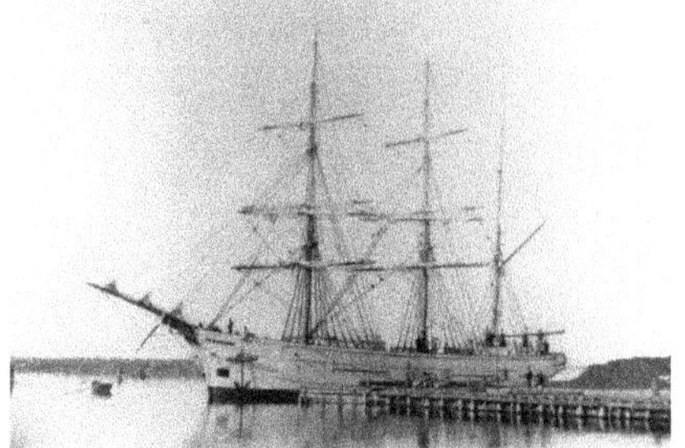

Great Grandpa Lillydahl's ship

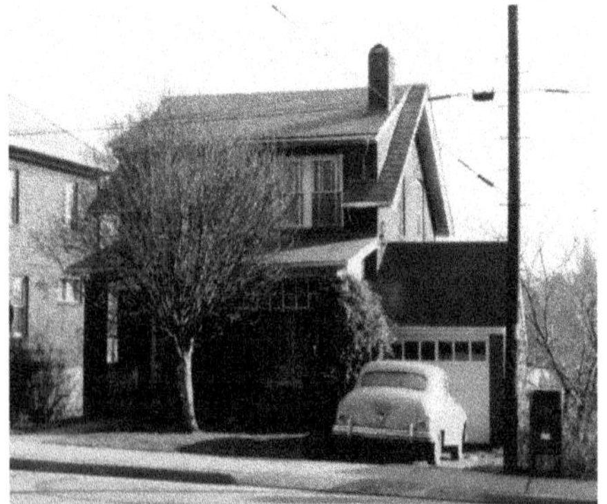

Our first home with the garage Dad built

In the front yard of our new home, mother planted a tree and named it "Faith Hope and Charity". My father used his building skills and added a garage onto the side of the building. As we were on that slope, the garage was on the street level, with an additional room underneath that became a garden shed. At one time an opossum moved in and had a batch of baby opossums, which was of great interest to the neighbourhood children.

There was also a vacant allotment beside the garage, where I asked Dad to build a swimming pool. Somehow he never said no, but that pool never materialised. But Dad did grow some vegetables there during the war. Of course the land did not belong to us. Eventually someone built a house there, after we had moved on to another house down the street.

Before long, Mary Gail's parents moved to a house down the street from us. But my mother was not so keen on the relationship remembering how I had been trapped in the cardboard box and tried to arrange with the school for us to be in separate classes. But Mary Gail's mother discovered this on the first day of grade one, and made a fuss until the Principal put us back together.

There were other children on the street that we played with. Nancy Archer was also an only child but a bit younger than us. Each of us at that time had a pet turtle. Turtle ownership was like a fad going around at the time. You could buy them at the dime store and they had paint with decal designs on their back. They were fed on lettuce leaves and bits of mince meat or a turtle food bought in a tin. On occasions we would have a turtle birthday party and take along our turtles. One time I came home from school planning to attend the turtle birthday party down the street to find no one home. I did not have a key. I tried the doors on different levels with no luck. So I actually broke a window to the cellar and climbed in, got Sammy the turtle and went to the party. I knew my Dad was handy and could fix anything. Luckily the door at the top of the cellar stairs up to the kitchen was not locked. I can't remember the reaction when I got home, so it couldn't have been too bad.

Susie Booth and her little sister were some of the other kids around. Barbara Buhrig lived there too. Our mothers were great mates and although she was the same age, she was much too grownup to play with us.

I loved bike riding and set about to earn money to buy my first bike when I was about 10. There were several projects I had. Each Christmas time, I went around the neighbourhood streets knocking on doors to show a range of Christmas cards they could order with their name printed inside. I had a brochure showing the range of cards as well as fonts and greetings that could be chosen. The next little business I had was making bird jewellery out of kits that were available with shiny metallic material. I tried this line at church with the ladies auxiliary and got some orders. I wonder what ever happened to my line of birds with long flowing tails? I could make a broach as well as earrings. Well I did earn enough for a brand new bike and loved riding off into the countryside in the summer holidays. No, I didn't have a helmet or a mobile phone. But I did need to be home for dinner. No one seemed to think it dangerous or even asked me where I had been.

I also loved the Saturday morning movies and would look around the house in all the drawers and pockets seeing if I could find 14 cents, which was the price of the show at the ticket office. I did have an allowance of 25 cents a week, so could have had some left from that. There was Shirley Temple, Andy Rooney and Judy Garland in the best movies ever. The shorts with Tarzan were rather good too. Later the price increased to 17 cents.

When I was younger my best plan for summer days was walking to the Municipal Swimming Pool, a distance of about two kilometers, and enjoying the water. Previously I had taken swimming lessons, so was considered perfectly safe. I seem to remember my hair turning green in the summer from the chlorine. As an only child, I was used to keeping my own company. And friends like Mary Gail didn't wander off on their own as I did. She wasn't allowed to go swimming during the heat of the day, as her skin burned badly, where as I tanned. She was driven there by her mother for a short time later in the afternoon and had to wear a shirt to cover her skin.

I continued through all the grades at Lincoln School, enjoying most of all the art activities. We had specialists come on occasion, both for art and music. But in grade five, my favourite teacher, Miss Dido, was excellent in art and included it in many activities. She also had a supply of special art materials that gave lovely effects if you knew how to use them.

I joined the Brownies and later the Girl Guides. When I was seven years old, I was signed up to go to Camp Redwing in Butler County. We lived in tents that had wooden floors and cot beds and were each big enough for four campers. One problem my mother was worried about was my tendency to sleepwalk. So the arrangement was that I had to have my leg tied to the bunk each night.

But one day I was called to the office by the camp counselor. It turned out that there had been an announcement on the radio that someone at the camp had been taken to hospital with Polio, the dreaded virus that crippled thousands of children and adults. My mother and father had driven the 50 miles from Pittsburgh to Butler County where they insisted on seeing me. The Director told them that I was fine but no camper was allowed to see their parents as it upset the settling down to life at camp. My mother told them that she and dad would not leave until they saw that I was well. And so I got a brief visit from home. I am still surprised that if there had actually been a case of Polio at camp, that everyone would not have been sent home. Looking at statistics, the 40s and 50s were times of real epidemics during summer. Then in 1954 the first vaccine developed by Jonas Salk, working at the University of Pittsburgh, was widely administered.

Another activity I had during primary school was singing in the youth choir of the Methodist Church we attended. We had rehearsal every Thursday after school. However the youth choir only performed on special Sundays. I remember some of the older girls arrived to rehearsal having bought dill pickles from the deli across the street as an after school snack. I had never seen anyone munching on a large pickle as if it were an apple or carrot. At that age the idea didn't appeal to me. When we did sing for the congregation, we wore large black robes, which concealed anything else we might have worn underneath and felt rather important.

There were opportunities to learn an instrument by the time we got to fourth grade and I was signed up to learn the violin with an instrument loaned from the school. The lessons were together with another student. I was waiting patiently while the other student was going through her exercise with the teacher. The room had a window opening internally to a corridor that went to the furnace room where the janitor was doing something quite interesting. As I was watching him, suddenly I was picked up by the hair and carried to the other side of the room by the music teacher who said I was not paying attention to him. That was the end of my violin experience. But my mother hadn't given up on me yet as she was so musical and couldn't believe a child of hers wouldn't have talent. Later we tried the flute in Junior High, but it made me dizzy when I played and gave it up.

However she hadn't given up on me with another of her interests, which was acting. I took drama lessons from Mrs Lawrence who organised opportunities for her students to provide entertainment for various group functions. I performed monologues, some of which were serious and emotional and others were comical. I rather enjoyed performance. My mother had given dramatic book reading and programs for many years and was registered with an agency.

After I had been married and moved away, she had actually had a major role in a TV drama that was shown around the world. Even the Swedish relatives contacted her and said they had seen her in the film. Unfortunately I could never find it and in later years contacting the TV studio was told they no longer had the footage. However I have a copy of the Pittsburg Press critique of the production stating that June Spicer, is a non-professional who fairly steals the show in her role.

Roller-skating was a big social activity at an indoor rink with lively music and special items like partner's events and Congo lines. There may have even been one where we had to skate backwards.

Birthday parties were sometimes held there. Some skaters could do fancy dance steps but most of us would do well just to stay upright and stay out of other peoples way. Our sixth grade class had an outing to the rink once and I spent hours trying to decorate a blouse to wear there with appliqued ribbons and designs. In the end, my mother discouraged me from wearing it, as my sewing skills were rudimentary. Some kids had proper costumes with short flaired skirts.

Lincoln School went from kindergarten, through to grade 6. The students moved on then to Melon Junior High School, which covered grades 7, 8 and 9. It was quite a change, as we no longer had one teacher all day, teaching the various subjects. Now we would have a homeroom to report to, but travel around the school to other classrooms according to a schedule. And in addition, we were mixed in with students from all over the district, so we met many new people. There were new subjects like civics and home economics including cooking and sewing. There was a large gym with a trained physical education teacher. We had to bring fresh clothing for gym each week and keep it in our locker, which could be a challenge each week to stay out of trouble with the teacher, Mrs Root, a strict disciplinarian. As my mother had a job teaching, I was considered to be old enough to do my own ironing.

Toward the later years at primary school there had been some excitement on Valentine's Day, seeing whom we had received cards from. It could be surprising to see some especially grand cards sent from boys in other classes, not that they had ever paid any attention to us. There was starting to be some attention from the other sex in a limited sort of way. But at Junior High I had the attention of someone who hadn't worked out what girls like. Andy Millington had never spoken to me, but one day walking between classes, he came by and smashed his large pile of books over my head. Well it was one way to get my attention, but not with the best result. I carefully avoided him for the entire three years. But I never forgot about the incident. It did get my attention and made me think about people and relationships, shyness and insecurities later on.

The Methodist Church also had a summer camp for youth at a complex called Jumonville, down past Uniontown, Pennsylvania in lovely countryside. This was available to us when we started Junior High. There were classes in Methodist things like teaching us the evils of smoking and drinking. But there were so many fun things like square dancing, hiking, swimming and craft activities that I looked forward to this every summer.

VISITING DAD'S FAMILY

When I was about thirteen, our family decided to drive to Magnolia, Arkansas for Christmas to visit Dad's family. Originally they had lived in Dahlgren, Illinois, where most of the relatives were Scotch-Irish farmers.

In about 1915 there had been an opportunity to obtain land in Columbia County, Arkansas, and grandpa acquired 301.5 acres. I had only met my grandmother Spicer once when she visited us in Pittsburgh when I was about four years old. When I was seven we had word that Dad's father had died. He suffered from Tuberculosis (TB) and my parents had not been willing to visit while he was alive for fear of infection. Mother also had a brother-in-law with TB who been sent out west to a sanatorium for a rest cure, but had died from it back in 1910. At that time the only treatment for TB sufferers had been rest and fresh air. In late 1943 the discovery of Streptomycin was the first drug to be effective in the disease, this was developed shortly before grandpa Spicer had died. But now in 2020, TB still persists in many areas, as there are drug resistant strains. I was shocked to read that around the world, 1.5 million people still die each year from TB.

The trip to Arkansas was also the first time I had met Dad's three brothers and their families. There were cousins about my age. So it was a big family around the table for the festive Christmas dinner. Out in the garden of the family home was a large pecan tree. Through the years we were always sent a large box of pecans at Christmas, which mother roasted to make sure no germs came with them. What impressed me as we drove around town that week was the central town square of Magnolia, with large Magnolia trees all around. There was no question of how the town got its name.

BOARDING SCHOOL

When approaching senior high school years, my mother had investigated private girls schools for me and became interested in Winchester Thurston in Shadyside a district on the other side of Pittsburgh from Mt. Lebanon. The motto of the school was "Think also of the Comfort and the Rights of Others". As well, there was chapel every Friday morning with the Dean of the Episcopal Cathedral delivering the message. It seemed like a school with good principles. As mother had always been a Sunday school teacher wherever we lived, she may have hoped to keep me in good company. We were instilled with an attitude of service.

Because of the distance, she thought it would be better if I were a boarding student at "The House" on campus. There were only about 12 boarders with a house mother and Mrs Fanny Hovey who was headmistress and general manager of the school which her two great aunts had founded. Mother's brother Walter Lillydahl was a bachelor and considered to be patriarch of the family. He had an interest in his sibling's children and was known to support their education in various ways. So Uncle Walter helped send me to boarding school.

My interests at Winchester Thurston included the Northfield spiritual fellowship, art club and drama group. I took the part in several school productions. We didn't have Art as a school subject, but did have Art History taught by Miss Harris. It was an extremely good course thought to be of a university standard and gave me a good base when eventually majoring in Art at university. All subjects were demanding, as they were in small classes with about 10 students. One had to be alert and ready at any time to answer questions and enter discussions. And I had to learn good study habits. But lunchtime was always saved for playing Bridge, so we would hurry up and eat quickly.

I had three happy years there, but for the senior year decided to become a day student and travelled each day in a station wagon supplied by school, picking up six students along the way. It was a fun social time in the vehicle, which was driven by a university student. One of my friends, who started out as a boarder, was Sue (Zenade) White who also lived in Mt. Lebanon and she became a daygirl, joining me in the station wagon back and forth.

Towards the end of Senior year there was a tradition where each student's family invited the entire 44 classmates to a farewell party. So Sue's mother and mine got together and hosted a luncheon at a club they belonged to. For a favour at each place, Sue's mother had made a layered felt needle holder in the shape of a girl in a bonnet with lace and bead trim. I still have that favour which my mother had incorporated into a framed memory box with glass front holding small treasures from the family that had held special memories. Sue and I did eventually go on different paths but have kept in touch over the years, and she even came to visit us in Australia.

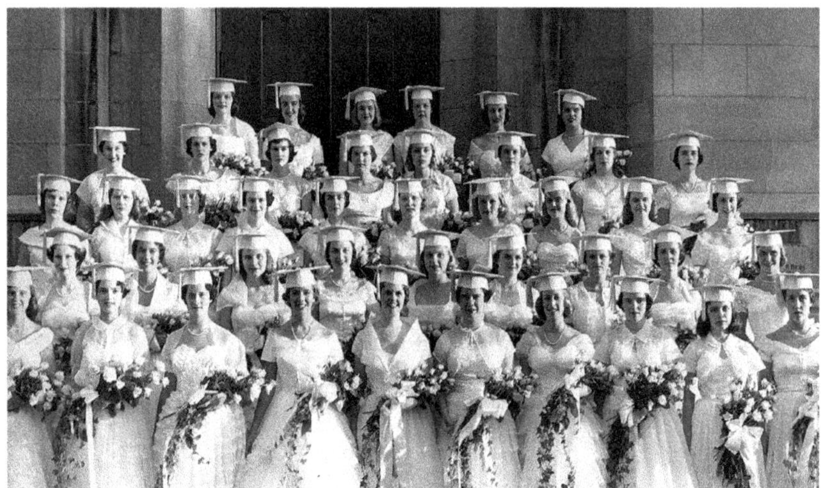

Dana third row from top and third from right side, Sue second row from top, and second left

During high school holidays, I became a volunteer at the Magee Hospital as a Candy Striper. That description was given because we wore a pinafore with a pink and white vertical striped design. The tasks given were varied, but often involved taking incoming patients to help find the ward assigned to them and other non-medical jobs. The hospital had a cafeteria that was known for their delicious cream pies so, after duty, I would reward myself with a treat.

UNIVERSITY OF LIFE

During our senior year, it was time to apply to universities. Although Pittsburgh had a multitude of tertiary institutions, I wanted to go further afield and experience campus life. My senior class had 44 students in total, all female. (However, in recent years the school has become co-ed.) Several other of my friends were applying to Centenary Junior College in New Jersey, which had been suggested by the head mistress. It seemed like an easy entry to tertiary study. So I followed that path.

Arriving at Hackettstown, New Jersey by car with my parents, I found I was assigned a room that held five students. We were all given the task of decorating our room for a competition. We had a huge room with high ceilings and a big bay window. I took the task upon myself and went shopping for fabric to make curtains for the five tall windows in the bay area. I bought cheap bright red fabric with enough extra to make cushion covers for the beds. It was pretty simple, but looked bright and cheerful. And we won! But my mother hearing of the win said *"It would be very nice to give the prize money to the Cancer Fund."* I admit I was rather deflated, but my conscience got the better of me.

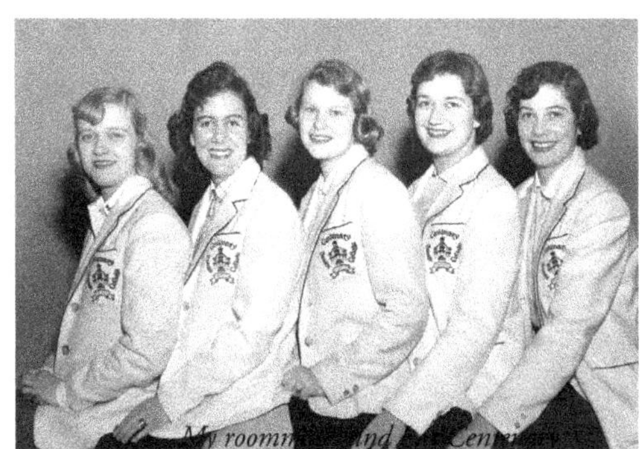

My roomm[illegible] and [illegible] Cen[illegible]

We had orientation week and functions with other colleges, and soon I was invited to week-end parties at Lafayette College, Princeton University, Rutgers University, Mt Pocono resort and New York City. There were days at the races, football games and fraternity club parties. I thought the class work was easy and so relaxed my way along, with barely enough time to do assignments. At mid-term my grades were among the top and I was one of five invited to the "President's Club" and selected as chair of that club. But of course by the end of the year the social life took its toll and I badly needed to pull my grades back up.

While I had been in New Jersey, my mother got the idea into her head that I might meet what she felt was a suitable range of young men, if I became a debutant and entered into society with the multitude of the season's balls, luncheons and garden parties. She had actually called her sister-in-law Alice in Milwaukee to find out how to go about organising this, as my cousin Grace had had her debut. When she called to tell me about it, I was aghast and said no, I was not interested. But the retort was that all had been organised and the dates were all in the social calendar. I did not have the backbone to stand up to her. Perhaps I may have had mixed feelings. But in fact I was somewhat embarrassed about it all. In the end, mother did the shopping and bought the ball dresses I would need. The summer of social events culminated in the Winter Cinderella Ball, with parents attending where we all had white gowns and long white gloves. For my own party, there was a dance at the Edgeworth Club in Sewickley with a wonderful band playing all the music I liked. My roommates from Centenary came, as did my uncles from Milwaukee and some older cousins. The biggest limitation to the evening was that my parents did not drink normally and did not want things out of control. Drinking age was 21 in Pennsylvania, so the only alcoholic drink provided was champagne punch which mother thought was refined. Eventually the young men

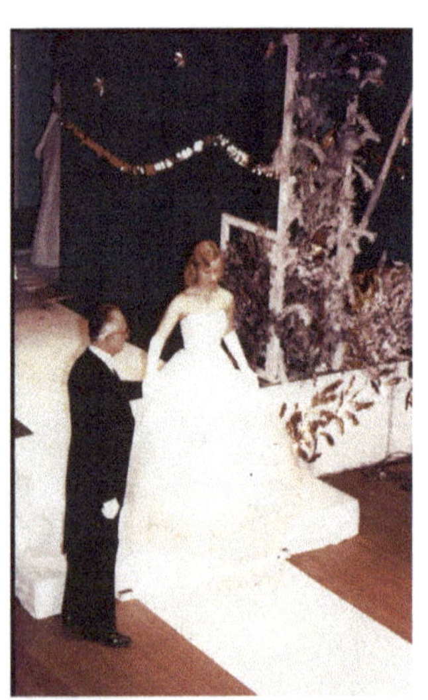

With Dad at the Cinderella Ball

decided to head off to another venue for a beer, but it was getting late and a good time to go home.

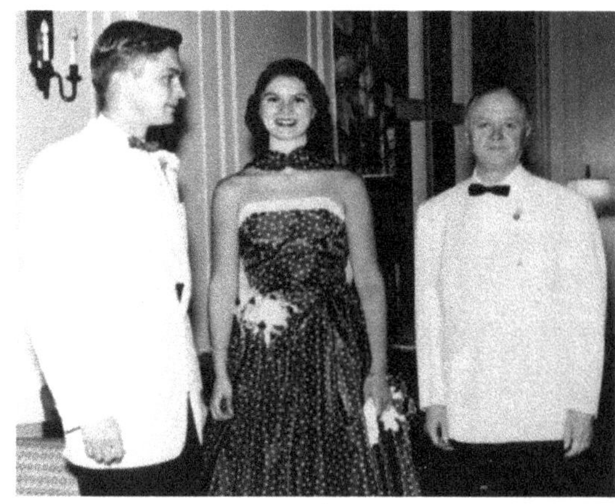
My Cousins and Uncle Walter at my dance

During the summer, my mother also had ideas that perhaps I needed new directions and suggested I might be interested in attending the University of Wisconsin, my birth state. In actual fact, it seemed like a lifeline to me, as I was re-evaluating my relationships and thought a change would be good. We went out to Milwaukee, visiting the relatives and then going to Madison where the main campus was located. Accommodation was going to be the most difficult thing to arrange, but my cousin Earl knew someone who actually owned the popular independent woman's residence called Ann Emery Hall, named after the first Dean of Women and was able to get me a place.

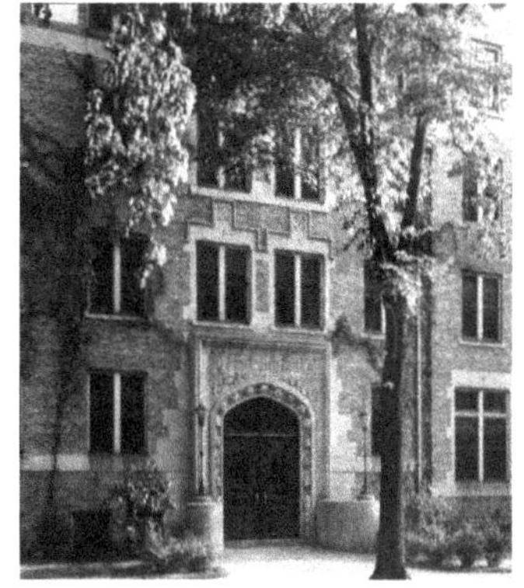
Ann Emery Hall

Having already taken first year courses, I was ready to choose my major. As I had had straight A in Math so far, I thought this was my strong suite. So I did enroll in Maths and started in Calculus, entering into the class after it had already begun. It was actually filled with all men who turned around and stared at me. But this was a type of math that was beyond my comprehension. Needless to say, I headed back to registration and formed a new plan. So Art turned out to be my strong suite and I enrolled in Art Education, having seen how well becoming a teacher worked for my mother. It was fun looking at the many offerings of units and making decisions. I have always loved the architecture of Frank Lloyd Wright and was surprised to see that one could take a course just on his work. Perhaps that is not so surprising as Frank Lloyd Wright had his architectural school and studio called Taliesin in Spring Green, Wisconsin. I had the opportunity to visit Taliesin while at Madison, and felt the beautiful relationship with buildings to earth and surroundings, enhanced by local stone and materials.

As for practical work, I studied 2-D design, 3-D design, sculpture, painting, jewellery, and even furniture design and construction. I took more courses in jewellery, as I liked the 3-D aspects and skills of learning to use materials in construction. But of course there were many units in educational principles, psychology, museum techniques, testing and student teaching. I have always enjoyed hands-on activities - creating things, so had found my niche.

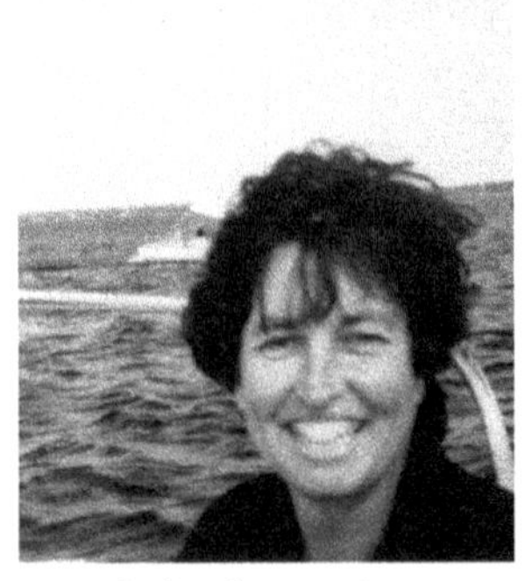
Carla, always sailing

In my second year there, a friend from Centenary arrived at Madison and looked me up. She had enrolled but couldn't get any dorm space. I had a single room, not very big but got the idea that they could put in a double decker bunk and so friend, Carla Kelly could move in. She grew up in Scarsdale, New York, but family had a summer home at Barnstable, Cape Cod, where she had been ocean sailing all her life. It didn't take Carla long to become captain of the Wisconsin University Sailing Team. My knowledge of sailing was non-existent, but Carla encouraged me to come along to the club and start learning the ropes. The club had various regattas scheduled around at other universities. On occasion she would invite me to go along and "crew" for her.

On one occasion we travelled to the University of Illinois to be in a regatta and were away the whole weekend. Eventually I took the test to try and get a license to skipper the boats myself on Lake Mendota along the side of our campus. Somehow I did pass the test. However my father came to visit from Pittsburgh soon afterward and I wanted to show him my new skill. I only had permission to use the dinghies. We climbed in and I started to steer the boat out from shore but a strong gust of wind pushed us back somewhat out of control. The loudspeaker came blaring on to tell me to get control. I think I took the boat back and ended my demonstration of skills for Dad, quite red-faced. Another time I visited my Uncle Bill and family who had a summer home in Oconomowoc, Wisconsin. Aunt Helen suggested I take the young cousins for a sail on the lake. I was very nervous and felt the responsibility of those young lives. So we had a very short sail.

I joined a sorority and moved into the Alpha Phi Sorority house making new friends. We have balls every year and other activities I am trying hard to remember. My aunt Helen had been an Alpha Phi as a student and had given a recommendation for me. It can be difficult to be asked to join without some connection. I roomed with Diane Roussey and was a bridesmaid in her wedding. I don't think I was a very good member, as I didn't stay long enough, having built up enough credits with some summer courses at the University of Pittsburgh to graduate early. But once an Alpha Phi, you are a member for life as alumni groups are around the world and they have a journal sent to all. I did get to participate in an alumni group in Pittsburgh when I had finished my degree.

FIRST JOB

As I was graduating in the middle of the university year, I was able to get a job teaching art for the second semester, starting later in January. I had applied to the Pittsburgh Department of Education and was offered a position at Wightman School in Squirrel Hill, on the other side of town nearer to Winchester Thurston. To get there each day I had to take a trolley into the city, change to another trolley out to Shadyside, and then take a bus to Squirrel Hill. Needless to say, I had to get up early to arrive in time. Wightman was a primary school covering grades one to six and had a dedicated art room, which also served as a homeroom for grade five. The arrangement was more like the Junior High I had attended with students moving to different teachers for subjects. And so each hour of the day, a different group of students from grade four through six would come to me for an art lesson.

I knew that it was important to be organised, especially on the first day. So I had all the materials prepared and distributed on the worktables. When the first class came in, I was not prepared for what happened next. They came filing in, jumped on the first table and leapt from one table to the next, throwing the art materials in the air. They said, *"We have gotten rid of the last four art teachers and we'll get rid of you, too."* I should have asked the Department of Education how there happened to be a vacant position in the middle of the year. I went home and cried all night.

The other teachers didn't seem to have any problem with these students. Why did it have to be me? I did not have any support from the Principal, Mr Shrock. He felt I had to be able to take control myself. I had to have a plan. So by the next morning I had put away all art materials and told the students we would now be having academic art. And we started with art history and continued for quite awhile.

The actual art room supplies were very meagre, in my opinion. I wanted to order coloured construction paper and numerous other papers and materials. There were large sheets of grey heavy card and a selection of powdered paints. And there were carving tools with rollers, but no lino to go with them. When I contacted the Principal with my concerns, he had no sympathy but said he would organise someone from the Dept of Ed to come and work things out with me. A very experienced teacher did come to give me some advice and to show me how ample my supplies were. In actual fact, she wanted us to do painting all the time with that supply of grey paper and powdered paint.

I had more interest in integrating a wide range of activities. So I brought newspaper from home and asked students to also bring some. I went to a wallpaper store and got paste. We did paper mache animals for one project creating a zoo out of cardboard cartons that the kids painted and turned into cages. These we displayed in the school library. Another time I went to a tile shop and bought lino tiles for the students to carve and print. We made a book of scenes of Pittsburgh landmarks, with each page created by a different student. I suppose I was taking a risk having this group of students handling sharp tools, but no one cut their hand or injured anyone else. The book created we also presented to the school library. There were many other lessons that did not require supplies, but I did buy a set of 25 mirrors so each child could use one to draw their own portrait.

I had one incident where a large grade six boy who looked old enough to be in Junior High School pulled out a switchblade and was having an argument with another student. I successfully talked him into handing it over to me and felt a great sense of satisfaction. I breathed a sigh of relief, but it took me the rest of the day to fully recover from the incident.

By the end of the school year, I felt like I had won, but the amount of effort, just to get to the school and home again was wearying. So I applied for a job in the suburbs near my home at a higher salary. I guess those students who on the first day said they would get rid of me also won.

TRAVELLING BUG

Having a long summer break coming up and my first money in the bank, I decided I wanted to take a trip to Europe as there were many tours available to the places where I could see the marvelous art I had learned about studying Art History. In addition, it would give me the opportunity to visit Sweden and meet some of the relatives that mother had been writing to. She had an interest in genealogy and loved everything Swedish. She had grown up listening to her father's stories and then had met Great Aunt Sigrid of course, who brought the tablecloth. All that older generation had passed on, but there were many cousins to meet. When contacting school friends to see if they had interest in coming on a trip, it seemed that they had all lined up summer jobs. The idea of heading off on my own did not worry me or hold me back. In fact it gave me freedom to plan it exactly for my interests. I took a cruise ship from Canada to England. Then I joined a bus tour through Europe. At the end I flew to Stockholm and was met by cousin Ranghild. Then I travelled to Uppsala and Norkopping to more relatives.

Originally I had the idea of seeing Europe on a bicycle. I joined the American Youth Hostel organisation and went to their meetings. They offered worldwide accommodation for youth but had tours as well. At the meetings I met others who were going that approaching summer and I came home excited about the idea. When my parents heard my plan, I got a strong negative reaction and in the end gave it away. My new bus trip itinerary overlapped in a few places and I did meet up in Venice with one young man whom I had met at the AYH meetings in Pittsburgh. Later on returning home telling of all my travels and mentioning the Venice meeting up with the AYH tour member, my mother looked at me and said, *"Dana why didn't you go on that bike trip?"*

The visit to Sweden, staying in relative's homes and meeting cousins my age was bringing together all the stories I had heard all my life. I took photos of us all together and realised I had the stereotype Swedish colouring. In group pictures I was sometimes one of the the few blondes.

Back home in Pittsburgh, it was time to get ready for the new teaching position. The new job had a different job description of an Art Supervisor. There were new demands, as I had to work in five different schools across the community and teach in all grades one - six. Each school had numerous sections of each grade. I had no designated art room, but went to each classroom around the school. However the Supervisor part was not something I was looking forward to. What it entailed was that twice a year, I had to have the classroom teacher present an art lesson to her own class, while I sat in the back and evaluated her lesson and wrote a report. Many of these teachers had vast experience and were much my senior. I didn't feel comfortable doing this. I needed more confidence.

There was an art cupboard filled with supplies for many types of projects. So I bought a trolley and made wooden boxes that sets of paint could be packed in with brushes and paper, or what ever else we might be using. The only problem was going to be getting from one school to the other in the suburbs without public transportation. So of course I needed to buy a car. I really wanted a Volkswagen Beetle, but was told there was an 18-month waiting list. I looked for the next available small car, which was a Fiat 500, much the same size as the VW. I bought it without ever having driven a car with gears to shift. The first day I lurched down the road, but soon got the hang of it. That little Fiat could zoom all around the suburbs and then some.

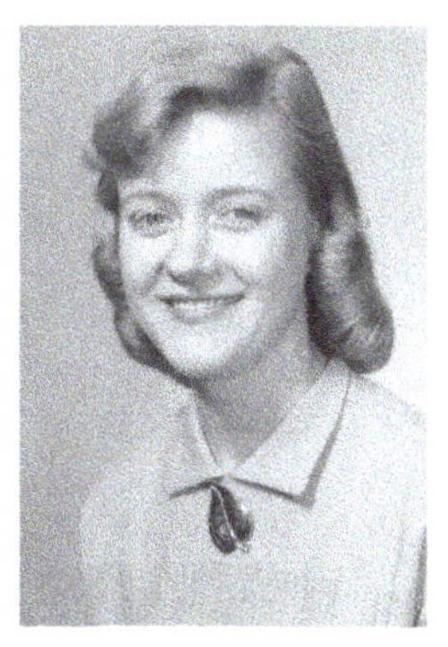

LOGAN SCHOOL
1958--59

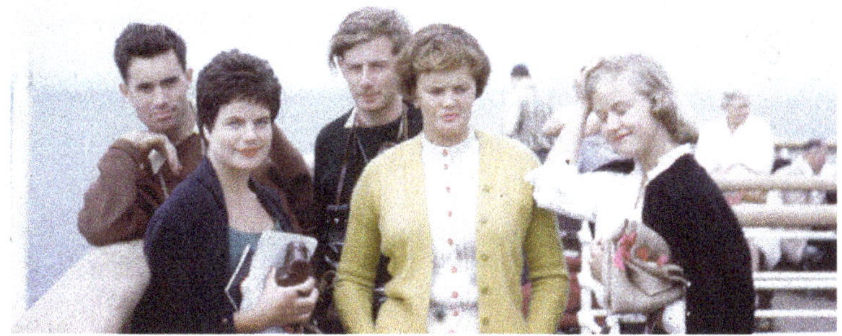

New friends on the deck of the cruise ship to England

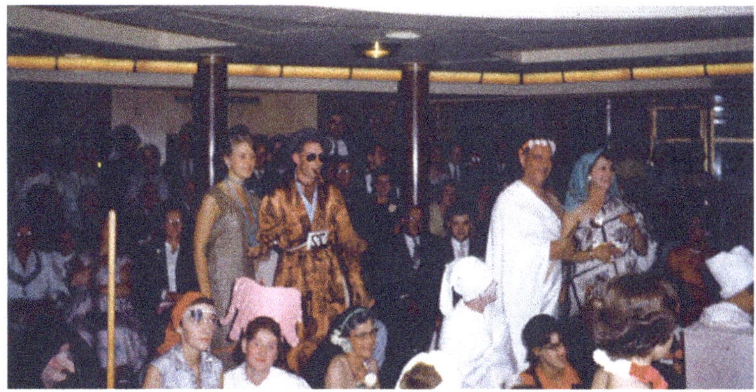

We were finalists for Fancy Dress on the ship (standing on left)

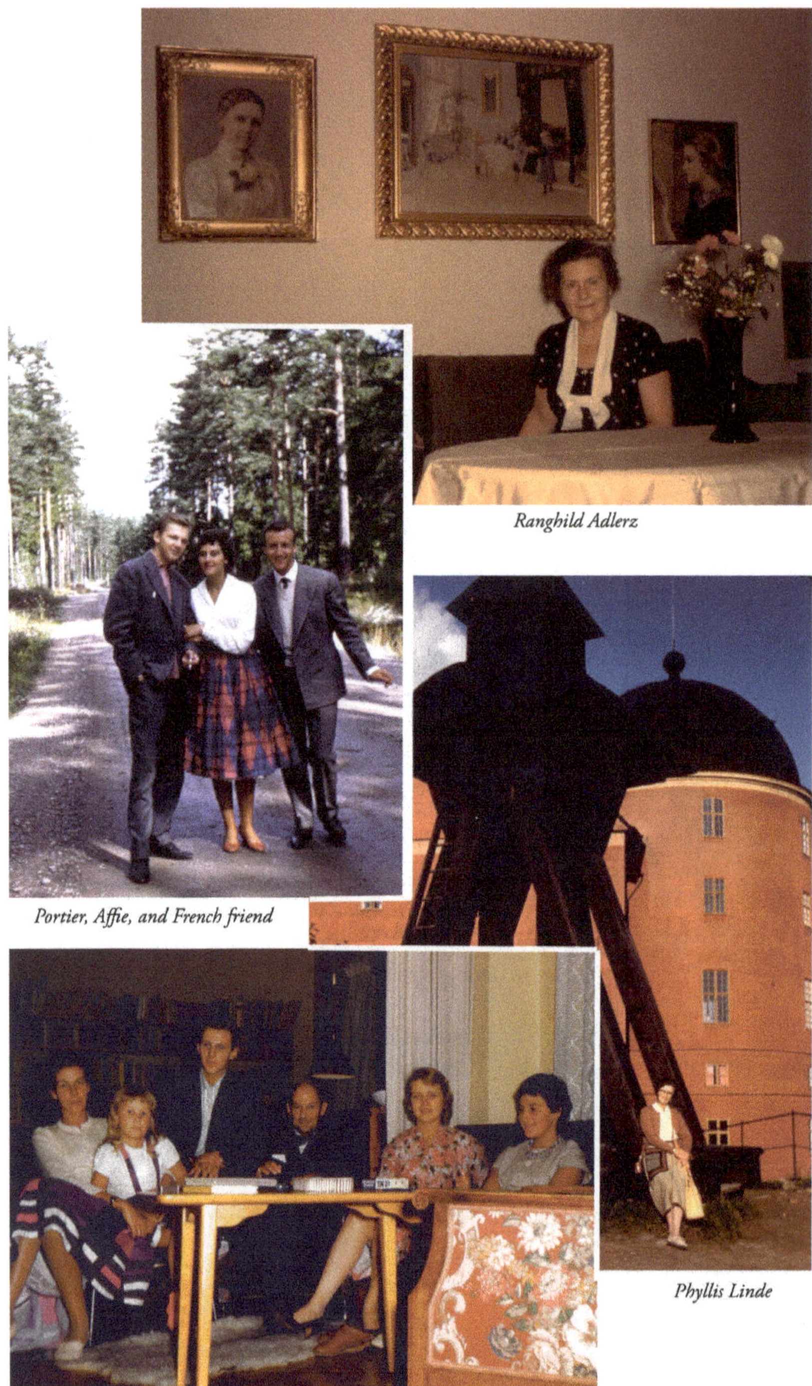

Ranghild Adlerz

Portier, Affie, and French friend

Phyllis Linde

Carle Family

SWEDISH COUSINS IN 1958 AND LATER

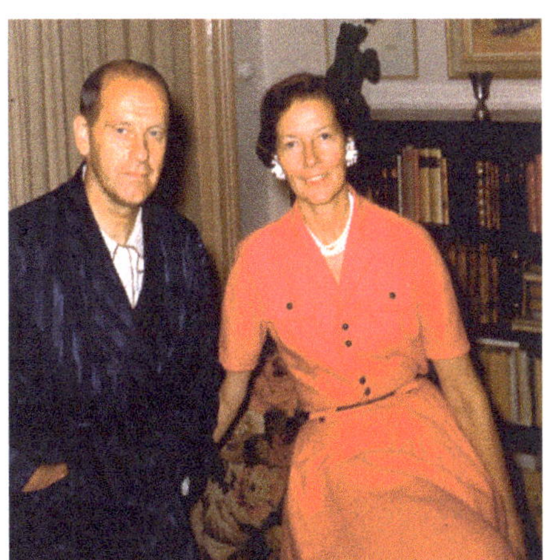

Harriet and Rangar Frolinder

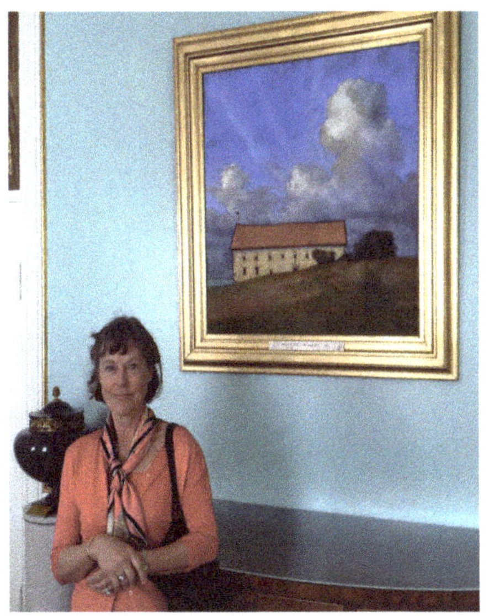

Charlotte von Axelson

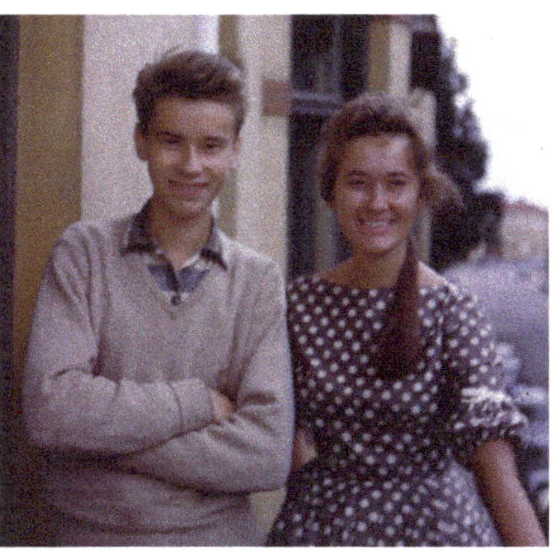

Hans and Kirstin Frolinder

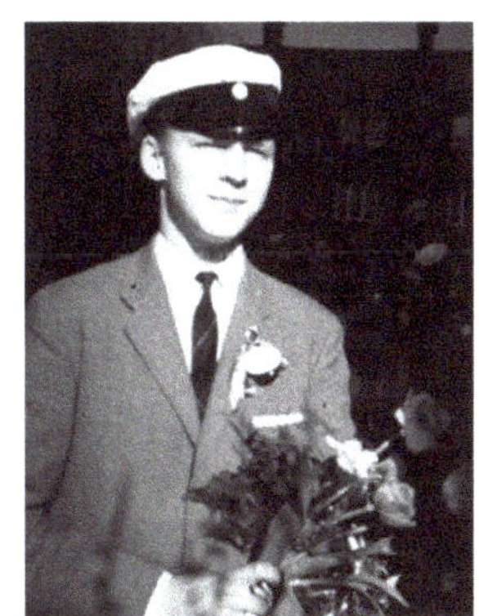

Magnus Carle graduation day

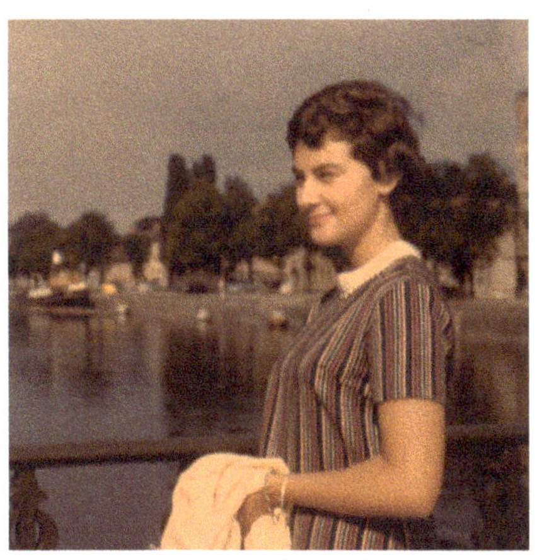

Ann-Sophie Carle

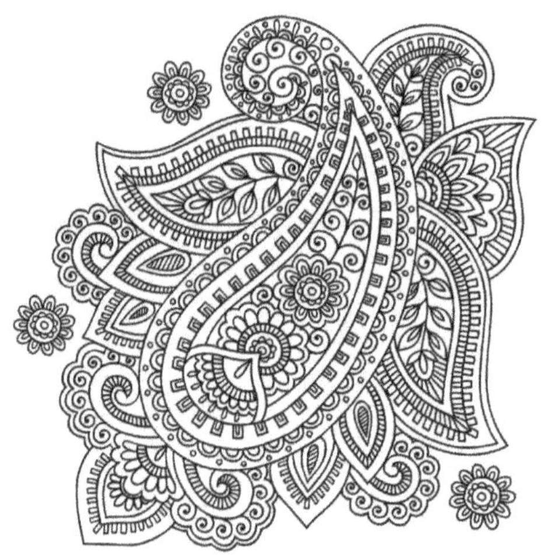

02

Unexpected

SUMMER EVENTS

Although I had been brought up in the Methodist Church, in later years I attended the Episcopal Church near our home, as we had moved to a different area. They had a young adult fellowship and bible study where I made new friends when I first returned home after university in 1958. But my very old friend Mary Gail, who now had dropped the Mary from her name, convinced me to attend an active young adult group at the Mt Lebanon Uniting Presbyterian Church. So I started to attend church there and met another group of young working adults who invited me to many outings for theatre, meals and out to play golf. Of course I had never played golf and tried to learn to actually hit the ball.

Sometime in 1959, I was invited to go to see the young associate minister at Mt Lebanon UP who was starting up a summer program for Junior and Senior High school and college students. He was hiring a staff of seven to run the program that had activities and outings throughout the week. He was offering me a contract to work with the university students. There would be staff meetings every morning to plan and have spiritual nourishment. Outings such as cave exploration were planned among ball games and picnics and of course, bible studies. The culmination of the summer program would be attending the New Wilmington

Missionary Conference, which was a highlight of the year with missionaries on home leave telling of the work they do in remote and exotic settings.

I was pleased to receive the invitation, but stated that I really thought I would be better working with Junior High age group. As Jerry Kirk explained, someone had already been signed up to work with that younger group. So I had one opportunity and had to either accept it or not. Well, I signed the contract.

ROMANCE AND NEW LIFE

Among the staff were some people I had met in Junior High School but others were quite new to me. Bob McCown had just returned from spending a year in Ethiopia as a volunteer at a small mission in Pokwo, out from Gambella. I knew who his family was, as his father was an elder Of the church and sang in the choir.

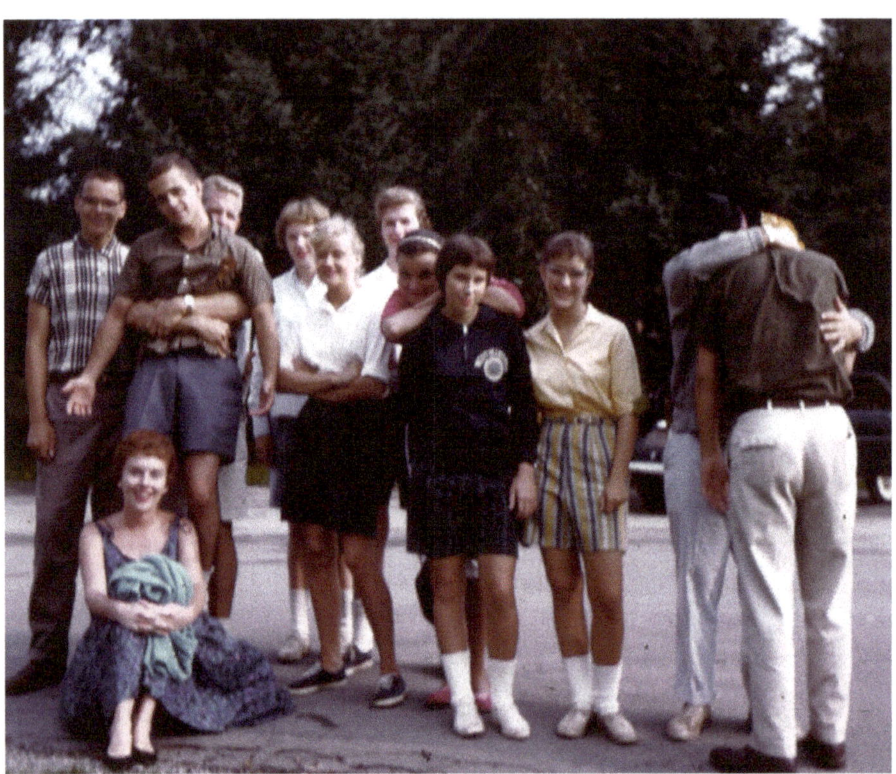

Fun loving summer staff gang and the university kids

His brother Dan was finishing high school, but I had never seen Bob before. He had been attending Penn State University but worked during summers on dairy farms where he boarded. One day Bob came along and said that a few of the group were going golfing and would I like to come. Well I had had those other golf dates previously, and hadn't really gained any skill, but I wasn't going to let that keep me back. Bob's best friend Carl was going along with another girl, so it was just the four of us. Carl had gone with Bob to Ethiopia, as an educationalist and had helped set up the school there. Then the next week Bob asked if I would like to go play golf again. It was always nice to get out on a lovely golf course and get fresh air, even if I wasn't any good at the sport. But there was another attraction of course.

In my recollection, that was about the total of our dates until attending the New Wilmington Missionary Conference at the end of summer. I seem to remember sitting out in the dark one night talking for hours. After that, Bob asked me to go with him when he was speaker for a group talking about his year in Ethiopia. I was very idealistic and impressionable. His photography was excellent and the stories quite exciting. When he took me home afterward, he leaned over and kissed me, saying, *"I vowed that the next girl I kissed I would marry."* He didn't ask if I would marry him, but must have known I was willing. So that was our first kiss. But I was going to be marrying someone I really didn't know very well at all. I was jumping off into the unknown.

He then was off to finish his undergraduate degree at Penn State. His father had been very worried he would never go back to complete the course after heading off to Africa. But Bob came back after spending the year doing agricultural work for the mission with determination to learn more to take back to Africa. Although he had been a Dairy major, he had decided the way to improve food production in Africa depended on improving feed for livestock. So he changed his major to Agronomy. He wanted to do graduate study at the University of California. Our plan was to get married after graduation and then head out to California. He did come home for the Thanksgiving holiday. And there was talk about having me

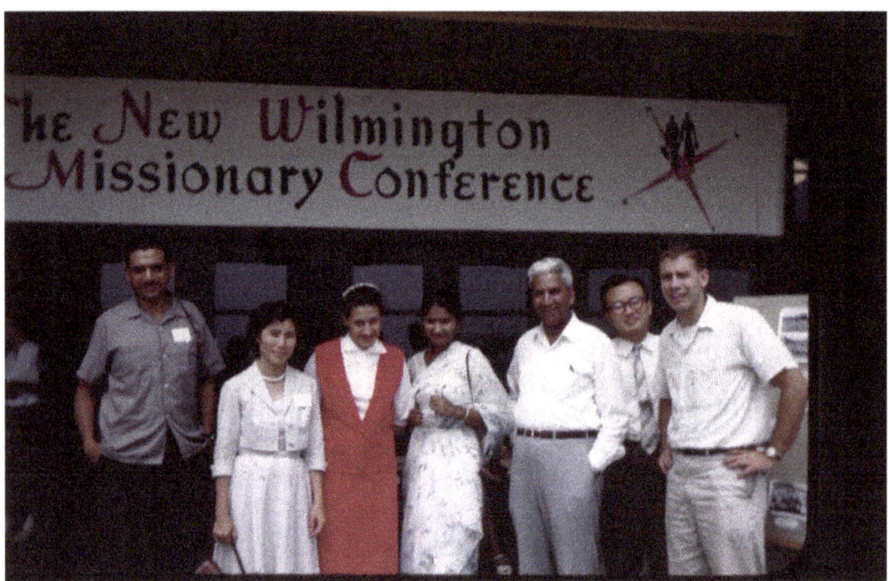

New Wilmington Conference with delegates and old friend Keith Brown

out to Penn State for a weekend. But when it came down to the line, Bob said that he had to work selling peanuts at the football game as he was saving money to buy me a ring and we better wait. Another project that would gain some ring money was entering a speech contest. He won the contest of course. One thing that helped along the way was the fact that his father gave him the diamond from his mother's ring. Another of his moneymaking projects was delivering mail over the Christmas Holidays. One morning while working he was bitten by a dog, often a hazard for mailmen.

Bob's mother died when he was 14. She had been a nurse and caught Scarlet Fever, which developed into Rheumatic Fever and damaged her heart. She had health problems all through Bob's early life. Once she asked Bob to call his father at work to tell him his mother was dying. In fact she had been told it would be dangerous to have children. After Bob's younger brother Dan was born, she was hospitalized for a period of time with what may have been called post-natal depression these days. Bob's father did eventually marry again and Betty Bush helped hold the family together, becoming an important member of the family.

Betty actually went with Bob to buy the long anticipated ring.

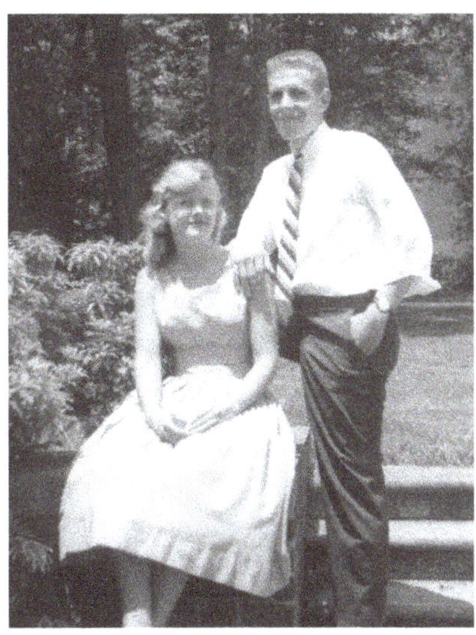

Penn State for graduation

I did receive the ring and also had a chance to visit Penn State for graduation. I drove out with his parents, meeting his friends and feeling proud seeing Bob graduate with distinction.

The next week was the wedding, which was held at Mt Lebanon United Presbyterian Church with Jerry Kirk conducting the ceremony. The two families had worked together to make a list of invitees to the wedding. They came up with a total of 600 people. As there was ample room in the church that was not a problem. My parents had organised the reception at the Mt Lebanon Women's Club for a simple event with tea or punch, cake and sandwiches. But the line of people trying to get into the building and shake hands with the newly weds, stretched out for several blocks. Among them were numerous relatives of Bob's that I had never met. And my little cousins from Milwaukee came to be bridesmaids along with three of my friends.

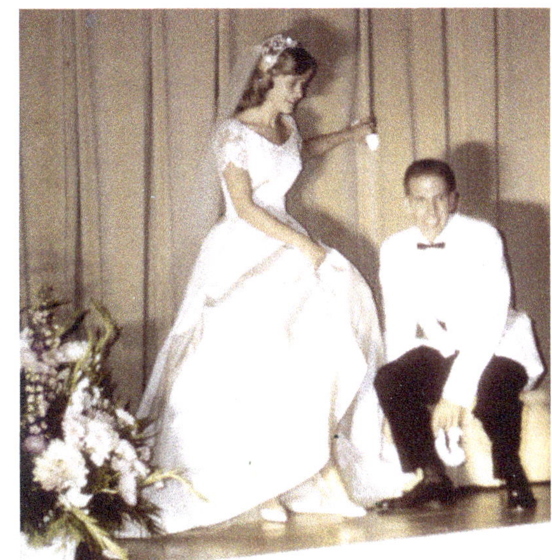

Who will catch the garter?

HONEYMOON FOIBLES

Our honeymoon was going to be at a cabin along a creek that the McCowns had rented for holidays over many years. It was in a picturesque setting only a few hours from home. Bob's parents had prepared a box of supplies to take to the cabin. Along the way we stopped and bought punnets of strawberries, as it was prime season.

When arriving, I had washed and halved the berries, then sprinkled them with sugar to create some juices. When we went to eat them, discovered that the loving family had played a trick on us and switched the sugar and salt, therefore our beautiful strawberries were in brine. That was bad enough, but later in the week, it was discovered that neither of us had changed the labeling and the brine was created again.

When returning home, it was time to deal with the wedding presents and we counted about 42 bed sheets and multiple numbers of other things. I had chosen a sterling silver dinner cutlery set, quite different to most, as it had black nylon handles and a modern Swedish design. The department store had a gift registry where people could see what we had desired or needed. It was possible to buy just one spoon for a gift, so in the end we had quite a complete set that had been monogrammed. But the duplications of sheets had to be returned along with numerous other things. We exchanged the duplicates for things like camping gear and even a sewing machine. You could see the saleswomen moaning when we came in carrying our items to return.

CALIFORNIA ADVENTURE

Bob had been accepted into the University of California for a Masters Degree program. His professor at Penn State had friends on the staff at Davis, and had arranged with someone who had an apartment vacant for the summer to be available when we arrived in Davis.

To get there we felt that the Fiat 500 was not going to work for us. So we looked for a second-hand car and one of my teacher friends was selling a blue Chevrolet convertible. It had a strong engine and could pull a U-Haul trailer with all of our earthly possessions across the United States. We had our camping gear with the plan that we would camp our way across the country. Now Bob had no interest in commercial campsites or community campgrounds.

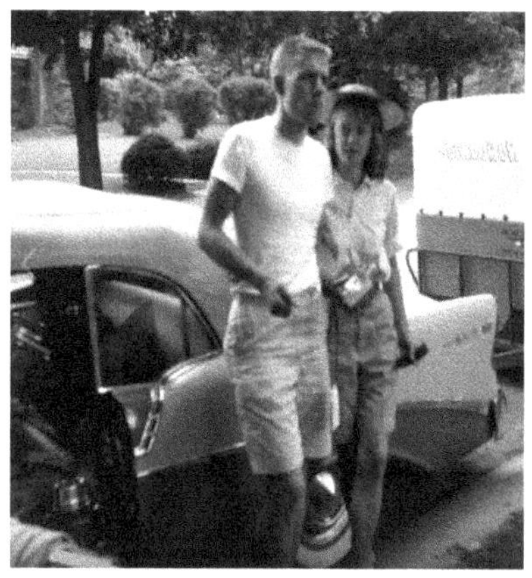

Having last farewells before heading off

His idea was to pull into some out-of-the-way piece of land and set up. This did work well to begin with, but along the way it started to rain. What we did discover was that our newly acquired convertible leaked around stitching that was deteriorating.

Bob had applied for an assistantship, which could also be used toward his research project and importantly, provide a salary as well. And the work started during the summer break, giving him an immediate full-time job. I meanwhile tried to find work for the beginning of the school year and contacted the local Education Department only to find that California did not have special art teachers in the schools. It was pointed out that there were some vacancies for teachers in other areas I could apply for. One was for a kindergarten teacher in a school one block from our apartment. The other was for a Special Ed class of intellectually disabled students. I felt completely incompetent to know how to work with the disabled, but thought my experience of living over 20 years with a kindergarten teacher was a benefit. The proviso was that I would have to attend summer school at the University to obtain units in early childhood. That appealed greatly. So now both Bob and I had activity for the summer to move ahead.

We had quite a different activity for the evenings. I had looked into getting a new cover for the Chevy, but Bob had an idea how we could re-stitch the entire cover. He found a nifty little hand held stitcher gadget that required two people to use it for this task. One pushed the threaded needle into the doubled canvas, and the other person was on the backside threading an additional waxed linen thread into the formed loop. Then Bob on the topside pulled the needle back out and pushed into the next hole. Luckily the holes provided by the near rotten stitching that was removed made the job easier, rather than having to create new holes through the tough doubled canvas. This was a task that took most of the summer and filled up our lounge room with the project.

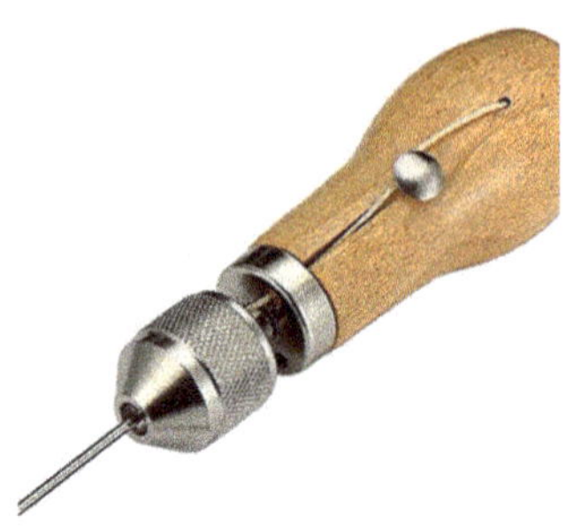

Nifty gadget

We loved the little modern apartment, which was one of three in a row, with an attractive garden of petunias along the front. But we knew at the beginning we would need to find a permanent home by the end of summer. So eventually we started looking.

Just down the block was a complex of past army barracks called "Aggie Villa" which now had become married student housing, but it was completed filled. So we looked in the paper every day. With the University year nearly ready to start and students arriving back, not much was available. We followed up on an advertisement and were shown an efficiency apartment on the side of a garage. So in the end, that was all we found and we lived in part of a garage for three months.

Eventually a place in Aggie Villa became available and we moved there and met many other married students. Aggie Villa was made up of many wooden two-story buildings with about six apartments on each floor, consisting of a living area, and a corridor kitchen connecting to a bedroom. Some of the buildings had two bedroom apartments. There was an indoor bathroom, thank goodness. Davis was a nice size town, about a half hour drive from Sacramento, our biggest nearby city to the east. In the other direction was San Francisco, a much longer drive away.

Life was very busy with both of us working and Bob studying at night. But summertime was a reprieve for me as the schools had such a long holiday. We met so many new students and their wives from countries all over the world. The Agronomy Department had social events, mainly organised by professors at their homes. And some of the staff took us under their wings, relationships that lasted all their lives. The graduate students were a small group and got to know each other very well.

Our first week after moving into Aggie Villa, Bob called home and said he was bringing along another student whose bicycle was broken. At Aggie Villa, there was a pile of bicycle parts that had been discarded by past residents. Bob had a great set of tools, mostly acquired through the exchange of those wedding gifts. So in no time at all he had fixed the bike of John Tothill, a student from New Zealand who was also in his department. Then the two came up for lunch.

Another student in the department was Don Faris, whose family lived in Aggie Villa in the bigger apartments as they had two children and were expecting a third. His wife Dawn was a nurse who was working and needed a babysitter for a while. So I took on that responsibility for a short time in the summer. In our building we had students from China, South America, Sudan, as well as America. In the department there were single guys from India, Egypt, and other areas of Africa from what I can remember.

Along an avenue leading up to the University was a row of walnut trees. In the autumn when the wind started blowing someone told me the walnuts were falling off the trees and were there for the taking. So I gathered together a bucket or two and rode my bicycle down the avenue. It was easy to pick up enough to fill my buckets rather quickly. At home I shelled them all and decided I would make Christmas cakes to send to my aunties and uncles. As I was now a married woman, I thought I should keep the connection with the wider family going. I must have had too much time on my hands, as I also collected coffee tins, which I painted and decorated. The cakes were baked in the tins so they fit perfectly.

When we had been married for six months, we started to think it was time to start a family. It seems, looking back, a bit of a rash idea. But we saw other students around that had young families and made it work. So we decided to take a little Easter holiday and drove down past San Francisco along the beautiful coastline. We admired Pebble Beach and finally stopped and found accommodation in Aptos, an attractive little town featuring beaches as well as state parks. It was a lovely interlude before going back to the demands of graduate school.

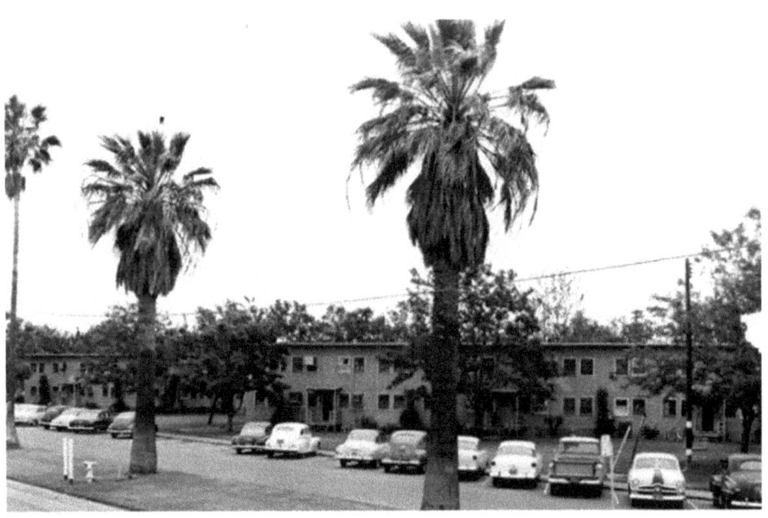

Aggie Villa married student housing, UC Davis Library Special Collections UAP00308

THE FAMILY GROWS

It wasn't too long after returning to Davis, that I thought I might be pregnant. By the time a few months passed, there was no doubt that I was suffering morning sickness. So it soon became time for me to send in my resignation to the school board. As I was found to be expecting in December, I wanted the time to prepare and get ready for this new phase of life. To begin with, I wanted to get out the sewing machine and start making maternity clothes. It was fun to look at patterns and think about fabrics. And we went on a shopping expedition to see what we would need for a baby.

It was summer time again and the Agronomy department had baseball games on the weekend with other departments. These times were social outings for families and friends. Many of the men were on the team with the wives and sweethearts on the sidelines cheering them on. I started to feel better by then and enjoyed getting together with the other wives. There was also a club for wives with meetings and activities. And we met other couples at the local church.

It became clear that although Bob had enrolled to attend graduate school to earn his masters degree, he had research he wanted to continue to work toward a PhD. Instead of two years, we were looking at a timeframe of five years of hard work with a pretty tight budget. And I had given up a full time job.

My due date was in late December. But a few days after my birthday, Bob went off to work and I was being lazy. Finally I got up and went to the toilet only to find I was hemorrhaging. Panic set in and I called Bob who came home and took me to the medical centre. But the doctor told us to go straight to the hospital in the town of Woodland. The staff there seemed to take it in their stride and had me rest in bed quietly. This went on for a few days when finally some action started and on the third day Jenny was born. Meanwhile Bob had contacted family in Pittsburgh and my mother flew out to be there to help and enjoy seeing her first grandchild. Luckily we had found a sofa bed when we were furnishing our small apartment. I had a Dr. Spock book that we read from cover to cover, as I had never really had anything to do with babies. At the hospital they gave some basic lessons on bathing and care, which were very helpful. Bob took a great interest in being a father and helping.

Jenny was born about three weeks early, so was a bit small and needed feeding about every three hours. I was keen to breastfeed and gave it a good shot. But in the end the bottle won out. At least I could tell how much she actually had drunk. It was a very long time before she slept all night. Bob was keen to get up for night feeds, although once I heard the crying I was wide awake. We loved seeing each little development and milestone.

It was just sad that all the grandparents could not share in the experience so the following summer time we had a trip back to Pittsburgh with the help of Bob's parents. It was a time to make the rounds of relatives and friends. Grandfather Ray Hopper came for a BBQ along with Bob's cousin Beverley and her two boys. We had some informal four-generation photographs.

Back at Davis, when school started up again in the fall, I signed up to do substitute teaching. It was possible to get childcare for the times I got called out with other mothers on campus. That was a help to our budget, but it also gave me experience in teaching various grades. It was usually made fairly easy by the lesson plans all teachers were required to have on their desk.

We decided it would be good to replace our convertible Chevrolet and have a vehicle more practical for little trips. A VW Combi van was purchased and we

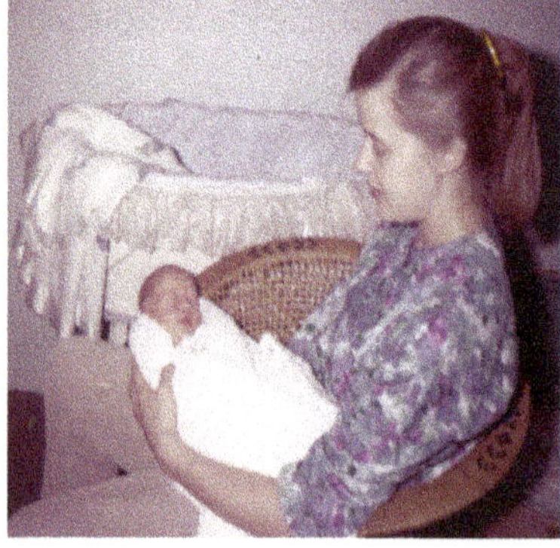

Just home from hospital

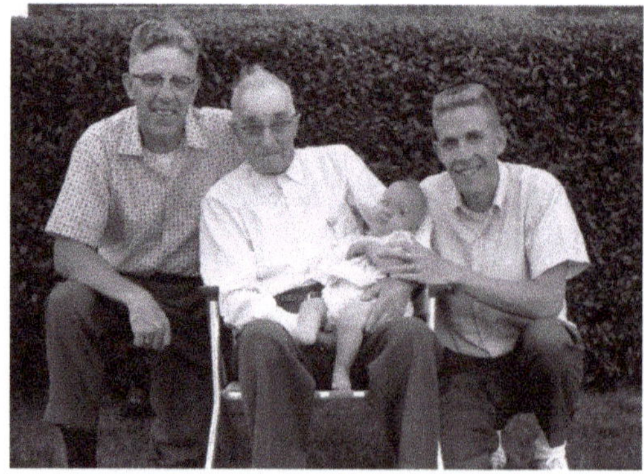

Grandpa McCown and Great Grandpa Hopper

loved the features complete with beds and kitchen space. We even drove the van to Nebraska to Bob's brother's wedding.

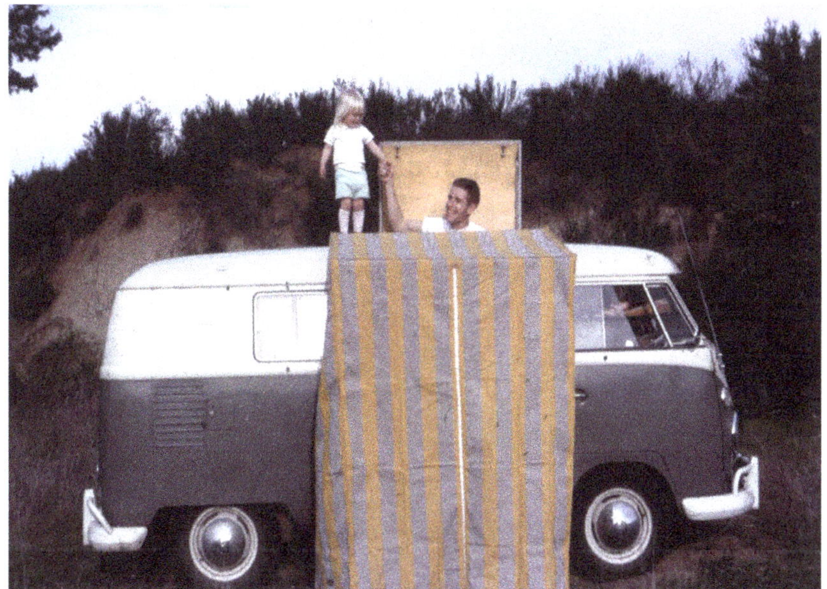

VW Combi complete with annex

Finally the University decided to build brand new married student apartments named Solano Park on the campus. We applied and were awarded a two-bedroom apartment set in attractively landscaped grounds with play areas included. We were fortunate to be assigned a ground level unit. All the families had similar aged children, and eventually three-year old Jenny was getting out making new little friends. Somehow Jenny always came home having been given food and not wanting to eat her lunch. In the end I had a sign pinned to her back saying "Please do not feed this animal".

Across the lawn, in the next building was a family from Mexico who had brought their maid with them. She seemed to be excluded from family life in ways that started to upset me and a few others. We decided to have her over for tea and cake one day. It was well intentioned but probably not a wise thing to do. The wife of the

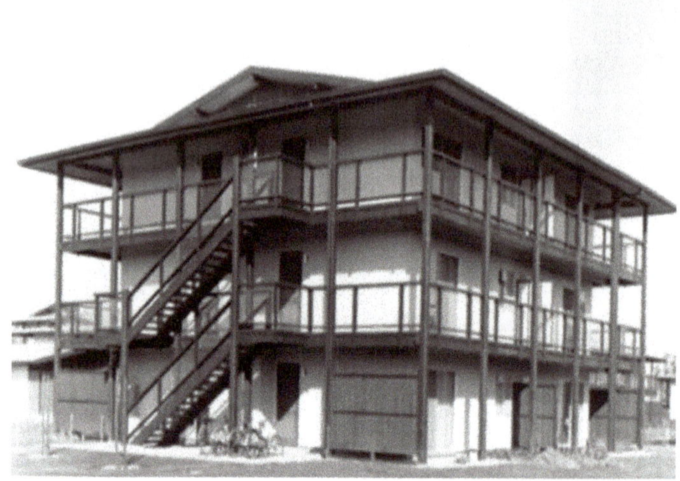

Solano Park, U Cal, Davis Library Special Collections 13030

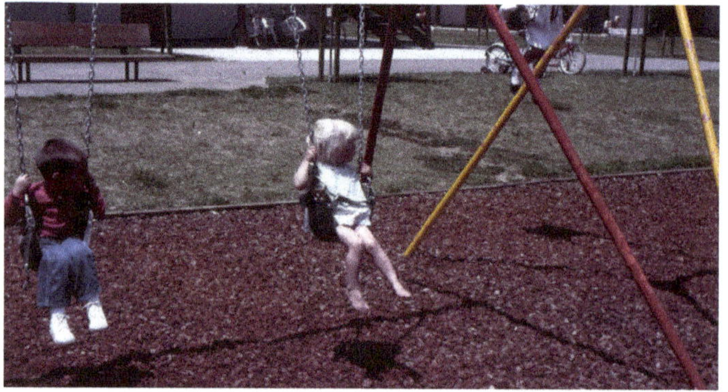

Jenny on the swings at Solano Park

family felt she was the one who should have had a social invitation. I had to learn not to take on all injustices I observed and acknowledge cultural and other differences.

Bob's parents came to visit that summer and we took a trip together through California. A big attraction on the trip for Jenny was visiting Disneyland. Grammie enjoyed having time with Jenny. She was very good with young children as she had been a grade one teacher for many years. She knew of good books for youngsters and spent time reading to her.

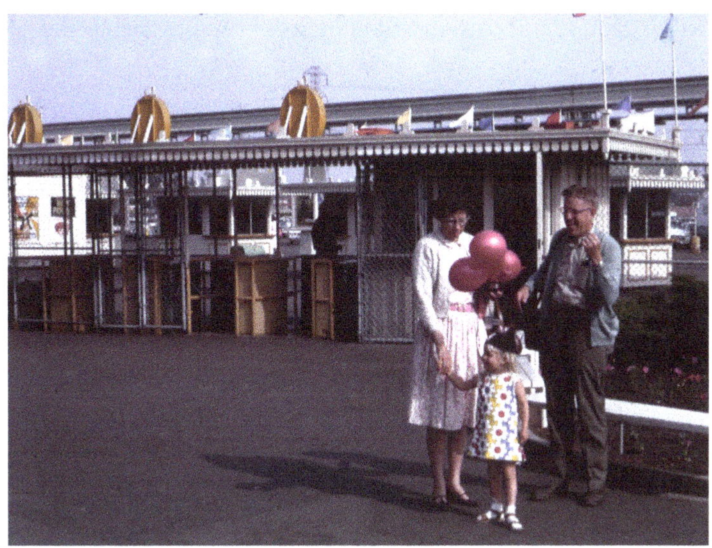

Grammie and Gramps enjoyed Disneyland with Jenny

We decided that Jenny needed a sibling and proceeded to make that happen, as we didn't want too big a gap in ages. It was going to be a big year with Bob completing his PhD by the end of 1965 and the baby being due in September. Bob was doing well with his program and thinking it was time to look for a job. He had hopes that with both a Masters Degree and a PhD he could find a job with an organisation like World Bank that would enable him to do development work in Africa. He was disappointed to learn that his training was nice, but what he really needed was experience working in the tropics. His friend John Tothill had gone to Australia to work with the Commonwealth Scientific and Industrial Research Organisation (CSIRO). John wrote back glowing reports of the opportunities within CSIRO. And then there were visits from CSIRO scientists headhunting young promising scientists. We met Wally and Maida Stern, living in Canberra and also working for CSIRO, when they came on a visit.

The attraction to Australia continued to grow. Bob had glowing references from the supervisors he had worked with and so he was eventually successful in his application. It was good to know that a job was secured and he would have a salary to support his family. But perhaps more importantly was the challenge of a new job taking him nearer to his goals.

OUR FAMILY GROUP CONTINUES TO GROW

Bob came home one day from Uni to tell me about his friend Sakti Jana who was having problems. Bob felt he needed to be with friends, not living alone and suggested we could fit Sakti in our little home as we had a sofa bed in the lounge. Sakti was a single guy from India and was also near to completing his PhD. I can't remember my reaction to the suggestion, but I was willing, in spite of the fact that we would also be adding another little one. Arrangements were made and Sakti moved in, making himself part of the family.

Our plan for the birth was to go back to Pittsburgh this time, giving both our families time to be with us before leaving for Australia. I was rather excited, because I knew I was going to have an epidural, making childbirth rather pain free compared to the last birthing that had lasted so long and with the scare of hemorrhaging.

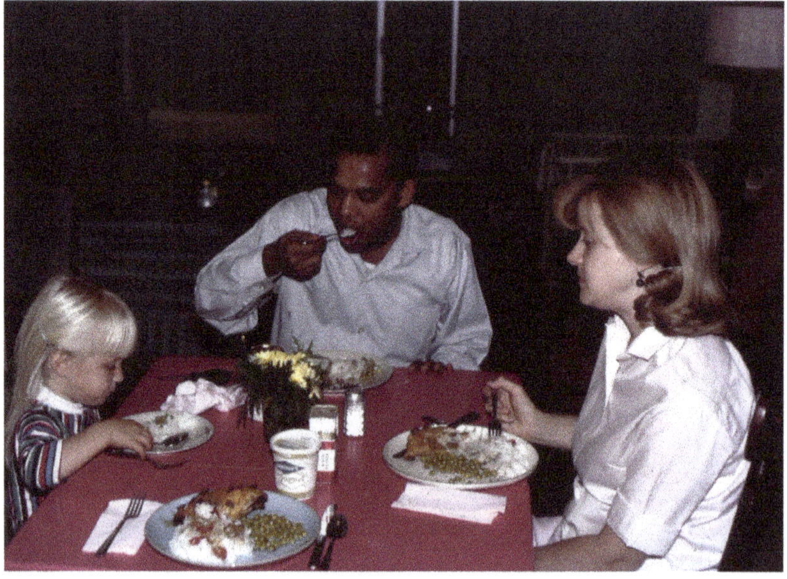

Sakti fit in well with the family

I had almost forgotten that when I was having my prenatal visits in Davis to the gynecologist, it was discovered that I had German Measles. I had been complaining about a red rash and when seeing it, the nurse didn't want me in the waiting room to infect other pregnant women. But what that meant was that after the birth, the baby was considered to be contagious and had to be in isolation. That made the feeding impossible and so we only stayed in hospital a day and a half taking little Jessica Loren home to Grammie's. It was a special visit with family knowing we were travelling so far away from America. California had been far enough.

My father had his own private appraisal business for many years and had become President of the MAI and SRA, national and international bodies of real estate appraisal and had number plates to match. While we were in Pittsburgh for the birth, seeing the possibility of keeping his family closer, Dad approached Bob about coming to work for him. He lobbied me about the possibility, but I had to keep reminding Dad that Bob was a scientist and had invested nine years of training to fulfill his dreams. In the end, Dad hired Bob's brother Dan instead.

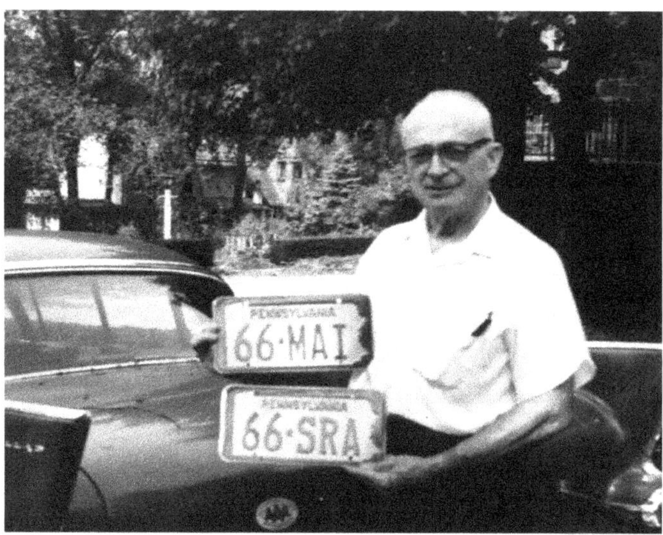

My dad with his personal plates, reflecting his presidency in the Appraisal Institutes

Back in Davis, Sakti was glad to welcome us. But when the baby would cry, it would upset him so, saying, *"Oh she is suffering."* He had a lovely sensitive nature.

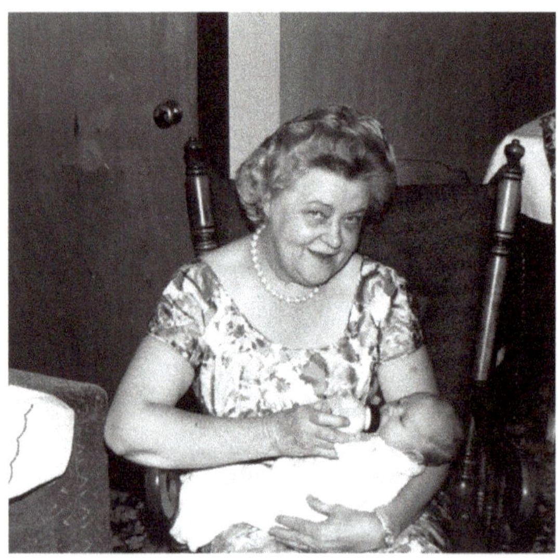

Grandma has the chance to hold darling Jessica Loren

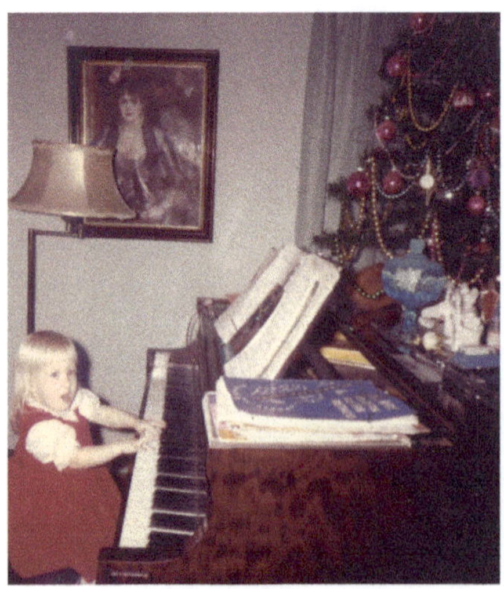

Playing Grandma's piano

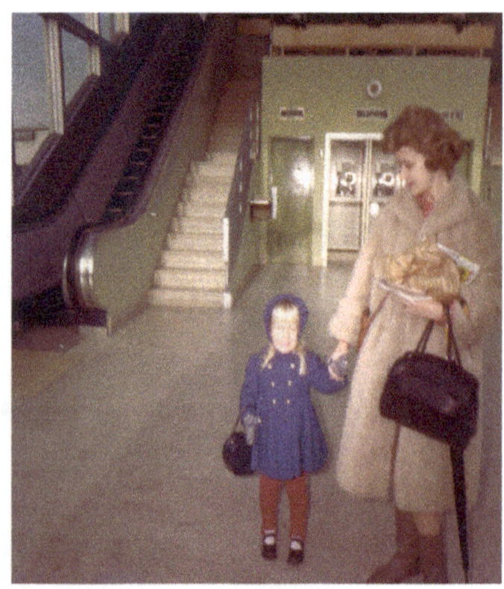

Arriving at the Pittsburgh Airport

SOME ASSORTED CHAPTER 2 PHOTOS

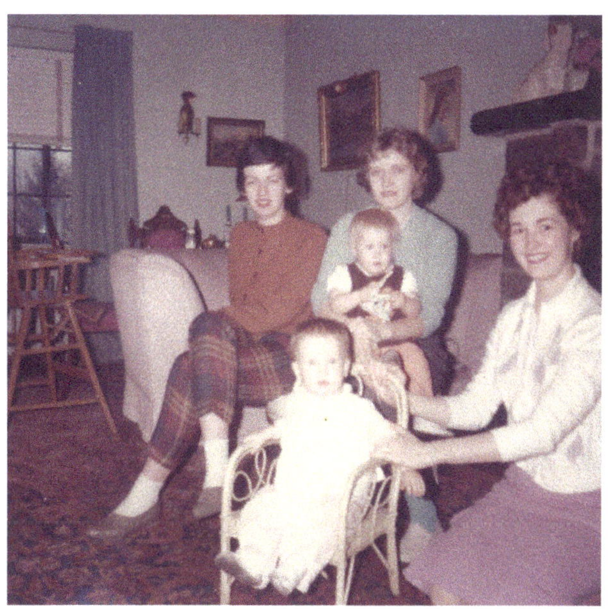

Mary Gail, Dana and Nancy with children Jenny and Suellen get together at my parents home

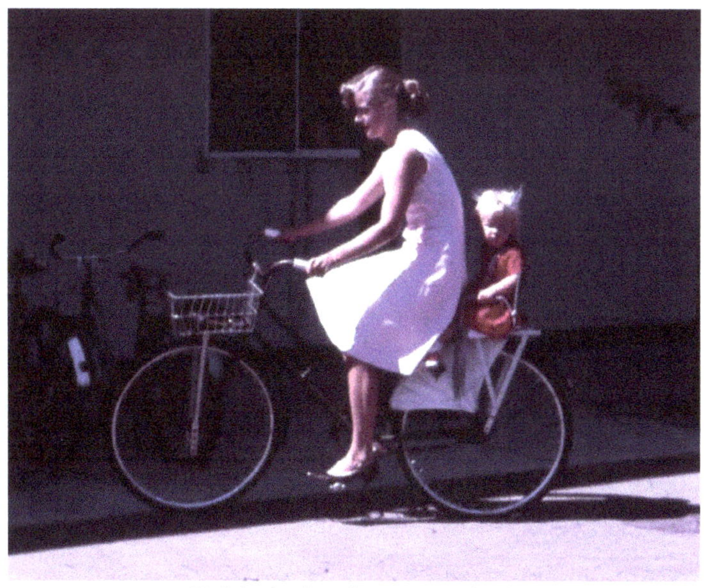

My bike that I used to get around in Davis

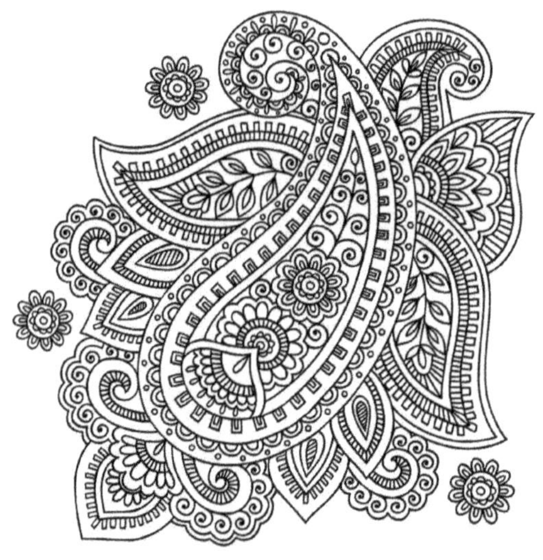

03

Australia

TOWNSVILLE HERE WE COME

Although I had dreams of taking a cruise to Australia, as that is how all the other Aussies studying at Davis were returning home, it wasn't going to happen. The beauty of going by ship is the ability to take a lot of gear in the ship's hold. In addition it would be a luxurious holiday with beautiful food and entertainment. I had been on a cruise to England when I went on that European trip after I finished working first semester at Wightman School and knew what fun it could be. However the idea of a cruise was torture to Bob. When he went to Africa in 1957 to the mission, he went by freighter and was extremely seasick the entire trip. So what could I say?

We had to start preparations for the trip. I couldn't pin Bob down to finding out what conditions he was entitled to concerning shipping personal affects and even salary. He didn't want to look presumptuous or greedy. There was a Miss Pennington at the Australian Embassy in Washington who made all the arrangements. She sent us tickets to fly with an overnight in Hawaii at a hotel with time to even go to Waikiki Beach. Arriving at the beach, we were pulled up by the lifeguard explaining that the sun was far too strong for a baby. We retreated and found some umbrellas to shelter under. I will always remember the breakfast of pecan waffles with maple syrup.

Upon landing in Sydney the next day we were taken to the Wentworth Hotel. It was a very proper old style hotel in the heart of the city. My biggest memory is that the pillows on the bed had hard lumps that seemed as big as basketballs. The other memory was of the breakfast dining room being very proper with lovely silver teapots and exemplary service.

We then flew to Brisbane where the Division of Tropical Agriculture was based to meet the staff at headquarters. We were met at the airport by Bob's old friend from Davis, John Tothill. Since we had last seen him, he had met a lovely Italian woman while on holiday at the Gold Coast. They married and built a home near Kenmore, out Pullenvale Road on acreage. We were taken to our accommodation, a place called Forest Lodge, with swimming pool and grounds with garden, which was the ideal place for a family to stay, and we returned many times in later years. John and Yolanda took us on an outing to Mt Coo-tha, a much-loved Brisbane landmark and we had our first Devonshire Tea at the kiosk. Another day, the Tothills had us over to celebrate Jenny's fourth birthday, presenting her with a lovely summer dress with a penguin in applique on the front. At the time, Yolanda was heavily pregnant with their son Sandro.

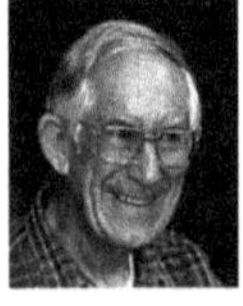
John Tothill

The Chief of the Division, Mark Hutton had us over for lunch. His wife, Gwen was a very kind motherly type with all kinds of advice. So we were having a very welcoming reception. This stop in Brisbane was only preparing Bob for our final destination, Townsville where the new Davies Laboratory had been recently opened. However upon getting indoctrination at the CSIRO office, Bob found out that we could have shipped all of our possessions. But in the end, the other Australian graduates heading home bought the things I hadn't been able to take, like my beautiful baby play pen and high chair, as they knew they had ample allowance from their employer.

NORTH QUEENSLAND REVEALED

Finally we flew to Townsville, and were met at the airport by Peter Gillard, one of the scientists who was originally from South Africa. Peter had kindly written to Bob in California, giving him information about the lab and the people there. So we felt we were being welcomed very nicely. A house had been rented in our name, so we had a place to stay.

When some of the Australians studying in Davis heard that we were headed to a job in Townsville, they said, *"Poor Dana."* They described all the houses as up on stilts. The reasons were numerous. First of all they were high to be above water in floods, or it was to keep the snakes out of the house, to catch the breezes, or simply it was to have somewhere to hang your washing. Or it was a cool place underneath to sit in the heat of the day. There was truth in all of it.

The house arranged for us was furnished, which was a blessing as we didn't own any furniture and were only shipping out a large crate with books and most of the wedding presents. I was intrigued looking under the house in the cemented laundry to see an item that I was told was a "copper". It was up on legs and had a round tub with a lid. It did seem to have a cord to plug into a powerpoint. It was in fact a boiler for washing clothes. There was a stick against the wall to agitate the items when needed. I was told I was fortunate it was not a wood fired model. One of the first purchases I made was an automatic electric washing machine to make my workload lighter. Townsville was a city located on the ocean with some shark enclosures where it was safe to swim. However there were warnings at times that there were jellyfish whose tentacles created painful stinging. Right beside the beach near our house was an Olympic swimming pool and Jenny had swimming lessons there. One big asset of the house was that it had fly-screens. At the time, fly-screens were a rare occurrence. The woman across the street asked me if it didn't get very hot behind all that wire. I had no idea how much hotter it may have been, but anything was worth keeping out flies and mosquitos in my opinion.

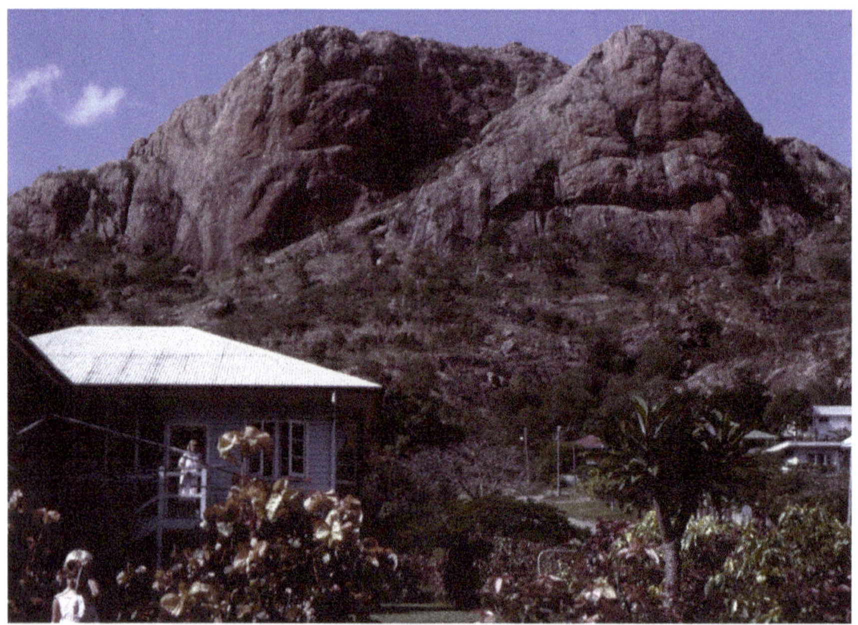

Our first house in the shadow of Castle Hill

Another typical feature of the house was the wooden louvres along the side verandah, which was also called a "sleepout," as there were beds along the louvres for extra sleeping quarters. Some sleepouts were used for sleeping on hot summer nights. We had arrived in the middle of summer, but discovered as winter approached that there was no way to warm the house. I commented that we had never been so cold at night when living in North America even when it snowed, as homes were heated usually with furnaces in the basement. So extra layers of clothing and blankets was the order of the day and night.

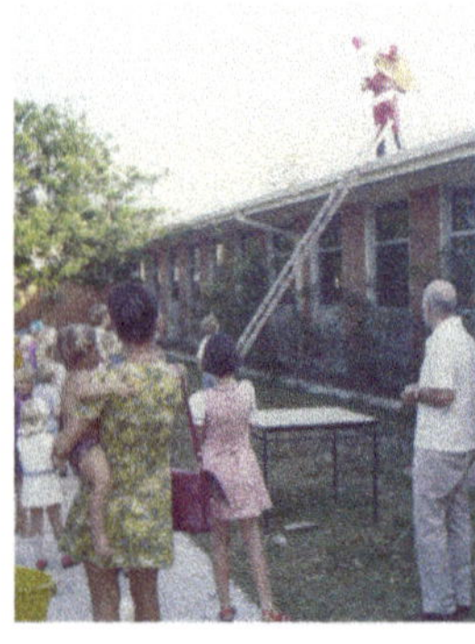

Not all kids were happy

It was getting pretty close to Christmas, and we discovered it was the party season. CSIRO had a Christmas party out on the lawn with Santa appearing over the roof of the lab. Most children were very excited as he had a bag of presents. But there were some who looked up and were terrified. It was always one of the staff acting as Santa. He never really looked too old and scary. Parents enjoyed the day too.

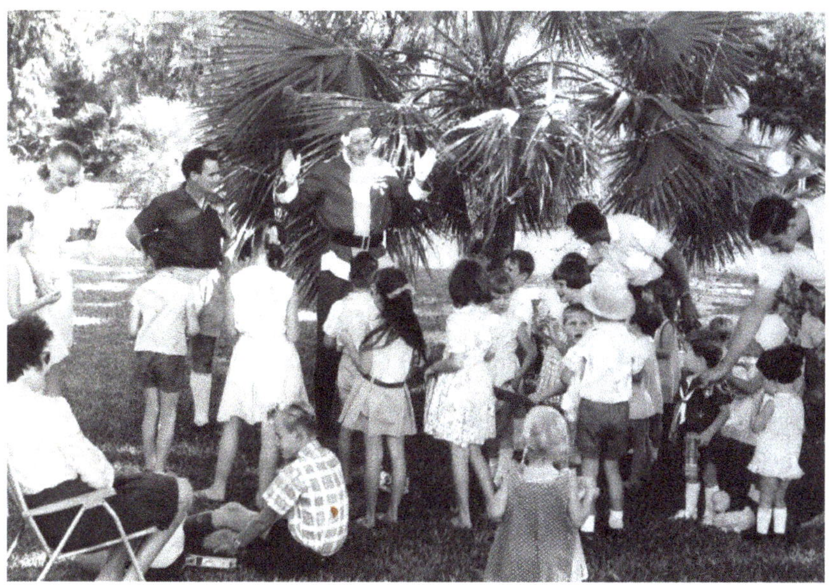

Santa came down from the roof with a big bag of gifts

We then rented in Aitkenvale, closer to Bob's work. In that house the open-plan lounge backed onto the kitchen. There was a sofa against a wall to the kitchen that was 3/4 height only. I came from the kitchen to see Jessie who was playing happily,

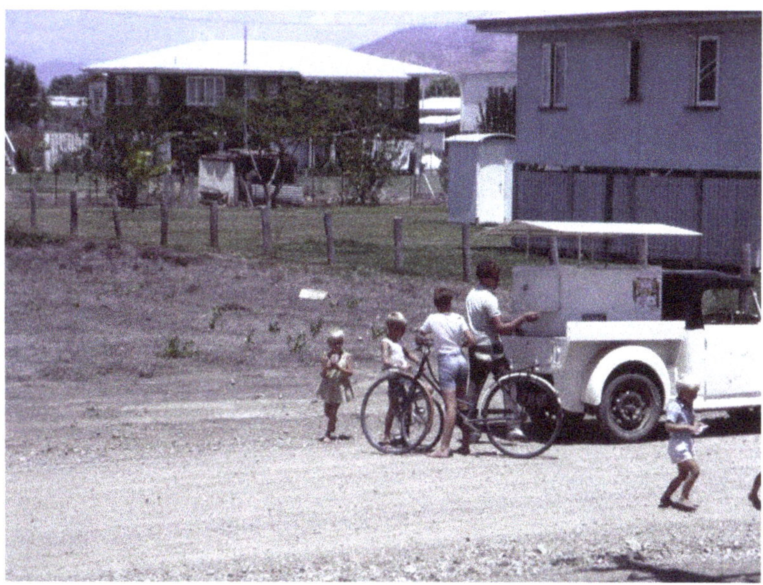

Jenny gets a treat from the pie van

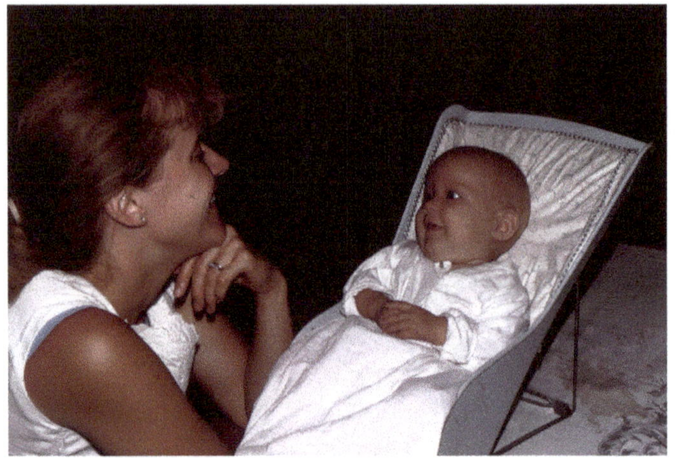

Sweet smiles of baby Jessie

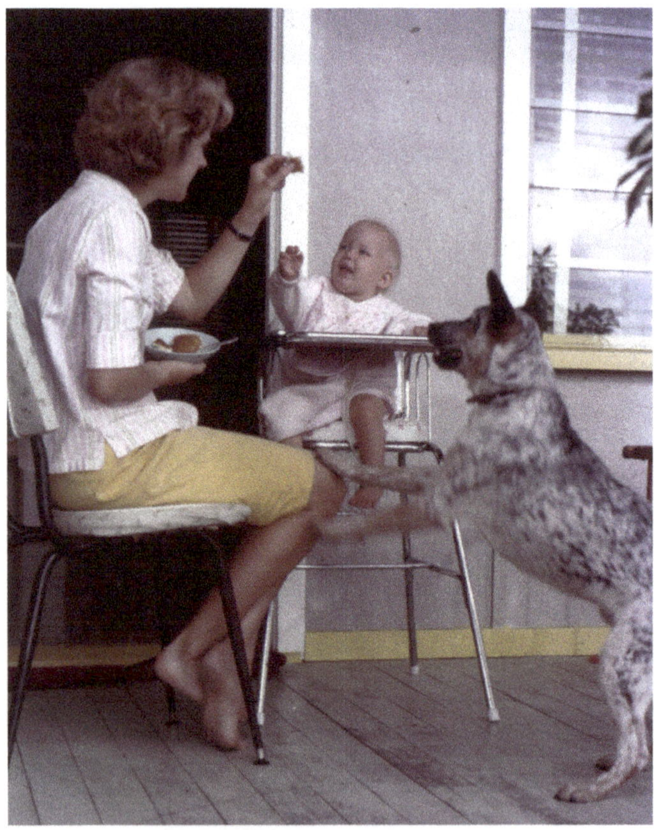

Our cattle dog, Jeff, was wanting a treat

but climbing up the wall, via the back of the couch attemping to get on top of the refrigerator in the kitchen. Her little legs had gotten quite strong and she had determination. By that time she may have been about six or seven months old.

The lab had been staffed with a predominance of young scientists with families. So all of these scientists had come from somewhere else and were glad to make friendships. We were invited to other couples homes for meals.

Very early on we met the Tonnoirs. June was the librarian at CSIRO and was married to Paul, a man of many talents. Their daughter Nonie was a little older than Jenny, but they got on very well with similar interests even at that young age. They invited us to their home, which was an interesting historic homestead with walls about a metre thick. There were always interesting discussions when we got together.

Other colleagues of Bob's also offered friendship and hospitality. Roger and Ann Jones had young children and similar interests. Bob always enjoyed getting to have some discussion of work and research, which was his priority. They lived in a traditional older style Queenslander with lots of charm. I will never forget an afternoon with the Little's, who had invited us for a meal. The children went off to play and we eventually discovered that they played hairdresser. Jenny cut off Belinda's gold ringlets. What a way to get to know people! Judith Little was shocked, as were Bob and I. Jenny may have also received a little trim, but nothing dramatic. Martin and Moira Playne had also arrived shortly before us. Moira was also an artist and so we all had a lot in common.

Several months later at home, I was shocked to go in the bedroom and discover that Jenny had decided to cut her own very long hair all off. It was a quick trip to the hairdresser to get some shape into what was left of her golden tresses. The result was a little pixie look, quite cool for the hot summer days.

After about four months I had a letter from Kay, a California friend asking me what were the differences I had found. At first that was all I could think of, the differences. But by that time I had become settled in, I couldn't think of any differences. Well, there was one difference to begin with that took some sorting out mentally. Australia used pounds, shillings and pence. I had no idea of what these things represented and put effort into mastering them. But two months later, Australia changed from pounds to decimal currency, which meant we were back to what I knew.

Also about that time, I opened a discussion with Bob about what we might do in three years, as I thought he had taken a three-year contract to prepare himself for work in Africa. He looked at me with bewilderment and said, *"What do you mean? This research I have started will take me at least 10 years."* That was the first I had heard about that!

We needed to find a local doctor, as it was time to get some of the baby's injections. We attended a practice with three medicos and were seen by Dr. Ian Dickson, who was originally from England.

I learned that mothers all take their infants to the "Baby Clinic" for injections and advice. And that some baby clinics were held in a special rail wagon taken to the outback for those families isolated by distance. Dr. Dickson mentioned that next door to his family was living an American family about our age, who had come for an engineering project. In fact he gave me their contact number, so I met up with Kathy Lowe who had a daughter Jenny's age. In fact, Dr. Dickson and his wife Susie had a holiday home on Magnetic Island and graciously invited us out for a Sunday outing and lunch. The Lowes were also invited, so we became friends with both families.

On another day Kathy took me to meet Anneke Silver, a very talented artist. In this way our acquaintances grew and grew. Anneka told me about the Townsville Art Society, which she was involved in and I joined and there made many friends.

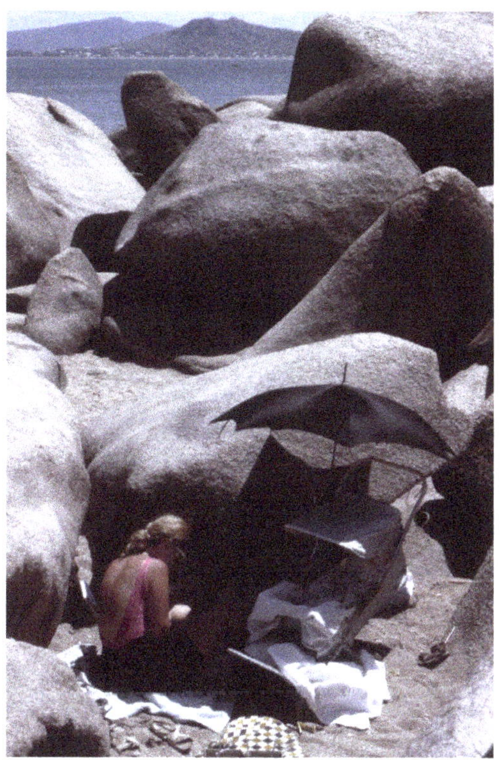

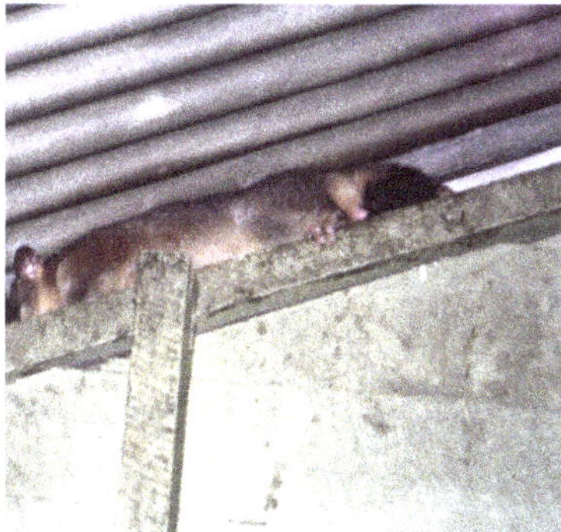

Possum on the rafters above our heads

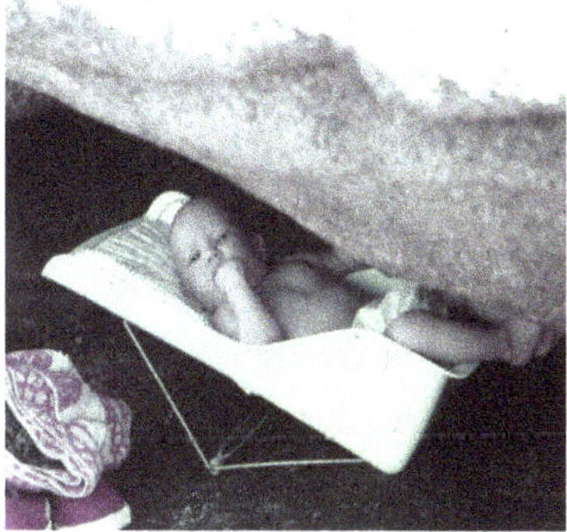

Jessica under a rock for protection on Magnetic Island

Our trip to Magnetic Island showed what an asset we had just off the coast of our own town. It gave us the idea that a little summer holiday to the island was just what we needed. It was possible to rent a little holiday cottage on one of the bays quite reasonably. We packed food and bedding, taking the Ferry, a 30-minute ride to Picnic Bay. It was an easy walk to the beach and bush walks were well set out.

The first night we were quite surprised to hear a growling inside our cottage. Getting the torch, we discovered that there were possums crawling along the rafters of the small dwelling. The growling was from one animal claiming territory from another. We made the mistake of getting a broom and trying to move them along to crawl outside. Instead it gave the impetus for leaping and chasing around inside the cottage. We were worried one would jump into Jessie's baby cot.

PROPERTY OWNERS AT LAST

We bought a 16 acre block of land out in the Upper Ross area along the banks of the Ross River approximately 20 km from the city centre. The road nearest to our block was only a dirt track. Many of the other residents in the area were on acreage blocks that had been in the families for generations. Both of us had grown up in the city. Bob had always had dreams of owning his own horse, but never had the opportunity. So this would now be a possibility.

Other work colleagues had built new homes. So we thought that was a great way to go as we were excited about the idea of designing just what we wanted. Before coming to Australia, my Uncle Oliver had died. He and his wife had not had children so he was generous to some of his nieces and nephews and left each $10,000. That was the exact price of the land. We decided to subdivide the road frontage and sell blocks to finance building a new home. In fact, that worked very well, getting us started as homeowners without a big mortgage.

We found that a builder some of our friends had used produced well-made and reasonably priced homes. We were able to use designs he had available and adjust them to suit our needs. He did make a verbal complaint saying, *"You scientists have millionaire tastes but very limited budgets."* Once construction started, we drove out every evening to check on what had been done. It turned to be vital that we checked the plans each time. Initially it turned out that the carpenters had got the plan switched entirely around with the main focus area not toward the river, but back across the paddock at the road. Luckily we caught it just in time. That sort of thing continued to happen all along. While planning the layout, I had actually made a proportional balsa wood model of the house with doors hinging to see how things would work. I also made miniature cardboard furniture shapes to see if rooms would be big enough or what size the furniture needed to be. It helped enormously in planning details.

Taking advantage of the river view, we placed the house on the top of a bank that sloped a long way down to the water. We had been told that across the river there were some rocky outcrops with Aboriginal drawings, so we crossed the

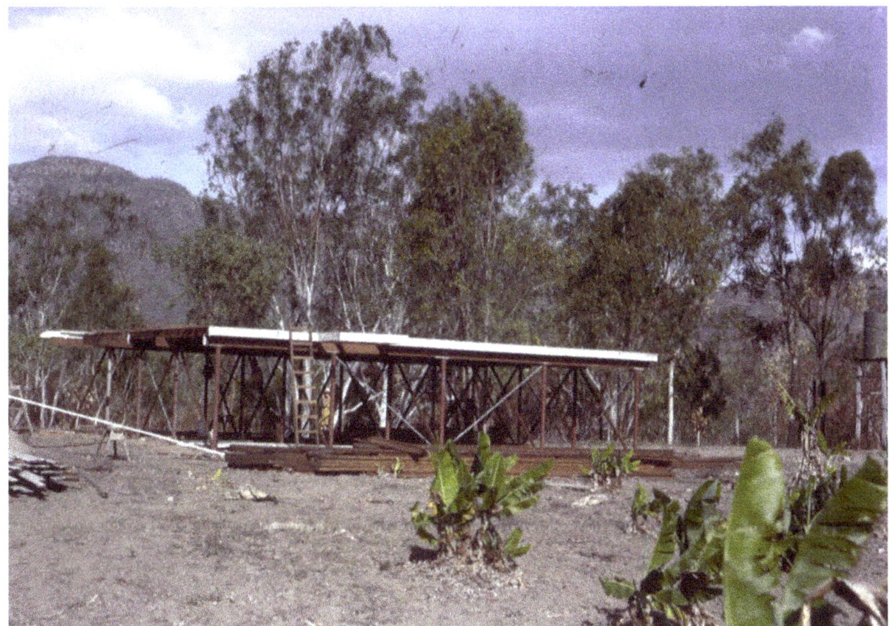

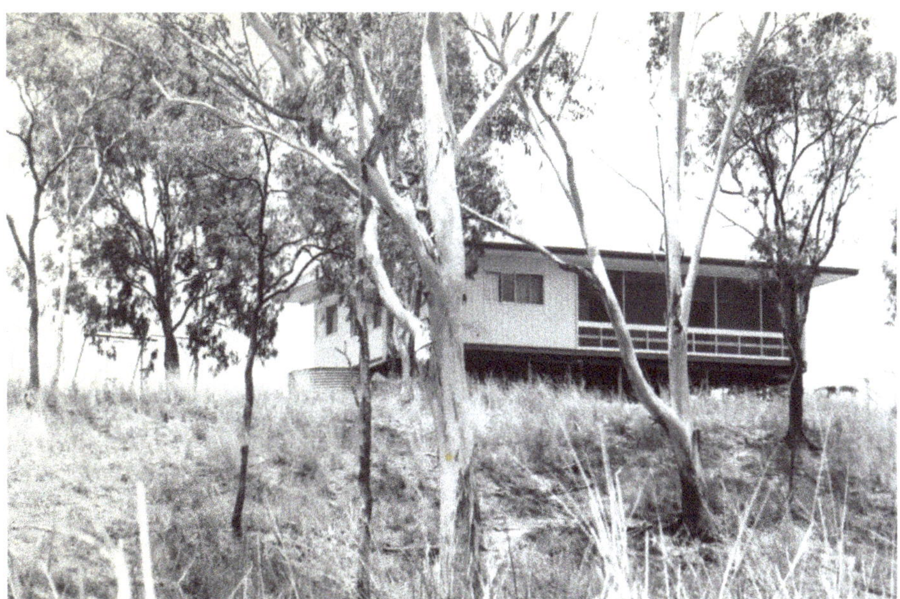

Looking up at our house from the river bank

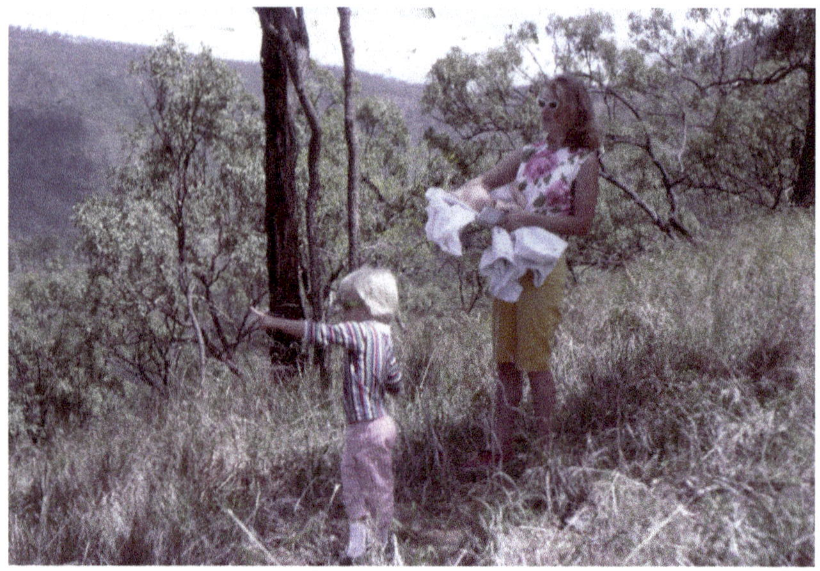

Across the river exploring for Aboriginal art

riverbed which was dry at that time of year and climbed the hill to explore. We did find some simple drawings.

NEIGHBOURS

On one of the weekend trips to see the progress of our building we had passed a truck carrying an old cottage. It was not unusual to see signs in the weekend newspaper of houses for removal. Considering that most homes were built of timber up on stumps, either short or tall, it was an easy process to lift off and take to another location once essential services had been disconnected. As we wandered around our land after checking what latest progress had been made, we suddenly noticed coming down the paddock beside our land was that little old cottage we had passed slowing travelling up the highway. And before long it was lifted off and placed on the riverbank, so we were going to have close neighbours. Later on, we were introduced to John and Marge Ward who would be living there. Marge was the daughter of the Hammond family, whose larger block of land had been divided to give her a place for her home. She had recently married John who was a railway worker. Maud and Stan Hammond were related to the McLachlan's down

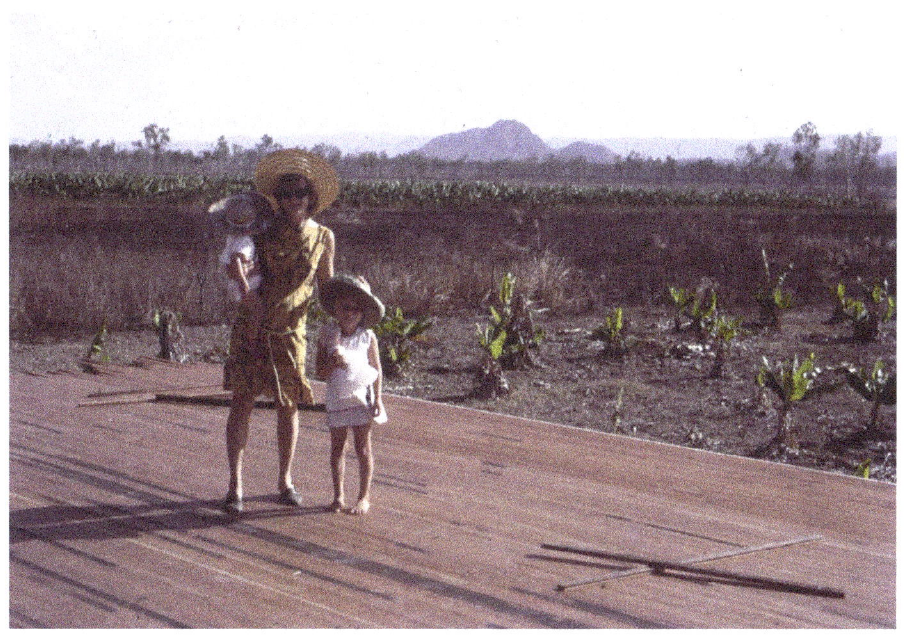

View of bananas in the dry paddock

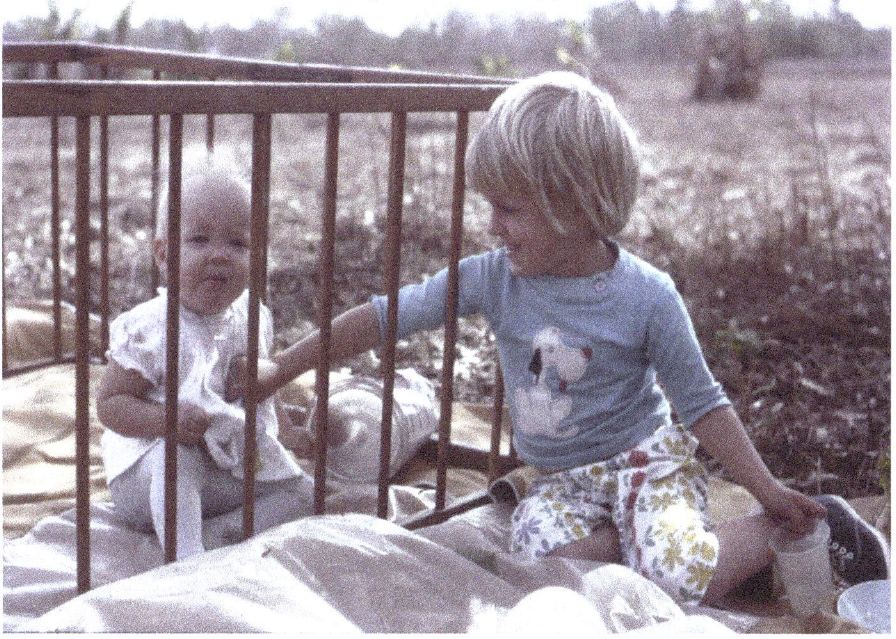

Jenny entertained Jess while we visited the building site

the road who had several married daughters living along the river and elsewhere in the Upper Ross area. McLachlan's also had a younger daughter Sharon, close to Jessica's age. Once living in the Upper Ross, people didn't want to leave. Marge's brother then built a home next to their parents when he married.

Our house on stilts would have a large screened-in verandah with both a dining area and a seating area situated to enjoy the view. The kitchen sink had a window above that opened right over the dining table so food could be passed through the window like a servery. Although we had an indoor dining setting too, the verandah was where we planned to have most of our meals. I was able to plan the kitchen with all the features I liked. And there was plenty of storage. I even added a built-in desk with drawers where I would sit and make phone calls and look at my recipes. To me it was my "dream kitchen".

Much of my free time was spent looking at fittings and fixtures for the final fit out of the house, as these personal touches made a house feel more like a home. But I had also joined the Townsville Art Society, and entered into their activities. They had an exhibition every year and had drawing classes in their clubrooms down by the harbour. Sometimes a special tutor was brought from Sydney. I started to paint a bit again and tried to capture the North Queensland landscape.

While living in town, I had been enjoying playing squash, a game I never knew existed until moving to Townsville. There were teams and fixtures. I joined a club that played once a week. I took baby Jessie along in her jump seat and other players would keep an eye on her while I had my time on the court. Jenny didn't come along as she was enrolled in the Western Suburbs Kindy. Toward the end of November all clubs were closing down for the summer holidays and had what they called "Breaking Up Parties".

NEW FRIENDSHIPS

The squash group was holding a morning tea at the Queens Hotel, along the Strand. I was setting out after parking my car and starting to cross the road to go to the hotel, when I heard someone call out, "*Wait for me.*" This woman who was one of the squash players introduced herself to me as Berice Morelli and we entered together. We found a seat together and started talking amongst ourselves, finding that we were going to be neighbours when our house was finished. And it turned out we both had children starting grade one at the end of January. We were both living quite a way from the school and decided it might be possible to share driving into Aitkenvale State School where we had decided to send the children. It was true that there was a one-room school much closer, but we felt the larger school had more to offer. This did sound like a good arrangement to me for the new school year.

Our home was completed and we needed to furnish it. Bob decided he would build a seating unit and I would need to get foam cushions and buy fabric to cover them. The cushions were firm square shapes about ten centimeters thick. Once we had the cushions, Bob could work out the dimensions and buy the materials.

I had a cane furniture maker build an oval shaped table that I designed with a walnut veneer tabletop edged in cane, and a bent cane base. Most other items we obtained from the second-hand shops. Curtains for the lounge were new proper pleated drapes, but for the bedrooms the sewing machine got a workout. There was a lot of satisfaction in creating part of the furnishings.

I found recently something I had written when we first moved into our new home on the Ross River.

"As I sit here on our verandah overlooking the north Queensland 'bush', the raucous laughter of the Kookaburra echoes back and forth.

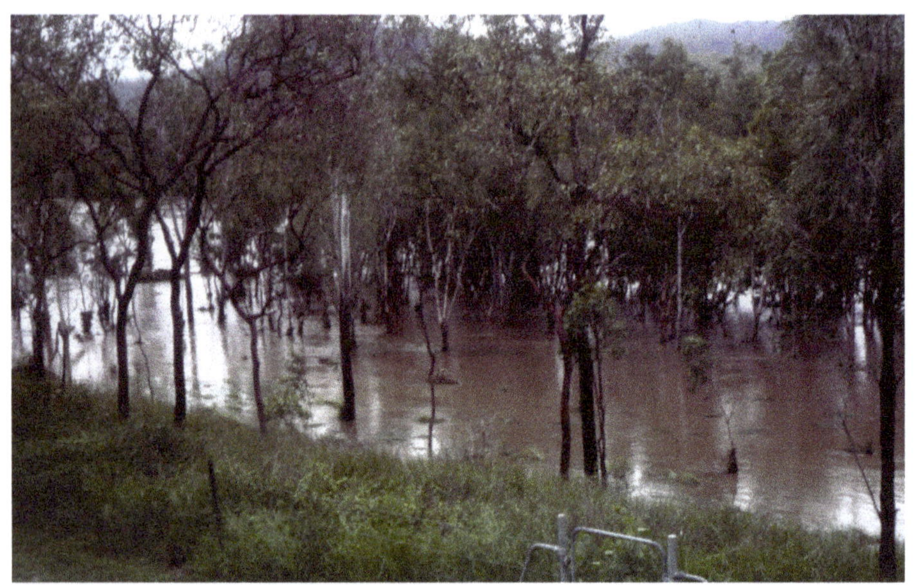

Our river in flood which happened every few years covering the lower terrace

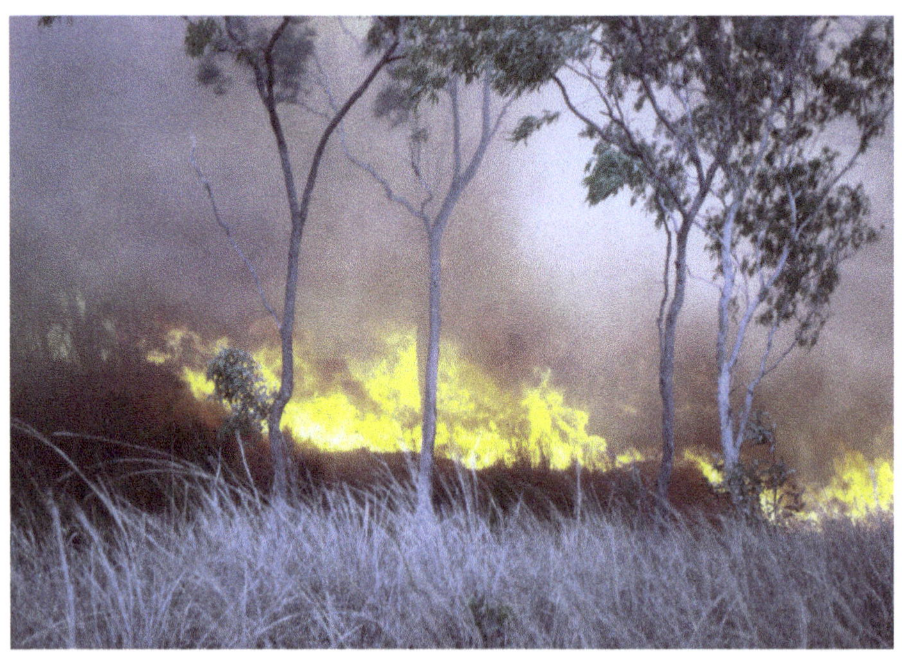

Fire travels so fast

It is so infectious, I usually find myself laughing too. Eucalyptus (or gum) trees line the banks of our river and now I understand the song I used to sing in grade school about kookaburra sitting on the old gum tree. This bird is only one of hundreds I watch with binoculars in my free moments. It is not uncommon to see kangaroos grazing among the trees. In fact, several nights ago I found them helping to "mow" our front lawn. These experiences living in Australia have been worth all the conveniences that may have been left at home."

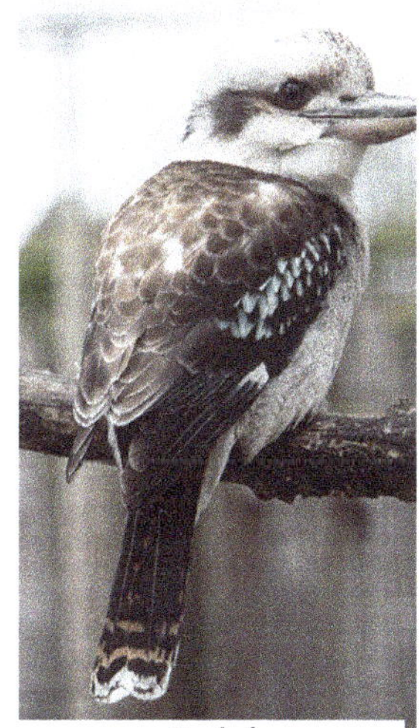

Kookaburra

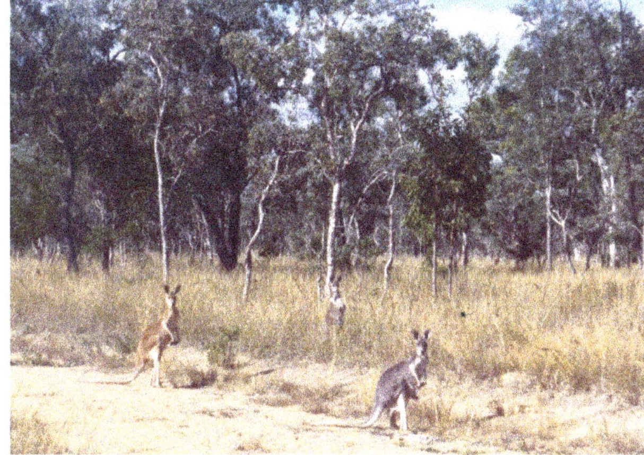

Kangaroos in our paddock

Bob had to drive into the Davies Laboratory that had been built out near the James Cook University each day for work. To begin, it was a long trip down the highway near the meatworks toward Wulguru and then doubling back along the other side of the river. But eventually the Nathan Street Bridge was built making it a quicker trip. But either way, Bob passed near the Aitkenvale State School and could drop off Jenny and Berice's son, Ricky. Ricky and Jenny became good friends. Then in the afternoons, Berice and I would take turns picking up the children. And we got to know each other better.

When living in the bush, fire is something to take seriously. At breakfast one day, Bob could see fire up river, in the distance. He told me to call him at work

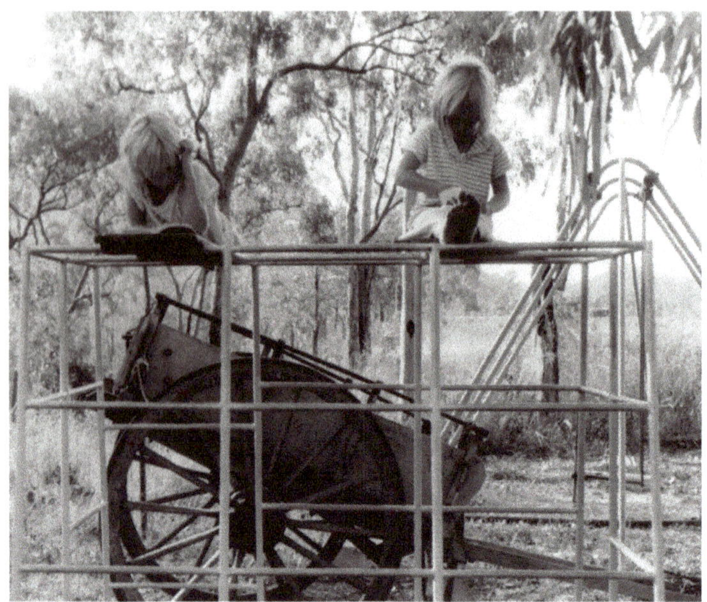

Reading can take place anywhere

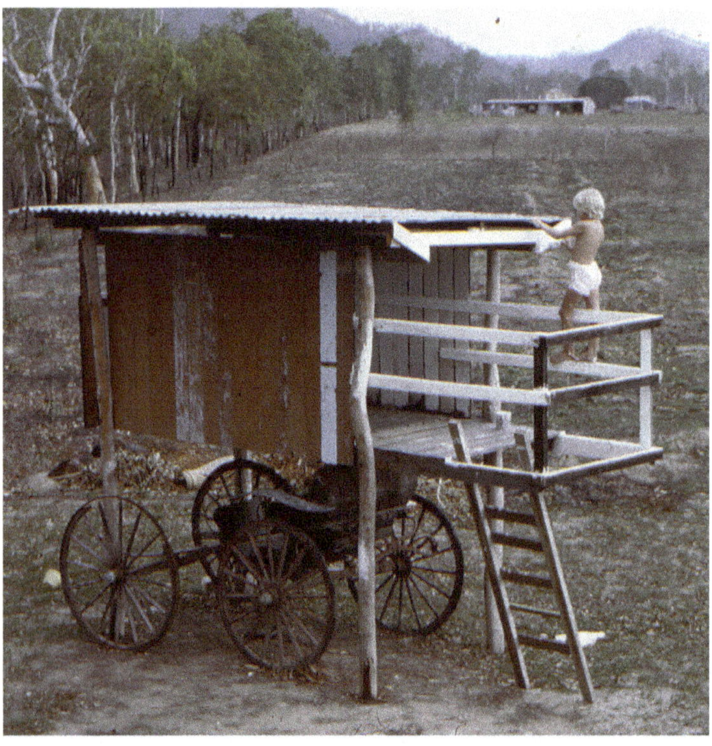

Bob built a cubby house up on stilts using recycled timber

if it got closer. But before we finished eating, it had arrived and all were out fighting it with wet burlap sacks and hoses. The neighbours came to help. The wind changed directions just after it passed our front yard and paddock or it would have engulfed our home. Of course it would have taken him 25 minutes to drive home from work and it would have been well and truly over. It is only until one has had experiences with fire in the bush, that the power of fire sinks in.

Jessie was not old enough for kindergarten or pre-school yet, but happily played around the home. We had tricycles, a swing set and the usual range of toys. Bob had built a cubby house up on stilts to copy the style of building in Queensland. I was busy cooking one day and got a phone call from Jean McLaughlin down the road asking me if I knew Jessica had come to play with Sharon, her daughter. Well evidently Jess had ridden her tricycle a kilometre on the highway and knew just where to go. So I was shocked, as it seemed like she had been here talking to me only minutes before. I quickly retrieved her and hoped that I emphasized that this was not allowed.

When Berice knew I had a background in art, she told how she had always wanted to learn to paint. So I encouraged her to also join the Art Society. They had monthly meetings in the evening at the clubroom near the harbour. We were organised to attend the next meeting, but she called and said she would have to wait until next time as Serge, her husband had to attend a meeting and wouldn't be home to care for the children. I said Bob would be quite willing for her to bring the children to us. In her memoirs she relates this story of feeling very apologetic about descending on Bob to babysit. I was rushing around getting ready with Jessica running around, minus her nappy. I was searching for nappy pins. Bob nonchalantly looked up and said calmly, "*Just go. If worse comes to worse, I'll put the nappy on with rubber bands."* And off we went. I told Berice who was apologizing and saying she should have stayed home, "*I learned if I stayed home over dramas, I'd be there forever.*" We enjoyed the evening and met many other local artists.

While living in California, I had seen a local painting rental program in action. It seemed like something that would work well for the Art Society, so with the group's approval, I set about organising it. Many of the members brought paintings to be displayed in a city centre location that also offered storage. Berice helped with that project. One of the benefits was that a number of city businesses decided to get paintings and could exchange them every three months. Some of the companies had never displayed artwork before. Many paintings were sold as well, since once they hung at home, clients liked them so much, they didn't want to give them back. The rental cost could be put toward the purchase price.

When we met Peter Gillard, he was still single. But eventually he met the right gal and we were invited to the wedding. Before long, we found that Peter and his bride, Maureen were building a house across the long paddock from us. They had adapted a design to have similar styling to South African Cape Dutch architecture from Peter's homeland, so it was definitely not up on stilts. It was built on a cement slab on the ground, which was becoming a more popular way to build. The construction of cement block had whitewashed walls. Eventually they built another new home on acreage, right next door to us on the river with a more Queensland style. These moves enabled the two men to have a carpool to work that lasted for many years. Maureen wanted to have a horse, and acquired Honey, so our families had many common interests. Jenny was very keen on babies and little children and enjoying going over to visit when Ben and Jane came along.

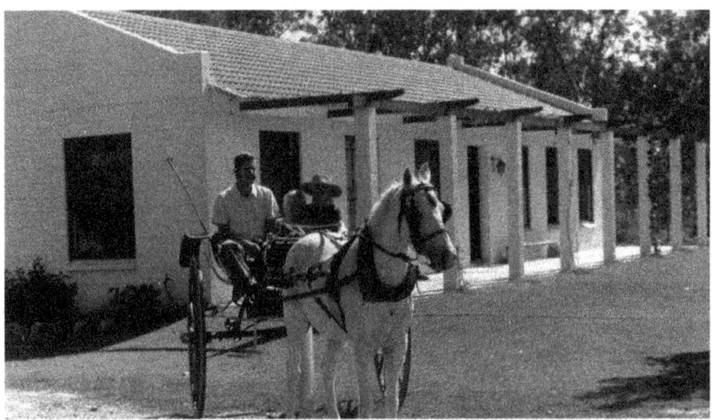

Gillard's first home, South African style

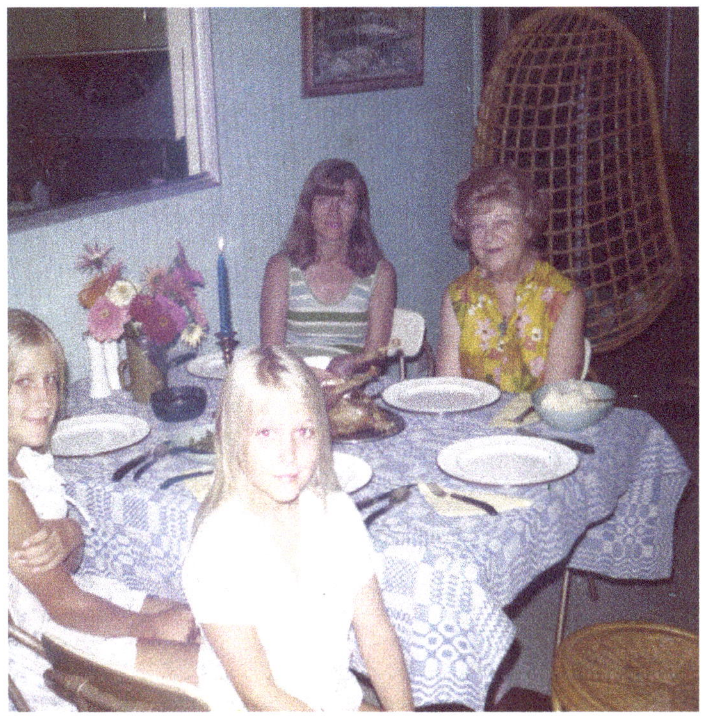

Mealtime on the verandah with Grandma

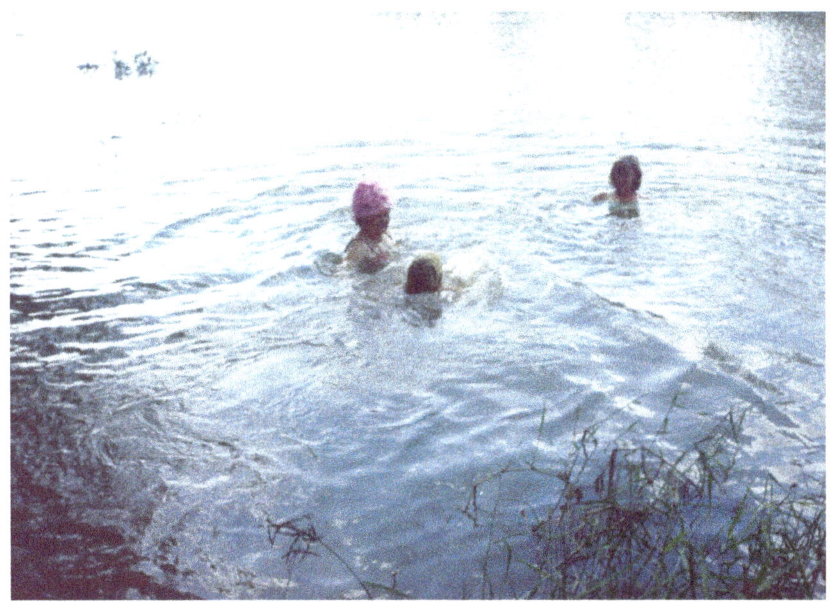

Swimming in the Ross River off our riverbank with Grandma

My mother came to visit in the early years and loved our setting. But the rest of the overseas family were missing these times with our young children.

OUR BIG HOLIDAY 1969

We felt an obligation to the older generation as we had taken away their only grandchildren and we also felt a need to see family and return to our roots. Bob saved all his holiday time for the first four years, so we had a big four-month block of time to make a trip in 1969. At the time, airlines around the world were very generous and flexible in making available around-the-world tickets for very little more than the cost of flying to the United States and back again. There were conditions about keeping going in the same direction and the number of actual stops that could be taken. In addition, Australia was very generous in the vacation time allotted to each worker after one year. We had a four-month block of time owing, but in addition to that we were given a 14% loading of salary for that amount of time. Well the attitude was, we were told, that while on holiday your expenses are higher.

I received brochures from Qantas to learn where stops were permissible and to try and chart out possible visits and adventures. First of all we wanted to head west, as there were many possibilities in that direction before we arrived to see family. So we planned to go to Perth in Western Australia and see the Ozannes, who were Aussies we had known in California and also the Sterns who had returned to Perth by that time. We weekended there before taking the overseas flight.

Our first destination was Sri Lanka to visit friends we had made in California. There was a driver waiting for us at the Colombo airport to take us to Candy, where the research station was located. The Thenabadou family had organised for us to stay in the Kandy Botanical Garden Government Guest House, complete with cook and housekeeper. The beautiful gardens are along a stream that lay just behind the guesthouse. Every evening the mahouts would bring their work elephants to bath in the river.

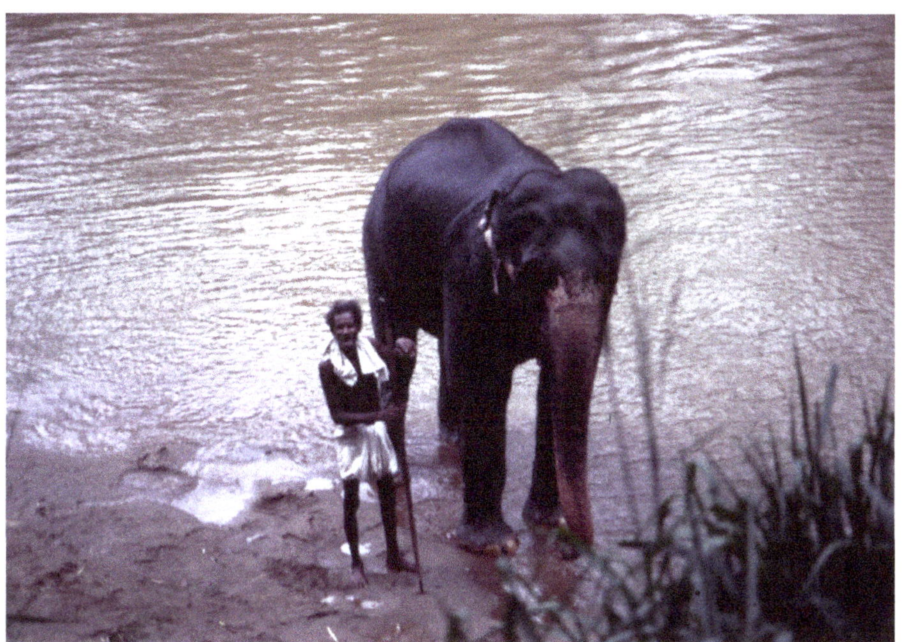

At the bottom of our garden the elephants were bathed

It was very exciting for the children to watch this happening, but they could not be convinced by the mahouts to have a ride on the elephants, until Bob joined them. There was a suspension bridge across the stream by our cottage that was fun to walk on.

We were taken on outings to tea plantations but most special of all was a trip to Sigirya Fortress, a monolithic rock with a fifth century BC palace and kingdom on top. The climb up is challenging but rewarded by seeing ancient rock paintings of beautiful women along the rock face. It is a world heritage site.

We had a delicious dinner one evening with the Thenabadous at their home along with another Ceylonese man we had known. Dinner was disrupted suddenly when blood-curdling screams came from the kitchen and out came the servant trembling. She was talking gibberish, but eventually calmed down enough to say

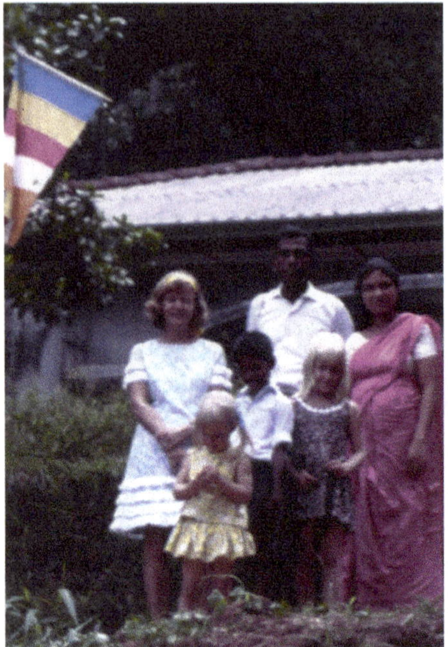

Thenabadu family in Kandy, Ceylon

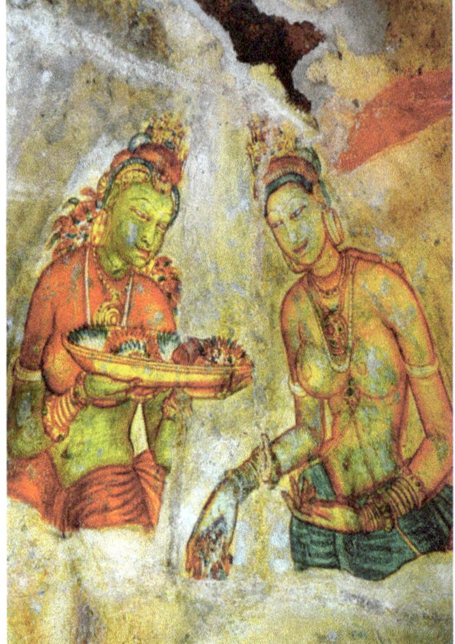

Sigiriya ancient rock fresco

she thought she saw a ghost. It did add a bit of excitement to the evening. But it became clear that the others did think ghosts were possible.

Our timing of the trip was fortuitous as there was a big Buddhist festival with processions of decorated elephants and musicians. I enjoyed shopping for a sari and getting instruction on how to wear it. In later years I wore it to balls in Townsville.

RENEWING OLD FRIENDSHIPS

Our next destination was Delhi, India. Our old friend Sakti had finished his PhD studies and had taken a job in Germany. But he was on home leave and arranged to meet us in Delhi for a week.

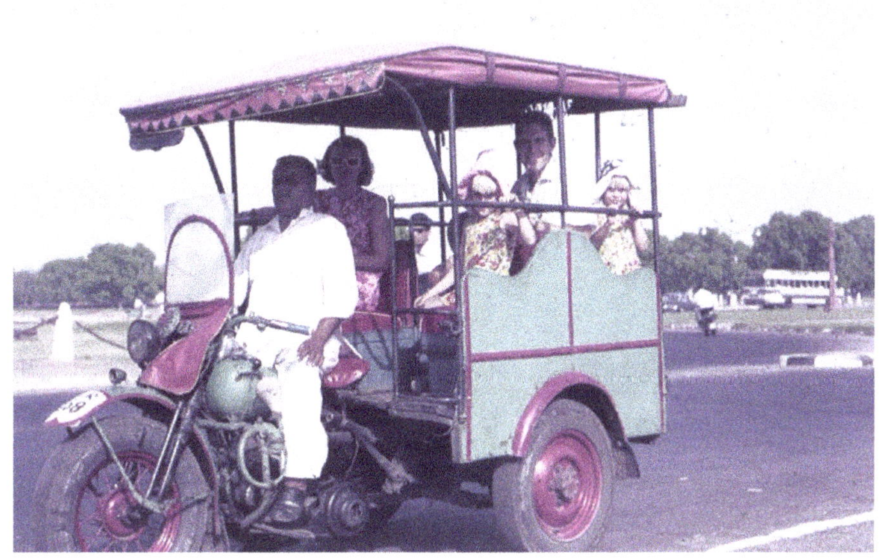

Tuktuk travels

We all stayed at the YWCA Hotel quite near Conneaugh Place, with shopping, monuments and life humming along. Bob had been travelling in his powder blue lightweight summer suit and felt it needed dry-cleaned. So we checked at the hotel office if this service was available and was given the paperwork to fill out along with a bag. The next day we had been out shopping and when back I opened the window hoping for some breeze, as it was quite hot and there was no air conditioning. Well to my surprise, in the garden below was much washing spread out over the grass. And among the many bits of clothing I spotted Bob's suit spread out like the rest. Well I was shocked and worried, wondering if the suit would ever be the same. In actual fact, it was returned later that day in perfect

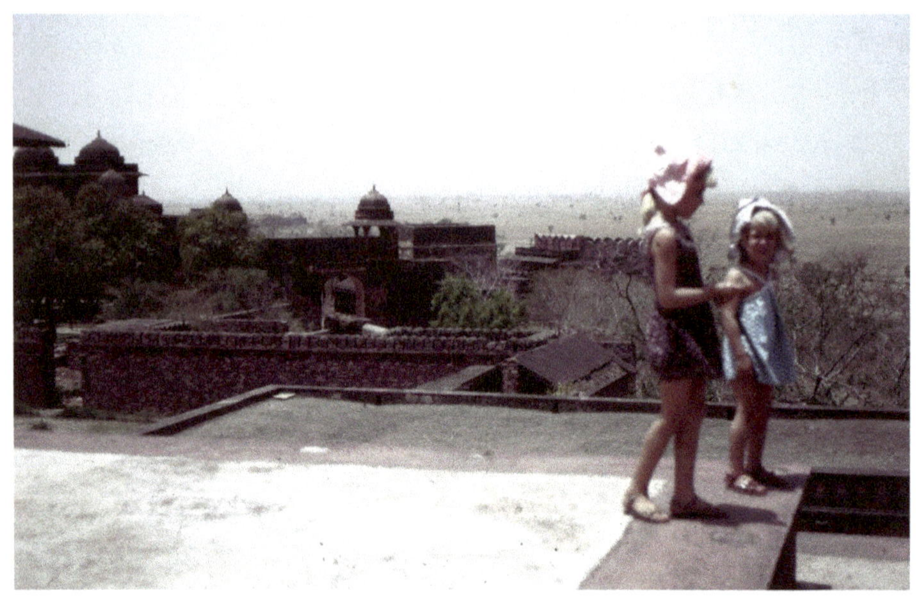

Rooftop India

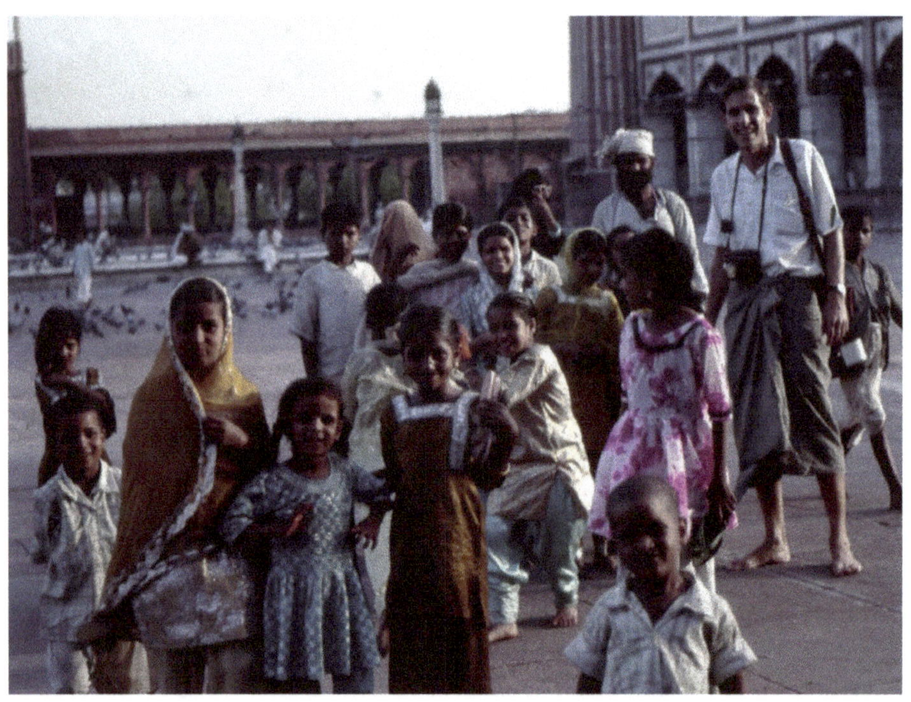

Bob and kids who loved to have their picture taken

condition. Our plan was to take the express train to Agra together to see the famous Taj Mahal. Sakti sent us to the train station to get the tickets, as he wanted us to see how long it took to get anything done in India as partly an explanation of why he had not taken a job in India. Bob had the attitude that the foreign students from developing countries travel to California to get training, but few return back to their homeland to help improve the living standards there.

We visited the Red Fort and went from room to room. Jessie was riding on Bob's shoulders. We would get to another area and Jess would pipe up, "*Oh another bootiful room.*" She was only three and a half years. When people say they are waiting to take family travelling when the children are old enough to benefit from it, I remember how Jess at three years loved it all. We must have been taking a sight-seeing bus, as Jenny was making adult friends on the bus and not wanting to sit with us. She was seven years old. In Agra, we walked along some roads at one point, and villagers from the countryside were coming along. One woman stopped Sakti to ask him something. Afterward we asked him what did she want. He said she had asked if our girls' platinum blonde hair was real, and he said, yes it was. She replied, *"How great God is!"*

ON TO IRAN

Our next planned stop was in Iran, where Ahmed and Brigitte Mokhtarzadeh were living. We were friends in Davis, California and there they were impressed with the fact that I was cutting Bob's hair. He had a crew cut and it actually wasn't easy. We were surprised late one night to hear knocking on the door and there stood Ahmed and Brigitte, she had red eyes. It turned out that Ahmed decided that it would be good for Brigitte to cut his hair too, to save money. Ahmed had wavy hair styled like the Shah of Iran. Brigitte's attempt had not gone well, and Ahmed thought I would be able to fix it. His black hair showed any little imperfection, where as Bob's more blond/brown hair could take a few mis-steps without looking bad. So my attempts to do anything to fix Ahmed's hair only made it worse. At least I took the pressure off Brigitte. The next day Ahmed went to the barber and got a crew cut, a style he kept for the rest of his life.

We liked going to the market and getting simple flat bread, which had been baked on a stone hearth. Then we bought large earthenware bowls with natural set yogurt. Their home was in the city of Shiraz, which is famous for grapes. One day Brigitte cooked a favourite dish, which combined rice with chicken, spices and dried fruit. When finished, the rice at the bottom of the pan formed a thick crust of crunchy delicious rice. I bought a cookbook and that dish became one of our favourites to make back home for special occasions.

Not far from Shiraz is Persepolis, the ruins of the 6th century BC ancient capital of the Achaemenid Empire. It covers large areas with ruins of the city and impressive carved murals in stone. We all went by car for a day's outing to this famous UNESCO World Heritage site we were so fortunate to see. The dry rocky landscape was good for grazing sheep, who were being watched by children. It was interesting to see many of the children were spinning wool as they watched.

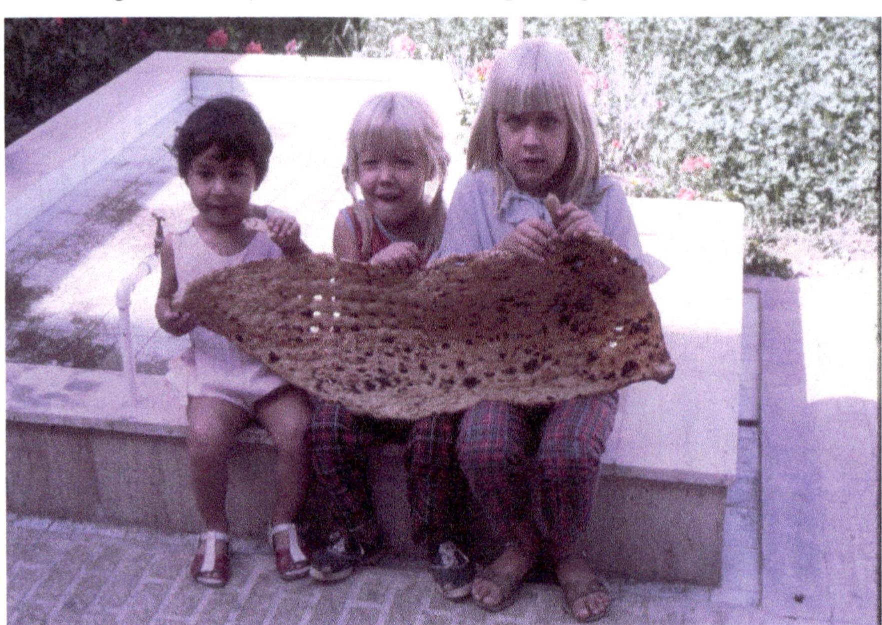

Mitra, Jessie and Jenny enjoying that wonderful bread baked on stones

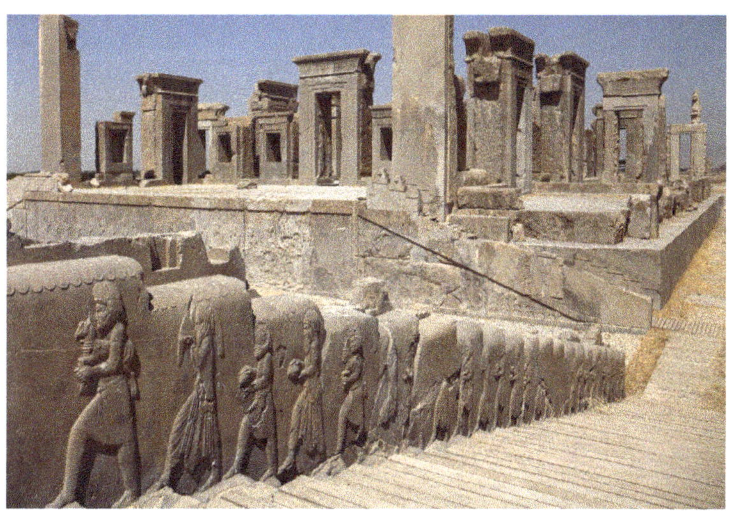

Ruins of ancient Persepolis

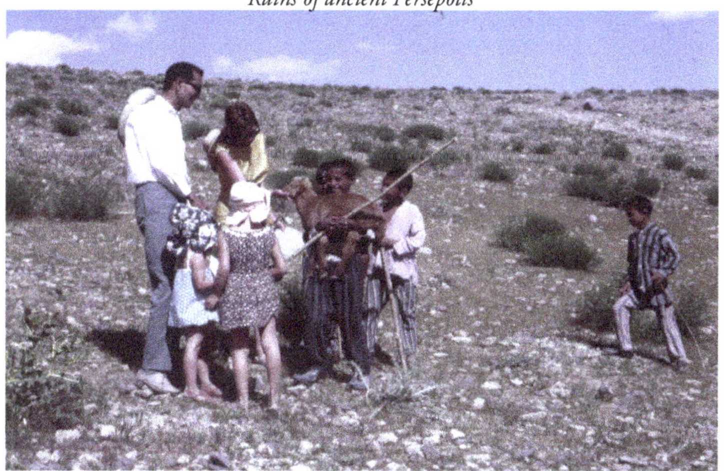

Ahmed and Brigitte, Iranian countryside

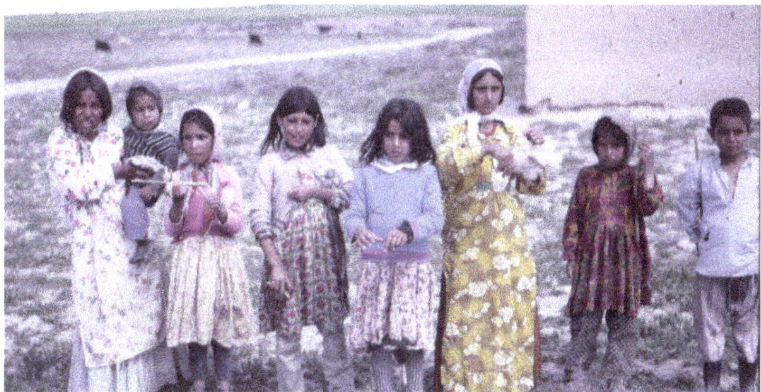

Girls spinning wool while they watch over the sheep

ON TO PITTSBURGH

The remainder of travel time was saved for Pittsburgh and families. We had planned it so we had the entire summer there, sharing time between our parents' homes. Luckily they lived fairly close to each other.

UNEXPECTED OPPORTUNITY

One morning, I saw an ad in the newspaper that Redwing, the Girl Scout Camp where I had once been a camper, was having a week long live-in adult holiday camp that was offering weaving and other crafts. Since my parents were available to babysit, it seemed the perfect opportunity. I had this romantic idea about weaving due to that tablecloth great Aunt Sigrid had woven so many years before. But I had no idea what even a loom looked like.

That first day we were taught to warp up the table loom provided. It seemed so tedious that at lunch break I went to the camp pool and swam, trying to get my shoulder and back muscles relaxed. But I vowed never to do weaving again after the course finished.

The course was designed in such a way that we had to warp up for a new short project each day.

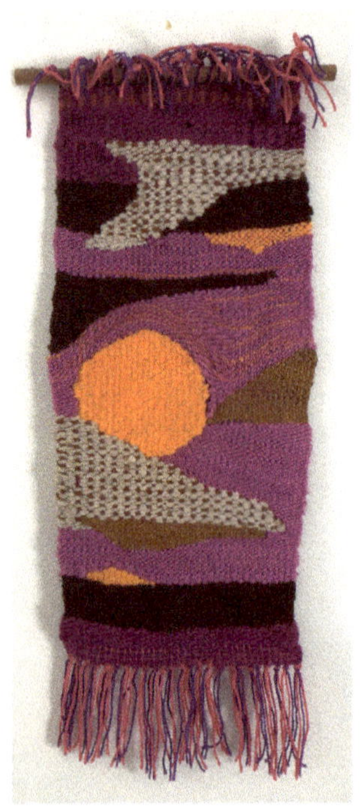

My first weaving made at camp

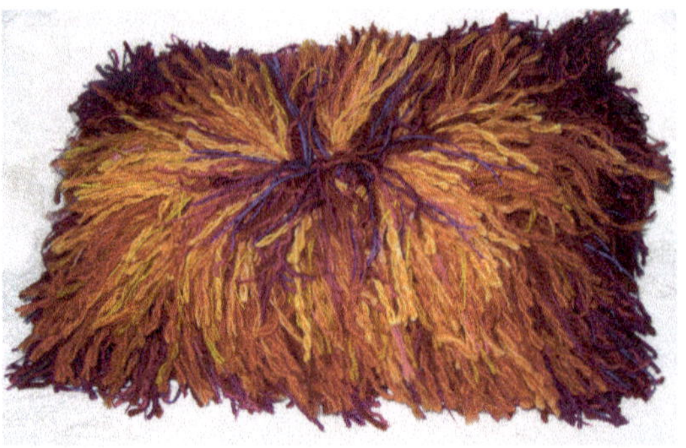

Rya cushion made at camp

By the second day it somehow seemed so easy and by the end of the week I was planning to buy my own loom as soon as I returned to North Queensland.

I did buy a table loom, but longed for a floor loom. So when I saw an ad in the Townsville paper for an auction, where there were three floor looms, I took note. The auction was being held at the Townsville Zoo, which was closing down. It had been set up by the Wirth Family Circus people to display their animals when the Circus quit operating. Evidently the grandmother in the family had been a weaver. The smaller looms were set up on display, but the biggest, with a supposed 51-inch weaving width, was still in a crate. The auctioneer said all the pieces were there as well as the directions for assembly. None of that was true. There were extra things in the crate like a Kodak film splicer and a big rope with a bolt. So I assumed the rope was for one of the animals.

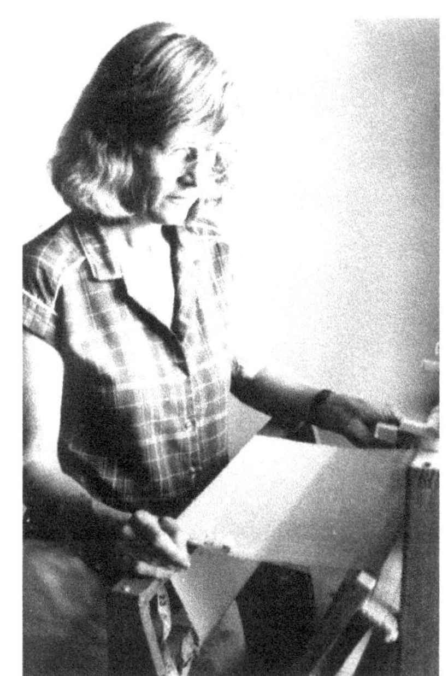

My first table loom

All pieces were wrapped in a 1949 Los Angeles newspaper, as the loom had been made there. To save weight for shipping, one leg was to be used to create the other three. All the hardware was present, but other items were meant as a pattern to complete the pieces. I took it to the local sheltered workshop to get it completed. They put it together as best they could. But it was not functional.

There was no large beam for the cloth to roll around, but Bob found a heavy piece of silky oak timber that would need to be turned on a large lathe. Berice's husband Serge suggested that a friend from church who worked at the Copper Refinery could turn the beam on the equipment there. It was Ken Northey who graciously offered to do the turning. When I wanted to pay him, he didn't want anything, but his wife Lesley suggested a piece of weaving would be lovely to have. So it worked out well for both of us. But still the loom was not functional. So I continued to work on my table loom and enjoyed the use of colour, texture and design. But finding suitable weaving yarns was not easy in Australia at that time. I then started to spin some of my own especially for textured wall hangings.

BOB'S LIFE-CHANGING GIFT

While we had been away for four months, Serge had come across a sulky buggy

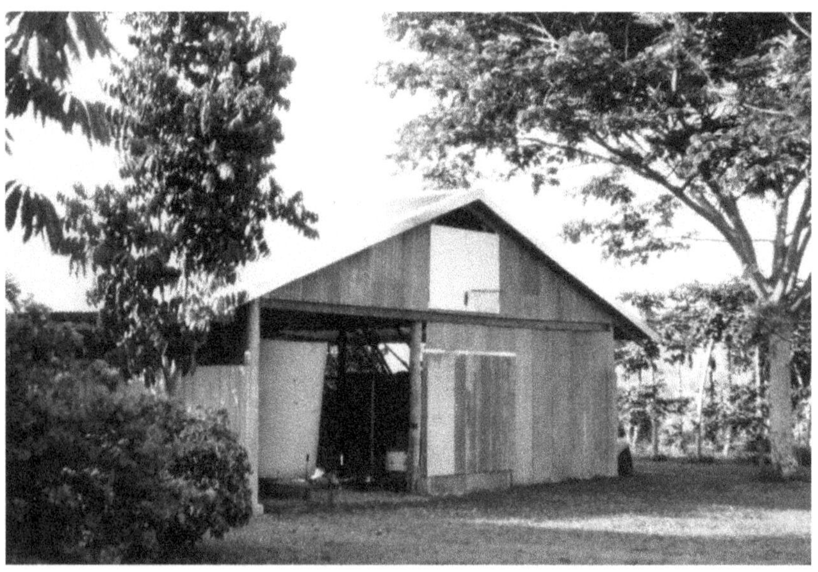

The shed Bob built complete with basketball hoop

that was available for sale with the original leather seats and lamps. He had bought it for Bob, thinking he would be able to use it with our ponies that we had been acquiring and we had even bred one. At that point Bob realised he needed a shed and went about building one that was as big as our home.

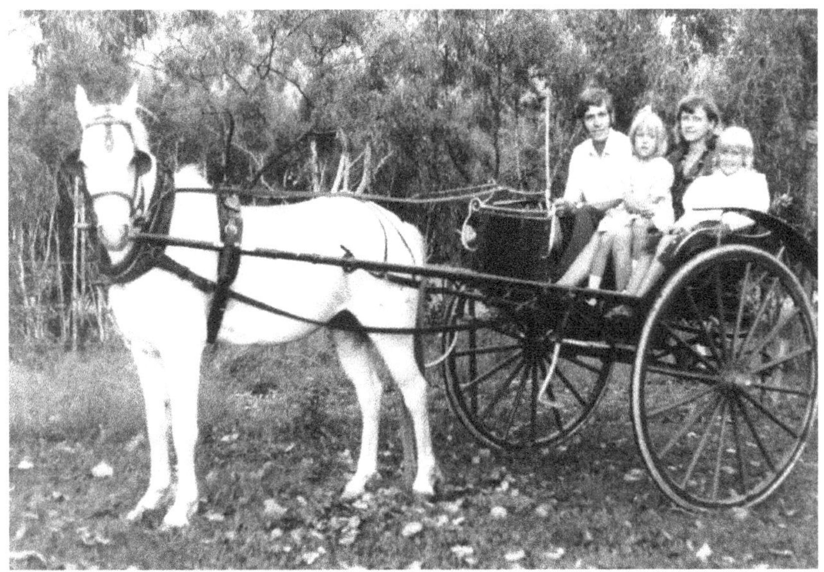

Our first horse-drawn vehicle drawn by Misty. Somehow the whole family fit in.

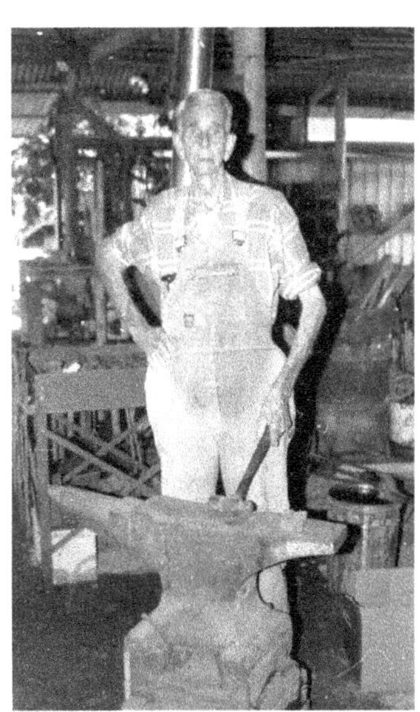

Dick Gelling with the anvil

Serge had a hobby restoring vintage cars and Bob started to find horse-drawn vehicles to work on himself. He would hear about a vehicle that needed rescuing from the white ants out on a property in the west, and would organize with a friend to go out and retrieve it. Eventually we found that we had a growing number of these and Bob needed to learn some skills. He also needed some appropriate tools. Finding out where there had been blacksmith and wheelwright shops took him around the older suburbs of Townsville where he met Dick and Cyril Gelling. Dick was in his 80s and Cyril had not carried on the business. Bob was able to buy his anvil and other tools to start building up a proper workshop. But Bob wanted someone to teach him the needed skills. Dick suggested another old-timer, Harry Pope, who had been a wheelwright. Both these men were agreeable

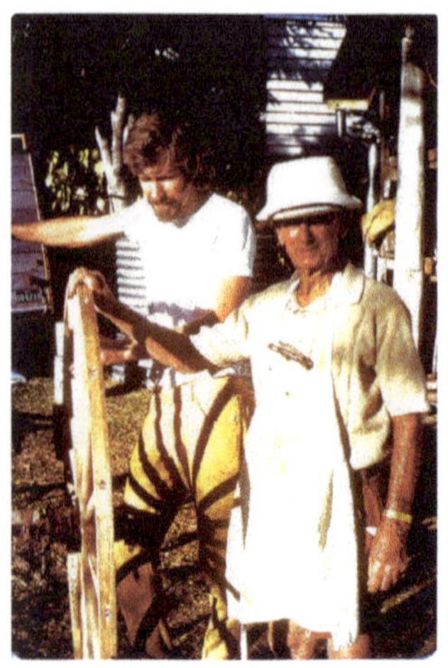
Bob and Harry Pope

to come out on weekends and give Bob some training. And I would provide lunch on the verandah. These men appreciated that someone was interested in their knowledge and enjoyed these outings. And now both Bob and I had hobbies that would be compelling. At one point Harry said to Bob, *"I couldn't do a better job myself. But you wouldn't want to be paid by the job with the amount of time it takes you to do it."*

Bob needed a horse to go with the hobby. We had started with the small pony, Choco for Jenny. She was a mare, so we decided to have her bred. The foal was named Pegasus. Jenny thought the whole process with the stallion was most interesting and wrote her grandparents all about it. Bob started off with a white horse called Misty. But he wanted a larger horse and decided to get one unbroken from our friends, the Clarkes, out at "Fanning River" near Mingala. It was love at first sight for Bob. He named the horse Xerxes, after the Persian king Xerxes the Great 518-465 BC. This was shortly after we had our

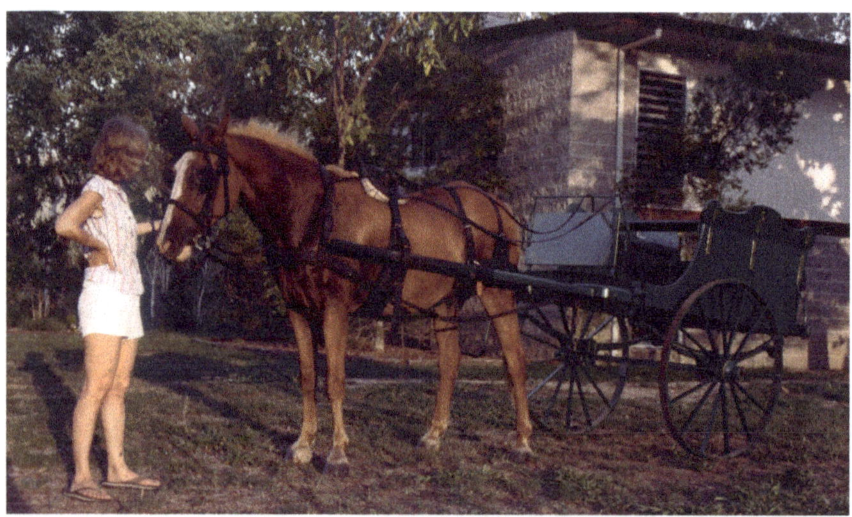
Xerxes and the Butcher's Cart

wonderful holiday to Persia and had been visiting Persepolis. The sire of Xerxes was Darius, so it was the perfect name. Bob then had the experience of breaking in the horse and training it. His knowledge was gained from books, as he had no previous experience. He was a beautiful horse. Unfortunately some years later, Xerxes got his leg caught in barbwire and never fully regained full movement.

The girls went to pony club and competed in Gymkhanas. Jenny inherited Misty and was very good at barrel races. Some American visitors came to work at the University for a year and the daughter was similar in age to ours and wanted to keep a pony at our place. The father was an expert Herpetologist and showed us an easy way to identify the snakes we would see around our property. It involved the scales between the eye and nostril. If there was an extra scale, it was non-venomous. If the scale surrounding the eye met up with the scale surrounding the nostril, then the snake was definitely poisonous. The only trouble was you needed to get pretty close to be able to see clearly. Bob and I started to catch snakes alive and put them in a jar with alcohol. We were relieved to see that many of them were not poisonous.

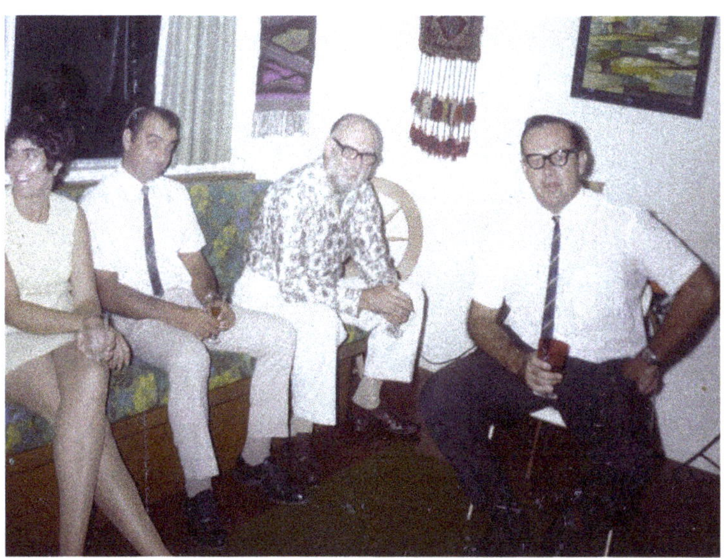

40th party with Berice and Serge Morelli, Dr Ian Dickson and Les Edye

My parents were able to visit in 1971 and it happened to be their 40th wedding anniversary so we had a party. It was a chance to invite some of our friends we had made by that time. And they were keen to see for themselves all we had done to create a home in the dry tropics. Initally we did not have reticulated water, so it was pumped from the river. Also there was a rainwater tank, but rain could

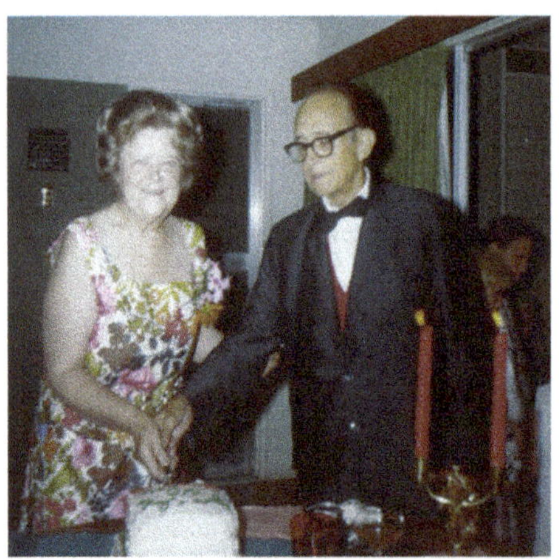

Cutting the cake

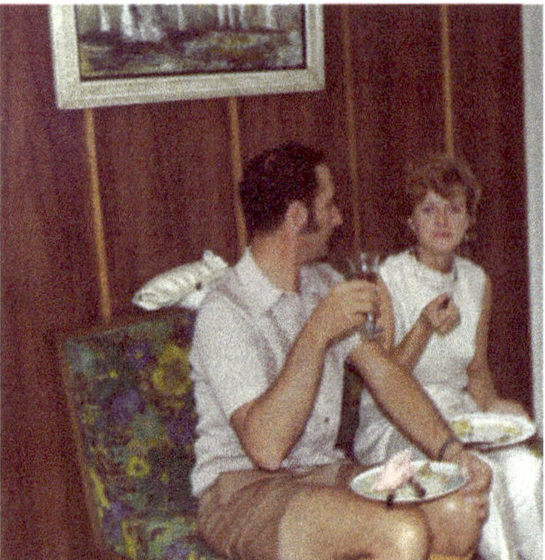

Paul and Dana

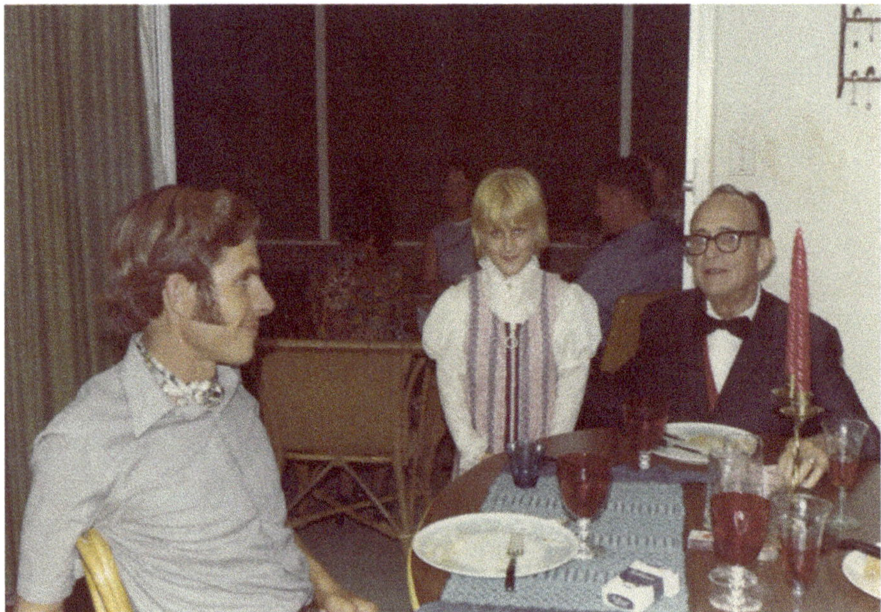

Bob, Jenny and John, my father

not be depended upon. Originally when we bought the land, it was only a dirt road out that far. But by the time we finished building, the road had been sealed.

ARIZONA

When my father was critically ill in 1972, I went back to Arizona where my parents had moved to see if the warmer climate would improve Dad's health. My mother said one day, "*Dana, take a break and go down to the 5th Avenue shops where there are lovely things like Indian jewellery and pottery.*" Well there I found a weaving studio and in the back workroom I could see the identical loom to mine. There was that "animal" rope which proved to be a vital part of the loom, controlling the warp advancing mechanism. So I sent pictures home to Bob who put the loom together in the correct way. I wove on that loom for the next 40 years. It was good in one way that the end of my father's life came with the experience that opened up a new creative life for me. After the funeral, my mother and I took a little trip together up to the Grand Canyon. It was an uplifting experience, seeing some natural beauty in life after going through the difficult experience of slowly watching my father's life slip away.

For the first years I was the only weaver in Townsville and slowly a few more came. Through grant money the Art Society group put on some workshops, bringing tutors from elsewhere. None of them could look at my loom and identify the brand, as it was different to most looms being manufactured. I wrote to numerous companies to see if they knew what loom I had. Eventually a James Gilmore from California wrote back telling me I had a Binder loom and they had not been manufactured since about 1949 when my loom arrived in Townsville. That was the date on the newspaper wrapped around the loom parts in the crate.

Janet DeBoer was invited to give a workshop on weaving in Townsville. She was an Occupational Therapist from Colorado and somehow ended up in Queensland. I billeted her at our home and that was to be the beginning of a long friendship.

She was also starting to write and edit a textile journal called Textile Fibre Forum. It started as a simple duplicated black and white newsletter type publication and became a full-colour glossy journal with feature articles and regular columnists within a few short years. But equally important were the Forums she organised several times a year, bringing in overseas tutors in a wide range of textile related subjects. These were held for a long time at Mittagong, NSW at a boarding school during the holiday break when students went home. Other locations were in Canberra, ACT and Geelong, Victoria. There were evening programs, bookstores, and shops set up with supplies we might need for our classes. But the mealtime entertainment that Janet provided with her flare for acting always made the events a fun, if not hilarious time.

During the years I took the opportunity to take various courses. One year I took Indigo Dyeing with Jim Lyle from USA who had written books on natural dyes. Although I had been doing indigo dyeing for quite a while, Jim brought an abundance of new information. Another time I did basket making with the Aboriginal ladies from Maningreda who brought plant material for us to work with as well as dyestuffs. It was a privilege to have the week with them. One year I organised for Bina Rao and husband Keshav to come to a Forum as teachers of a natural dye workshop. They came and shipped ahead numerous Indian dyestuffs. Jenny went with me another year and we did a course with a Cook Island woman on their style of quilt making. Janet finally decided to retire from all this activity, but is still very much valued for her wealth of knowledge. And we now see each other at The Asian Art Society of Australia (TAASA) events.

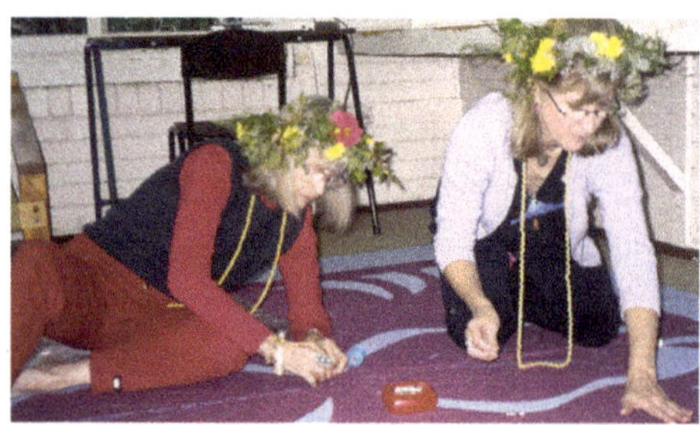

At forum working on the Cook Island quilt

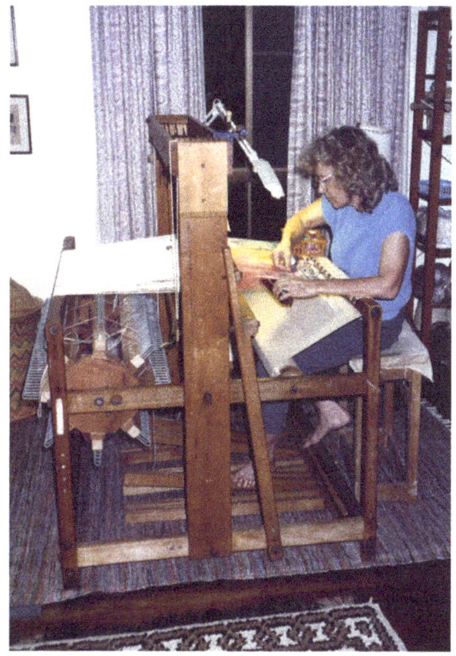

When the loom finally worked

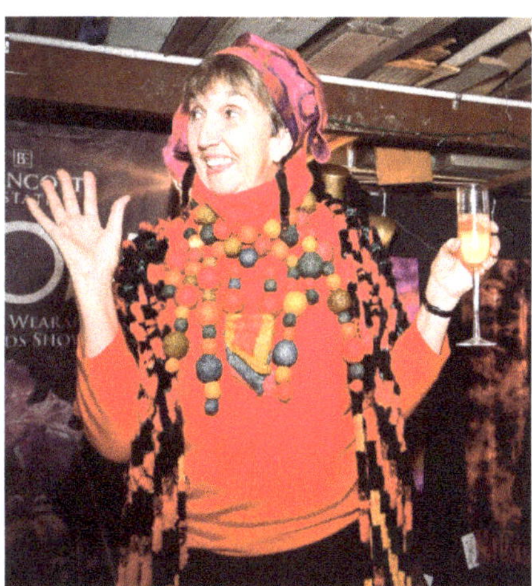

Janet de Boer in entertainment mode

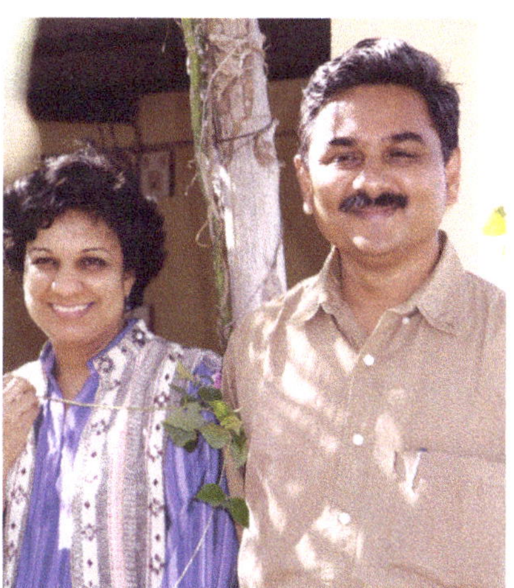

Bina and Kesav Rao

I had helped organise a new group in 1975 we called "Fibres and Fabrics Creative Textiles Association" (Fibres & Fabrics) in Townsville and quickly built up a membership covering numerous textile areas. During those earlier years I joined Queensland Spinners Weavers and Dyers Group (QSWDG) and the Victorian Spinners and Weavers. I anxiously awaited the newsletters from both groups each month to inspire me and give me contact with other weavers. Fibres & Fabrics held Exhibitions and Awards with grant money. Part of our reason for starting the group had been the reluctance of "The Art Society" to accept textiles into their Pacific Festival Awards. This group is still active and I continue to receive their newsletters, having been made an honorary life member.

Back to my Great Aunt Sigrid's tablecloth, I eventually wanted to weave one myself. I couldn't find a similar pattern anywhere, so got out graph paper and plotted it out. I wove it in two pieces as she had done with a join in the middle. However a few years later, I found a Swedish weaving book with the same pattern. The limitation I found was not having the same yarns available for the project.

I continued to find so many interesting things to weave. If I was feeling creative, I could make woven tapestries and entered textile exhibitions around Australia. If I wanted to make practical items, there were floor rugs, hand towels, fabric for clothing. And although I started out using chunky yarns and textures, I eventually moved more to fine threads of linen, cotton. silk and even tencil. As we lived in a tropical climate, creating lightweight fabrics was more logical. And I enjoyed wearing clothes that I had made with fabric I had woven. I also used raffia and indigo dye.

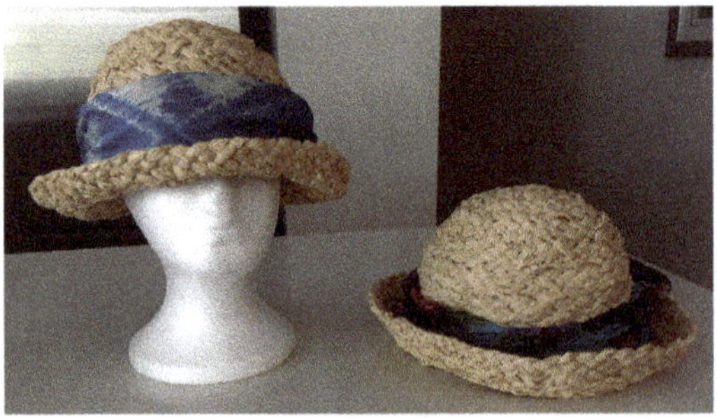

Raffia Hats by Dana and Uta

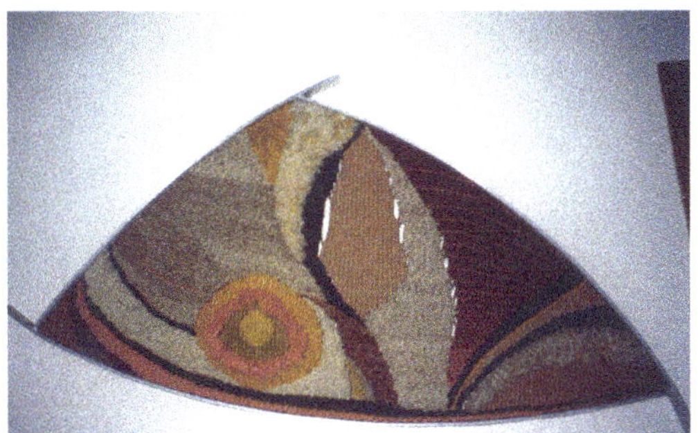

Solar Series

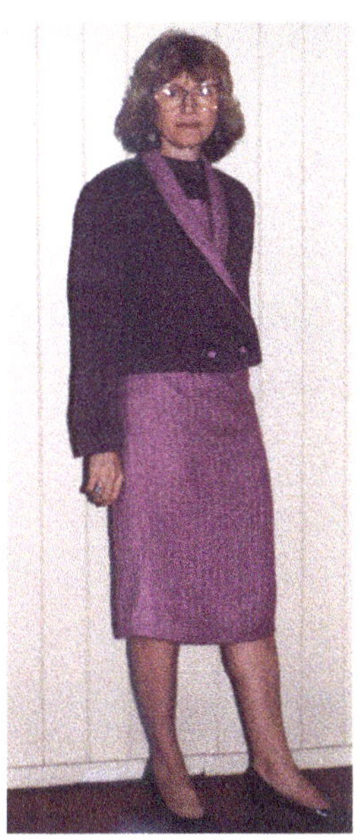

Two-piece silk blend outfit

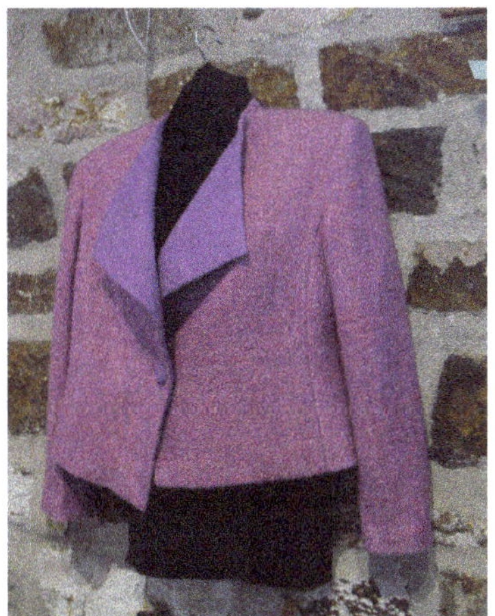

Woven and dyed silk blend

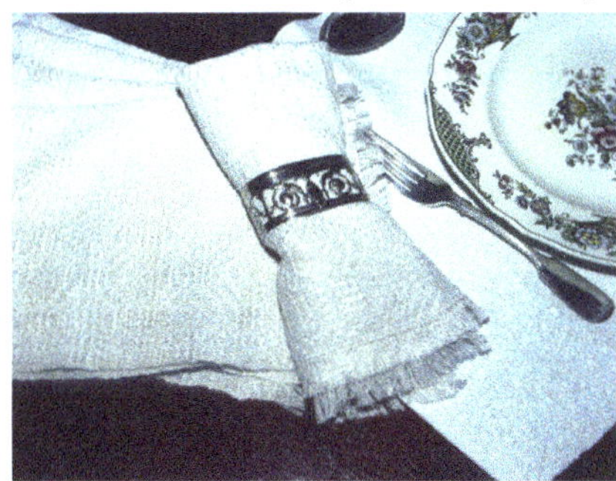

Table linen

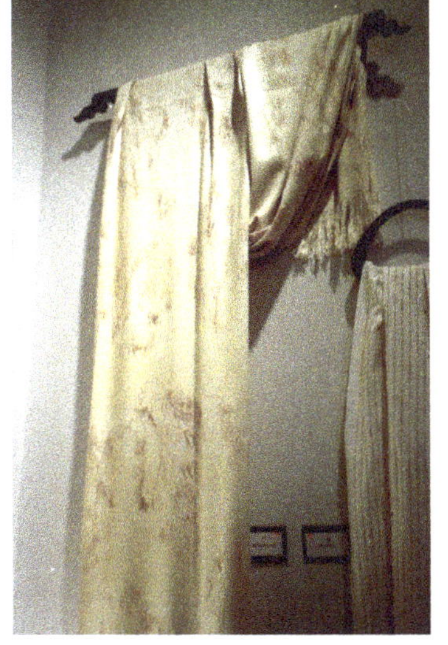

Pure silk stole warp printed

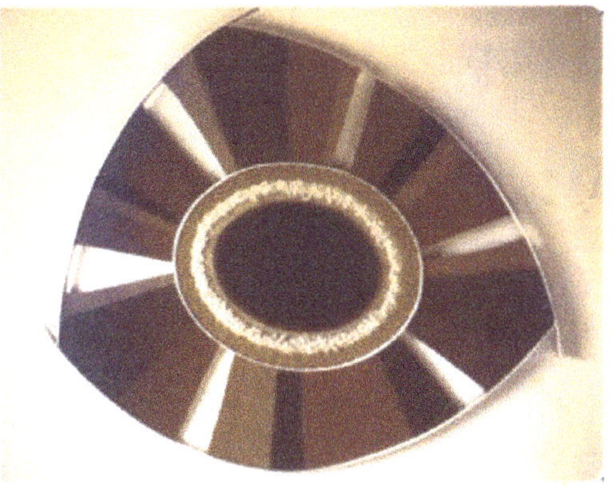

Sun Burst

A CHANGE IN DIRECTIONS 1975

One day Bob Reid, a colleague of Bob's from CSIRO came along with a friend from the Native Plant Association. He and John Donohue were both experts in knowledge of propagating and growing natives. They came to us because we had land and access to a water supply from the river to set up a native plant nursery. In fact our only water had been from the river, which we pumped up to a tank. They had the opportunity to accept a contract from the Copper Refinery to landscape a large area to screen a holding pond. It required growing appropriate species, setting up irrigation then planting them and caring for them until they became established. It provided a good return, which was useful to us, as we were getting ready to depart for just over 12 months to work in Ethiopia.

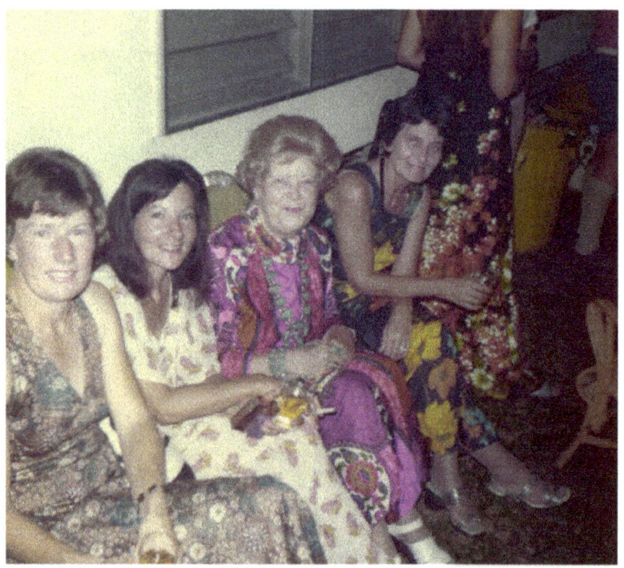

Maureen, Robin, Mother and June on New Years Eve at the Reids

Bob and Rhonda Reid were known for their great New Years Eve parties. Once my mother was here visiting at the right time and was able to attend.

MORE CHAPTER THREE IMAGES

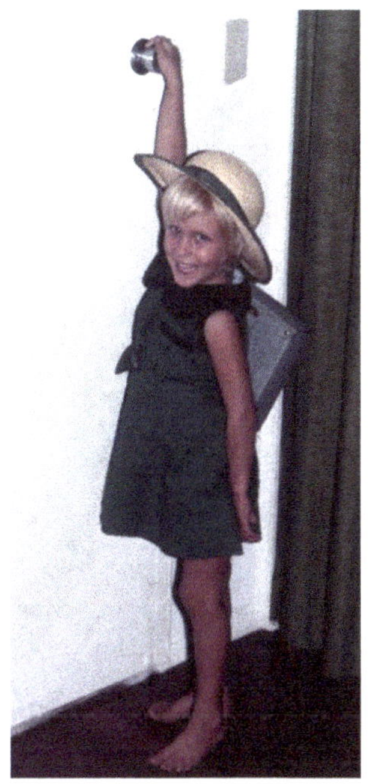

Jenny in her school uniform

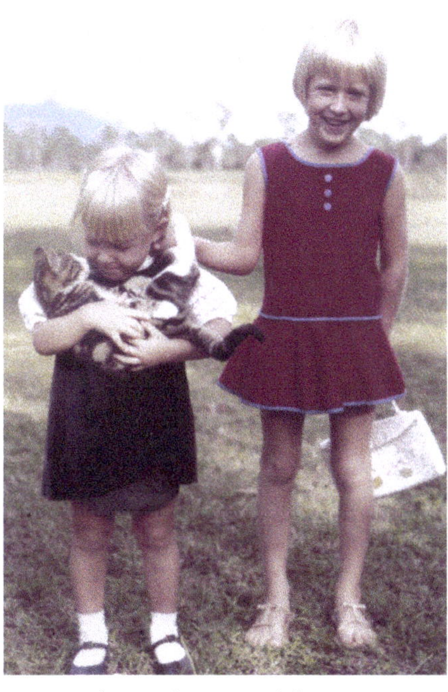

Jess, the cat whisperer with big sister, Jenny

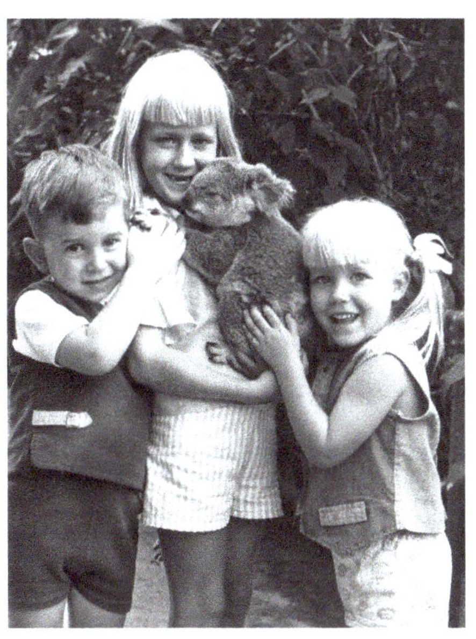

Sandro Tothill, Jenny, and Jessie at Lone Pine

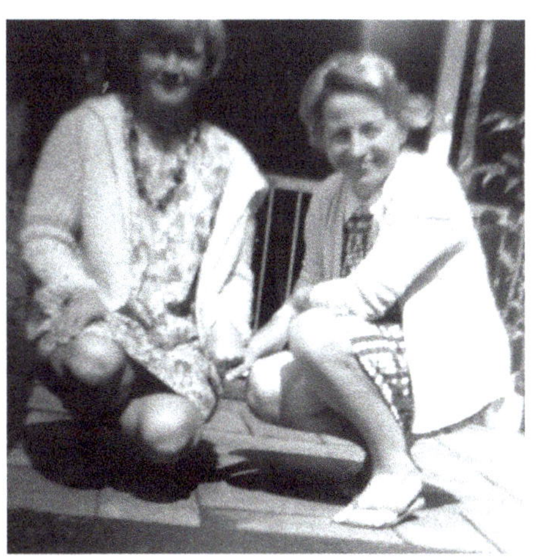

Dana with Yolanda Tothill

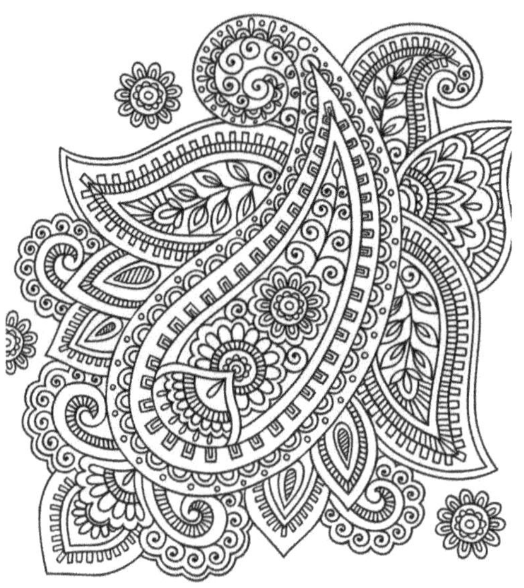

04

Africa At Last

ETHIOPIAN ADVENTURES 1976 -77

Bob was under secondment to ILCA, the International Livestock Centre for Africa, to take the role of Research Director, in Ethiopia. This was the type of opportunity Bob had been working toward. So the nursery project that would see the planting done before we left, fitted into our timeframe. John Donohue and his family would live in our house while we were away, making it convenient to have our own garden cared for and the cat fed. John would be there to water plants and keep the nursery expanding.

Bob did not have time to work among the plants, but he was happy to build an extra room onto the back of his shed to be used for a nursery office. In the end we all went to plant the thousands of plants and trees to form a three-layered screening just before we departed for our year away. The group was comprised of wives, husbands, children, and even some friends.

We travelled to the USA before going to Africa. First stop was Arizona to see my mother and then Pittsburgh to see the McCowns. We arrived in 1976 in Addis Ababa, the capital of Ethiopia where the offices of ILCA were located. When Bob had lived in Ethiopia nearly 20 years earlier, Haile Selassie was the Emperor.

In 1974 there had been a military coup d'état and the communist Derg ran the country. Outside Bob's office building was a soldier with a machine gun and when entering there was a body search. It was the same at government buildings like the post office. In spite of security of persons entering Bob's workplace, that did not stop events happening outside the building. One day after work as staff were leaving, the husband of a secretary was parked at the curb waiting for her. Suddenly a motorcyclist pulled up and shot him, riding off in a flash. It was said to be a political execution. But this was the environment during our year in Africa.

We were given rooms in the Ghion Hotel until a house could be located for rental. At the time, it was difficult to find anything, so we stayed at the Ghion for about three months. It had a lovely hot springs swimming pool and an excellent dining room, so we were very comfortable. But the search was on, as we preferred to be in a normal neighbourhood.

The girls had been settled into school. In the middle of the city area was the Lycée Guebre-Mariam, which we thought would give Jenny an opportunity to become fluent in French. It was a large school with international students, but a large number of Ethiopians as well.

Although we had originally signed Jenny up for lunch in the cafeteria, it turned out, she never got there. She had made many Ethiopian friends who went out on the curb in front of the school and their maids brought lunch, which they shared with Jenny. The national dish was based on a sourdough large crepe made out of teff flour and called injera. This was eaten with a stew-like dish called wat using pieces of injera to scoop up the stew with the hand. It could have chicken, lamb, beef or lentils and vegetables. It did have hot spices, but was very delicious.

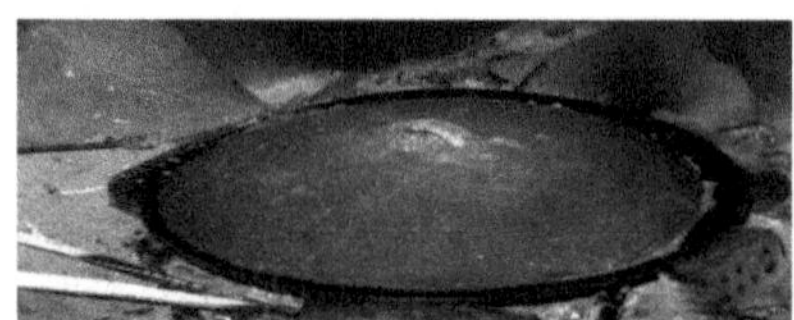

Injera is cooked on a large ceramic plate over open fire

Jessica was ready for grade six and we chose quite a different experience for her at the American International School, so she was mainly making international friends. There were some other children whose parents also worked at ILCA, which was nice, as she would also meet up with them at work related social functions.

FURTHER EXPLORATIONS

We decided to have a little holiday by car, driving to the east visiting the towns of Dire Dawa and Harare. Bob's assistant Abiy came along to drive. His lovely wife and baby, came along as well as Seble, a dear Ethiopian friend of Jenny's. At some point we came across a roadblock. While we were stopped to show our credentials, another car came from behind us and knocked over the barricade and sped through without stopping. Immediately the soldier with his riffle insisted in getting in our car and chasing the vehicle that sped ahead. We drove along for quite awhile but finally the solder said we could take him back. How lucky that we never caught up with the other car.

We found a popular juice joint in Dire Dawa that blended wonderful tropical fruits like "Soursop", mango, and pineapple together for refreshing drinks. In Harare the people were more Somalian and wore different clothing than the Amharas. They had wonderful woven injera baskets for serving the food. We found one we loved with natural dyed colours to take home.

We were told there was an attraction to see at night on the edge of the escarpment of a Hyena Man feeding wild hyenas by hand. We went along and watched as he started to call the animals to come. He had a basket full of bones to carefully offer the wild animals whose jaws can powerfully crunch large bones. He would feed for a while and then invited people sitting on the hillside behind him the chance to feed with him. Suddenly Jessie jumped up and ran to sit with him before we could even realize what was happening. One could see that Hyena Man did not have all his fingers, but luckily Jess returned to us with all of hers. What a scare and a relief that it was all over. But later that night Jess woke up with a nightmare that was more like "night terrors". It took a long time for them to stop.

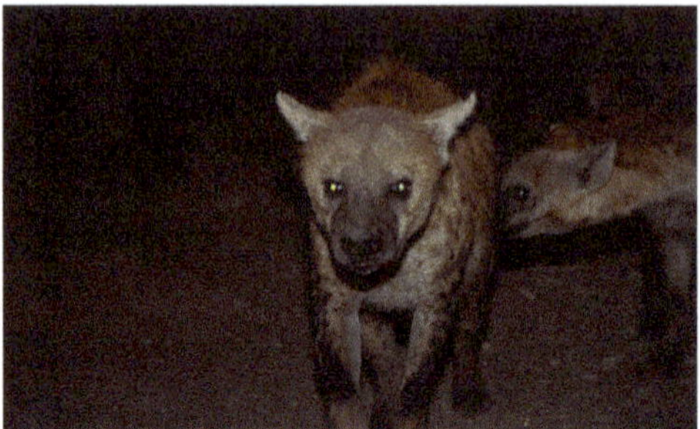

Hungry hyenas

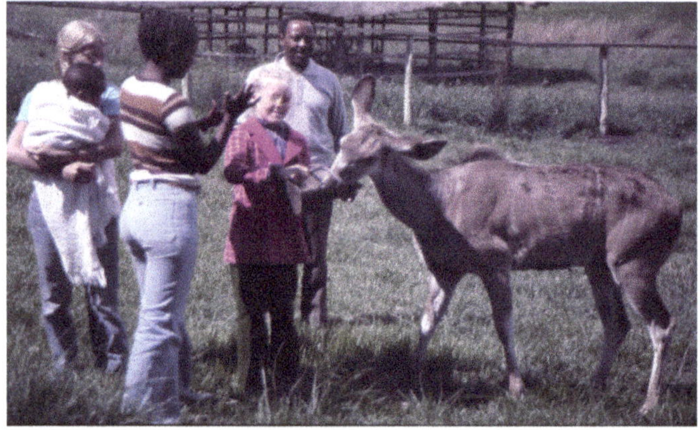

The girls with Abiy and his young daughter

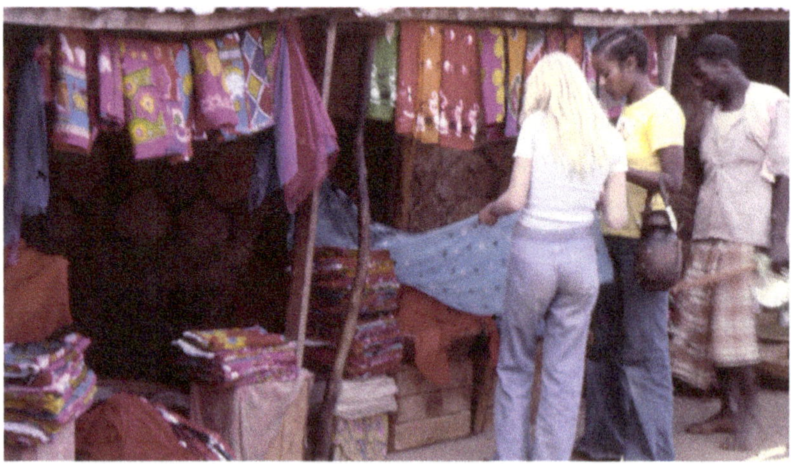

The girls enjoyed the textile markets

Back in Addis, to make life more interesting, the Africa Cup of Nations finals would be held at the stadium and the Ethiopian team was staying in our hotel. And of course Jenny and Seble somehow had met a number of the players and the German wife of the football coach. The first of the competitions were coming up and Jenny and Seble were invited to go with the team and sit on the bench with the coach's wife. I was absolutely stunned by the idea of this happening, as I was worried about riots that one hears about happening around such games. The coach's wife called me and assured me that she would be well taken care of. And she went. Several weeks later, late one night there was a knock at the door. When opening it, there was one of the football players with a gift of a bronze Egyptian statue for Jenny. She was asleep long before.

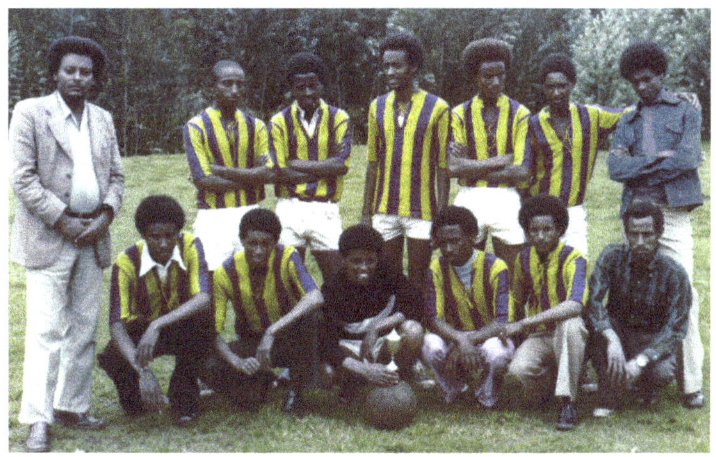

Ethiopian National Football Team

The Ghion pool had a lovely setting and was a place the young crowd frequented. That is where Jenny had actually made friends with Seble, who had come on the road trip with us. Seble had finished high school and was awaiting the communist government to send her to university overseas to another communist country. Upon finishing school, she had been sent out into the countryside to work with farmers like the other students for "Zemeche". This was a development through co-operations plan to make everyone on an equal level, socially and economically. Now she waited. Her choice was to study dentistry in Yugoslavia. Meanwhile Jenny got to know her and her lovely family.

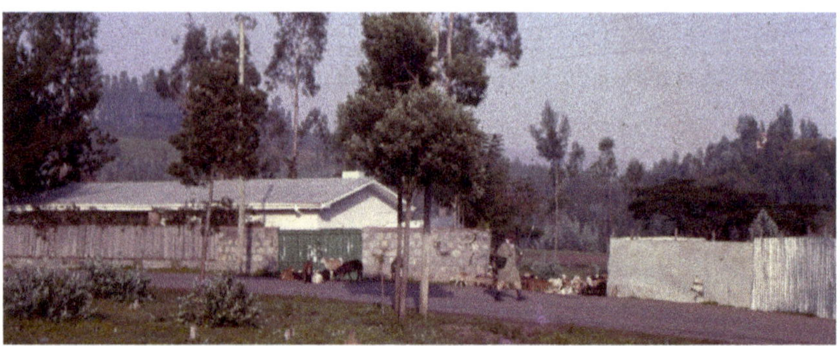

Our home in the village

We finally found a house to move to in the outskirts of the city. One of Bob's Dutch colleagues lived in the same village. The house had been empty for while and the local government committee had been using it to store corn and grain. We went out to have a look before moving in. When we came out, we were met by a man who introduced himself as Abraham, who had worked in the house for many years when it was the home of a woman doctor who was professor of Gynaecology at the University. He had a reference describing his many talents such as cooking, flower arranging, ironing and general housekeeping. House occupants were also expected to hire gardeners/gate keepers 24 hours a day. That meant that there was a shift of two men who would take turns. One would take day shift for a week and then trade for night shift. So suddenly I had a staff of three who had worked for years for the English professor. She had left because the communist government had shut down the Universities.

In the garage area was a laundry and extra room. Abraham had lived there with his family, so when the professor departed, she built him a basic house further along in the village as a thank you for his faithful service. Next door to us was a large Ethiopian family with children close in age to ours. So Jessie had her opportunity to play and have fun with local children. Jenny also got friendly with the older girls.

In the village, Bob soon got to know the neighbourhood boys who had a football team. He became their sponsor and got the team matching shirts for their

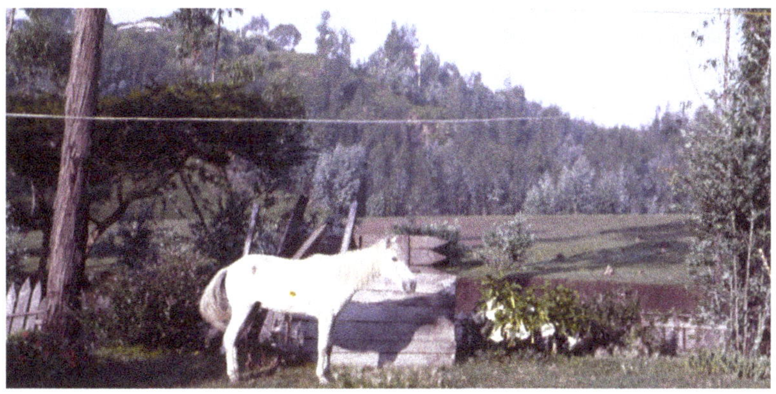

Zemeche in our backyard garden

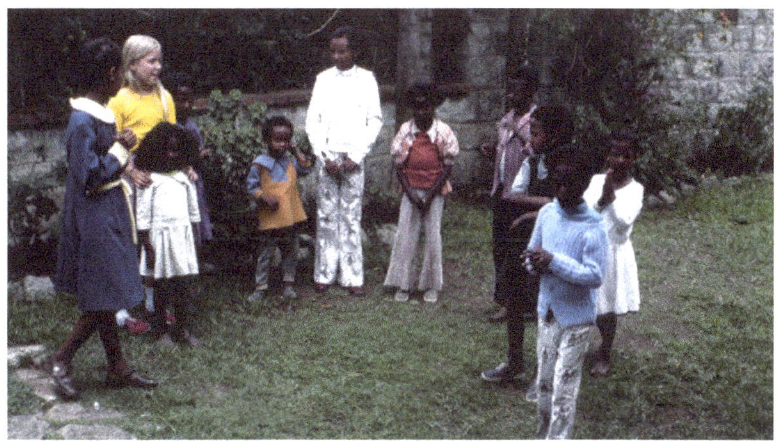

Jessie plays fun games with the village children

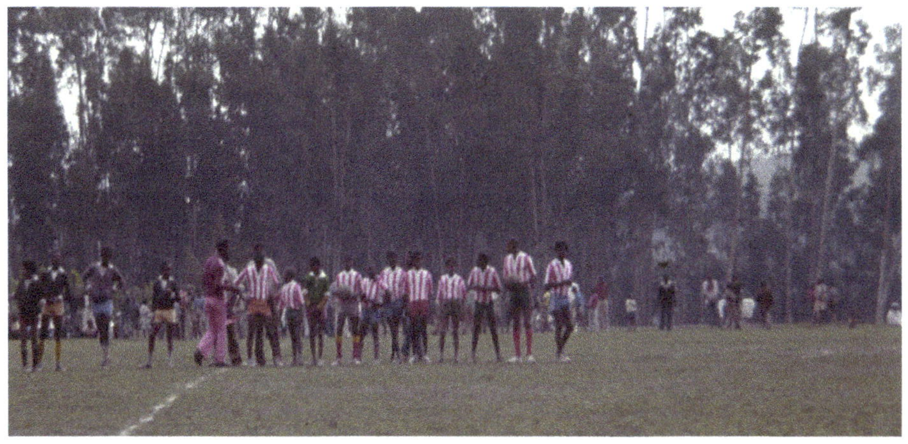

Village football team that Bob sponsored

competitions. At some point we acquired a pony for Jess which we kept in the back yard. There was a gymkhana she went to and also rode through the village. Jenny went to an event competing on a borrowed horse.

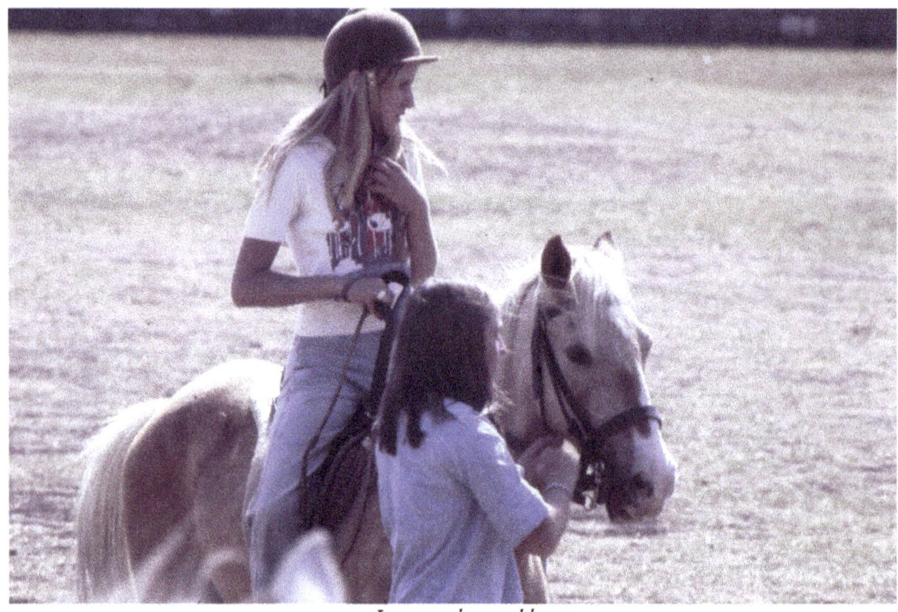

Jenny at the gymkhana

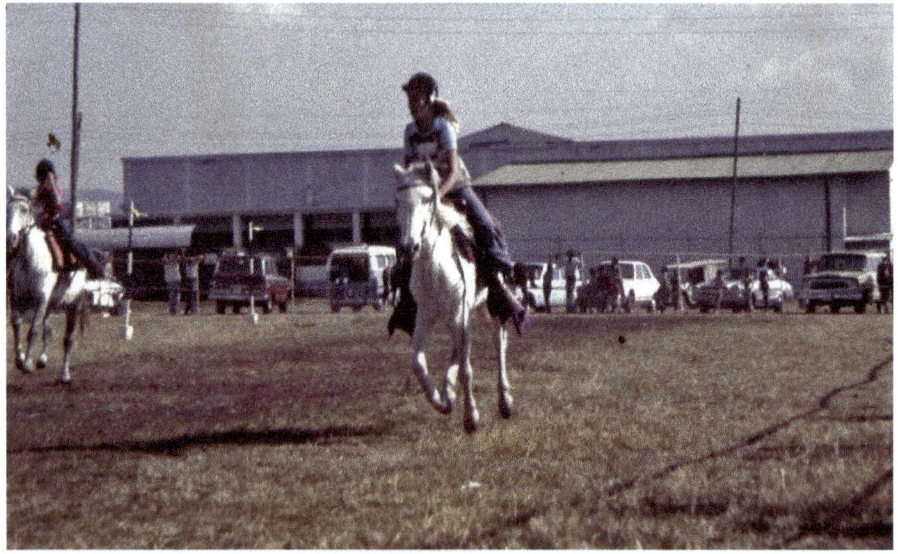

Good fun on the weekend

MY YEAR AT THE PIAZZA

I knew that Ethiopia had a long tradition of making filigree jewellery and was hoping to learn the skill, so I brought along my hand tools and set about finding

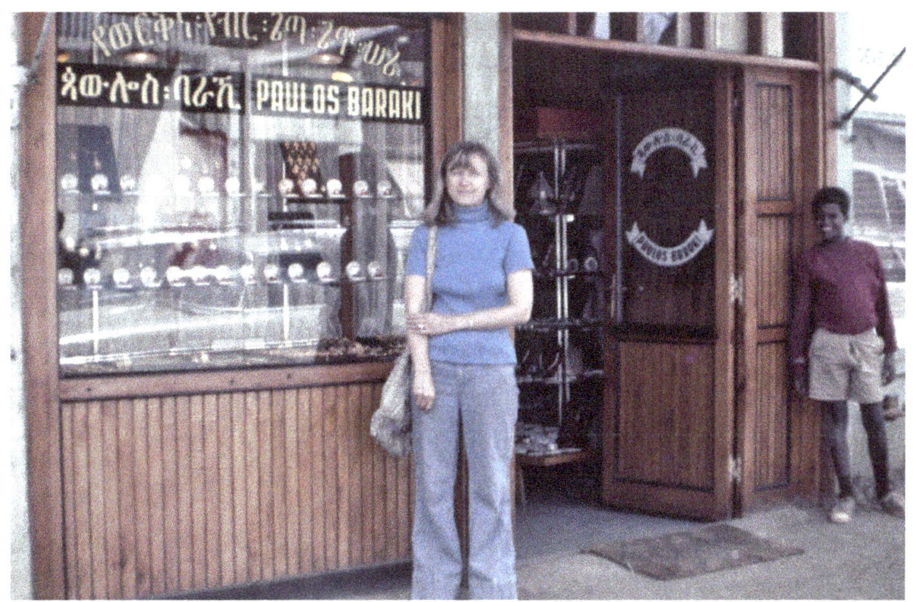

Paulos Baraki Goldsmith shop where I spent 12 months making jewellery

where I might learn. Bob's office was up Churchill Avenue and the Lycée was quite near. I dropped both Bob and Jenny off in the morning then continued up to the top of the road to the Piazza area where all the goldsmith showrooms were located. My plan was to park the car and set off stopping at jewellers until I found one where I could learn. All of the shops had sales staff with good English, so I gave my little story at the first premises to see what was the reaction. The sales fellow told his boss my story and came back saying, *"Impossible"*. So I went to the next shop and started all over again. The sales person asked the boss and turned back to me and said, *"Come tomorrow."* This was a jewellery shop called Paulos Baraki Goldsmith. I learned I would pay to use my workbench for the year and buy my metal from Paulos.

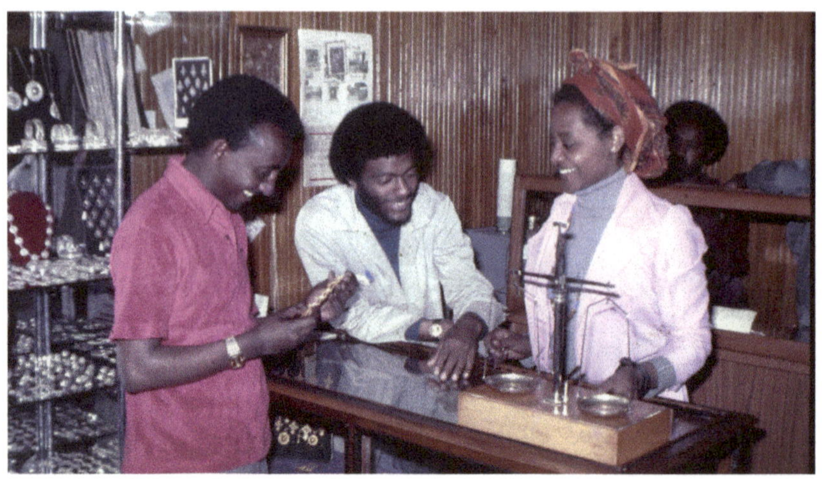

Makonnen and Nigest, the sales team behind the counter

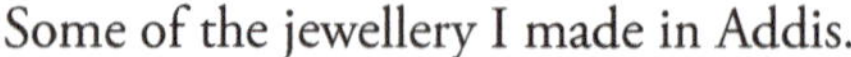
Some of the jewellery I made in Addis.

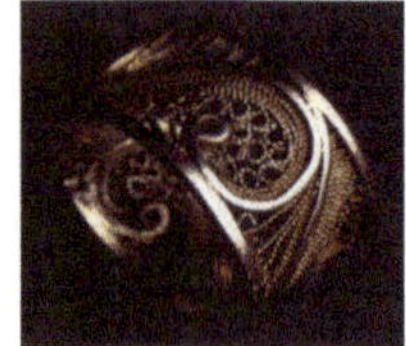

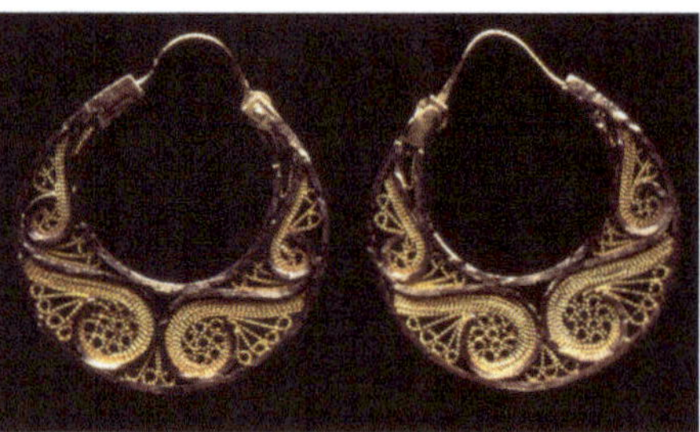

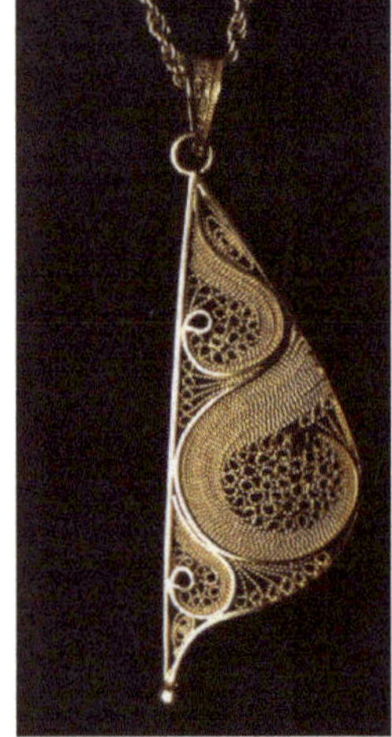

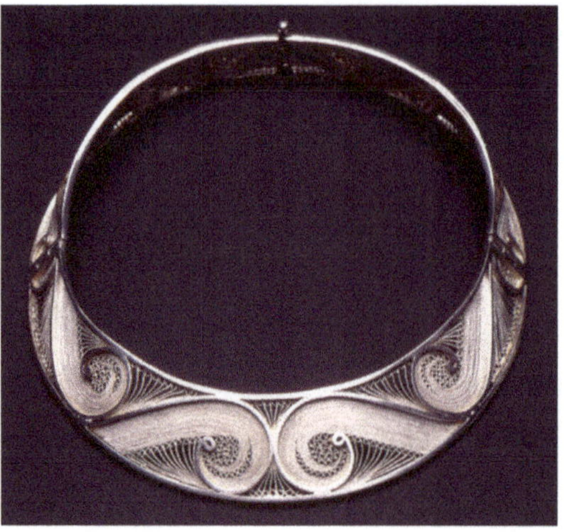

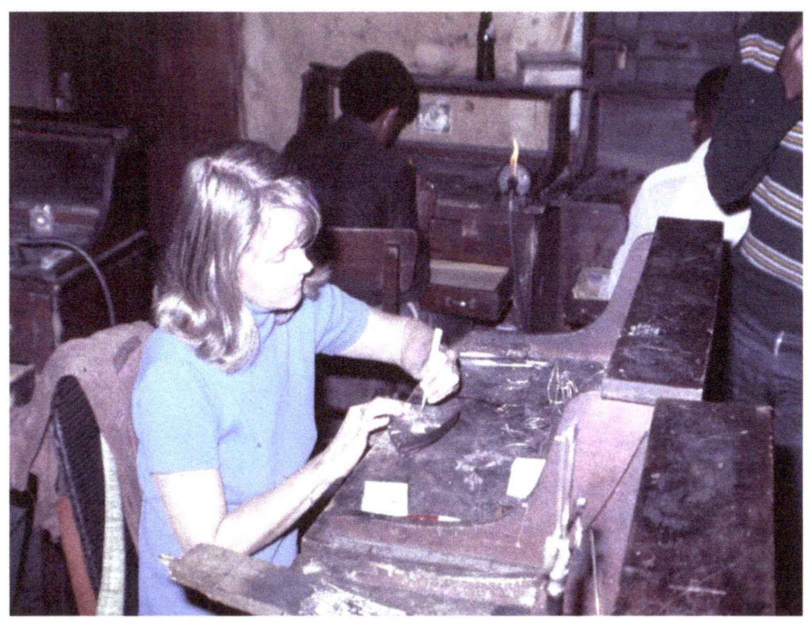

My workbench for the year

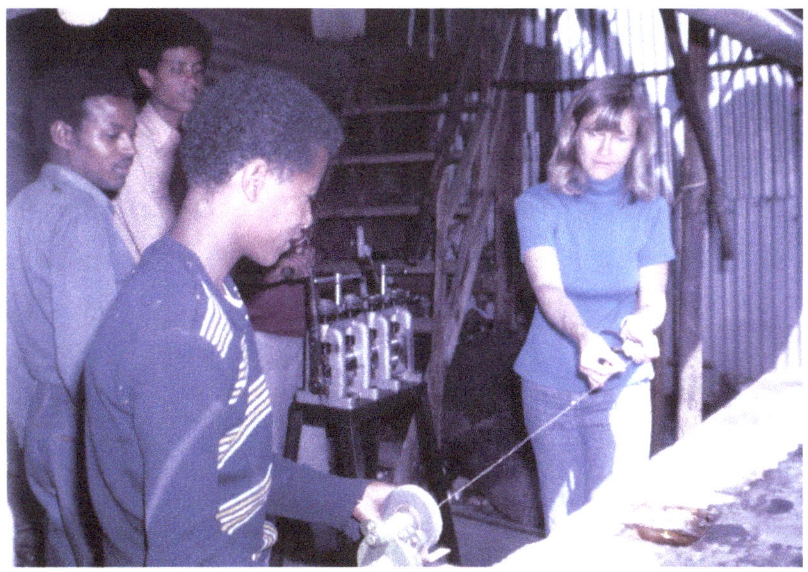

Twisting the filigree wire

In the past, I had been able to buy wire of various sizes and sheet metal of different gauge, depending on what I needed. So the next morning I was very surprised when the salesman, Makonnen, handed me an ingot of pure silver to create sterling for the framework to hold the filigree wires, by adding some copper.

He told me I would go down to the cellar area where the apprentice would melt the metal on the forge and help me pour it into a rectangular mold. Then he would show me how to put it through a roller with a square profile until it became smaller and smaller. So I worked with that until he came to show the next step. Rolling hardened the silver, so then it had to be softened with annealing by placing it back on the charcoal and then turning a handle on the blower bringing in oxygen, making the fire burn hotter. When the metal reach a certain temperature, judged by colour or pink glow, it was ready to work with again. So then it could be rolled smaller. Eventually the long wire with a square profile would be pulled through a metal drawplate to create round wire. For the filigree wire, the round would become thin and then doubled and twisted. The twisted wire would then get put through flat rollers creating a beaded edge on the flattened wire. I never expected there would be so much work just to get the materials to use. I had expected to be handed a spool of filigree wire.

I worked with 12 men who didn't speak English, in the workshop directly behind the showroom. So I started learning the Amharic word for the tools I had or needed to use. These men did not have all their own tools, but could pick what was needed off the rack on the wall. After my materials were all created, I was shown a simple task creating an open circle with a dividing bar, then filling in both semi-circles with pieces of filigree wire that had to fit together firmly. I had to be able to pick it up so nothing would fall out. I had to turn it over and using a torch, solder them in. I think it took me all day to get the first one made. I felt relieved having success, but was taken back when then I was told I needed to make 20 more as the project was for a bracelet and earrings. However once I had made the first, the rest were easier.

As the men did not speak English, when I needed help, I could get one of the two sales persons to come in and translate. The young male, Makonnen, who had been a university student was usually available but there was also a young woman named Nigest, who I became friends with and she visited us at home.

JENNY AND SEBLE'S HOLIDAY

Jenny's friend Seble had an auntie living in Dire Dawa, down from the escarpment toward Somalia. It had a warmer climate with lovely tropical fruit and we had been there on that family holiday. The girls wanted to take the train and go stay with Seble's auntie. Well, we tried to think of ways to squash the idea and said something off-hand about the need for her to have the money for the trip. Well Jenny was never short of ideas. We had friends from ILCA who had decorated their home with wonderful large macramé hanging baskets they had made and filled with lovely plants. Jenny asked Janine Temple if she would be willing to give her and Seble lessons in creating the macramé hangings. So the project began and the girls then went to the Mercato area where they could buy rope and beads. Little did Bob and I know how this was developing, but soon learned that the creations they made sold well at the Ghion pool to African diplomats. It is only now that I learn they actually had to hang them in the

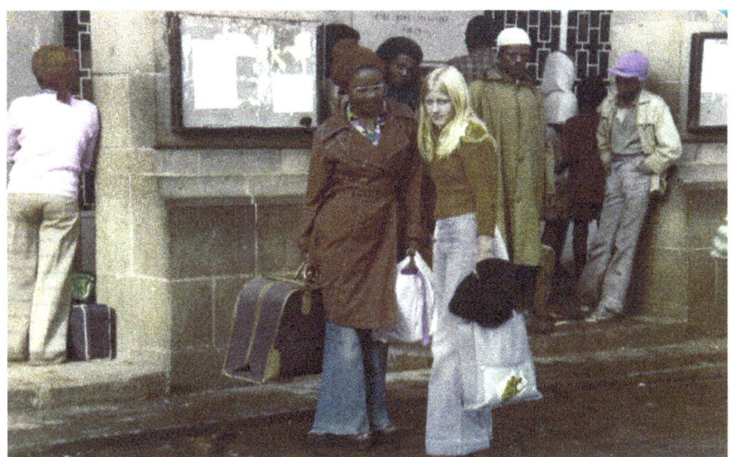

The girls off on their adventure

diplomat's residences, and they were taken there in the official vehicles with flags furling. So the money had been raised for the trip and what could we say?

Jenny and Seble finally made plans for their trip to Dire Dawa. But I was somewhat nervous about the timing, as we were going to Kenya soon afterwards meeting up with my mother. The two girls did go on their trip, but at the end of the week Jenny phoned. She said they wanted to stay another week and she would see her grandmother another time. Well that didn't go over well. At work Bob was discussing the situation and his assistant, Abiy said, *"Get her out of there. I was down there last week and the place is swarming with secret police. Something big is stirring."* And so then Jenny was given the ultimatum to get home. She arrived bringing something with her - she had acquired nits. We did the treatments and hoped that nothing was left. She told the story of the train down to Dire Dawa with wild looking Afar tribal daggar men, goats and pigs. And a woman they befriended had nits.

MOTHER IN AFRICA

I had wanted my mother to come visit us in Ethiopia, but she had had a severe heart attack previously and the doctor was against this happening because of the high altitude in Addis of over 9000 feet. However it would be possible for her to come to Kenya. Bob had meetings to attend and the altitude in Nairobi was just over 5000 feet. So the doctor gave approval for her to come. To get there, she decided to stop along the way to places she had wanted to see all her life. The first stop was Greece where she climbed up

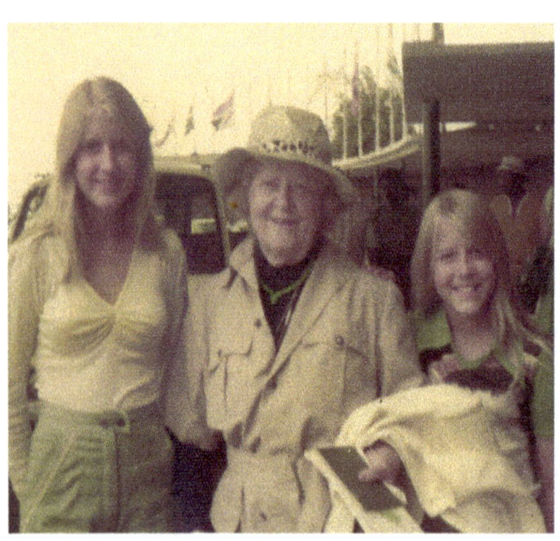

We picked up Grandma at the airport

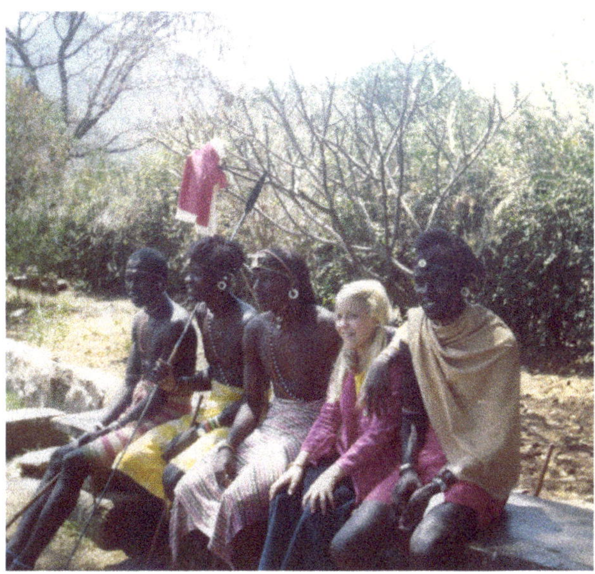

Jess meets the maasai warriors

to the Parthenon. Then she went to the Holy Lands and walked everywhere to see all the places she had been teaching about as a Sunday school teacher. These are all things we thought she would never be able to do, as her last heart attack had been so severe we were told that if she recovered, she might have trouble walking across a room.

We met mother at the airport and did warn her about the episode of nits as we couldn't be sure there weren't any left. She laughed and told us a story of when she was a girl getting nits. She slept in a bed with her older sister and then both had to have their heads dabbed with kerosene. She had long golden ringlets and did not want her hair cut off, which was a common happening for the problem.

We combined the trip with some safari time for the girls and me with mother. When we met up with the young Maasai warriors, they noticed the turquoise beads Mother always wore and nudged each other to have a look.

It was a lovely time together and the last time we would see her as she died six months later. Jenny would have lost her opportunity if she had not returned then.

THE WEDDING

The trip was over and I returned to the goldsmith shop to find a little paper note with small Amharic script on my workbench. Nigest came in and told me it was an

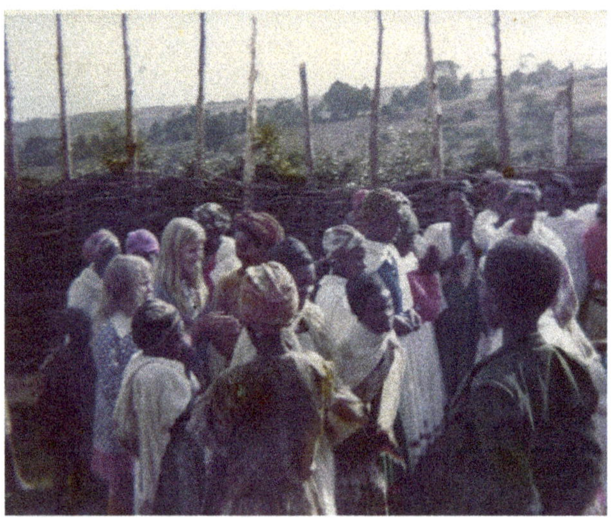

At the wedding in the mountains

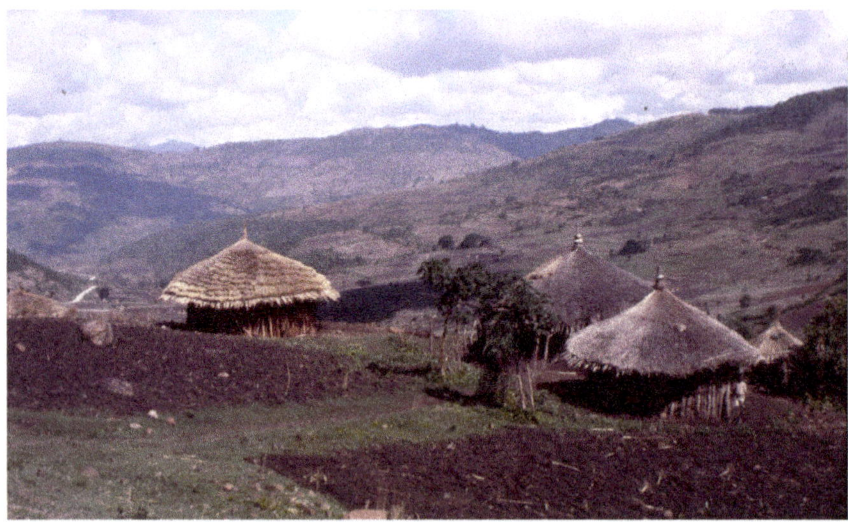

Tukuls up the mountain side

invitation to attend a wedding. It was from the charcoal man who came every week on his donkey bringing fuel to burn in the forge. His daughter was being married and all the goldsmiths were invited. Nigest suggested she and I could go together with Jenny and Jessie. I asked her where was the wedding held and she indicated the way to go was out by the Mexican Square, past where we lived. So we made arrangements to pick her up where she lived, not far from the shop. I had told Bob we would be gone to a wedding for the morning and would be back in the afternoon. We started down toward Mexican Square and Nigest pointed further down the highway. We were headed toward another town.

Nigest knew a landmark where we were to pull over and we asked at market stalls where was the wedding. They pointed up a mountain. So we were to park the car and continue by foot. We did ask the man at the market if he could show us the way. But he said, *"No, I have to sell my produce."* That should have given us some indication what was ahead. We walked quite a way thinking we were reaching the top of the ridge, to discover there would be another and another hilltop to aim for. It took us all morning to reach the little cluster of Tukuls, houses build with poles in a circle and a thatched roof, where the wedding festivities were occurring.

The charcoal man greeted us and could see how thirsty we were after climbing the mountain. He brought Jessie a glass of milk and immediately I could think of unpasturized milk and what it might carry. I tried kindly to explain that Jessie didn't drink milk. He explained that the only

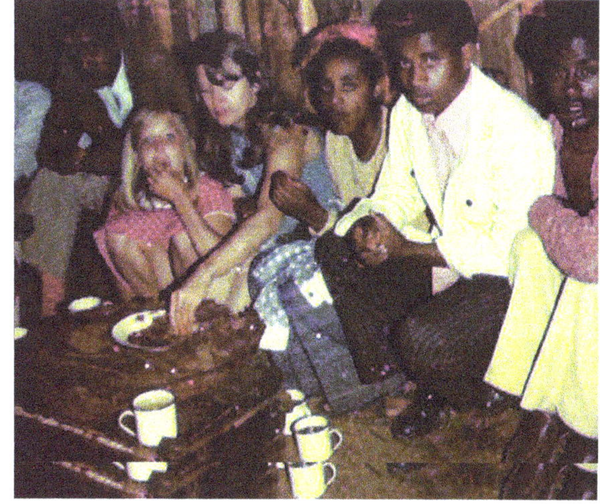

At the wedding with the other goldsmiths

other option was homemade beer in a barrel. It was weak and had plenty of twigs floating around in it, but it was wet and the alcohol would help make it safe. And we all drank some. There was traditional dancing happening. I don't think we ever met the bride, but it was a special opportunity to see how remote communities lived and celebrated. The other goldsmiths had arrived before us, having an earlier start and were headed home shortly after we arrived. I started to think about Bob expecting us back soon. So I asked one of the goldsmiths to phone him when back home to tell him we would arrive closer to evening. However we discovered he never received a message, but wasn't thinking about us anyway. He easily got carried away with work and research.

Eventually the Ethiopian government got things organised for the university students to go overseas. Seble did not get her choice and was sent to Russia where she studied political science. After she left, her family came to our place for dinner. At the time, Bob's parents were also visiting and enjoying getting to see first hand the beauty of Ethiopia and its people. We also took Grammie to the marcato and bought beautiful handwoven traditional Ethiopian dresses.

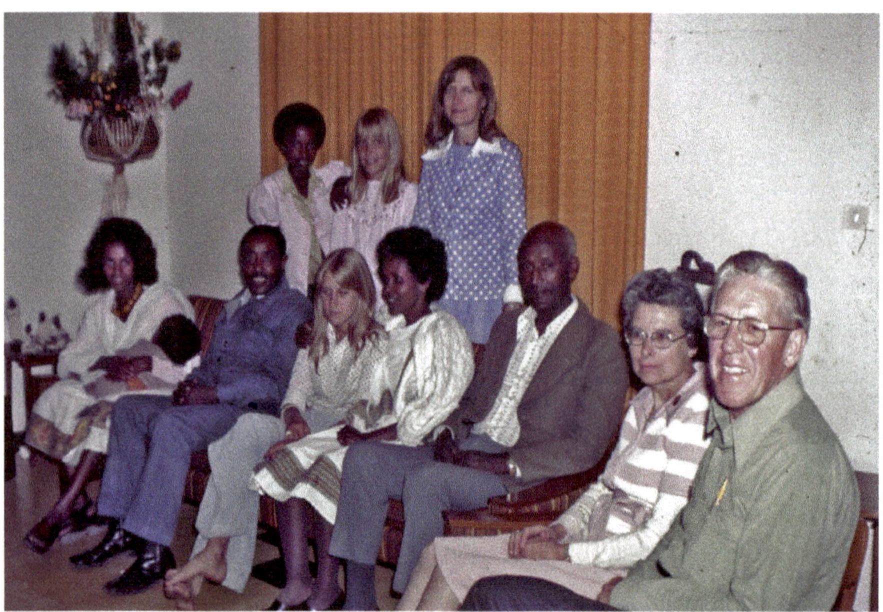

Abiy's family and Seble's parents came to our home for dinner to meet Grammie and Gramps

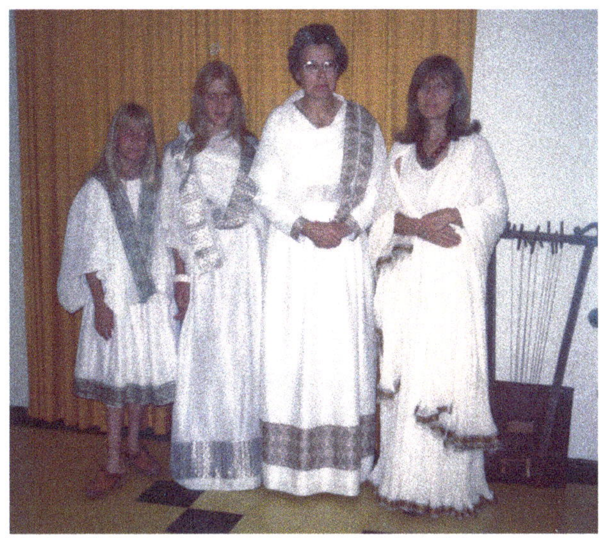

Our handwoven cotton traditional Ethiopian dress

Bob had such wonderful memories of his year spent in western Ethiopia working with the Anuaks at the Presbyterian Mission, Pokwo run by Don McClure. As it happened, Don had been given land by Haile Selassie, before he was deposed, to enter a new area closer to Somalia that had a Muslim population.

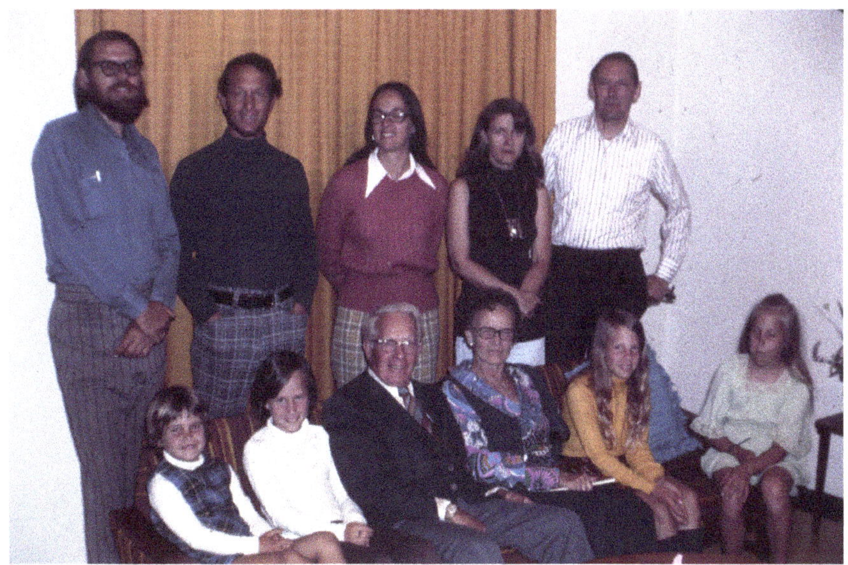

Don with his family and Al Achenheil (beside me) who sponsored Bob's first trip to Ethiopia

But when we arrived, Don was back in Addis making some arrangements. And so we occasionally joined him for a Chinese meal near our hotel. We all loved the toffee-fried bananas they served with ice cream. And it was a good chance for our family to hear Don's exciting stories. Later we were fortunate that his family was in Addis and they came to our home for dinner. Al Achenheil was also visiting from Pittsburgh. He had been the sponsor for Bob's first trip to Ethiopia in 1957. Al came to my work and took quality photos of my jewellery activities.

The mission at Pokwo was still active and the Reimers, a family that had been there with Bob, still managed it. Bob especially wanted us to see this remote place that had such an impression on him and influenced his future path. So we travelled west to near the Sudan border. Bob got to see some of the villagers that he had worked with. And we could all picture this environment that he had such affection for.

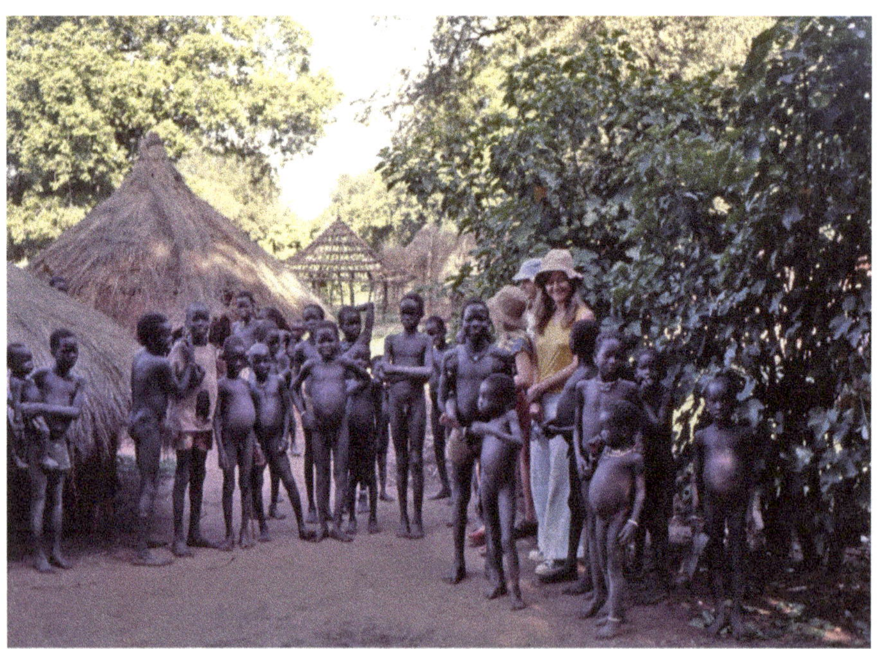

Walking around Pokwo village near the Sudanese border. Anuak tribal people live here.

We were later to get the sad news that Don McClure had returned to his new location in south eastern Ethiopia and had been killed by Somali rebels. His son Don Jr. was able to escape.

It was early 1977, and time to head back to Australia for the school year to begin. The girls and I had to go on ahead as Bob still had some important work to finish. One of the important things on his mind was the work there in Addis and whom the project really needed. Bob contacted John Tothill, in Brisbane and encouraged him to come and replace Bob as Research Director. In the end, John convinced his family this would be an opportunity for them. And they came. They stayed for quite a few years. Sandro did eventually go off to England for university, but they all became part of the ILCA experience.

We had discussed as a family the idea of Jenny going to boarding school in Brisbane. Our friends the Tonnoirs had sent Nonie to St Peters, a co-ed school from K to grade 12. But there was also a boarding facility for older students. Nonie had loved it. The Joneses, who by then were living in Brisbane, had also sent their children to St. Peters as day students. So after reaching home, we needed to get Jenny ready for boarding at St Peters.

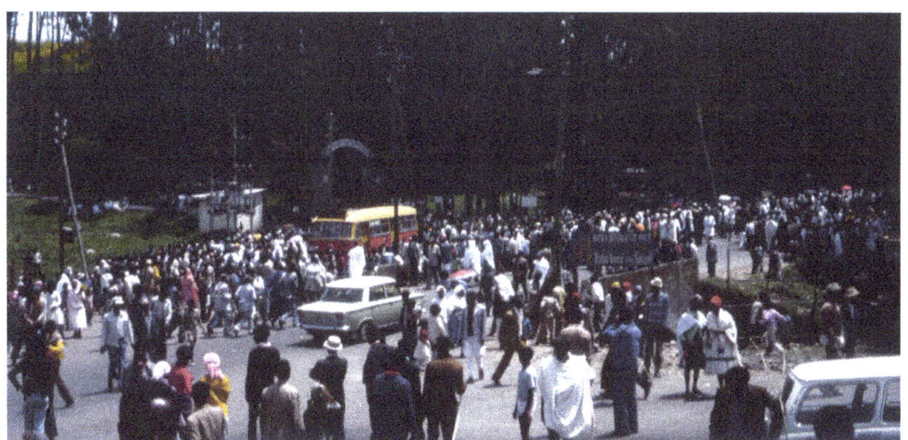

Bus stop on our corner across from the leprosy colony. We drove through the colony every day on the school run.

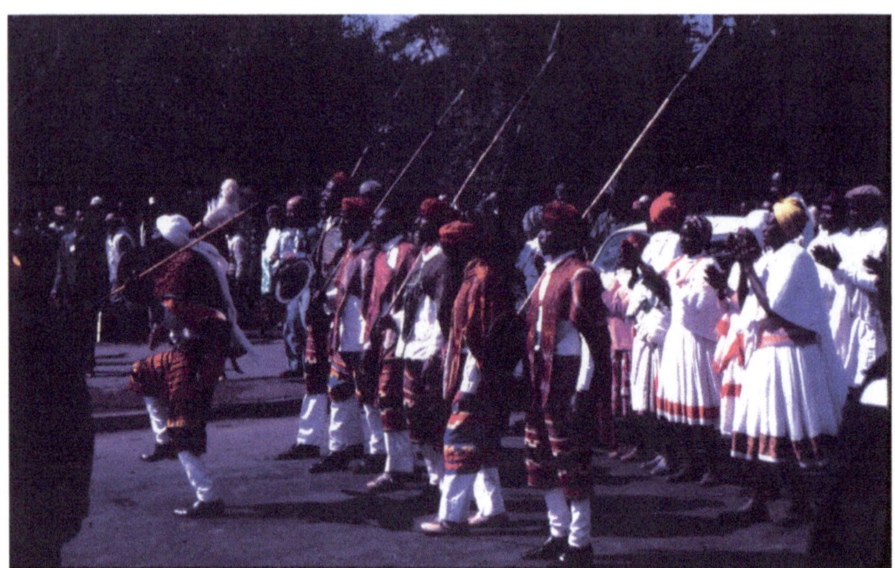

One of the religious festival processions

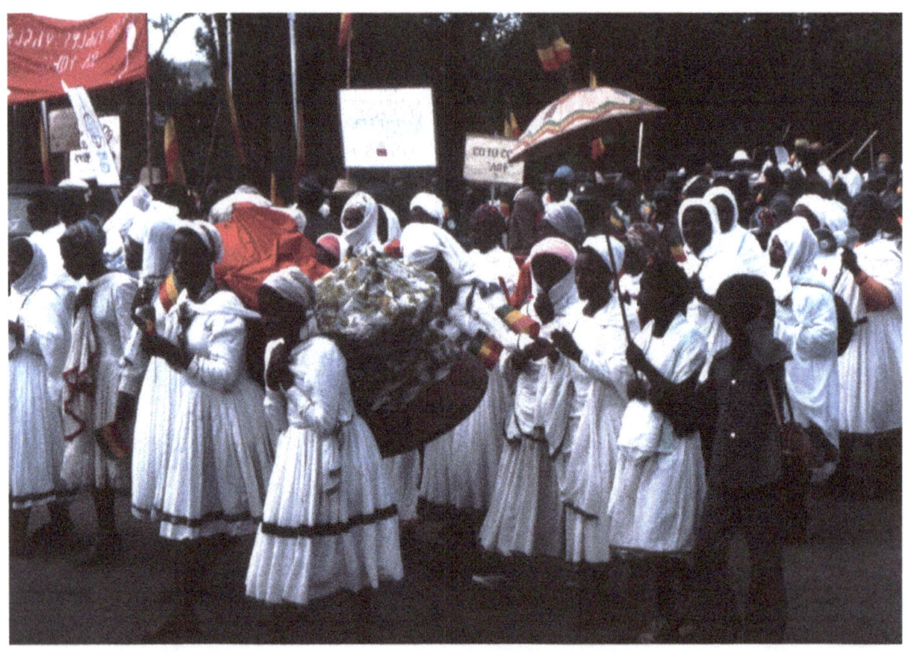

Religious festival with women carrying injera baskets on their backs

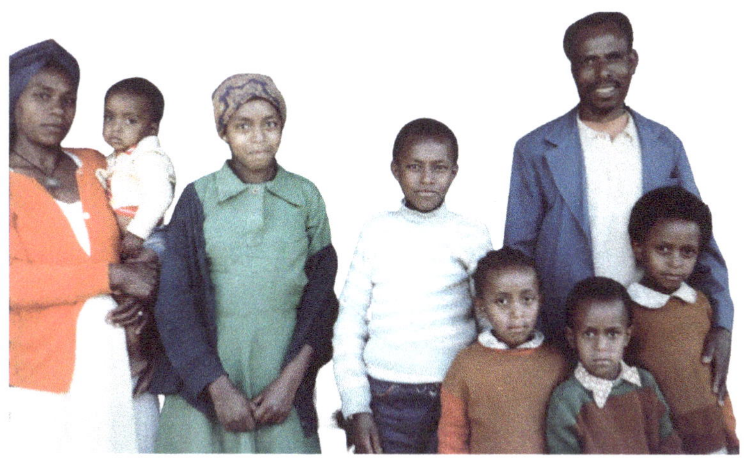

Abraham, our talented cook and his family

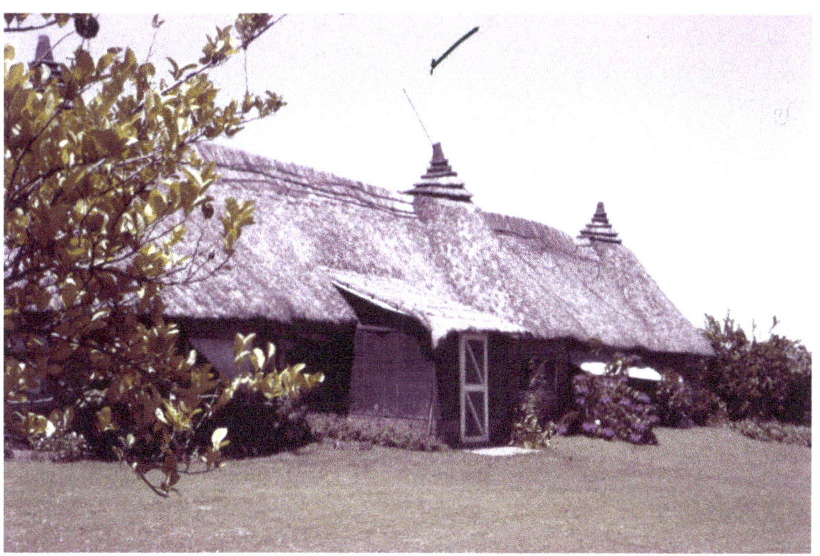

Don McClure's home in Pokwo where Bob lived in 1957-58

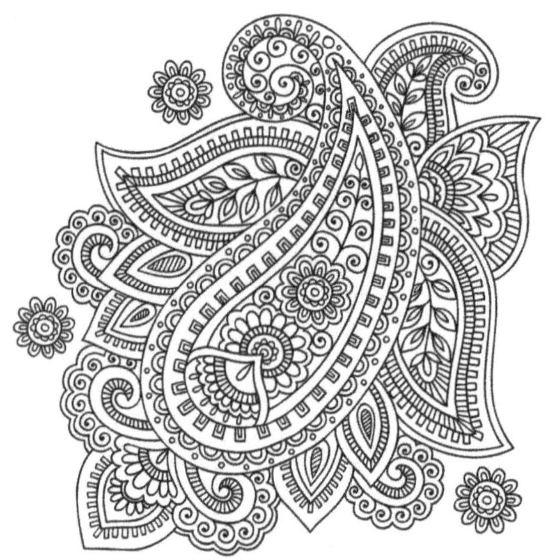

05

Back to Oz

TOWNSVILLE TROPICAL TREES

As for me, the nursery, which we named "Townsville Tropical Trees," had expanded while we were away and I took a bigger role in the management. As it dealt in wholesale, the orders came by phone from other nurseries or from landscapers. Each Monday we packed cartons to be taken to the rail. It got me outside doing physical work lifting pots, watering and working on the accounts. One of the memorable happenings during those years was developing a new Grevillea species for the market, which we named "Pink Parfait". It was a cross with two other well-known plants that my partners had created. From the seeds that grew, the plant that had the desirable coloured flowers was chosen and was reproduced only by cuttings. So it was a slow process. We had to wait until enough stock was produced as generations needed to be grown for the cuttings. Otherwise, seed from that plant could revert to either parent.

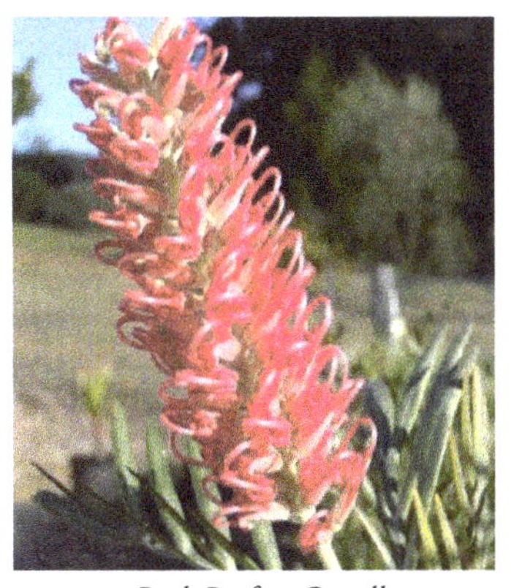

Pink Parfait Grevillea

We had so many small tubes that had been used for cuttings that then are transferred to larger pots. These tubes needed to be washed and used again so we hired very young Lindsey

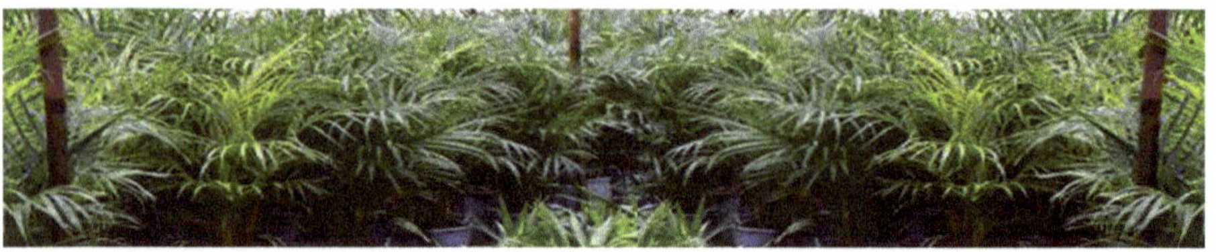

Williams and paid him by the tube. Later he moved on to mowing our yard with the ride-on mower. In high school he had been in Cadets and decided to apply to the Air Force. He still wasn't old enough to get a drivers license. But he did get into the Air Force and flew fighter jets and then trained other pilots. And now he flies for Cathay Pacific. Well he did eventually learn to drive a car.

One of the other partners, Bob Reid, decided he wanted to withdraw from the arrangement, so that left John Donohue and myself. We had also hired young Ricky Morelli to do mowing for our large garden, but eventually saw what a hard worker he was and hired him in the nursery. Ricky was a natural with plants with motorcycles on the side. He became an expert in cutting propagation with many of the native plants that were difficult to strike.

Later on John Donohue came to tell me that an opportunity in town had arisen for him to have a family nursery and wanted to sell his half of the business. So the idea developed that Serge Morelli might like to buy John's share, as Serge had gotten rid of his thousands of chickens and taken down the sheds to make room eventually for sub-division of his land. The demands of helping run a business greatly diminished my time for weaving and jewellery. But it was an enjoyable time out in fresh air with lovely plants.

So eventually when I sold my share to Serge and he took it all away to his own land, I had my creative activities back. And the Fibres & Fabrics group had expanded from the first group of 12 people who came to the meeting we advertised in the newspaper to over 80 members. In addition, I also taught some silversmithing classes in my workshop under the house.

Bob would occasionally go to Brisbane to the CSIRO headquarters for meetings and visit with Jenny. He would take her and her new friend Rose out to dinner on occasion. It turned out that our supposedly independent Jenny was homesick. By the end of the year she wanted to return to Townsville and finish her schooling there. In the end, it seemed the best thing about being at St Peters was the friendship with Rose. During the summer back home, there was time to swim in the river, paddle our kayak, and ride her pony with friends.

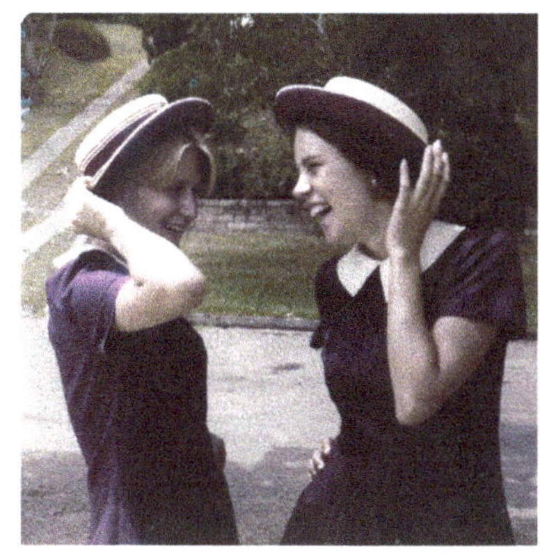

Jenny and Rose

BACK TO TOWNSVILLE

When school started, Jenny went back to Pimlico High School and was in a class with another student named Barbara, who had been away for six months in France. So both girls were settling back in and became fast friends. Barbara had a car as she had a weekend job at a coffee shop, so needed transport. Needless to say, she and Jenny liked to get around on the weekend to hear bands play. Then Barbara would come and spend the night with us afterward. I would lie awake waiting to hear the putt putt putting of the VW Beetle coming up our road. There were school formal balls they attended. Looking for dresses was always a discussion topic. The girls found patterns in Seventeen Magazine's special "prom edition", and then went looking for fabric. They found a white Swiss eyelit they both liked,

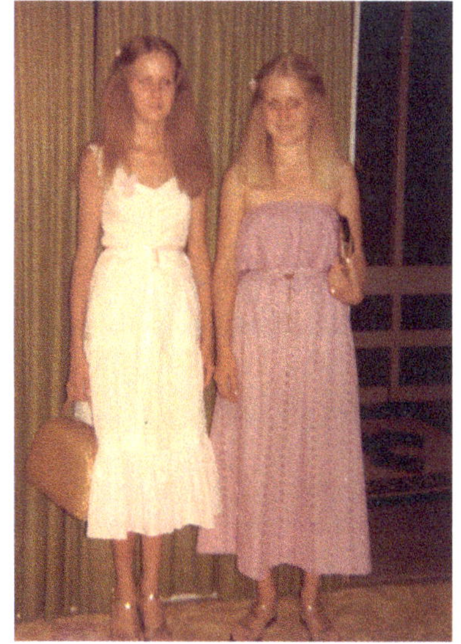

Ready for the senior prom

but Jenny had me dye hers. I made Jenny's dress and another friend, Judy, offered to make Barbara's.

Returning from Ethiopia, I changed Jessica from Aitkenvale School to The Weir State School, closer to home and no longer just a one-teacher school. But when thinking about high school, a brand new Kirwan High had been built and they were starting with only one class, grade seven. Each year they would add another grade. Jessica was in the first class and eventually graduated. Jessica had heard about a modeling school taught by Julieanna, a European woman, new to Townsville. She gathered a team of young people and found gigs for them to have opportunities to develop their skills. And she helped arrange photographic sessions for them to build up a portfolio, so important to get jobs. There were social outings and classes. This opened up new experiences and gave Jessica poise and more confidence. Everyone in the family was busy with interesting activities.

Meanwhile Jenny had always had an interest in music. Bob had encouraged this, getting her quality albums of musicians such as Stevie Wonder, Cat Stevens, Roberta Flack and Donny Hathaway. Jenny and Barbara seemed to know what groups were playing and were starting to get to know some of the musicians. But Jenny had a curfew around 11 pm. And so when she came with requests to go out with one of them to an after-party following a concert at the civic theatre, I reminded her of the curfew. I was told this guy ran the band, had a motorcycle shop, was a welder and wrote articles about music for the local newspaper. Well he seemed too old for Jenny but I tried to tread lightly. When I did ask him directly how old he was, I was shocked. I asked him why wasn't he finding girls nearer his own age.

Before long Jenny decided she was quitting high school and took a job at the Townsville city childcare centre, in town. And then marriage was being discussed. I have always felt it is best to keep communication open and relationships intact. But as a parent it is hard to know the best path. But in 1979 Jenny and Larry proceeded to have a lovely wedding with Jenny's friends and Jess as attendants. In the end Ricky Morelli was in the wedding party. Grammie and Gramps came for the occasion bringing the little cousins, Kyle, Katie and Chad from Pittsburgh to be in the wedding.

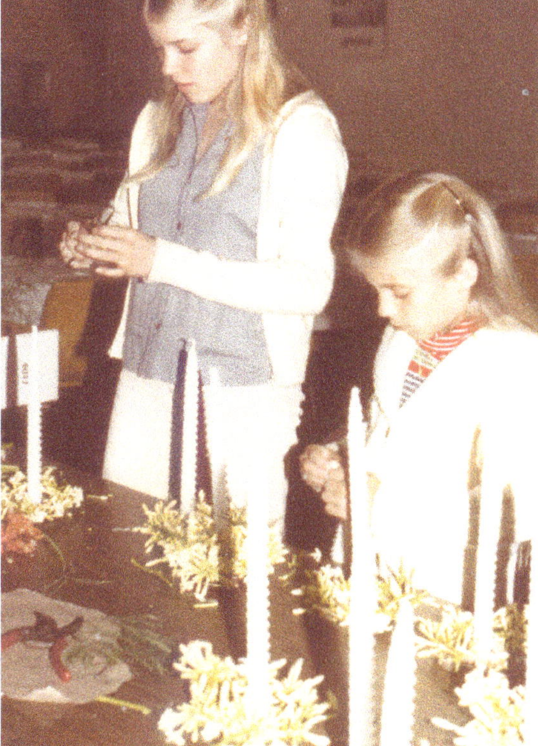

Jessica and cousin Katie help decorate the church

Eventually Larry sold his business in South Townsville and they bought the house next door to us. Larry then went to James Cook University to get a teaching degree. Jenny threw herself into landscaping the garden and creating an environment with her own touches. After a year or so, she wanted to start a family and Jordan was born in 1981. He was an engaging baby and then a young toddler with a head of golden curls. The neighbourhood gang of children liked to come play with him. But on his 2nd birthday they arrived to say he was now old enough to come run with the gang for an hour or so for the first time. It was a marvelous neighbourhood of families with young children of various ages that could have fun together. When Jordan was about three, he announced he didn't want to be "Goldilocks" any more. He just wanted to be a normal boy.

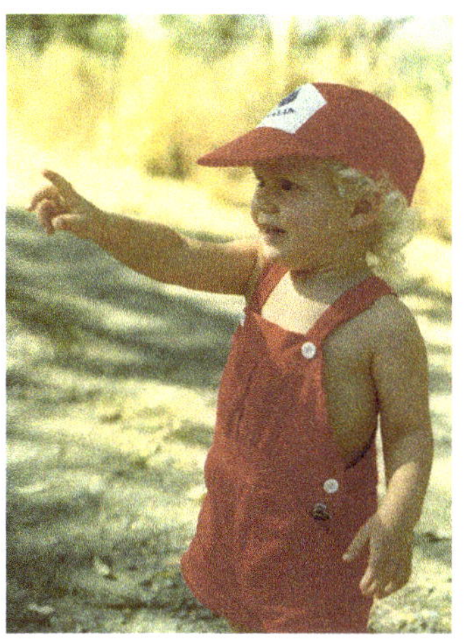

Jordan at 2 years

Jenny made friends with a new young woman who bought the cottage next door that had seen a series of changes since Marge and John moved that building down the highway in 1967. They sold the cottage to our dear CSIRO friends John and Joy Williams who renovated to suit their family needs. But with a still growing family, they needed more space and built a new home along the river a few doors down. They sold to Jennifer and John Carleton. Jennifer was a friend of mine from Fibres and Fabrics, who was very talented in quilting and anything to do with textiles. As Jennifer and Jenny were young women with common interests and a child, they became fast friends. About that time, Jenny was pregnant with a second child, who was named Samuel Jesse. Both Jenny's boys became water babies, starting swimming from the age of two months, as they had a pool in the backyard. My own children had wanted a pool, a request always laughed at, as we had a river and in summer swam several times

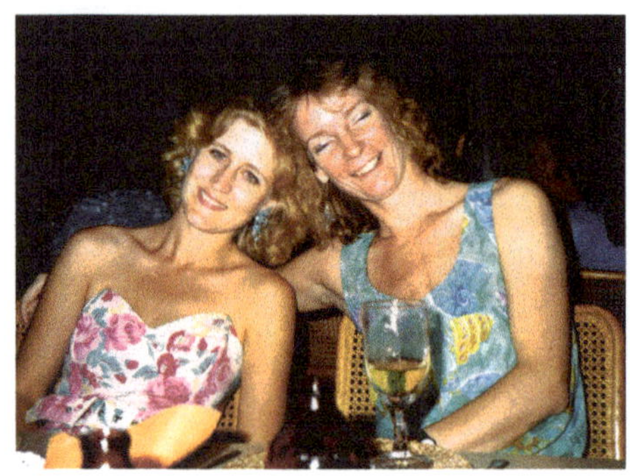

Jen and neighbour Jennifer Carleton

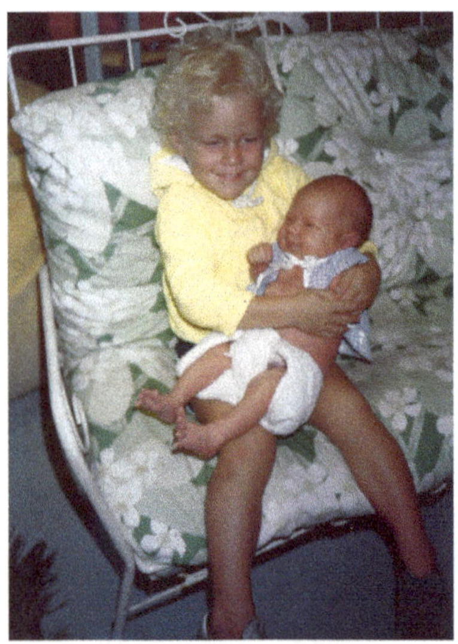

Jordan is now a big brother

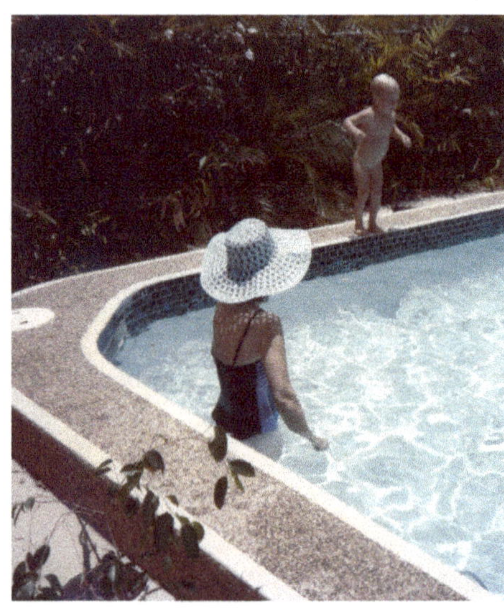

The pool was well used

a day and enjoyed our "Red Devil" kayak. Jessica always claimed everyone in her class had a pool - all except her.

About 1980, Bob had been asked to start a new project in Kenya for The Australian Centre for International Agricultural Research (ACIAR). The original idea Bob had of gaining the experience in Australia to get other jobs working in developing countries, turned out to be completely unnecessary. The Australian government made all this happen for Bob to have opportunities, but to still retain a family homebase in Queensland. Bob had decided he wanted to become an Australian citizen, which at that time would mean losing his American citizenship. He continued to feel Australia was his true home, but also was travelling for work around the world and it would have been better to be on an official Australian Government passport. He talked about it with the family, but the rest of us had reservations and didn't feel it was the right time for us.

When Jessica graduated from high school in 1983, her plan was to have a gap year, travelling to America to spend time with grandparents and to get a job. As Bob had meetings to attend in India and Ethiopia, we thought about combining a trip for the three of us to fly first to India where we visited Bombay. In actual fact, Bob had flown ahead for meetings and Jess and I arrived at the Bombay airport late at night alone and hired a taxi to take us to the beautiful Taj Mahal Hotel, where we would be staying. The driver piled our luggage on the roof of the car and occasionally would lean out his open window to try and see if the luggage was still there, as he was driving at break-neck speed, dodging cows and goats along the way, seeming to turn bends on two wheels. Jess and I were actually screaming in fright. He thought we were laughing in pleasure and would turn around looking at us with a big grin, as if we were having fun together. Upon arriving at the Taj, we had taken down the taxi number and reported him at the reception desk describing the terrifying journey. Little did we know that was the way the taxis were normally driven. I'm sure the receptionist threw away our report on the taxi ride as we got in the lift. While at the hotel, a wedding party was held with the groom coming on a white horse decorated for the occasion. The guests all arrived dressed in colourful array. We were dazzled.

Then we visited Hyderabad where we met up with old friends from Davis, California, Don and Dawn Faris who were now living at the cropping research station. Dawn took us to local markets and the esteemed

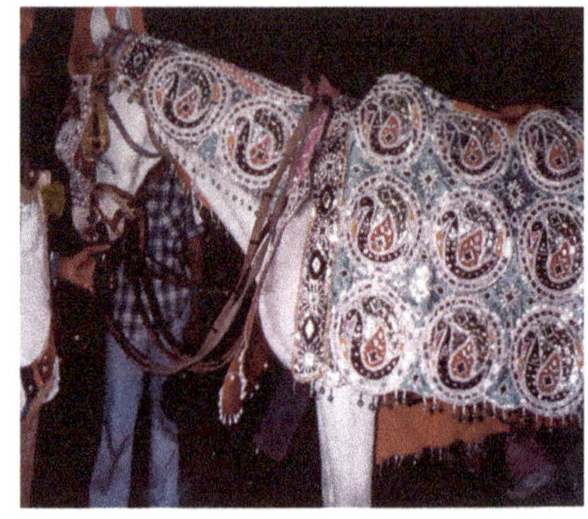

Wedding horse

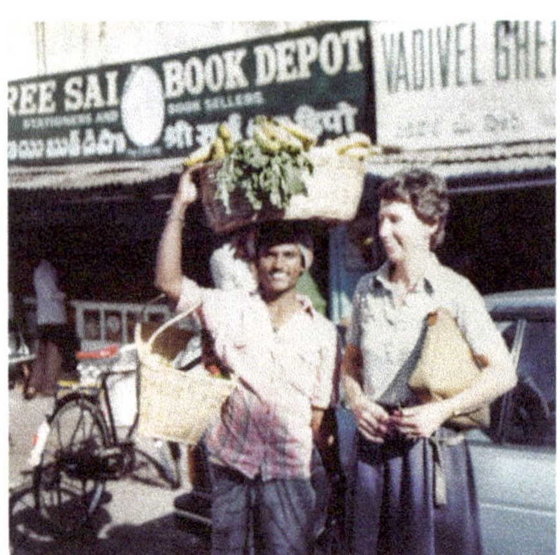

Dawn showing us the markets

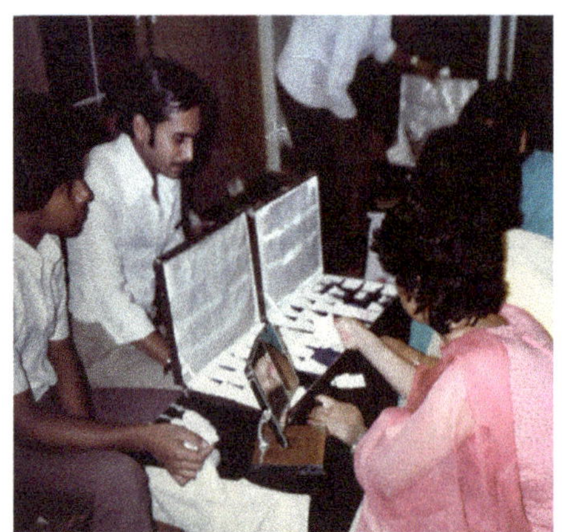

Pearl merchant

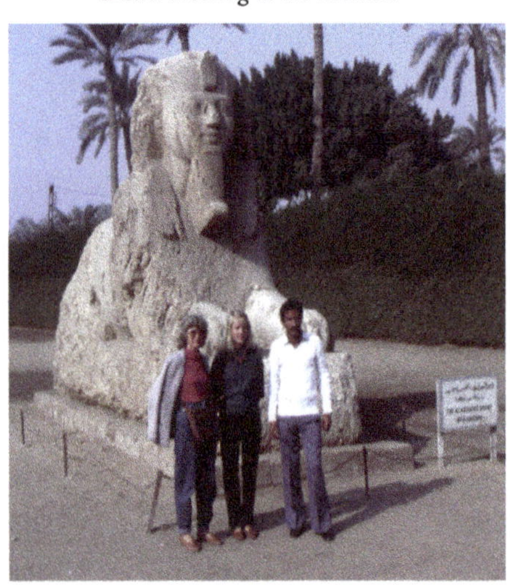

At the alabaster sphinx

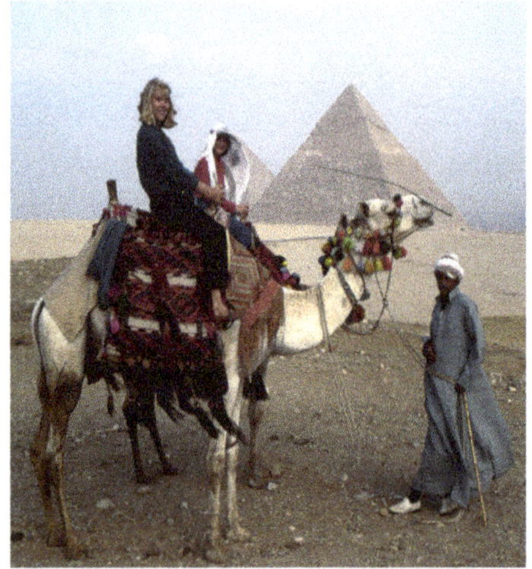

Jess and Dana near the pyramids

Mangatrai pearl shop, then to Ponchampalli to see the ikat weaving. Seeing this most remarkable process started my deep interest in researching Ikat.

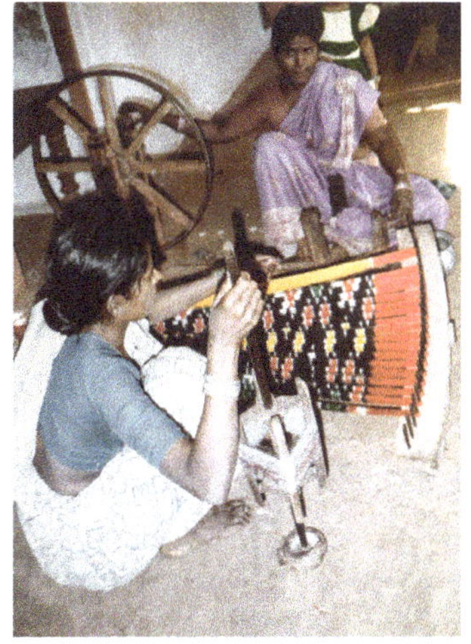

Winding yarn for weft

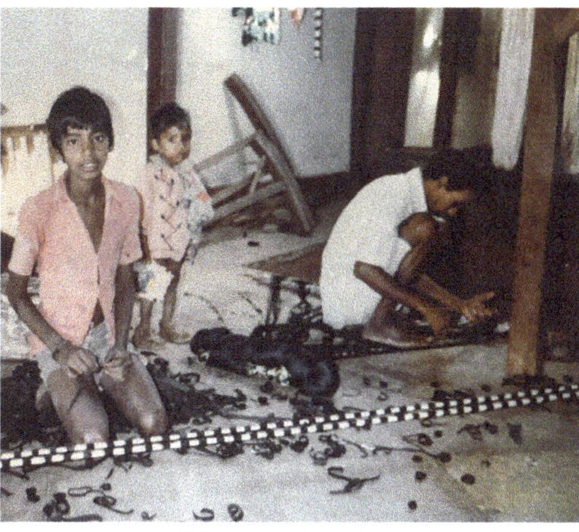

Warp yarn that is being resist tied

Because in high school Jess had studied ancient history, we thought this would be an opportunity to go to Egypt next and see what she had read about. Bob and I had never been there either. Bob thought he would really spend the time at the hotel getting ready for his next meetings, but a trip to the museum and seeing Tutankhamun treasures caught his imagination. We then went to see the

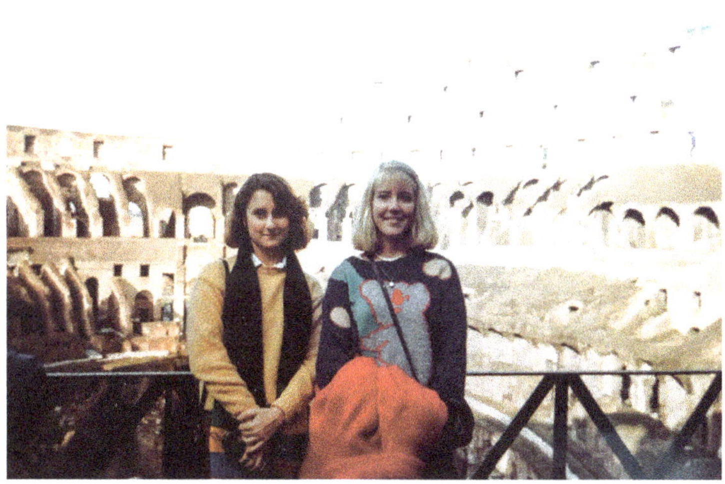

Jessica and Lorena at the Colosseum, Rome

pyramids and had a train trip down the Nile to the Valley of Kings. Next we flew to Ethiopia for more meetings. While in Addis, Jessie and I had a visit with Nigest in her home where she invited some friends to meet us. And then we went on to Rome. Again the ancient history could be revisited. But it was also a chance to make contact with friend Lorena who Jess had met at school in Ethiopia, now living in Rome. So this trip was full of reunions with old friends.

The last stop was Pittsburgh and Grammie and Gramps greeted us with open arms. We arrived without any baggage, due to a mishap at the Rome airport, where we got separated and our plane departed without us. So it was Christmas approaching and our gifts were in the bags, but more importantly so were our clothes. Bob and I were staying for three weeks and the bags only arrived when it was time to return to Australia. Bob could easily wear his dad's gear, but my mother-in-law and I were quite different sizes. Jessica went off to the local mall and got a job working in a Bridal Shop. So her plan was working out. Bob and I returned to Townsville.

UNIVERSITY IN BRISBANE

Jessica had been accepted into the University of Queensland to study Occupational Therapy, within the School of Medicine. We felt lucky to get her accommodation in Cromwell College, under the auspices of the Uniting Church, as places were hard to get. That arrangement meant that she would be living in a community with new friends and activities. To begin with, there were touch football games with the men's colleges or otherwise she may never have met David Hoey, her future husband. On a trip to Brisbane to attend a workshop at the Spinners and Weavers Guild, I shared Jess's dorm room and I was briefly introduced to David when we went for a breakfast picnic. Bob had trips to Brisbane CSIRO headquarters and Jess would get him to take her and David out to a nice restaurant. So slowly we were getting to know him. Then he came to Townsville for Christmas. Jess wanted to introduce David to the American family so they planned a trip to visit the USA.

Jessica and I had decided we wanted to also become Australian citizens. We had the ceremony privately in the Thuringowa Shire Mayor's office in 1986. We were proud of our new country, but still had affection for the United States. But at that time there was no dual citizenship opportunity. A visa was required for Australians to visit USA at that time, so Jess applied to get one. She was contacted by the American Consulate and told to bring in her documentation. They then told her they could not give her a visa, as they did not recognise her Australian citizenship. The reason was she had become naturalized three months before her 21st birthday and she wasn't mature enough to make that decision. In Australia, one becomes an adult at 18. So instead, they gave her a new USA passport. So just quietly, Jess kept both passports. And they went on that trip for David to meet the rellies (Aussie slang for relatives), and while there became engaged.

In Townsville the Fibres & Fabrics group was going strong with some new younger women who had many talents. One project to raise money for our Pacific Festival prize money was to be a joint effort native flower quilt designed by member Andi Cairns, in all curved pieces. It was planned out on graph paper, and each participant received a section. In the end, the quilt was very beautiful and raised $10,000 through a raffle. Another project was the Allan Cunningham Floral Embroidery designed by Barbara Douglas who drew images of plants the explorer Allan Cunningham had collected in North Queensland in 1819. It was planned to have a local focus to coincide with Australia's bicentenary celebrations in 1988. I ordered the linen yarn from Sweden and then wove fabric for the embroidery to be stitched onto, with

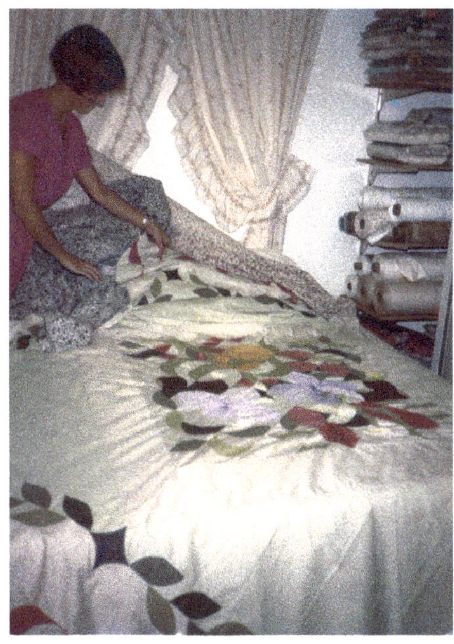

Andi with the North QLD Floral Quilt

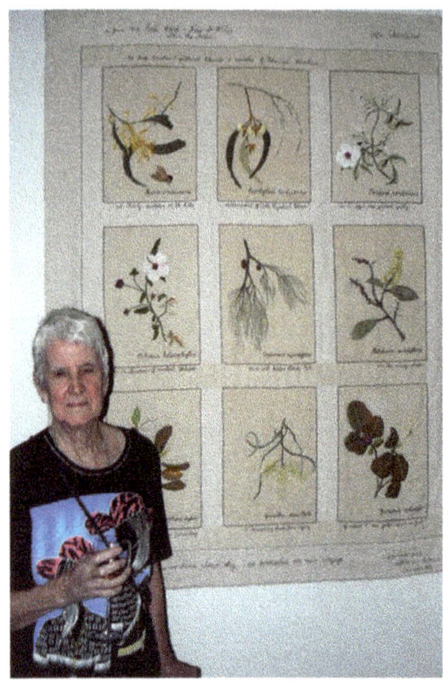

Barbara with the hanging

help from Amy Casey and Laurel Squire. That embroidered hanging travelled to other locations and even was hung for a time at the Botanical Gardens in Canberra. Now it resides in Townsville at Federation Place on Sturt Street. Barabara had done much research about Cunningham and created a book about the project.

I found a bicycle trip to China that went to all the wonderful textile areas I wanted to see and asked Bob to go with me on this trip. He said that if I got fit, he would go. So I joined a gym and attended classes. When it came time to sign up for the China trip, he said he couldn't possibly go as he had too many work obligations.

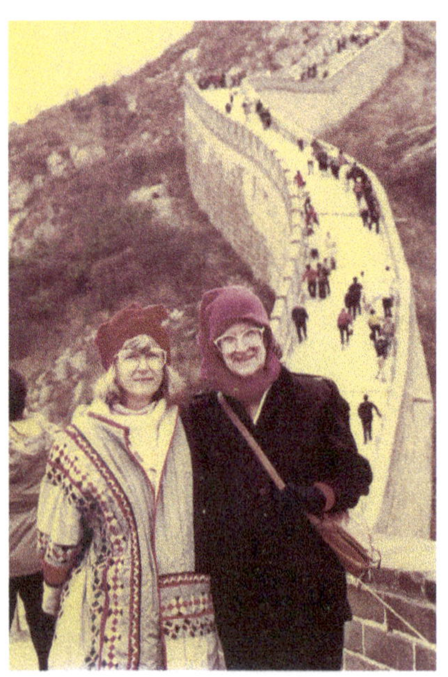

Dana and Barbara at the Great Wall

So I attempted a project that would enable members of our Fibres & Fabrics group to have a cultural textile exchange experience in China. After many meetings and letters going back and forth, this did not eventuate either. So I decided to use the knowledge gained of special Chinese textiles and planned a trip to China for a group using the Australia-Chinese Friendship Assoc. In the end, only Barbara Douglas and I went from Fibres and Fabrics, about three from the Brisbane Spinners and Weavers, and then textile enthusiasts from all over Australia joined to make a group of 22. This was in 1987 and while we were away, the stock market crashed, news that was hard for some of our group. As we were arriving in winter, we knew it would be cold and needed to be have the right clothes. My friend, Gai Copeman kindly offered me the loan of a quilted coat she had made. It kept me snug and warm. And on my head I used the red tights I had brought to keep my legs warm, but found a better use.

NEW BEGINNINGS

Jenny had turned 25 years old, had gone back to university full time, studying history and politics. Several years before she had gone back to finish high school and had already done several subjects at James Cook University. Jordan was now at school and the university had great childcare facilities for Sam. Having ended her marriage, Jenny needed to get a job and support her two young children.

In late 1989, toward the end of her studies, it happened that Queensland was getting ready to have an election. Candidates were all out and about promoting themselves to the electorate. As Jenny was driving home from university, she saw an election caravan on the side of the road promoting Ken McElligott, Labor Parliamentarian and thought she would stop and inquire about possible government jobs. Ken said that if Labor won the election, she should get in touch with him at his Brisbane office. The elections were held in November and by early December Ken had been named Minister for Health. Jenny and the boys moved to Brisbane in December and she contacted his office in early January for an appointment. She had the appointment and then the wait was on. Eventually the call came to say she had a job as Personal Secretary to the Minister for Health. All this was wonderful luck and timing. She had landed on her feet. She had two years in the Ministers Office and then move to the department and became a Policy and Planning Officer.

AFRICA AGAIN

Bob had taken up the Kenya work, travelling as a representative of the Australian government. The location of the project was in Machakos, about 60 km southwest of Nairobi. He recruited a good team of Australian scientists to live in Kenya, and would go himself periodically for five or six weeks. Roger Jones was project leader and took his family to live on location. The project also involved some of the Kenyan scientists coming to Australia to further their qualifications. And so our family got to meet them, in our home. This project lasted until 1990 when it finished with workshops in Zimbabwe and Nairobi.

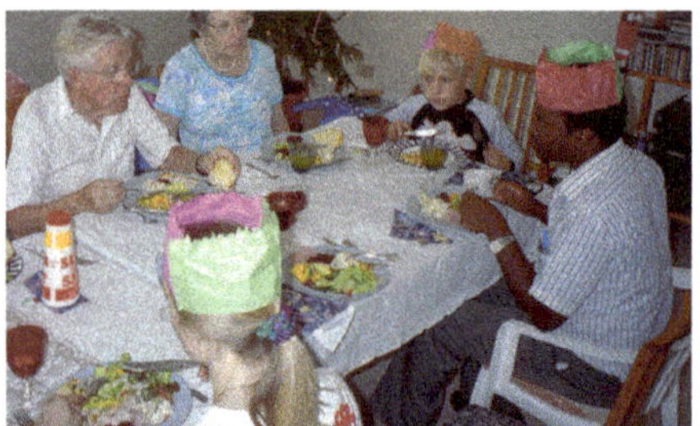

Christmas guest far from home

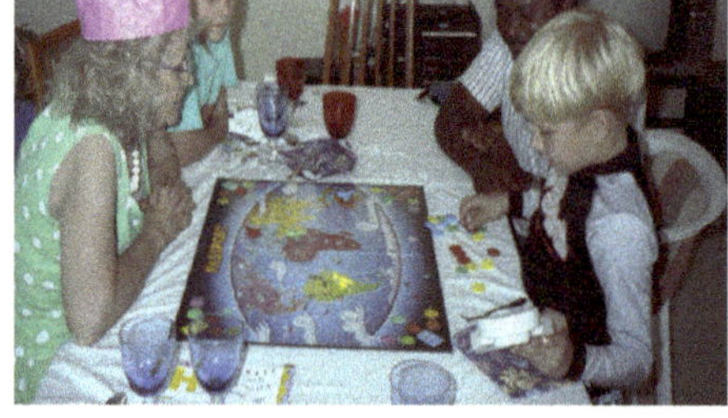

Game time fun

We decided to take the two young grandsons along when the workshops in Harare, Zimbabwe were being held. Bob had gone ahead and so I followed later with the boys, aged five and nine, meeting up for the social activities at the end. We stayed in a resort that had a moat around the buildings. Jordan found a length of pipe he decided he could use as a snorkel in the moat and must have taken in some of the dirty water. Sam played in the moat as well and they both became ill. Medical attention was required but they recovered enough that we could go on to Victoria Falls and

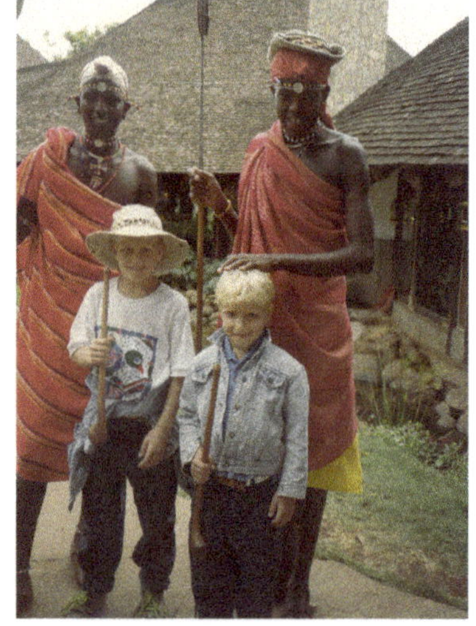

Where did Sam's hat go?

afterwards fly to Kenya where Bob had more workshops following on from the project's end.

In Nairobi, I had read about a wonderful baby elephant orphanage. These young elephants had lost their mothers to poachers. So I signed up with a tour company to be picked up in a mini-bus at our hotel with some others and taken to the area. We were told to climb up the path, where the staff would be waiting. We were divided into groups of five with an expert to tell us how each baby elephant was hand-fed and cared for by a personal attendant. Elephants are very smart and have similar life cycles to humans. After awhile, I turned around and

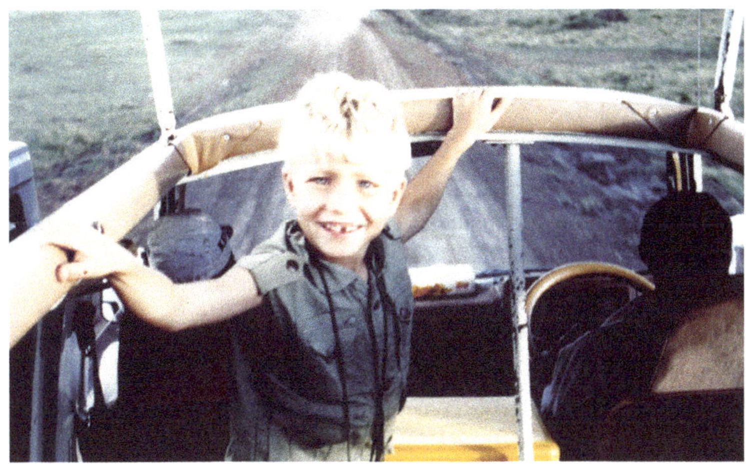

Sam out looking for lions

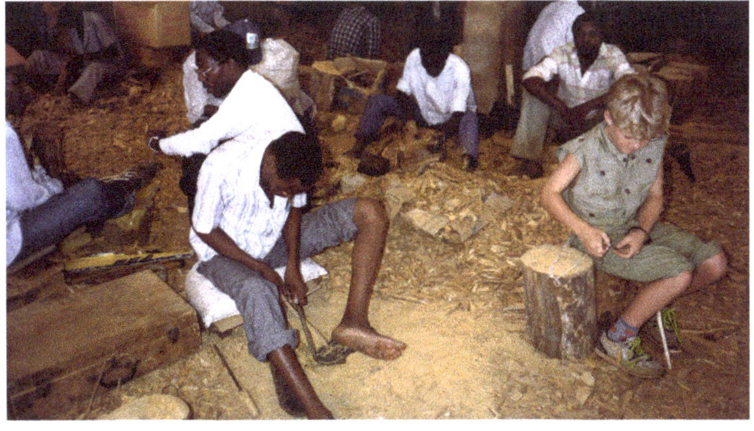

Visiting the wood carvers and having some hands-on learning

discovered that my young grandsons were missing. I ran along to find the other groups of five to see if they had joined them. No one had seen them, but the head organiser was very upset. She said, *"This is a wild game park, part of the Nairobi reserve with lions and tigers freely roaming. It is a dangerous place for young children roaming."* I thought I better first go back and check out the mini-bus. Well, there they were, waiting to go back to the hotel. I really needed them on a leash.

The final destination of the trip was to arrive in Pittsburgh for my father-in-law, Willard's 80th birthday. A big party was planned which also gave us a chance to see relatives and friends all in one location. Jessica and David, who had been married in 1988, also arrived from Australia for the event. They had graduated and had jobs in Brisbane. And Jenny came as well.

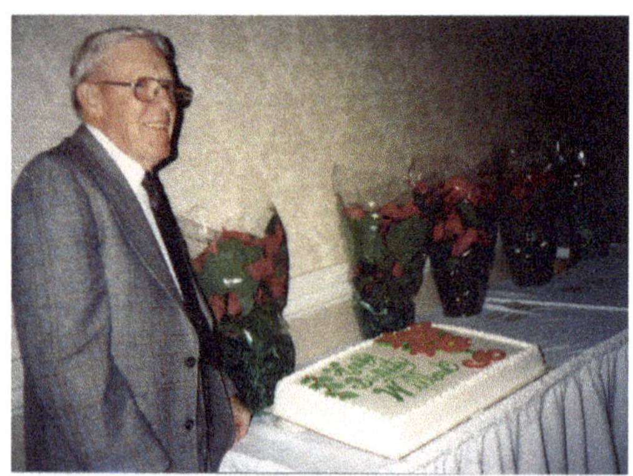

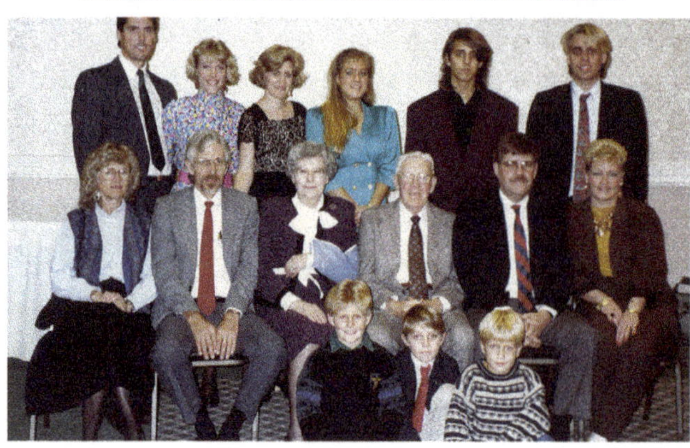

All the family - four generations

LEAVING THE TROPICS

We arrived back in Townsville in time to get ready for a move to Toowoomba, as Bob had decided to shift his project there to co-ordinate his team's Decision Support application development with the Department of Primary Industries (DPI). Instead of both groups working in parallel to each other, there could be a joint team effort. Toowoomba is in the heart of Queensland's cropping area so it seemed a logical location. The development of FARMSCAPE software for Bob was developing nicely.

As Toowoomba has a much cooler climate, it was a break for some from the tropical heat that lasted so long in the year. Bob and I took a trip beforehand to look for a new home and the westerly winds started blowing. Bob's asthma flared up and he thought Toowoomba was going to be too cold for him. So we looked for land below the range where the climate was quite different.

We each had our list of features for a residence. Bob was going to be leaving a huge shed behind and bringing his collection of horse drawn vehicles, his blacksmith shop and wheelwright equipment. So Bob needed a big shed. I wanted a house that would have a lounge room big enough to fit the Persian carpet my parents had sent me when they moved to Arizona for Dad's health. They bought a condominium with pile carpet installed. They tried putting the carpet on top, but it moved as they walked. So I was the lucky recipient. And I also wanted to have wooden floors for the carpet to rest on.

We found a 10-acre block in the area of Iredale along a little creek called Monkey Water Holes. The first redeeming feature was a large shed, which could hold everything we would be bringing. And it gave Bob some projects of adapting the spaces for his needs. There was a large area with a raised platform that had been previously used to hold feed for cattle. Inside the house, it had the features I was most interested in. The floors were wooden and the lounge was large enough for Mom's carpet. There was a recreation room that would make the perfect loom room for me. In Townsville my loom had resided in a garage area that had been enclosed for my workshop. So I was outside the actual living area of the house. I really enjoyed my Toowoomba weaving room being integrated into daily life. In the shed on the deck area was a good storage area for equipment I had for jewellery making, quilting and large supplies of yarn. We bought the home from the Luther family, who had subdivided our 10 acres off their larger parcel. They had built a new home on the other piece. A nice aspect of having them next door was that their three children were similar ages to our grandsons who would be coming to us for school holidays. So there were some local children for play. Besides that, the parents, Barbara and Roger, were very nice people to have as neighbours.

I joined the Uniting Church in the city and learned that they had a program called "Enablers" working with people with intellectual disabilities with a monthly evening program and needed helpers. I went along and enjoyed the experience and helped organise activities. Another Uniting Church involvement was with the Social Justice Network, and I agreed to be their representative in the Toowoomba group. Bob and I attended a program they held one evening with a speaker about "The Lost Boys of the Sudan". Toowoomba had been an area the government had resettled numbers of these boys who had walked across Africa, been shot at by Ethiopian police and ended up in a Kenyan refugee camp. The Catholic Church had given them access to a high school education at St Mary's when they arrived. We saw a film and then after hearing the speaker, Bob asked what was the biggest need for this group and was told jobs were hard to get. Bob thought about it for a while and decided to provide work experience for one person for a six-month period in his program. The organiser thought he could suggest someone who would benefit. So Susan (or Adeng Alei) started to work in Bob's office with CSIRO to learn new skills. Susan had come with her uncle, aunt and cousins to Toowoomba and did have good English, but she was very shy to begin with.

Sometimes a friend would come to give Susan a ride home at the end of the day and want to talk to Bob. He was a young man from this group of lost boys who had walked hundreds of kilometers to safety during warfare. Paduol Ater told Bob how at St. Mary's High School he had taken a unit one semester in Aviation and had done well and loved it. His dream was to become a pilot and he needed a sponsor. As a child, Bob used to have dreams that he could fly and soar through the sky. He had sympathy for Paduol and his dream so did enable him to have some private flying lessons. We had Paduol come on Saturdays and do mowing and garden work to earn some money. Through the next years this continued and Paduol eventually got his pilot's license. Then of course he needed his commercial license. It turned out easier to achieve the qualification passing all the government tests than it was to get a job. Jenny arranged with a journalist to write an article for The Sydney Morning Herald magazine that was published nationally in the hope of generating employment. But in the end, Paduol had to survive picking tomatoes or onions in Helidon to keep going.

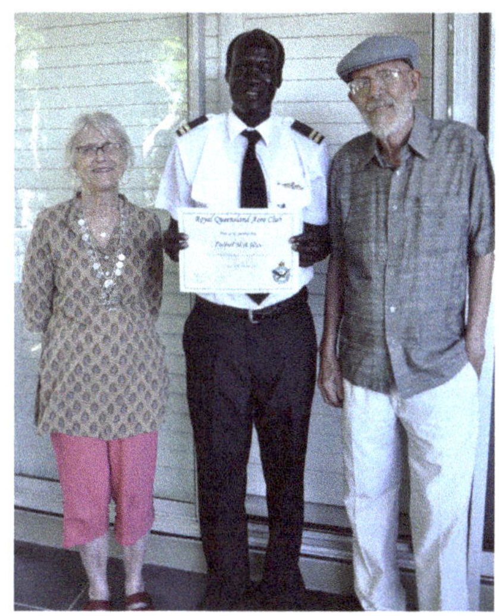

Achievement!

Meanwhile Susan had wanted to get married to a man she knew who had been accepted with refugee status in America. She went to visit him but

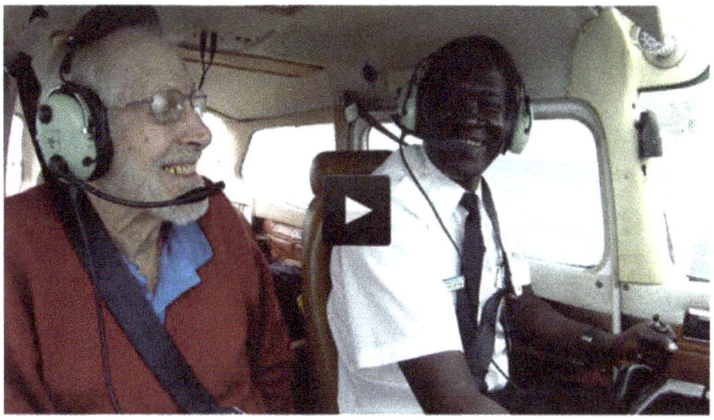

Bob had a flight with Paduol

getting a visa for him was going to be a problem. He then came to Toowoomba on a tourist visa and they had a lovely wedding at St Anthony's Catholic Church with a big reception at St Mary's school hall. But John's visa ran out and he had to return to America. Eventually it turned out Susan was pregnant and going to have to go through the whole experience without John with her. Nancy (Ajok) was born at the Toowoomba Hospital, and cried a lot. Susan was just coping and waiting for the day for John to arrive. It finally happened to her relief. Susan and John now have four children and John is an Australian citizen.

Through the years Susan has been actively getting more training and skills.

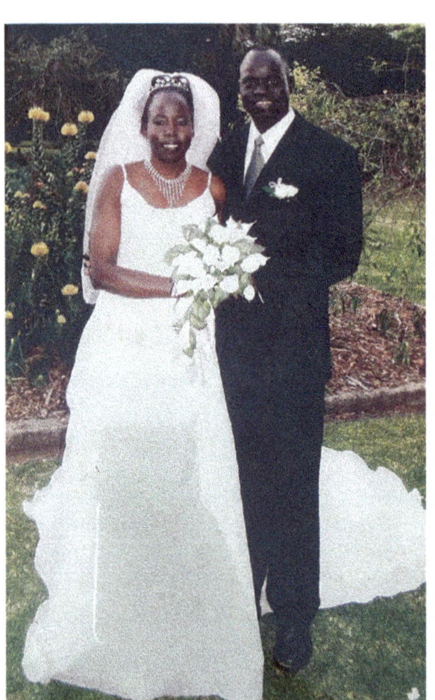

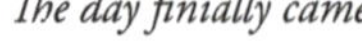

The day finially came

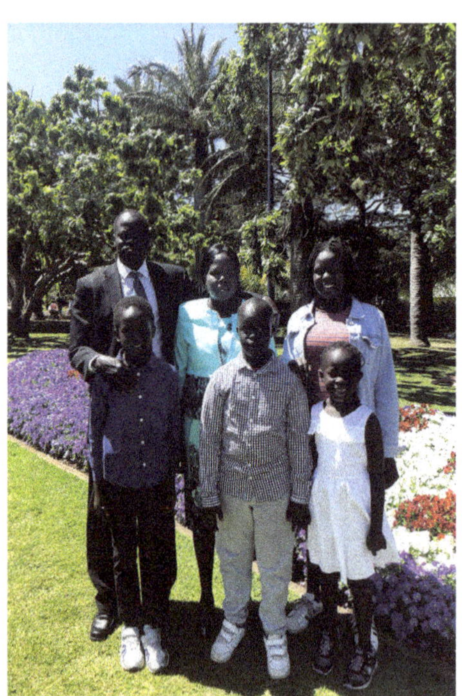

Family in Queens Gardens

I helped her gain the skill of driving. We would go for many sessions around Toowoomba in my little blue Astra. It was a happy day when she finally passed the driver's test. Now she drives a people mover from Toowoomba to Brisbane with ease.

In fact I have had other experiences of teaching driving. In Townsville I belonged to the Uniting Church in Aitkenvale which started a program of helping to settle refugees. Eventually the committee was very fortunate to become the recipients of a grant to buy a three-bedroom home in Aitkenvale to settle new refugees into when first arriving. Previously we would be given notice that a new family would arrive and have the difficult task of finding rental accommodation. There were many areas that parishioners could help with the process of settling in. There were doctor visits, government forms to be filled out, teaching English. The first wave of refugee families came from Vietnam. One of my friends taught the young wife enough English to use in hospital when she went to have her baby. Beside taking people to appointments, I did teach one Vietnamese man to drive. It did take a long time for him to actually pass his test. But unfortunately, the next day, he had a prang. Luckily no one was injured.

I also taught the mother of a friend who arrived from England never having driven, as she had been employed and the boss sent a driver to take her to work every day. I have to admit that one day when we were out practicing, she sideswiped a vehicle while practicing parking. But she eventually became a skilled driver.

Being new in Toowoomba, I quickly found the Spinners and Weavers group and joined. It is easy to make friends with people who have similar interests. There were weekly meetings. I joined the Gallery Society, a support group for the Toowoomba Regional Art Gallery and was a volunteer there. Eventually I curated some textile related exhibitions in the gallery as well. Bob and I joined the Willows gym and we would often meet there after he finished work. I found yoga for the first time, joining Leslie's Yoga School and started going to class once a week without fail. And finally I had found a bridge club and started playing again after nearly 40 years. I was lucky to have Kim Nicol for a partner and learned many of the new bridge conventions, which had changed over that time. And sometimes I played with Betty Goodchild. So I ended up driving up the Range highway quite often. Betty and I met up again for more activities after we both moved to Brisbane.

NEW LIFE

As we were having new experiences and a full life, our children in Brisbane were equally busy and productive. We loved the fact that we could drive to see them in an hour and a half. Jessica and David had their first child Maddison Dana in 1992 and I was honored to be there for the birth. She was a happy healthy bundle of joy for everyone.

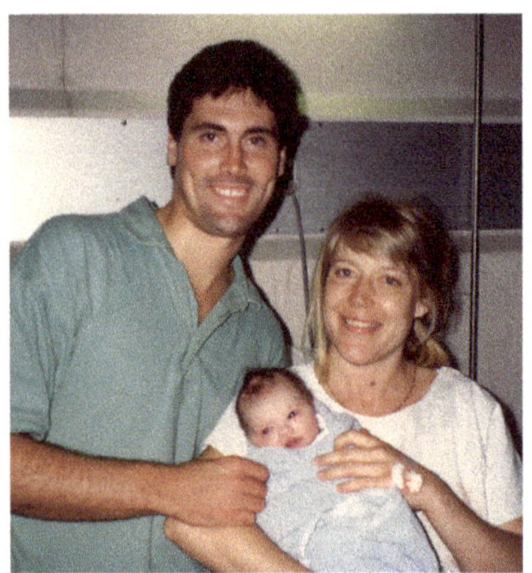

Welcome Maddison

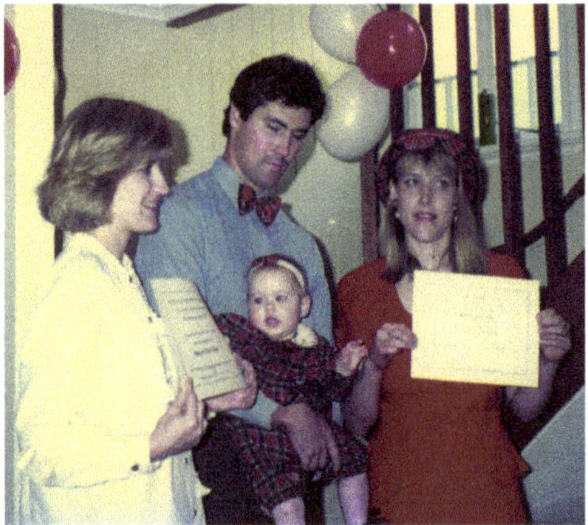

Naming ceremony

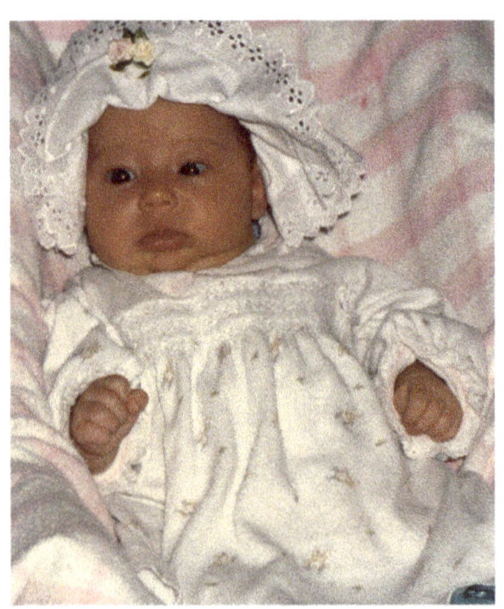

Bright eyed little Paris

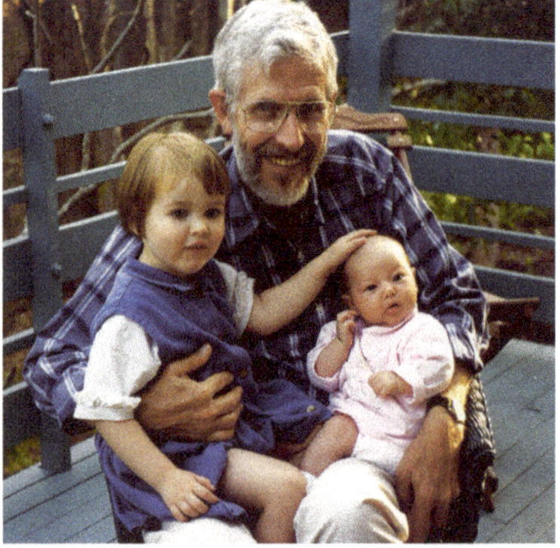

Pa greeting little Paris

And three years later Paris Elizabeth was born and was equally adorable. I did go to Brisbane to help Jess after her birth, but the first night there, I injured my back and was bedridden. Poor Jess had to take care of me as well as the new baby and Maddie who was a toddler.

It was easy for Jess and David to bring the family for a weekend at "the farm," as they referred to our place. Bob had set up a swing for the girls and we had a little red wagon and a billy cart that was fun to play with, especially when it was hooked it up to the ride-on mower.

Not long after moving in, we added two additions and a gazebo to make the home suit our needs both aesthetically and practically. We had room for everyone to sleep, although it involved stacker beds and a sofa bed in addition to two proper guestrooms if one included Bob's office.

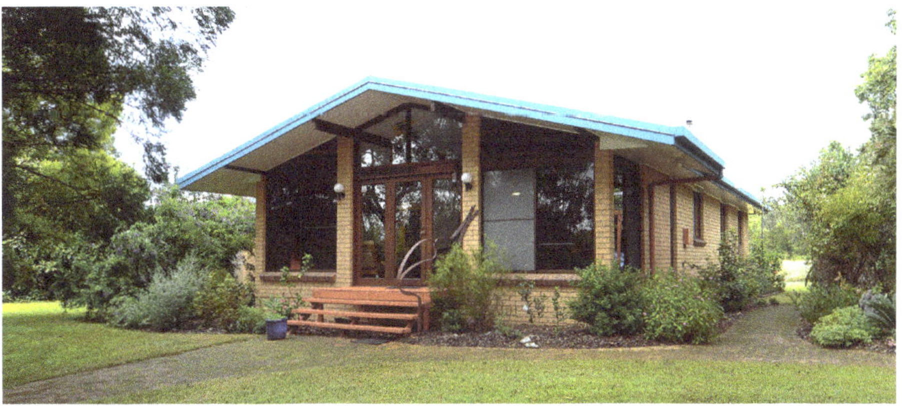

The new family room was wonderful and spacious

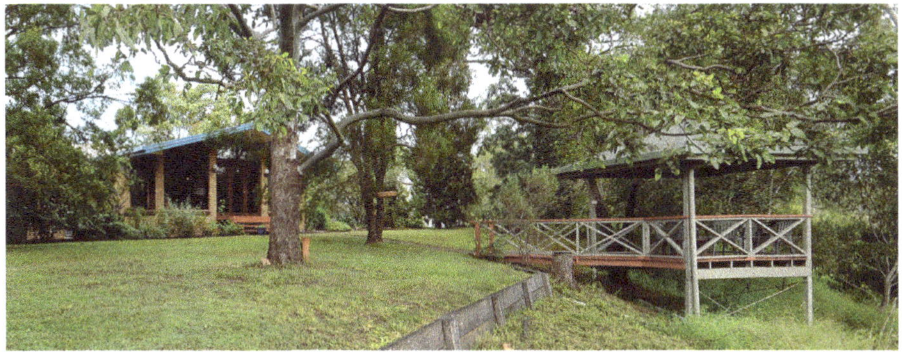

House, yard and gazebo overlooking the creek

Sam and Jordan usually came for the school holidays as Jenny was working. They were old enough to get involved in projects in the shed, often school driven assignments. And both families were often there together.

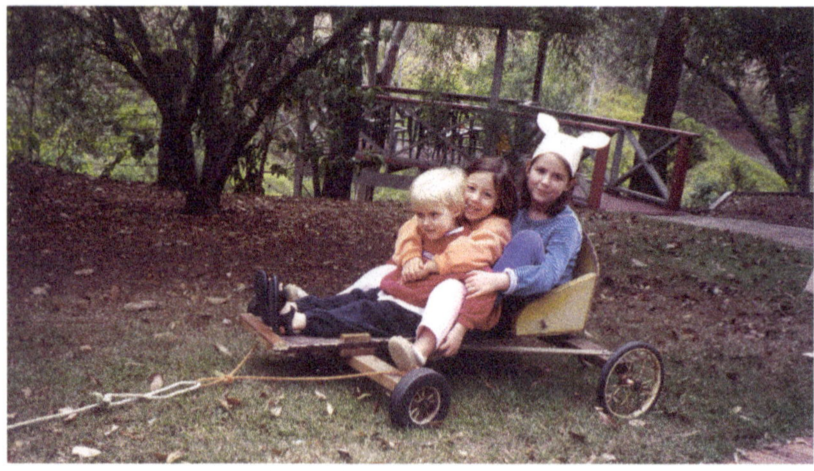

That simple go-cart provided lots of fun

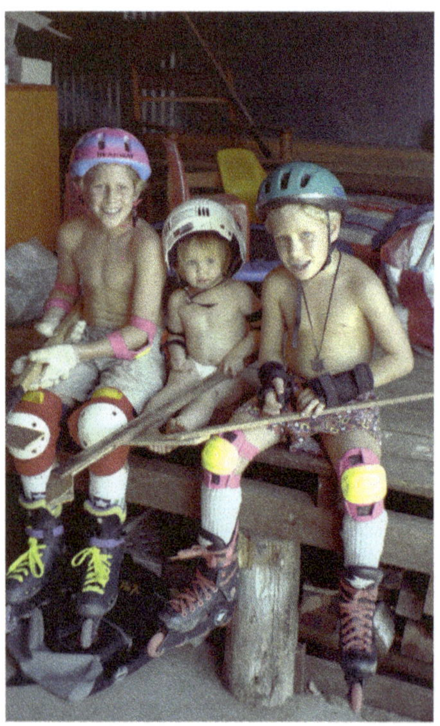

Shed floor was great for hockey

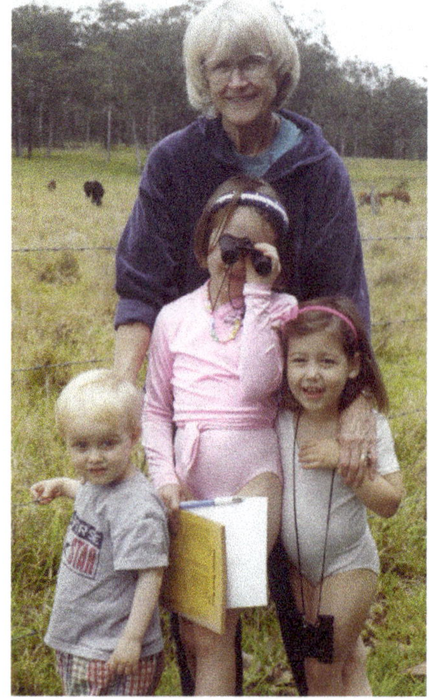

Birdwatching with Ma was fun

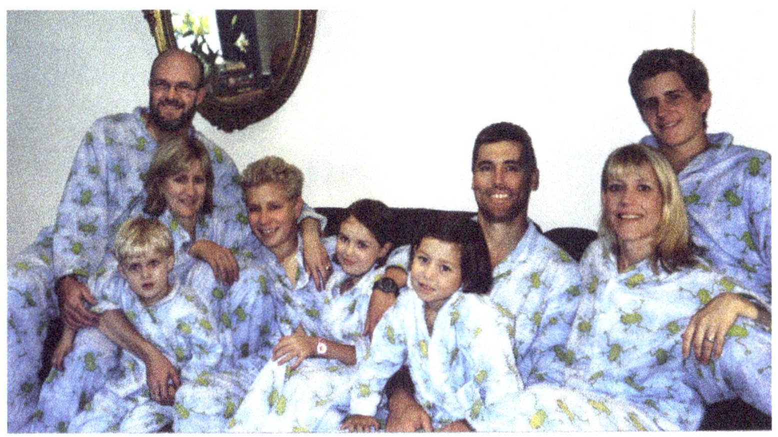

Guess what everyone got under the Christmas tree? Yes, Frog Pajamas.

In 1995 Jenny married David Butt, whom she had met working in the Minister's Office. So another year or so later after they had moved to Canberra, Conor was born. The family had grown. There were lots of celebrations and events. Jessica was the master of putting on special birthday parties and one year she flew down to Canberra to put on a Pirate Party for Conor.

Christmas celebrations were often held in Brisbane with our girls' families and everyone contributing to the meal with favourite dishes. After Jenny's family moved to Canberra, some were held in Canberra and Mossy Point, the beach house the Butt family acquired. Easter always brought an Easter egg hunt, using the American tradition of dyed and decorated boiled hen eggs. Beforehand the fun was in the dyeing and decorating. The next morning the eggs had been hidden and the challenge was to find them all. Usually there would be one or two never found until weeks later when they started to smell.

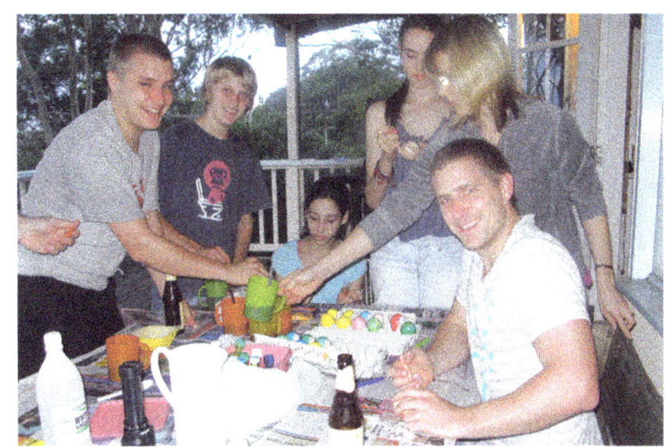

Big and little kids enjoyed the fun

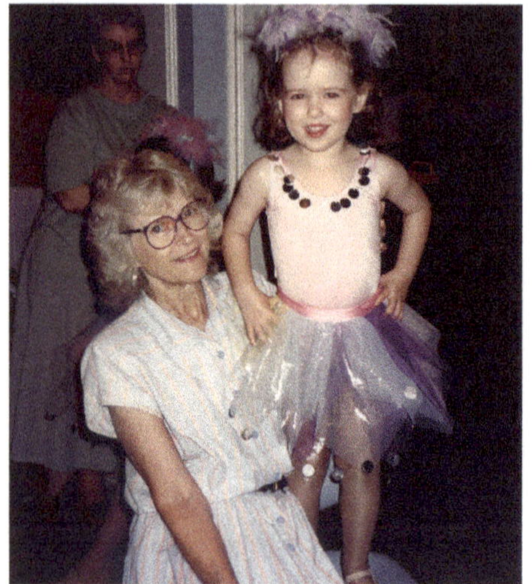

Maddie in a Christmas performance

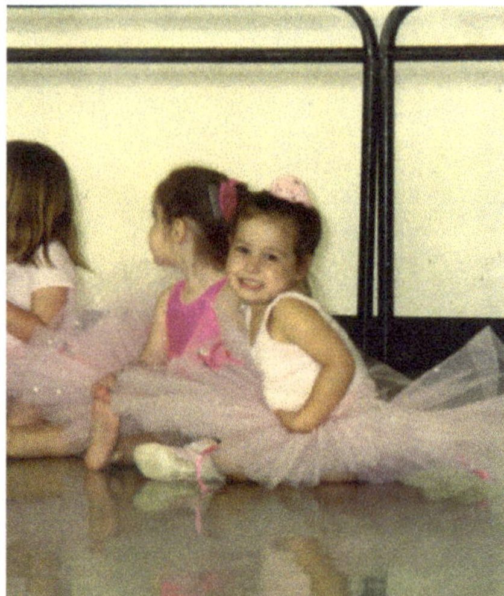

Early beginnings for Paris

Bob and I enjoyed attending the younger grandchildren's activities. Conor was an avid soccer player and the girls enjoyed ballet performances wearing lovely outfits and learning skills. The older boys were in school. They were enjoying being not too far from the snow fields and had the opportunity to learn snow boarding.

Bob and I always drove down to Canberra in his ute (Aussie slang for utility). Usually there was a load in the back that Jenny had organised such as furniture from the secondhand shop in our area. We liked the drive, often listening to stories on tape. I always had to stay awake to keep Bob from falling asleep.

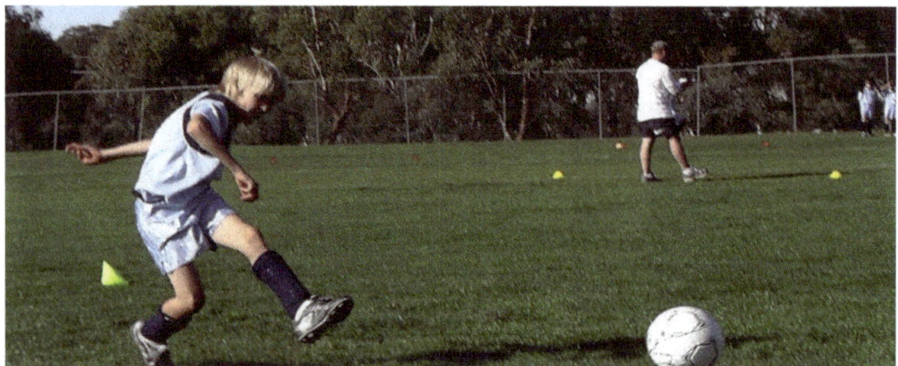

Conor played for the Woden Valley Club in Canberra

TECHNOLOGY

Bob was always working on his laptop and devising new ideas for computer software programs. I decided it was time for me to have a computer, learn some skills and get on the internet. I went to a TAFE course in building websites and built mine, calling it Dana's Textile Travels. And then I created websites for others and was webmaster for some organisations' sites.

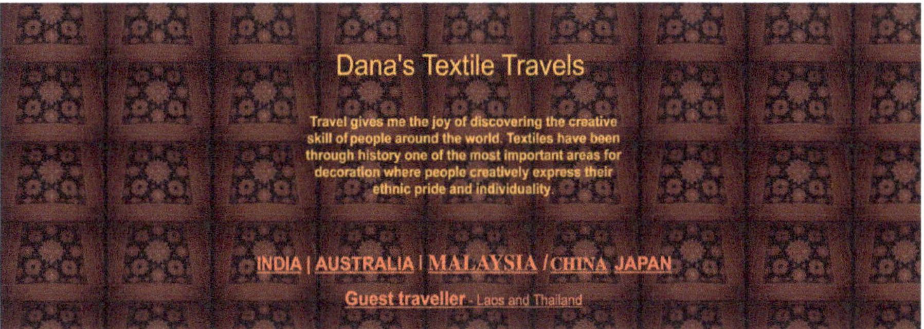

Before long I found on the internet a weaving group that gave me contacts all over the world. It was exciting to discover weaving experts such as Peter Collingwood from England posting in the Weavers Forum. I met people I would follow up with on overseas trips. When I told my daughters that I was meeting up with a new friend in New York City, they were alarmed and wondered if it could actually be "Jack the Ripper". I assured them that these new friends were really weavers. I met one at the Museum of Modern Art who had a business selling tencel yarns. I ordered a large box of these yarns to be sent to me and loved the qualities combining the best of cotton and rayon in one fibre made from trees. We had a great day in New York going to textile related colleges and exhibitions. We learned how permanent pleating is done in a small Manhattan business.

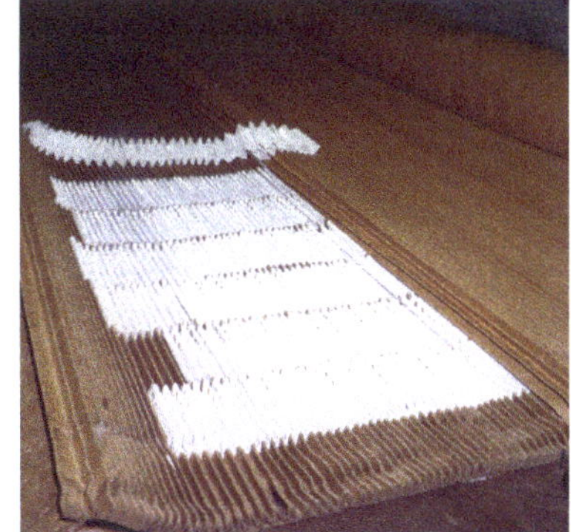

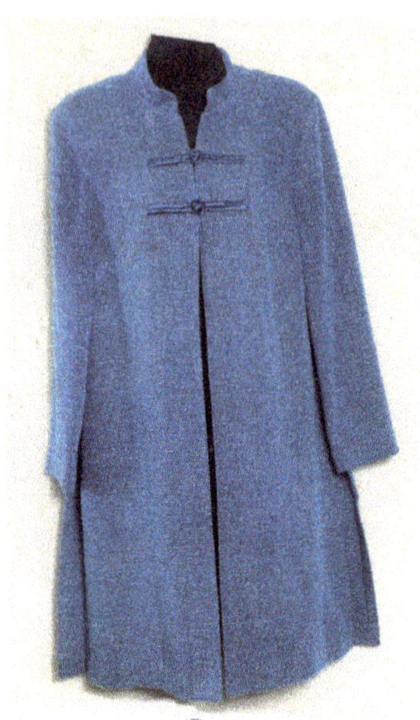

My weaving with tencel

All of the tencel yarn I had ordered was white, so that I could dye it to suit my needs. One of the tencel yarns I had ordered was a blend with silk. After dyeing half the yarn a turquoise blue and the other deep blue, I wove enough yardage for a coat. I was always thinking of projects that would be useful to wear or use. But I also needed to think of what I would exhibit with the Dozen Weavers Group each year.

TRAVELS WITH BOB

These sorts of trips usually worked out for me, travelling with Bob for work. He was often a speaker at a conference. Then he would have appointments around the county. So I would make a different itinerary. After a conference in Baltimore, I visited my cousin Sandy Lillydahl at Amherst and friend Carla in Cape Cod. Carla and I then had some days in New York City, a place Bob always wanted to avoid. When he was speaker at a conference in Denmark, afterward we drove to Sweden and went to Lund. There I spent time in the archives doing family history. It was fascinating seeing the original records kept by the Lutheran Church that even recorded scores of literacy and numeracy for the parishioners. Following that, we drove up to Solvesborg and visited with Nilsson relatives. Folke Nilsson took us to the cemetery and showed us the family headstones, which had been maintained for over 200 years. Most space in a cemetery, I was told was only available for 25 years and then someone else could have the space. In the church I was shown a silver chalice made by my great uncle Jacob for the church. Birgit told us the story about when my mother was expected to visit in Solvesborg and

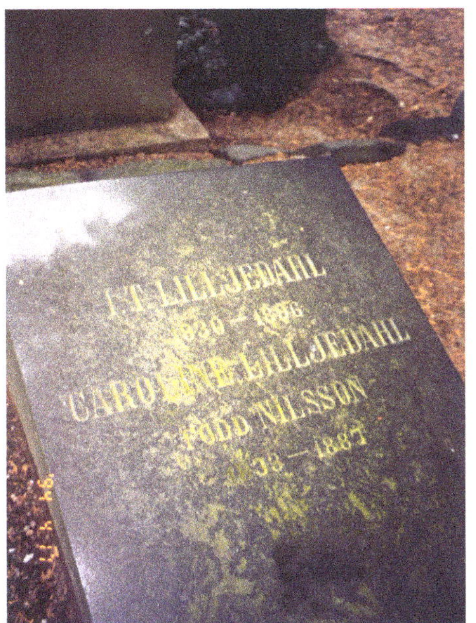

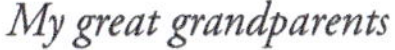

My great grandparents

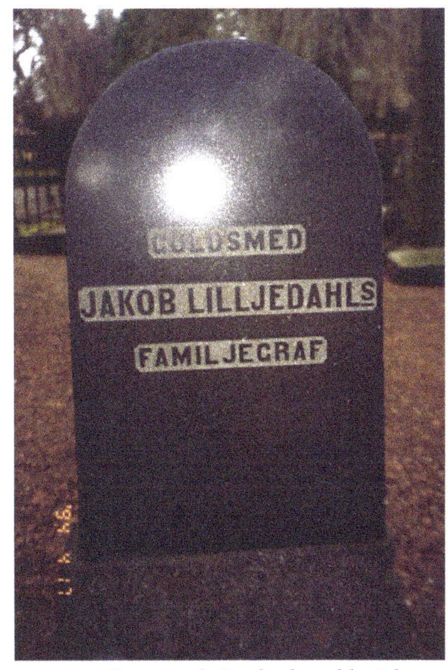

Great uncle Jacob, the goldsmith

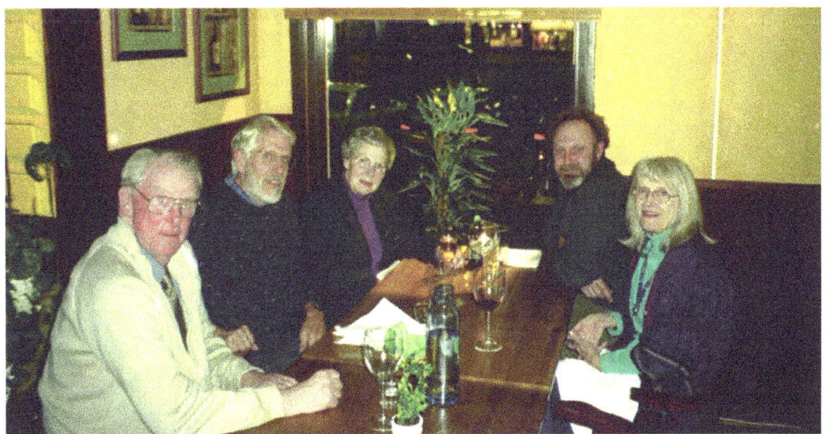

Visiting with Folke and Birgit Nilsson and their son Stefan

was arriving by train. Evidently they had never seen a picture of her. Birgit was at the station platform waiting and there were some others she knew and was telling about this American relative arriving and wondering how she could identify her. Well the train pulled in and out came this person small in stature but "bigger than life". And Birgit, said *"that must be her."* She had been described by some as an "Auntie Mame".

Then we went to Stockholm visiting cousin Charlotte and her husband Karl Von Axelson who invited cousins Karin and Lisen and their own daughters over for lunch. Previously Karen and Lisen had come to Australia and stayed with my daughters. Bob and I were in India at the time and missed them, so this was an opportunity to meet.

The sea was frozen over near Stockholm. Ice skating on the sea is a very popular wintertime activity and this was going to be the last weekend considered safe for skating. So Charlotte and Karl had a morning on the ice while Bob and I did sightseeing around the city. It was still extremely cold in our opinion.

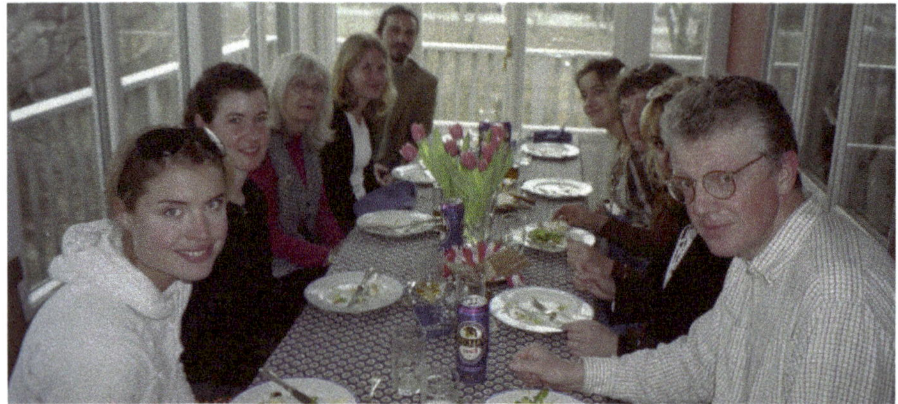

Cousins enjoy lunch with Von Axelson hospitality

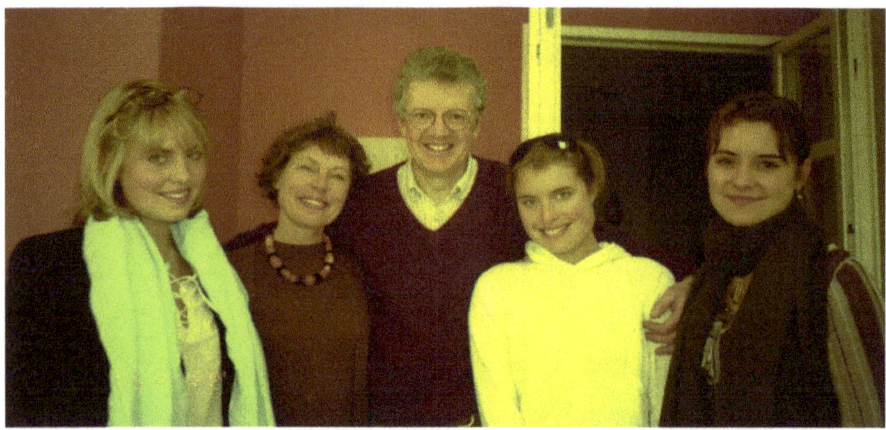

Charlotte, Karl and daughters

Another year we were in the USA and decided to fly up to Saskatoon in Canada where Sakti lived with his wife Bharati and children, Kunal and Arup. We continued to have contact through the years with them. Sakti visited us in Queensland as well.

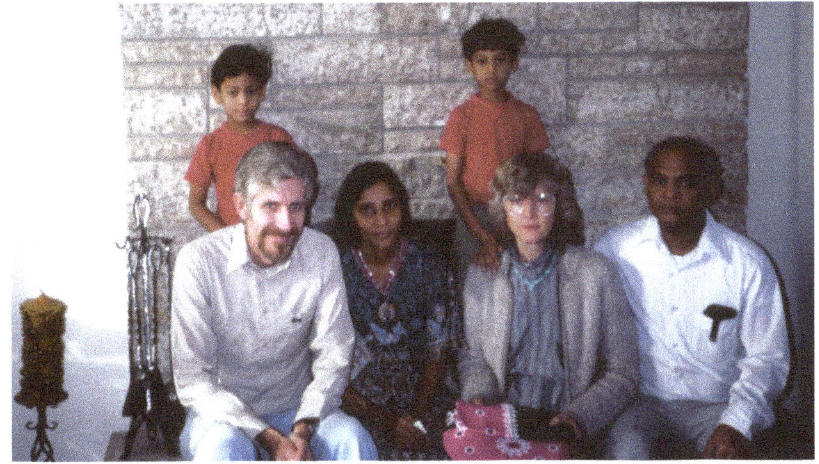

Visiting Sakti's family

One of the new and exciting internet applications was a program called "Skype" offering free phone calls. Better yet was the facility to make calls to another computer that included video during the talk. We would call Bob's parents every Saturday morning and have a chat with them for an hour. Sometimes the unexpected is captured on the video. I remember one session where we were talking to Grammie on her own, when in the background the bathroom door opened and out came Grandpa wearing only his underpants. At least he had those on.

Having these chats made the distance seem to disappear and we kept up to date with daily life. I just felt bad that such technology wasn't around while my parents were alive. In those days phone calls were so expensive, but I did write home a proper letter every week and we sent voice tapes with the children telling their stories and singing with new guitar skills.

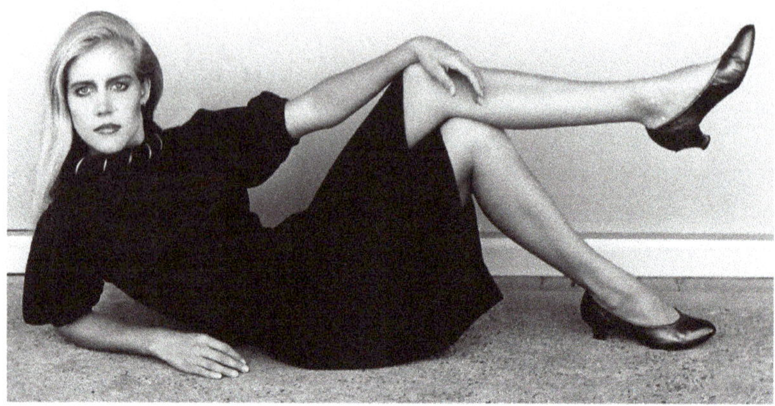

Jess in her modelling days

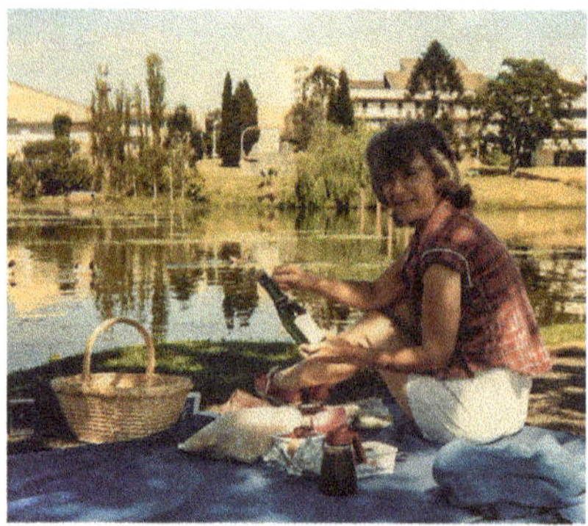

Champagne breakfast picnic

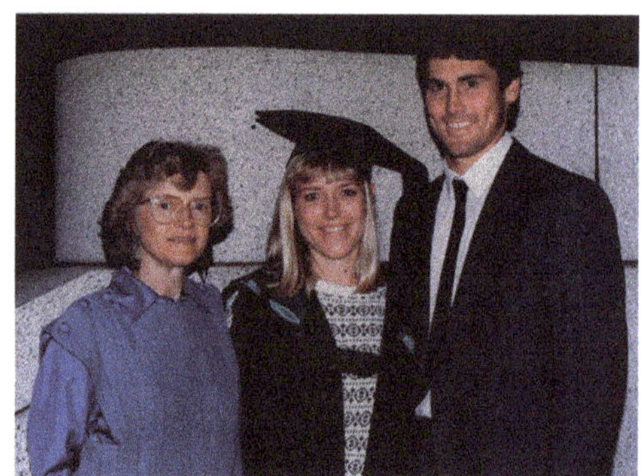

Graduation and meeting David

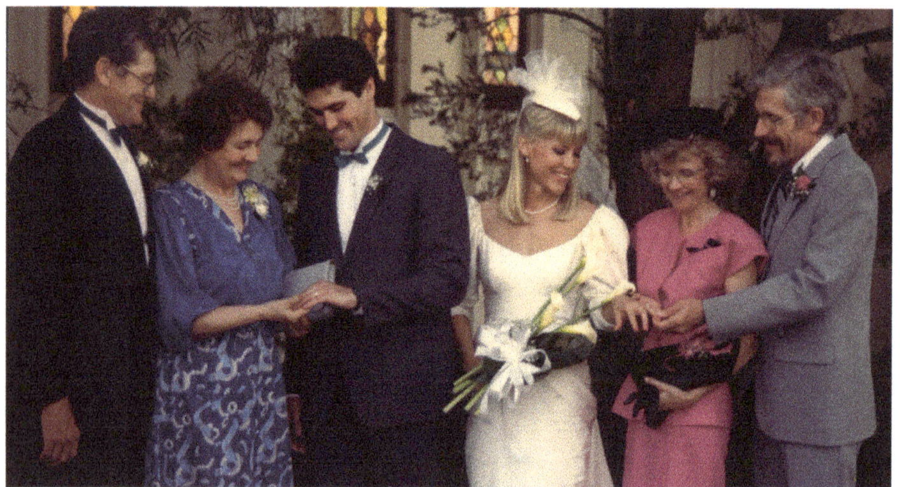

Parents admiring the wedding rings

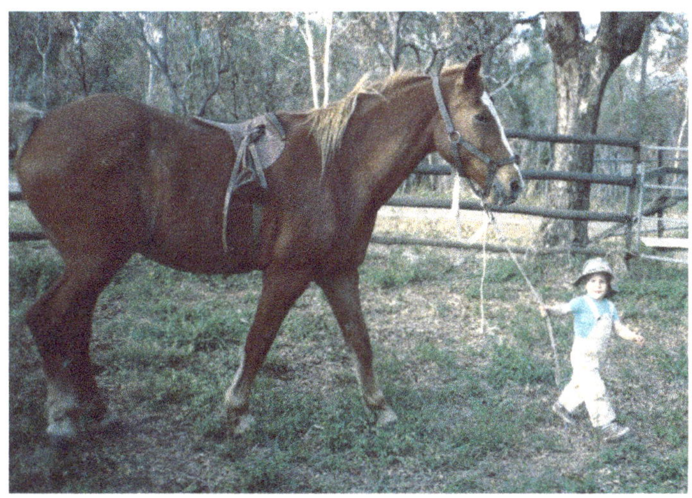

Jordan learned horse skills

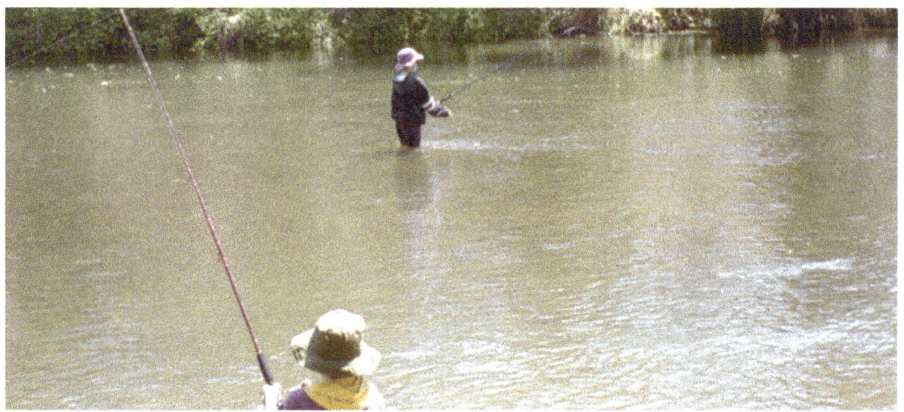

Fishing in the river below our home

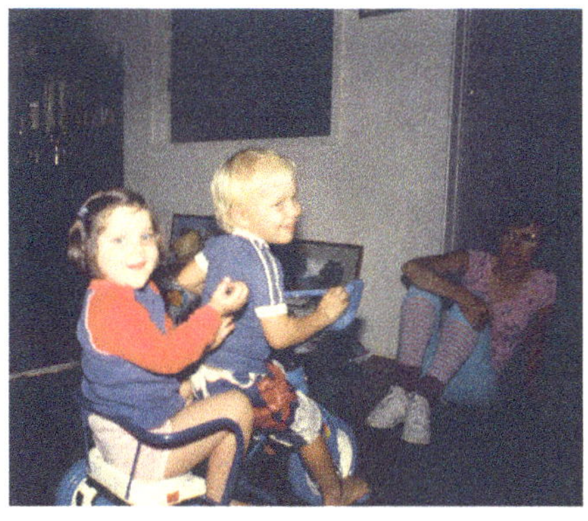

Erin Patrick and Sam riding in my dining room

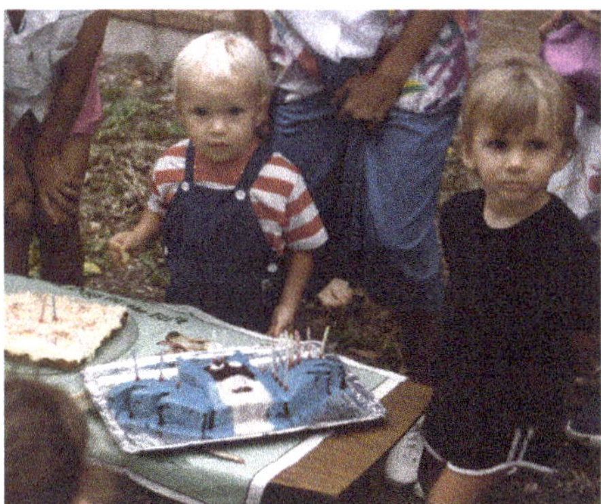

Sam and Sean sharing a birthday

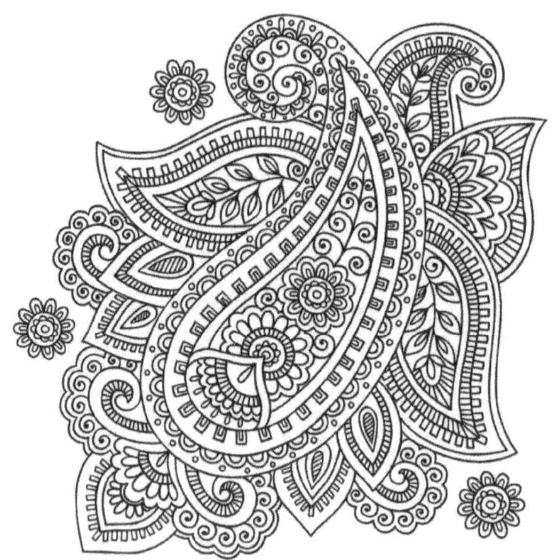

06

Indian Opportunities and More

1994 HYDERABAD

Bob, who also had numerous Indian projects, decided he needed to spend a part of each year in Andhra Pradesh, near Hyderabad, South India. Although Bob was hesitant asking me to tear myself away from my activities in Toowoomba, where we had been living then, I could only see the opportunity. I had a real interest in bird watching. In India we would be living on a research station with fields, lakes, forests and residential environs, so various species were prevalent. There were over 150 species on the listed sightings. And remembering the trip Dawn Faris took me on to see ikat villages in 1983, I knew that my weaving interests would be satisfied.

Arriving at ICRISAT, before long I met Sue Byth, whose husband Don was the Research Director. They were from Brisbane and were helpful in our settling in. Don's ICRISAT driver, Rama Rao, turned out to be the same driver our old friend Don Faris had, during his time at ICRISAT. Rama Rao was an outstanding driver and man. Both families had helped with educating his children. So Sue and I were able to use Rama Rao on a trip further afield to explore a type of ikat I wanted to research called Telia Rumal. I had just read about it on the plane flying to India. I then actually bought some fragments of the cloth from a dealer and collector

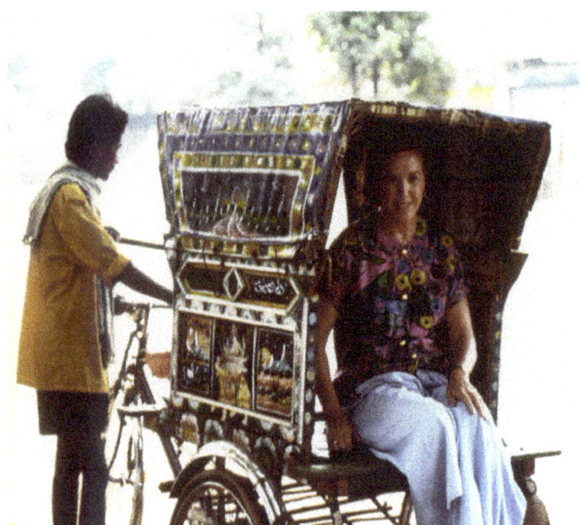

Sue and I headed off on adventure

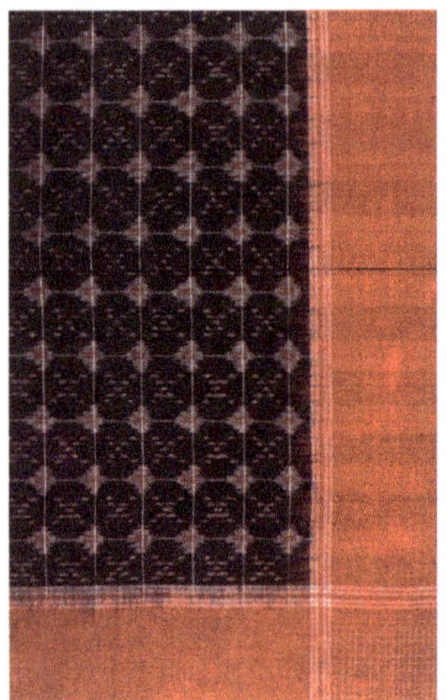

Antique fragment

Jagdish Mittal, who supposedly had a museum collection without a home to place it in. And I used these pieces to try and find weavers who knew the skill.

Our destination was the town of Chirala, on the other side of Andhra Pradesh, where Telia Rumal supposedly first developed. But along the way we stopped at Koyalgudam Weavers Co-operative. I walked in holding my samples and a designer from Delhi happened to be there, giving design classes to the weavers. He saw my fabric pieces and grabbed them, showing the weavers. He told them that when you see something with good colour combinations use those colours but don't throw in additional colours. Use them in a different way. Perhaps make the design bigger or use different yarns. He was there to get them to design items for the World Vision Christmas catalogue.

We continued on to Chirala, which looked like such a small dot on the map, but turned out to have 20,000 weavers. I showed my samples to weavers we came across and none knew of anyone weaving anything like them. One man did say he had seen one twenty years before. Rama Rao decided he would make some phone calls, and came back saying he had an address. I think he had called back to Hyderabad to the Weavers Service Centre. We met Gunti Bhasker Rao and his

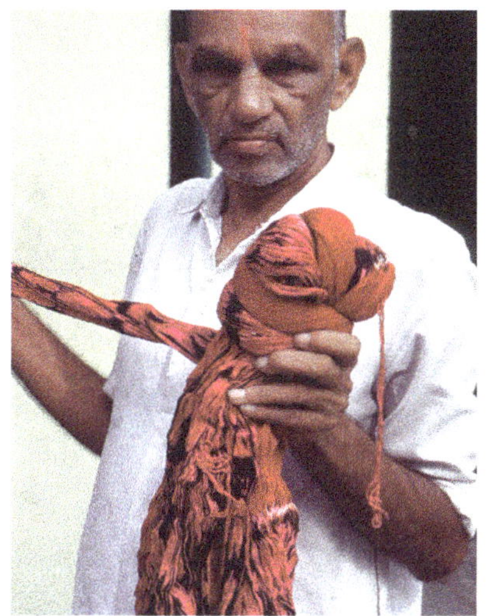

Gunit Bhasker Rao holding warp threads

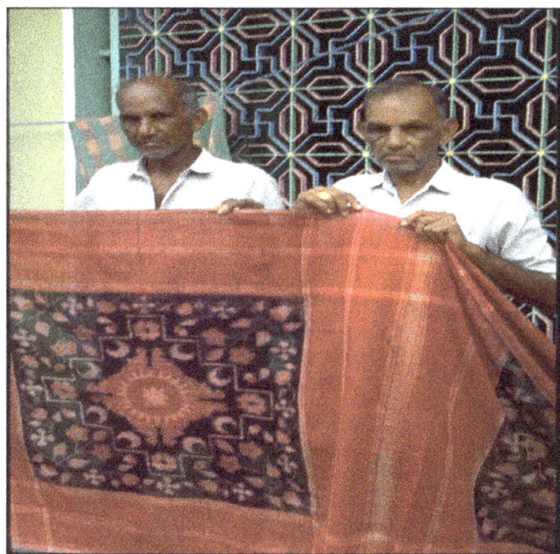

The Bhasker Rao brothers

brother, Gunti Venkata Subba Rao who were the last Telia Rumal producers in Chirala. Bhasker Rao was the designer and producer of the resist tied yarn while his brother was the dyer. They would prepare warps and wefts for a small group of women they had who would do the weaving. These people were all elderly and younger weavers were not involved. So we bought some pieces which they would only sell in the length they were woven on the loom called a "than", which would contain eight pieces of Telia Rumal.

THE HOLIDAY FROM HELL

Bob was going on another trip to Africa, so I decided to book a trip for myself to Bandipur Game Reserve in Karnataka. The office at the Research Station had a Thomas Cook travel agency and could arrange my trip. I caught the train at Hyderabad, about a 45-minute ride from Patancheru where we were living at the ICRISAT research station. The transport department had a bank of vehicles and drivers available for me to use. At the same time, I booked a pick-up on return. I had a lower level berth and had a woman above me. When I arrived at the Bangalore train station, a driver was waiting for me with a vehicle to take me for the rest of the trip. But he explained that I needed the vouchers for the Game Reserve, which needed to be picked up. We went to the location, which was an office up on the fourth floor of a building. The driver came back and said the office was empty. Thinking they might be gone on lunch break, we waited an hour and he went back. It turns out he found them in the back room playing cards. So we finally got our vouchers and started off.

We hadn't gone too far when we had an accident with a tuktuk full of little school children that actually ran into us and spilled the children over the road. The tuktuk driver did hurt his knee, but the children all picked themselves up and got back in. I asked would we be getting the police to come? No, we just went on our way. Our Ambassador vehicle was like a tank and didn't even get a dent in the side.

Again we started off and the rain started to pour. The driver pointed out the scenic hills where the movie, "A Passage to India" was filmed, but the rain was so heavy I couldn't see much. We arrived at Mysore where my hotel was booked. Registering, the receptionist asked for my passport, which I had not brought. Back in Hyderabad, Wendy Ryan had told me about her kids visiting, had taken a train trip and been robbed of their passports. So I explained that to the hotel staff and was told that I could not stay anywhere in Mysore without a passport. At that, I told him he would have to take me home to his place. I did ask to see the manager and was told he had called the manager from home. It was actually getting late as with all the events that had happened we were much later than planned. The manager did arrive and said everything would be fine this time, but to bring it next trip. Well the problem was I was headed to the Game Park and coming back soon. But he was OK with that. When the attendant carried up my luggage to my room, he said, "*Do not be upset, do not worry, that man is just a learning man,*" referring to the man on the reception desk. It was very sweet.

We then drove on to the Game Reserve to discover I was the only guest because in the wet season the elephants and other animals don't need to come in for water and food. Actually there was a film unit also there documenting something. I did have nice bird walks with the manager of the game park. I had expected to see herds of elephants coming into the lagoon by the dining room.

Driving back to the Bangalore train station we stopped to see the silk cocoon auction rooms and saw farmers bringing in bags of the cocoons they had raised from silk worms. I was shown my carriage on the train, again having a sleeping berth. But this time sitting in my compartment as my travelling companion was an Air Force serviceman. I sat down and said I was surprised they had put me with a man, especially as the carriage was half empty. He looked at me and said, *"In the next few hours you had better change your thinking."* Because I had a woman to share with coming down, I just thought that was the way they did it. In actual fact, this time we were in a 4-berth compartment and he explained that more people would be coming on at the next few stations. He did say he would go talk to the conductor and find out what was happening. In actual fact, he did make for a pleasant travelling companion. Several stops down the track a couple got on and had been assigned to our compartment. We started chatting and they told about just coming from a medical facility set up by one of the industrial billionaire to treat people holistically without charge. The husband had diabetes and had experienced lifestyle improvements as well as medical. He started to demonstrate the yoga poses he had learned, and the alternate nostril breathing is something I had been practicing in Toowoomba. In about an hour, they departed, having reached their station.

It was time to make up our berths and go to sleep. In the middle of the night more men got on the train and were in our berth, bringing big wooden boxes instead of luggage. These filled up the floor between the bunks.

Later I woke up and the train seemed very quiet without the usual clickety-clack. Well it was obvious we weren't moving. Finally at daylight we discovered that there was a derailment on the track ahead of us and eventually we would be transferred by bus to a station further ahead. We waited until about 10a.m. There were many buses they were trying to get filled and they had information to tell us.

We were finally assigned a bus and the organiser came to explain that soon we would be crossing the border from Karnataka into Andhra Pradesh where recently they had brought in prohibition. It was explained there would be very bad consequences for anyone going over the border carrying alcohol so they were asking if anyone had anything to declare and hand over. Well I had to put up my hand as I had a little miniature bottle of something or other. Everyone turned around and looked at me. I was somewhat embarrassed and started to hand it over, when the Air Force guy said, *"Well, could I have it as the services have an exemption?"* So that worked out fine.

Meanwhile we arrived on the side of the road and were told there was a platform to catch the next train. The organiser said to wait while he found out how to proceed. He came back saying there is a swamp we would have to wade through to get to the platform, so he asked the young children running around if we tried down 100 meters or so further would we get through. The children indicated down there it would be over our chests. My Air Force guy suggested I better take off my Reebok shoes, which I did and hung them around my neck. And guess who carried my suitcase! I had found my guardian angel. With us was a businessman, dressed in suit and leather dress brogues, carrying a suitcase in one hand and brief case in the other. He took about five or six steps in this swamp and became stuck in the mud, wobbling this way and that. He couldn't get his feet to free up and both his hands were occupied. In the end I don't know how he got free of the mud. I was very thankful I had been told to take off my shoes. How flexible the foot is without shoes and able to release from the mud.

To make things even better for me, there were Banjara gypsy women doing labouring work there and carrying in clean water to make cement. My Air Force guy talked one of them into pouring some water over my feet so I could get rid of the sticky mud. She wasn't too happy about that and indicated what would she do then for more water. But I didn't need a huge quantity.

So eventually we were back on a train headed to Hyderabad. We arrived at about 10 or 11 at night. I looked for my ride back to the research station but no one was there. I just assumed they would have arrived for my earlier train and discovered about the derailment and late arrival and found out the new plan. I was able to get the staff at the train station to call the transport department at ICRISAT to find out what happened. I was told there never was any booking to pick me up. But they would try to help me out. One of the transport workers was in Hyderabad at a party and he would come and pick me up, taking me to the ICRISAT Club in Banjara Hills where a driver from the research station would drive in and get me there to return to the campus. So I went out to the curb of the train station to wait for my ride. This man arrived in a white silk outfit with gold chains around his neck, looking like a movie star coming along and I tried to look the other way, avoiding eye contact. Eventually I came to realize this was Gopal from transport who I saw all the time in his blue uniform, looking nothing like a movie star. So I did get back to our apartment and discovered there was Bob! He had returned from Africa and the staff had told him I was away and would be back the next week. So he never was worried about me.

Most days I had a local driver, Ravi Kumar and went into the city exploring local possibilities. I met Bina Rao who was a designer working with weavers through

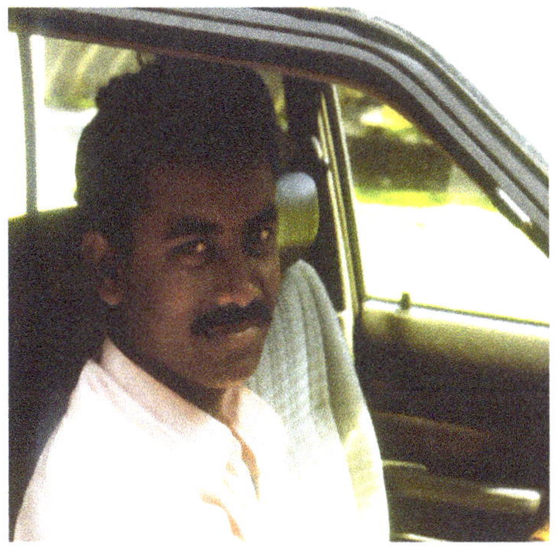

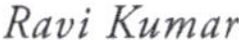

Ravi Kumar

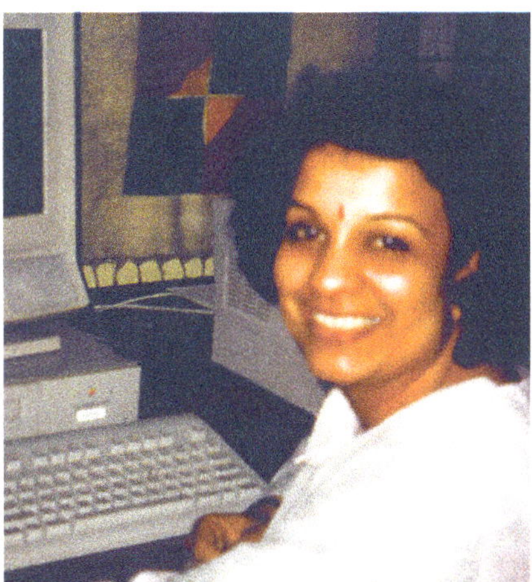

Bina Rao designer

Mrs Nanderaj who had a printing studio. Then Dastkar, an NGO working with crafts, introduced me to Jagada Rajapa who designed saris in natural dyes on silk, so my contacts were increasing. I found many contacts through the Weaver's Service Centre (WSC), an organisation helping artisans in various ways. Eventually I got to know Govardhana, who worked at the WSC and was a member of the Gajam Family who are traditional weavers of the double ikat, Telia Rumal. I offered to write about his family's work on my textile website. It takes time for such artisans to trust that you are not trying to take advantage in any way. As we were only spending two to three months at a time in India, this all fit in with a busy life back in Queensland. But I would pick up the pieces the next year when returning to India and build on that.

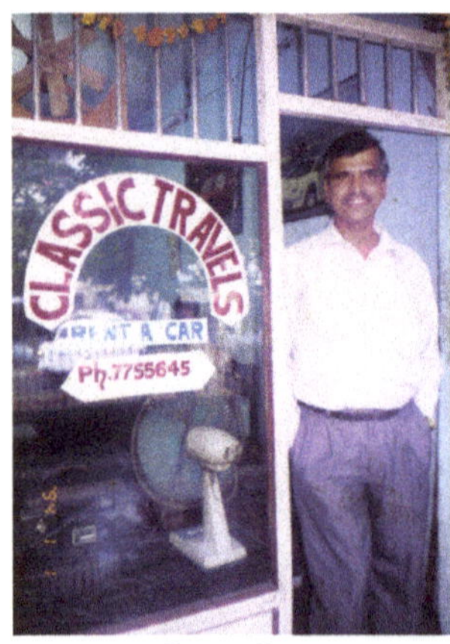

Rama Rao

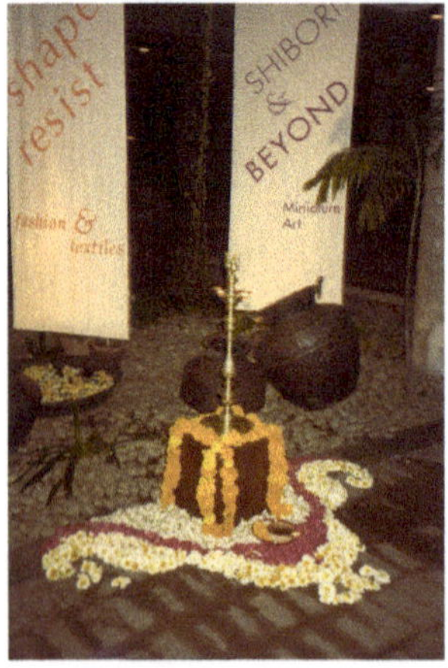

Shibori Symposium

Eventually Rama Rao took a redundancy from ICRISAT and bought one of the older vehicles to start his own travel business in Hyderabad. It went so well he ordered a brand new Indian Ambassador off the production line. So that year Barbara Douglas flew out to Hyderabad with us and the two of us had a wonderful trip to Orissa with Rama Rao for the new car's maiden voyage. Ambassadors are built like a tank and don't have all the comforts of many foreign cars, but parts are available and they can be repaired anywhere in India. Travelling with Rama Rao meant there would always be lots of interesting conversation. And it was such an advantage to have him on any trip as he spoke five different Indian languages.

In 1997 before heading to Hyderabad, I went to Ahmedabad for the International Shibori Symposium with textile friend Margaret Barnett. It was a wonderful week of seminars, workshops and exhibitions. Margaret had work displayed in the beautiful exhibition that was arranged with artists from around the world. We then had more adventures around Gujarat, meeting more artisans and visiting the city of Patan where the Salvi family produces the wonderful Patan Patola, famous around the world. It is a double ikat on silk with natural dyes created on unusual floating looms. Eventually we arrived at the ICRISAT research station for Margaret to see what the Hyderabad area had to offer.

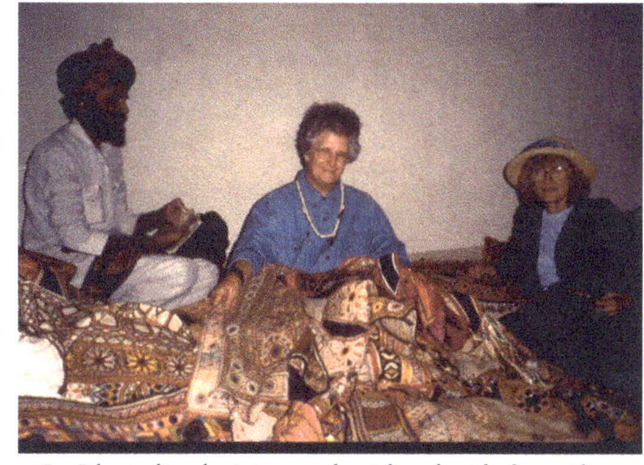

In Bhujodi admiring embroidered tribal textiles

On another of my trips, going to Karnataka to see the historic ruins at Hampi, I invited Rama Rao to bring his wife Janaka along so they could have a nice time together. No matter what the destination or aim of the trip, it was always the unexpected along the way that enriched travelling in India. Although this trip was of historic interest, I managed to find some unusual textiles being woven and even a cultural event of a funeral procession with the dead person sitting upright in a decorative chair.

Bob had been thinking of his work in India as a project leader and decided it was time to withdraw. I was rather shocked, as I had just really gotten into the research I was doing. He had had enough and wanted to stay home. He had contacted Bob Myers

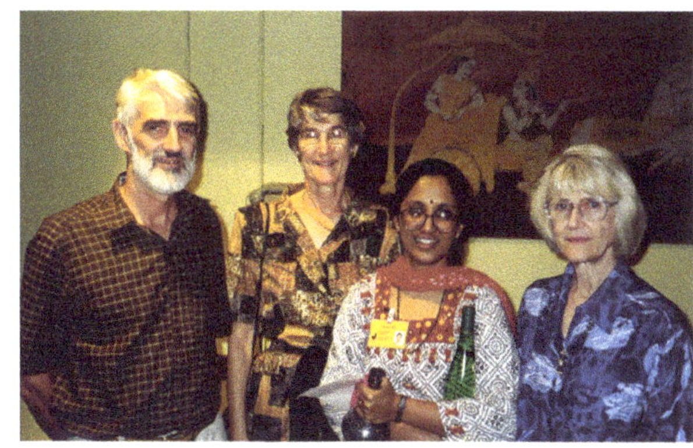

Bob and Margaret Myers with Gayatri Devi and Dana

who at the time was working in Thailand and living there with his wife Margaret, who I had known from CSIRO, to encourage him to come and take a substantial roll in the ICRISAT work. Well Bob did come with Margaret to live there and my Bob felt the project was in good hands.

Back in Toowoomba, in 1999 on the internet, I saw an announcement about an International Ikat Conference to be held in Sarawak, Borneo. It sounded too good to be true with my interests. I could see by the flier that my friends Bina Rao and her husband Keshav from Hyderabad would be involved. It was coming up very soon. Bob encouraged me to go, so how could I hesitate? It was organised by Edric Ong, a local architect and lover of textiles and culture who was able, with

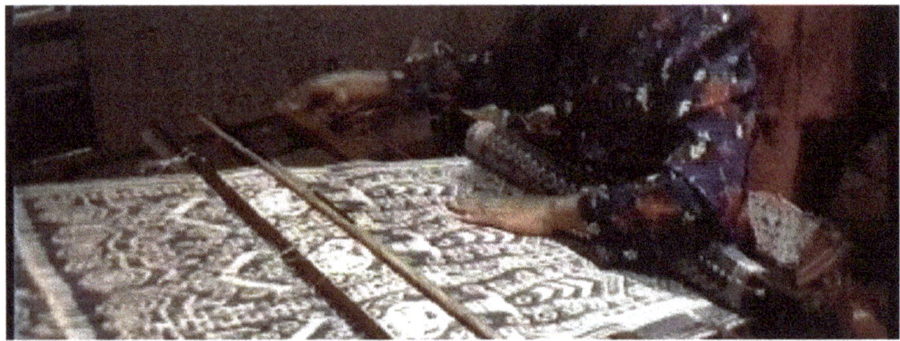

Weaving Pua Cloth on a backstrap loom

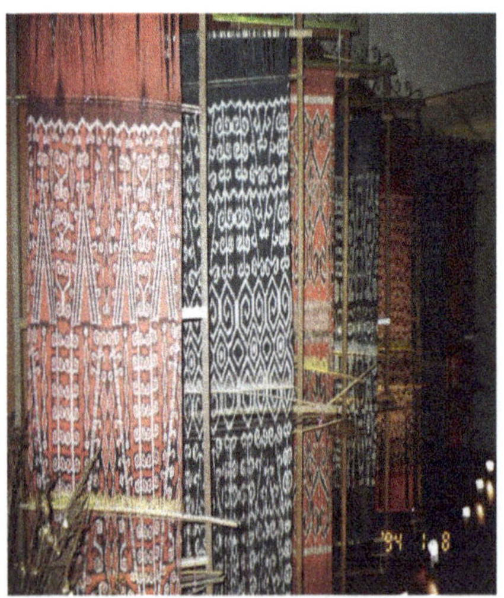

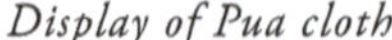

Display of Pua cloth

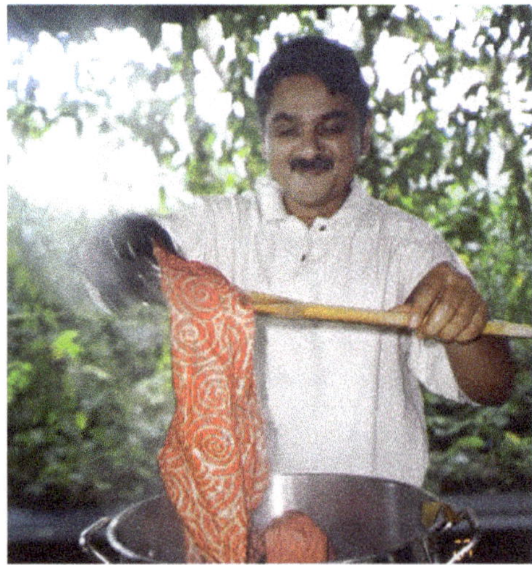

Keshav Rao vegetable dyeing conference

the help of his cousins and friends, get together a week of wonderful events. There were demonstrations, exhibitions, dinners, and entertainments around town in various locations. An added bonus of the trip was the opportunity to go on a side trip, to stay in a "long house" in the jungle overnight and see the Iban tribal culture and learn something of their spirit world and rituals, especially involved in their weaving. The Iban tribe weave Pua cloth, which has a long history of being associated with headhunting.

Most delegates stayed at the Hilton Hotel, so we were very comfortable. One evening a special dinner was at a different location and we were taken there by bus. I got on and found a seat next to Govardhan who was attending as a delegate and also there demonstrating his family's traditional weaving. I sat and chatted with him about my desire to document the entire process of the Telia Rumal. But I knew it would take weeks if not months to complete all the processes. Govardhan said that he could arrange for me to achieve what I wanted. He was one of five brothers and could have different processes already completed so that the timing could be cut down to just over a week living in their village. I was pretty excited. I went home and thought I needed to act on this offer quickly. So again Bob was supportive and encourage me to follow through. So I contacted Govardhan and told him that I would like to come later in the year. He offered his daughter Pushpa Laita as a translator and I proceeded to plan.

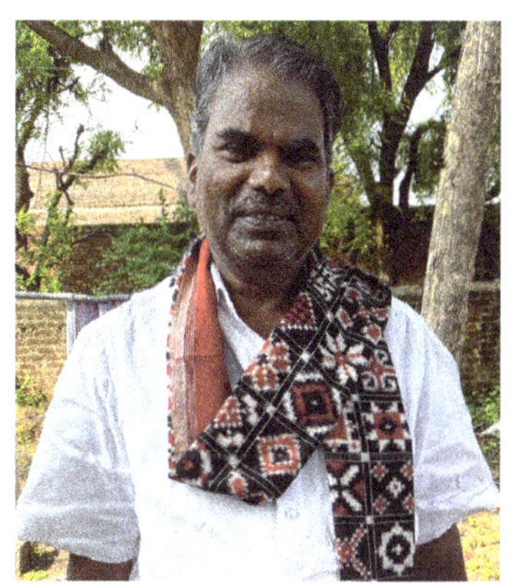

Gorardhan

I invited Pam Foale, another CSIRO wife to come along and Jill, another person at the QLD Spinners and Weavers was interested also. So the three of us flew off on Air Brunei stopping overnight. We were rather alarmed when taking off from each airport that a prayer was being sung. But we got to the point of view that it was reassuring, rather than a warning of danger. We did have time to visit some outstanding mosques with mosaic walls in beautiful designs the next day. It was not hard to believe that Brunei is one of the richest countries in the world, after seeing the beautiful mosques.

Our first adventure was to be a textile tour arranged with a company in Orissa. However the night before flying out of Brisbane, on the evening news was word of a super cyclone that had hit Orissa, closing all airports. Flying into Calcutta we had to have new plans. The company we were to meet in Orissa arranged for an associate to meet us in Calcutta and arranged a delay in our arrival in Bhubaneswar, Orissa for another week until transportation opened up. There were choices, but looking at a map, it seemed logical to take a train up to Darjeeling and go further up to Sikkim, viewing the Himalayas. This all seemed interesting and possible. We actually got to the border of Butan and thought some day it would be nice to visit.

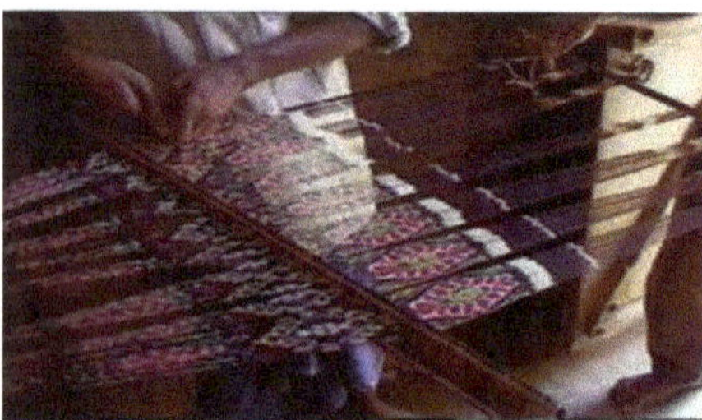

Orissa ikat on the loom

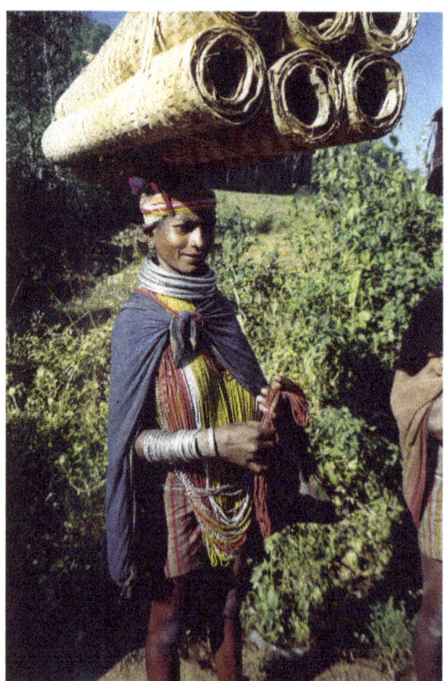

Bonda woman going to market

Eventually we arrived in Orissa and saw the worst affected areas of the cyclone, which sadly damaged property but also left people searching desperately for food. Despite the difficult circumstances, we still had a great visit as the country is so full of textile production and skills. There are institutes for silkworm culture. We visited a woman who spun silk off the cocoon twisting it on her thigh in a slow process. We bought some of the silk they then wove. We also saw commercial spinning units using mechanised process. Orissa has an ikat style different to that done in Andhra Pradesh, with more curved flowing lines. Generally each shape is outlined with white. We saw sacred scriptures being woven in ikat. Much precision and skill was needed and challenged me to think about incorporating it into my future weaving projects.

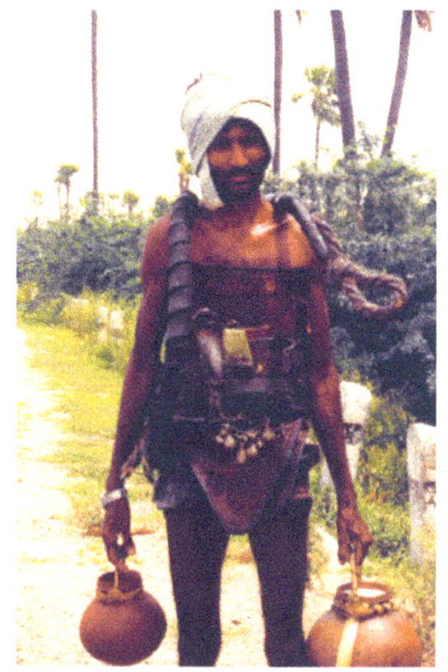

Toddy tapper

To me the most interesting group of people in Orissa were the Bonda tribals who looked to me more like the Africans I had seen in our travels. The women were bare-breasted with beads covering their chest and small handwoven loincloths around their hips. They also had series of large metal rings around their neck. It was only possible to see them walking to the market on a weekly trip to sell some goods. They live in a protected area, where it is practically impossible to get a permit to visit. We met some of them going to market. We learned, unfortunately these Bonda are financially in a difficult spot, due to debt from dowry and death customs.

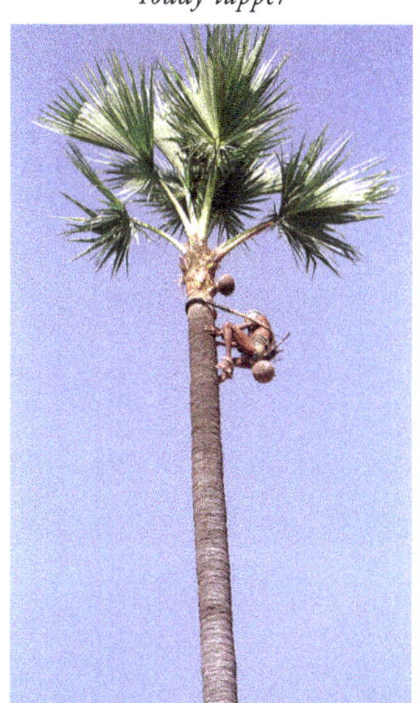

Palm tree producing toddy

We took a train headed toward Hyderabad and were met by Rama Rao at Koraput. It was great to see a familiar face and know he could help arrange any detail. We could then drive along and see interesting things along the highway. Growing along the way are many Toddy trees, a type of palm whose sap can be fermented into an alcoholic drink. Men called Toddy Tappers climb the palms and place terracotta pots under a leaf that has been cut at the base. Then a liquid drips into the pot. Next day the Toddy Tappers climb again and replace the pot with an empty one. The liquid by then is semi-fermented and makes a popular drink. The Tappers have bells to warn any snakes that could be in the tree that they are approaching.

Our plan was to contact Govardhan and learn what was our next step. He said there would be a slight delay going to Puttapaka, as Pushpa, his daughter had gone on holiday with a group of cousins and would be back soon. Their trip was more like a pilgrimage to special temples around the country. One often sees busloads of pilgrims travelling to sacred areas, but I hadn't expected that a group of young adults would be doing this for their annual holiday.

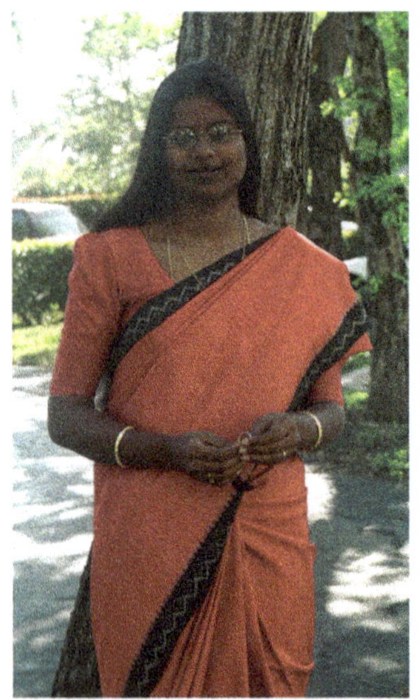
Pushpa

In the meantime we would enjoy the many interesting sites around Hyderabad. Before long, the young people were back and we went to Murale Saree Emporium where the Gajam's had their retail business and also their home in an apartment building they owned. Various members of the family had units with the downstairs all offices and showroom. The products sold were mainly the various woven items from Puttapaka, their home village. Govardhan explained that as Master Weavers, they had over 200 weavers working for them. I introduced my companions and we met Pushpa who was a recently married young woman. The car trip out to Puttapaka takes about an hour and a half. Arriving there we learned that we would stay with Narasimha, a brother of Govarhan, and his wife, Laxmi, who would provide our meals. Narasimha was not a weaver, but handled the business side, running around the countryside picking up weaving that had been completed on a motor bike. Next door to them lived brother Ramulu and his wife Rambiyamma. Ramulu was a master weaver and would demonstrate all the processes of the Telia Rumal, which was their family special skill and heritage. Ramulu was a rough diamond, who had a brash manner. He was balanced by his wife, Rambiyamma, who had an infectious laugh and made everything fun. Of course, I had to fit in with other things Ramulu might have to do. But I needed to be ready at the drop of a hat. One morning Ramulu burst in next door where we were staying at 6 am and said "Come now, quick quick." And of course I would jump up out of bed and knew how lucky I was to be having this time to document the process.

It became clear that the younger generation were not going to be weavers, as they were all educated through tertiary level. My concern and interest was to capture the information in detail so it was not lost. It was clear that the time consuming process of Telia Rumal was not economically rewarding any more.

In the office at Puttapaka we saw work coming in on a Japanese order of silk furnishing fabric, still done in ikat, but with a contemporary colour scheme and simple shapes. When a weaver would return his work, the fabric was weighed to correspond with the amount of silk yarn handed out to him. The fabric would be inspected inch by inch to see any possible flaw, which could be repaired. This type of work was beautiful and so much faster to produce. And more important was the fact that there was a market for it at a good return. The Telia Rumal had big overseas markets in the early 20th century to Arab countries, but the war had interrupted the shipping lines and the market never returned.

While I was busy during the day with the weaving process, my travelling companions found things to do. Pam visited a school where she was welcomed and was invited to talk to the students. The teacher then asked one of the boys to dance for her. Pam was so impressed she asked him to come to the house we were staying at and dance so I could make a video of it. Pam asked him if one day he would like to become a famous dancer. His reply surprised her. He said, "*How could a poor village boy like me become a famous dancer? No, I want to become a brain surgeon.*"

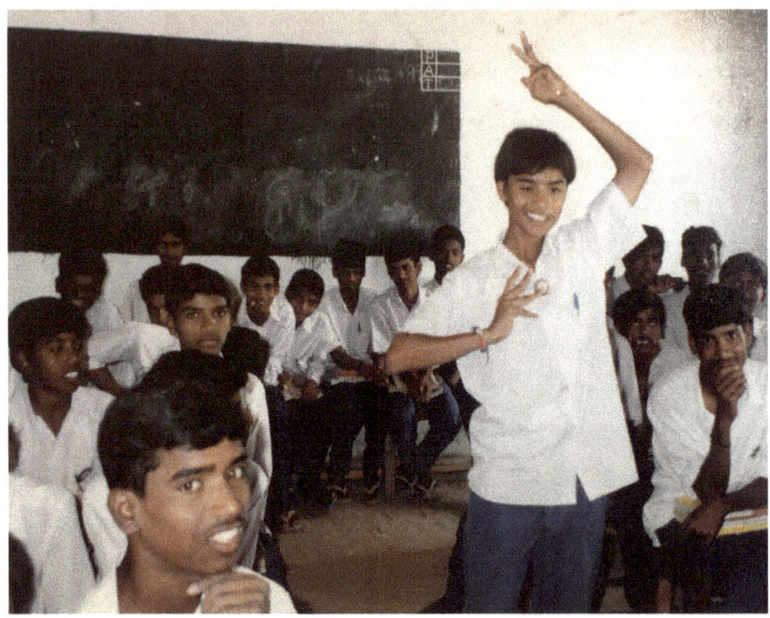

Village school boy doing a Peacock dance

Other days Pam would sit out on the front porch and embroider on a piece of silk purchased in Orissa, using discarded silk yarn that one of the weavers on our travels had given her. The villagers loved to see what she was doing. Jill found things to do at the house and even nursed Laxmi when she became ill.

Most of the Gajam family came to help with different processes. The tying of the resist areas before dyeing is very precise in order for the design to take the correct shape. It requires very tight wrapping and tying. Otherwise when the dyeing takes place, the colour will seep into the wrong place. When the warp was being wrapped, first with black bike inner tube to cover wide areas and then with fine cotton yarn for the

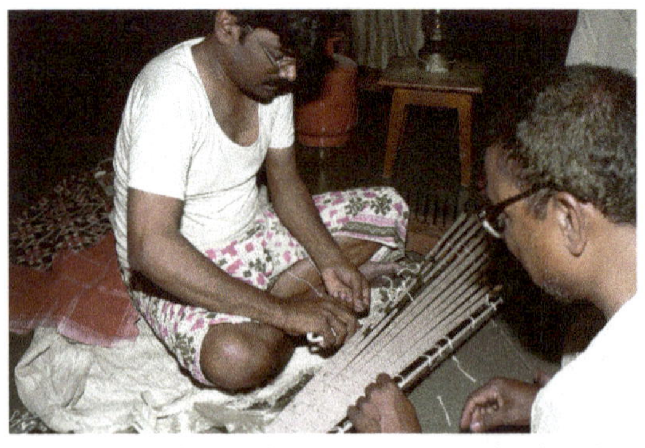

Shankir and Ramulu resist wrapping the threads

small areas, I wanted to help with the wrapping, but found I didn't have enough strength in my fingers.

Another brother, Shankir who is a naturopathic doctor came to help. Pushpa was amazed and said she had never seen him do anything like that with his hands. A sister, Mrs Ramulamma, also helped as did Narasamma, the family matriarch. Govardhan's mother, Narisimma, had related the story of being married to her husband at the age of five. She still lived with her parents until she matured. But she would come and spend the day with the Gajam family to get used to that family way of life. Her father-in-law would give her a task of preparing the sheep

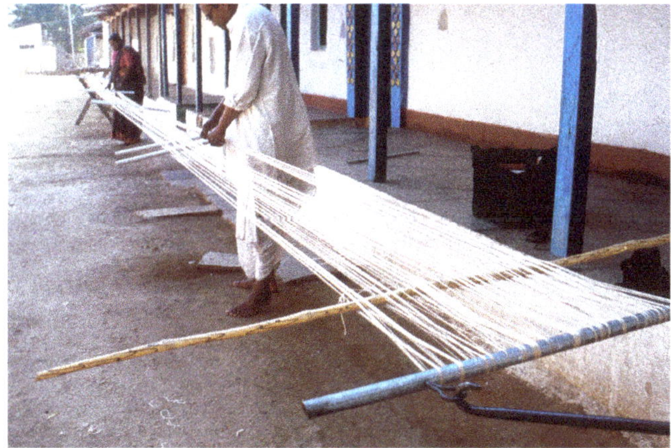

Auntie and Ramulu work on the warp

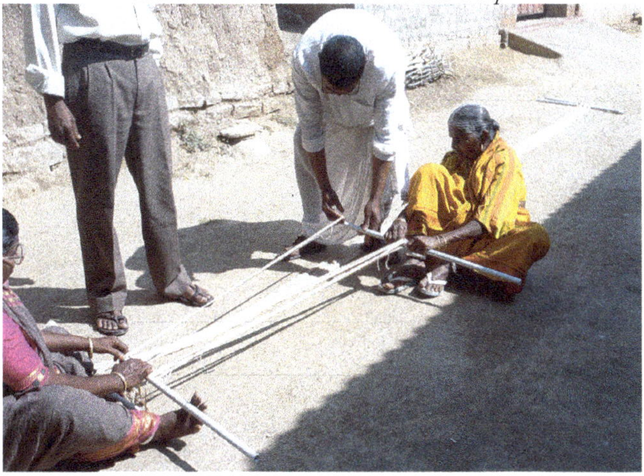

Auntie and grandma helping fold warp

dung into a slurry to use in the dyeing process. She was not so keen on that task. But in weavers' families, everyone gets into helping in different ways. When the children come home from school for lunch they all give some help, learning the skills at a young age.

One of the processes of organising the warp out along the street, I found fascinating. There was a technique of folding the warp into metre lengths to enable duplication of the resisted areas. A full detailed description of the process including dyeing, can be found in my publication "An Endangered Species: Double Ikats of South India".

Toward the end of our documentation of Telia Rumal, Ramulu and his wife had a puja celebration starting at their home. The village musicians had been invited to come and play. There was singing of mantras and chanting with echoing response. We all drank chai and enjoyed the music. At about 9 o'clock everyone got up and followed the musicians out the door. In the middle of the street there was some dancing around the musicians, and then we all proceeded to the Markandeye Temple. Ramulu and Rambyiamma carried a special food offering to the gods. We all went around the temple in clockwise direction, ringing bells hung at various locations. And then the priest gave a special blessing to the couple. In the temple I was shown the family tree of the Padmasali cast, showing direct

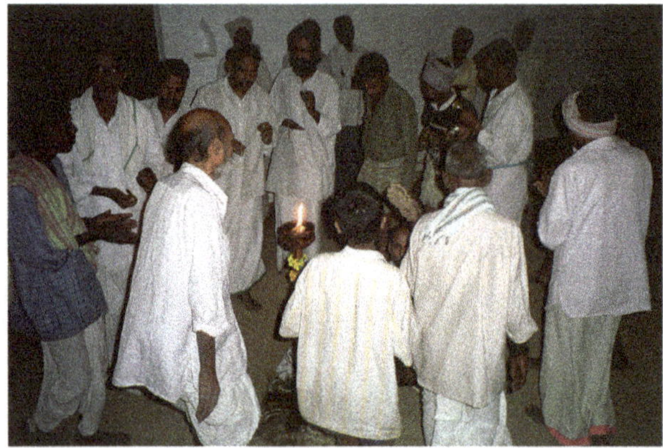

Procession of musicians

descent from the god Markandeye, whose sons were all weavers. And the Gajam family was in the direct lineage.

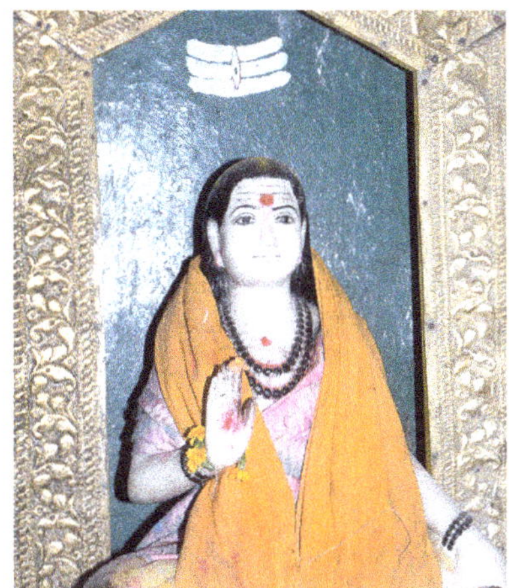

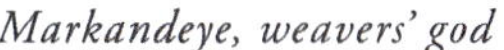

Markandeye, weavers' god

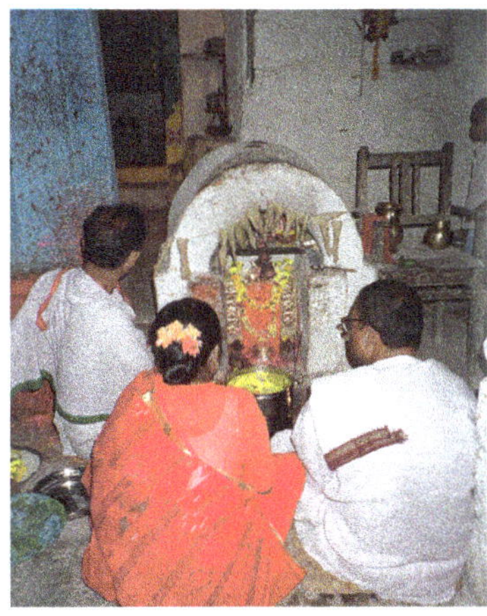

Blessings

A DOZEN WEAVERS

Back in Australia, I continued my membership in the Queensland Spinners and Weavers group, but could only attend a monthly meeting once in awhile. I was invited to join a weaving group in Brisbane called "A Dozen Weavers". They had meetings once a month at different members' homes to plan for a yearly big exhibition to be held at the Brisbane City Hall, Stephens Gallery, and various other venues. There were other events we participated in. In 1998 our 10th anniversary was coming up and we decided the theme would be "Cyber Fibre". As this was going to be a special event, we felt it would be good to have a professional gallery space that would be overseen and hung by staff. The Queensland Craft Council was able to arrange with the University of Southern Queensland for us to have the prominent space of the Arts Foyer Gallery and Craft Council staff came to hang. We put together a very nice catalogue that was printed professionally. It had a page for each weaver. One of the pieces I produced was called Cyber Scripture and combined the traditional dyeing technique of ikat with the imagery derived from the text of my website address using a format based on ancient temple scrolls of scripture.

Cyber Script Ikat

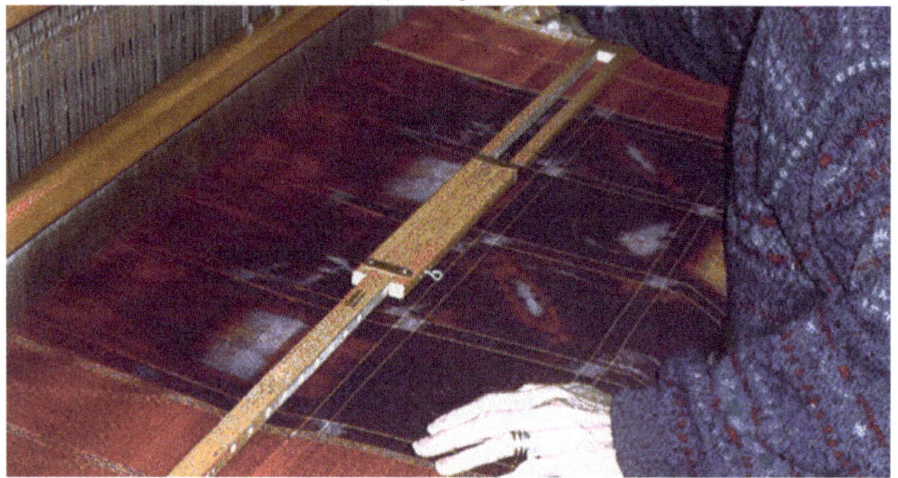

Weaving "Cyber Fibre"

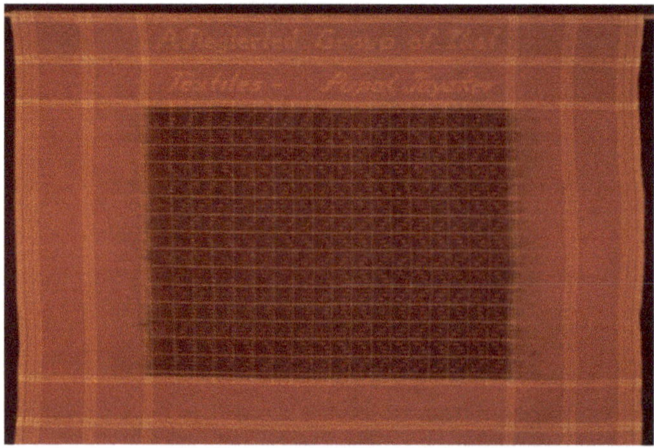

Detail of "A Neglected Group"

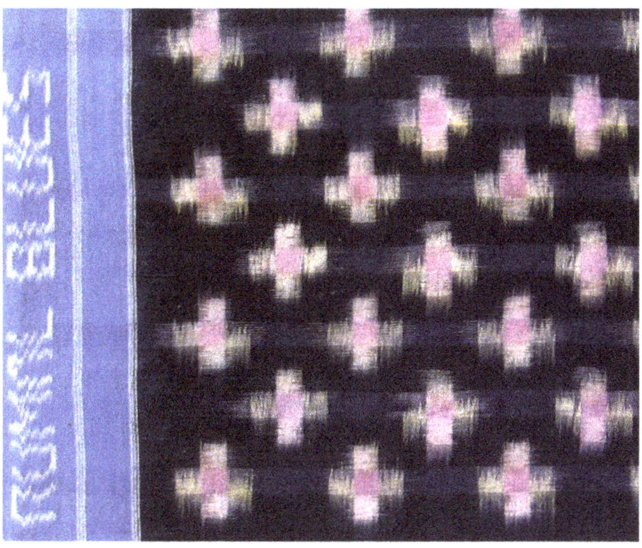

Detail of "Rumal Blues"

As I had been researching the Indian ikat technique called Telia Rumal, I decided to try and attempt a similar piece, but using imagery relating to computers. The original technique also introduced imagery that was modern at the time, such as clocks and airplanes. A piece called Rumal Blues was using non-traditional colours for the weaving, but the name referred to the problem that the weavers had with marketing the rumal, as the original buyers in Africa and Middle East had been lost long before during the war when shipping lanes were interrupted. The exhibition would be on display for nearly a month.

UNIVERSITY DAYS

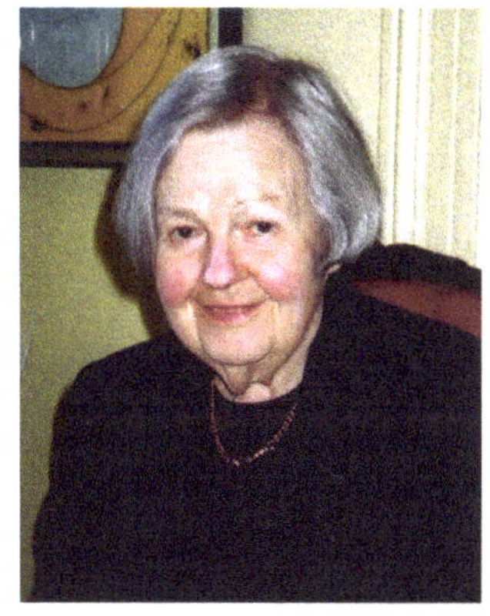

Joyce

Returning to Toowoomba, I had enrolled at the University of Southern Queensland (USQ) to work on my Masters Degree which was based on my research into this special double ikat. I started to attend conferences which were pertinent to my study, starting with "Close Ties" at USQ. There I met another delegate from Sydney, Joyce Burnard, who had written a book entitled "Chintz and

Cotton: India's Textile Gift to the World". She told me about The Asian Art Society of Australia (TAASA) and encouraged me to join. In the same year I attended the Asia Pacific Trienniel (APT) Conference at the Art Gallery of Queensland. There was an e-Textiles Conference at the University of New South Wales, and later, Sari to Sarong Conference, National Art Gallery, Canberra, and at the same time I could use their library for research. So it was a busy time for me.

As part of my work for the Master's Degree, I had built up a collection of the Telia Rumal for an exhibition that I was able to hold in the Toowoomba Regional Art Gallery. I made a 30-minute video of the process that was shown throughout the time the exhibition was held. There was also an interactive CD that anyone could sit at a computer and work through. It was an easy way to learn about the process, but it also included a design activity I created so that people could try designing a rumal themselves by combining various imagery. These multimedia skills helped document the textile in various ways. I also produced a book to be used as a catalogue accompanying the travelling exhibition. I increased my website building skills and started to build websites for others.

After I finished my Master's Degree, one of the lecturers then invited me to help assist with the Multimedia course, as he would be overseas part of the year. The course was entirely online which I found to be such a practical approach. Each student, and many were overseas, could login according to their time zone. We had discussion groups that were comprised of messages, each entered in response to the topic. It was interesting that you would feel like you were getting to know these students perhaps half way around the world from you. My mother-in-law, Betty, came to visit for an extended time while I was marking assignments. She said, *"Dana, you probably have had the professor to dinner, haven't you, as you do a lot of entertaining."* I had to explain that I had never actually met him in person. She found it all hard to believe.

Joyce Burnard contacted me about the Textile Group of TAASA that met in Sydney and invited me as speaker for one of their monthly meetings at the

Powerhouse Museum. Of course the topic was my research into the Telia Rumal of South India. It was a good opportunity for me, as I could then go on to Canberra where Jenny and family were living at the time. Joyce would at a later date come to Toowoomba to stay with me and be there for the opening of the "Two Hearts in Harmony" exhibition I curated.

THAI TEXTILE OPPORTUNITY

In 2002, one of the friends I made through the Weavers Forum or on the Internet somehow was Kathleen Johnston. She had seen my website and the opportunity I offered others to become a guest weaver on the website. Kathleen had travelled a great deal in Laos and Thailand and had an interesting story with pictures. I then included Kathleen's story on my website and we continued to communicate. She had been contacted by many people who saw her article. Eventually she decided to organise a symposium in Bangkok where she lived and invited me to come. As it turned out, Kathleen's husband Darrell was the ambassador to Thailand and I was invited to stay in the guest home on the American compound along with Carol Cassidy from Laos and Sigrid Piroch from USA. The program was carried out in several locations - The Siam Society, the Bangkok National Museum, and also in Chiang Mai. Some of the papers presented dealt with conservation of textiles, care of textile collections, development of Lao textile products, natural dye demonstrations, textile analysis - discovery and documentation. We visited Patricia Cheeseman at her Studio Nawenna in Changi Mai and learned about the traditional woven clothing in Thailand using ikat and natural dyes.

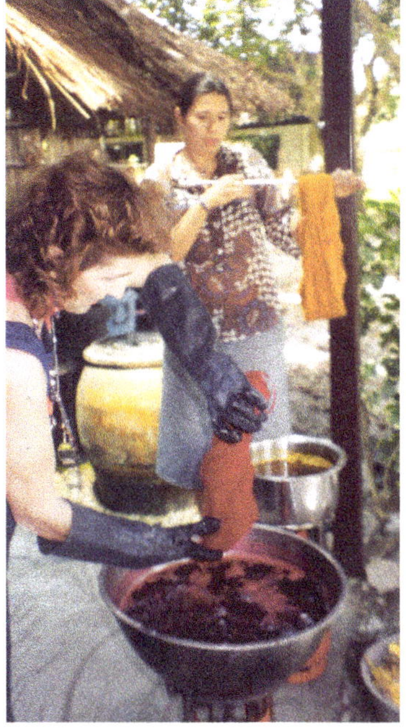

Patricia showing all natural dyes

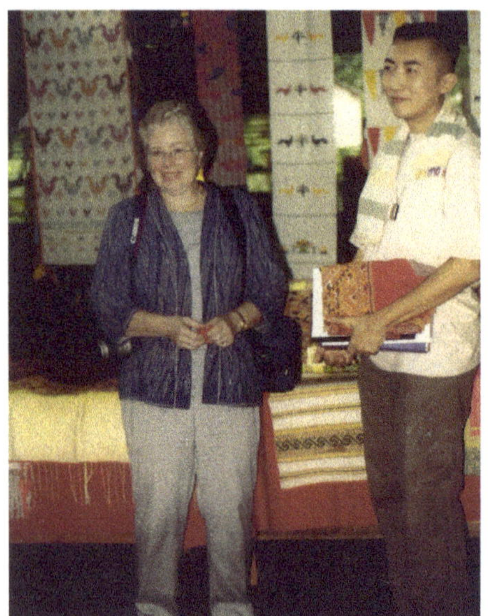
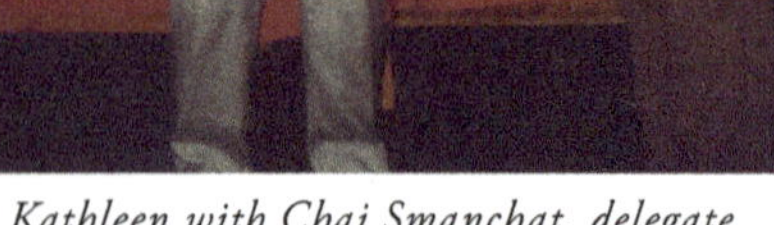

Kathleen with Chai Smanchat, delegate

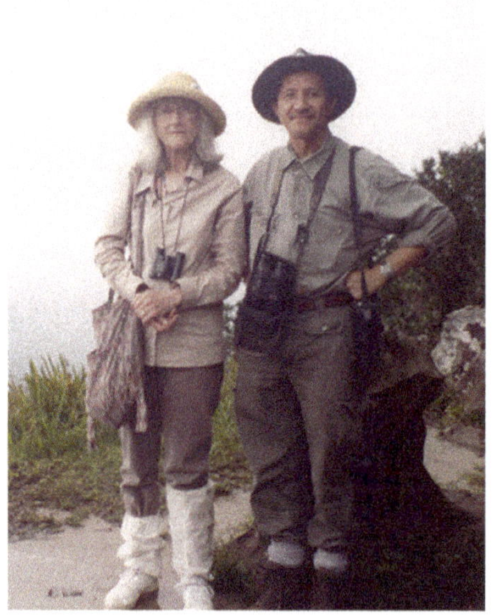

Birdwatching in Thailand

This group I travelled with were then going to Laos to present the same program there. But I had made arrangements with one of Thailand's expert bird watchers Kamol Komolphalin to go on a trip with him. We saw many different hornbills, which interested me greatly after seeing their relationship in Borneo with the headhunters. You will note that in the picture of me with Kamol, it is easy to see that I am wearing "leach-proof gaters".

After having several days birdwatching, I had arranged to spend time in a village that wove ikat, known as Mudmee in Thailand. The opportunity was arranged for me by the university to go to Ban Kwao and stay at the home of Khun Darunee, a teacher there. She provided her young

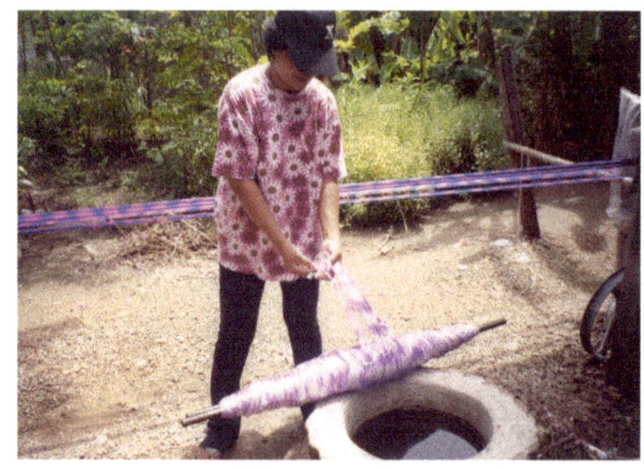

Making a long resist dyed warp

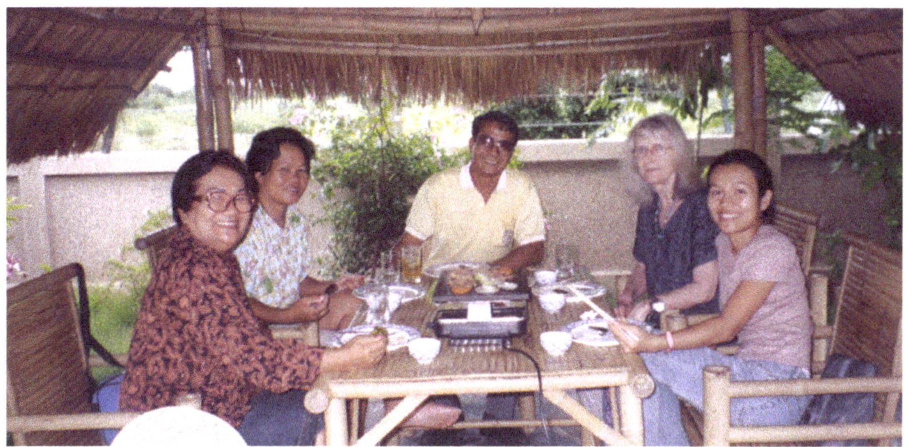

My hostess in Ban Kwao and my translator Prissadang with her parents

niece, Prissadang, to translate for me and take me to see dyeing with Lac, an insect producing red dye and some local ikat. At night a guy on a motorcycle came bringing all the ingredients for a hotpot, which we ate outside with her students who had a textile project going on. Prissadang and I then travelled further east to the Khon Kaen area looking for some of the most famous Mudmee artists. It was a great benefit to me, as little English is spoken the further one travels from Bangkok.

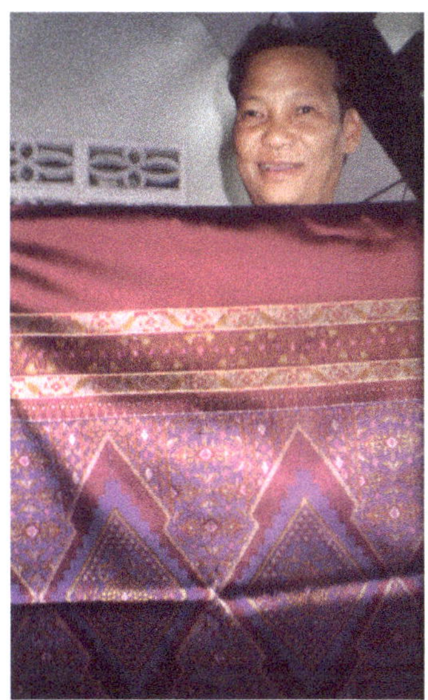

Expert weaver Khun Songkram

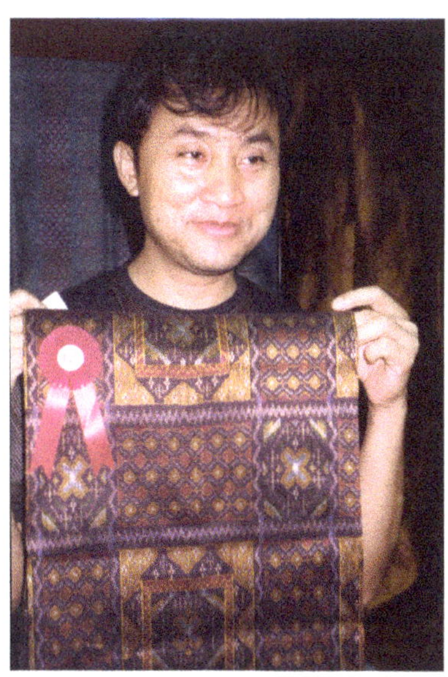

Award winner Khun Chin

BOOKS CAN INFLUENCE

My friend Barbara Douglas had come to visit and gave me a book she loved entitled, "Grandmother's Footsteps: A Journey in Search of Penelope Betjeman". The book by her granddaughter, Imogen Lycett Green, recalls a wonderful trip with her grandmother when she was younger and then retraces those travels as her grandmother had died leading a group trekking in the Kullu Valley. Well I loved the book too, and decided after reading it, that I would take each of my grandchildren to India when they turned 21 years old.

The first to accompany me to India was Jordan in 2003. I realised that my grandchildren will not have interest in one of my usual textile trips, so I planned an itinerary to be varied and interesting for them. To begin with, being on the highway is most often an experience to get used to. To us, having gained our drivers license meeting rigid standards and road rules, what happens on the roads in India is astounding. But it requires drivers with excellent reflexes and skill to cope with the possibilities of animals suddenly appearing in front of you or huge trucks coming at you. There is a rhythm of ebb and flow that one gets used to and maybe one can eventually relax. This was Jordan's biggest hurdle.

We started in Chennai with a car and Mani, the driver, travelling around South India. Mani told me that his boss was an Australian lady, who gave much better

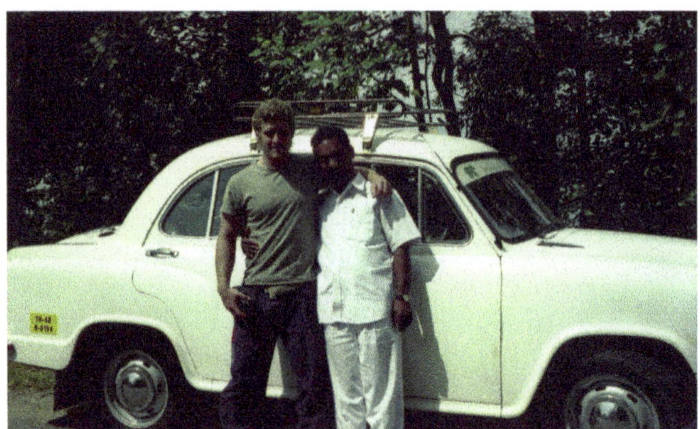

Jordan with Mani and the Commodore

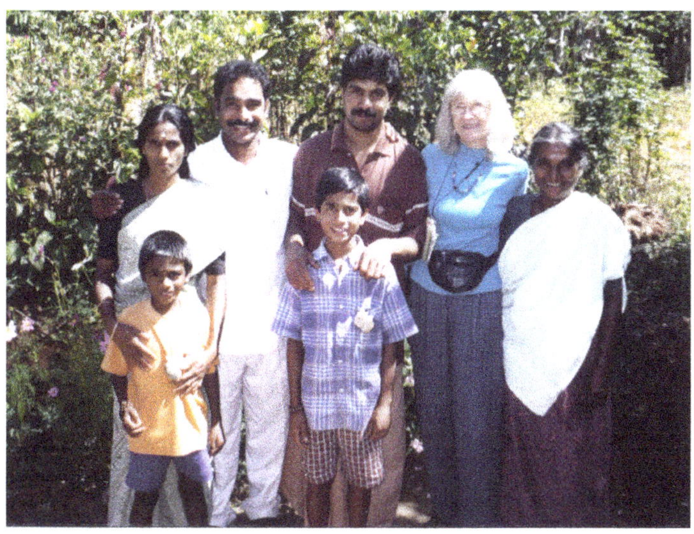

Mani and his family

conditions to her drivers than other companies did. He continued to sing her praises and I took note. After a few days we arrived at the town where Mani lived and he arranged to take us to his home for lunch and to meet his mother and wife. He showed us his garden and nursery of medical plants, telling us that eventually he wanted to retire from driving and concentrate on his plants. As we were leaving, his two young sons returned from school so we met them too. He earlier had told us the story about how his father had died and his mother had taken him to work, at the age of five to a trucking company. He helped wash the vehicles and they would feed him. These were desperate measures of a mother who needed to keep her child fed. I never found out how he got schooling and learned to read. Or did he? But he learned to drive at the trucking company. He grew up and wanted to get married. So he went to the Catholic orphanage in Kerala, the state where he lived. He told the sister that he wanted to have a wife. She offered to provide a choice of two young women. Mani told her, *"Just pick who you think would be right for me. If I choose between two, how would the one feel that I didn't choose?"* This story has stayed with me and I still get teary over it. In later years, I tried to follow up on Mani with Faith. She told me he had resigned from her company to go home and develop his medicinal plant business, that he had shown Jordan and me at his home. So his plan came to pass.

Our first destination after arriving in Chennai and meeting up with Mani, had been Mahabalipuran, commonly known as Mamallapuram, one of my favourite places in India. It is very close to Chennai, but has impressive sculpture, from rock temples to monolithic size granite statues and chariots called the five Rathas. It is a UNESCO World Heritage site along the ocean front, and one of the most famous tourist destinations. But it still has a small town atmostphere and is easy to walk around to see the attractions. In addition, it is also a fishing village. The boats go out early in the morning and the fishermen bring in their catch and sit along the beach working on their nets. It adds to the colourful atmosphere. Seafood restaurants, naturally are also excellent and popular.

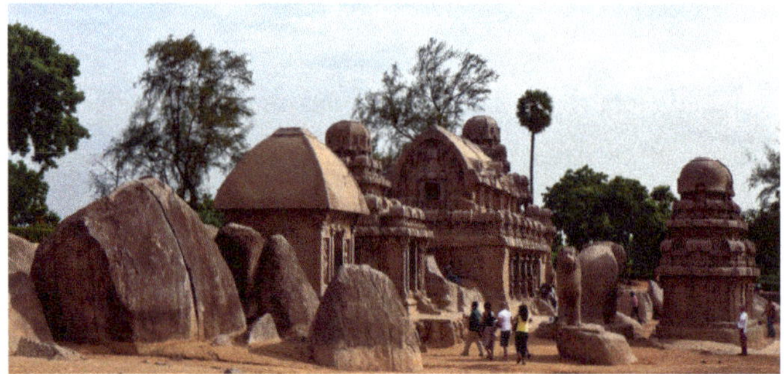

The Five Rathas archeological site in Mahabalipuram, India

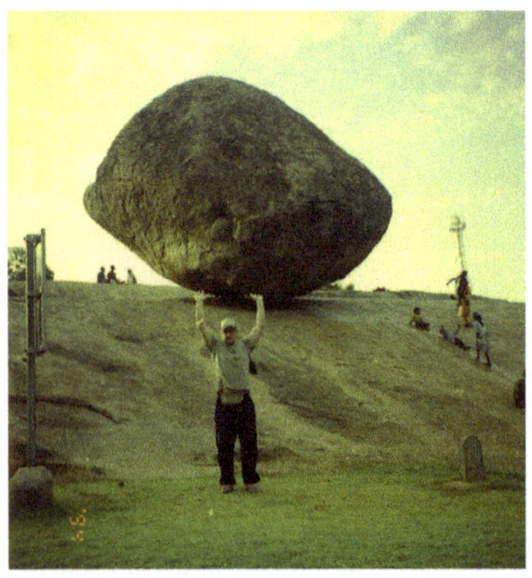

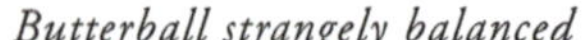

Butterball strangely balanced

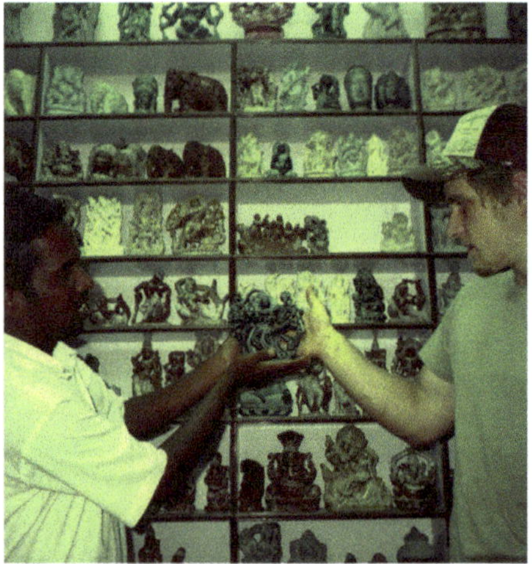

Jordan shopping

We travelled to Kerala to have the experience of staying overnight on a houseboat travelling on the canals and river at Alleppey. These picturesque boats are made of wooden frames with bamboo poles and cane woven matting. We arrived at the pier and found we were assigned to a two-story high boat with lounge and two bedrooms and an extra mezzanine on the higher level. There was another couple getting assigned a boat, but the woman, who turned out to be a new bride came and wanted to see our boat. She was outraged that they had been given a smaller boat and it was their honeymoon. Nevertheless, we did not offer to trade. I felt sorry for the new husband.

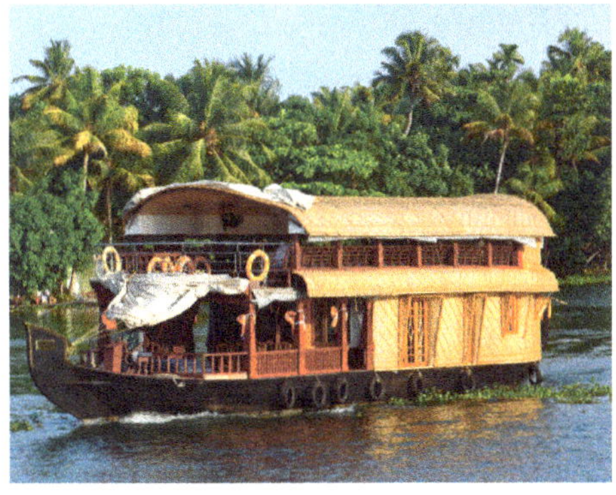

Houseboat on Kerala backwaters

The cook came and told us that at 10 o'clock the staff was going to a local temple that was having a fire-walking ceremony only held once a year. We debated about how late this would be lasting and whether it was better to get some sleep. Well we decided to go and forget about sleep. We walked carefully on paths through tropical vegetation in the dark, following the cook. We got to a small humble temple with chairs set up that were mostly filled, but we were lucky to get a seat. I had taken my movie camera and was a bit worried that I might offend the congregation by filming this ceremony. In the front of the church there was a large pile of wood being lit. There were men wearing white loincloths or lungis, circling the glowing fire and chanting. Now and again the priest standing at the side would offer sips of liquid from a bowl. Some men had young sons with them. The chanting continued as the fire got hotter and hotter. I was worried that some of the children seemed ready to pass out. I was feeling very hot myself, and I was not so close to the fire. The wood had burnt down to embers and suddenly there was wild running across the glowing embers by these men with only bare feet.

Suddenly it was evident that some of these men had gone into trance, and were shaking and falling over. Some were lying on the cement in spasm with eyeballs rolling. At the end when the fire was all but out, other men were trying to get those in trance out of the condition by pouring water on them. I had been hesitant about filming, so had not tried to push in to get a good position. However it seemed the congregation wanted me to capture the event and encouraged me. It was a phenomenal happening that we never could have imagined what it would be like. Lucky we didn't miss it. A man who had been in the ceremony walking on hot coals came and showed me his feet. The bottoms were not blistered or damaged.

The ride through the canals during the day had been relaxing and also interesting, seeing people living along the waters edge. Local canoes would pass us by and people would wave. On occasion, they grabbed hold of our stern and got pulled for a short distance. The lush green vegetation along the canals was just as lovely as we had been told it would be. Kerala is a beautiful state.

We went to spice gardens and nature reserves. There were tea plantations we saw in the Ooty area. Silkworm culture was very active in South India. Rubber was another industry. Jute or sisal was processed along the road. Much to see.

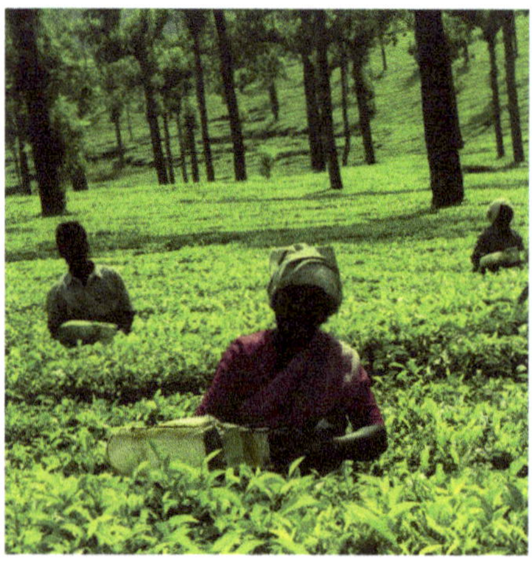

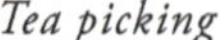

Tea picking

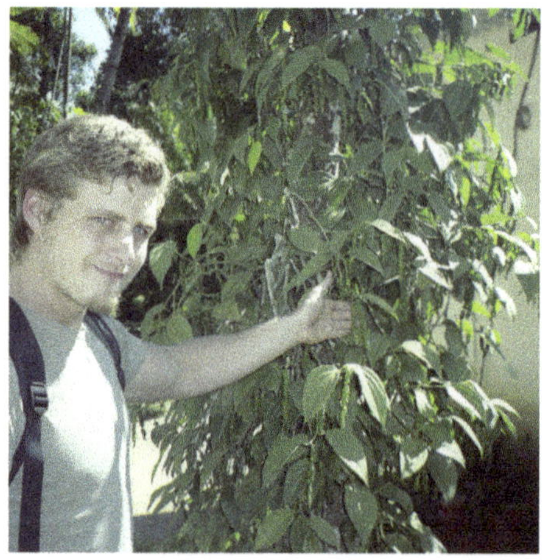

Black pepper growing

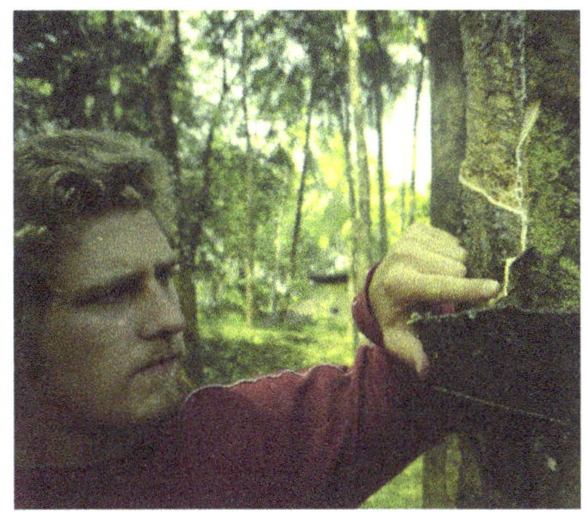

Sap from the Rubber Tree

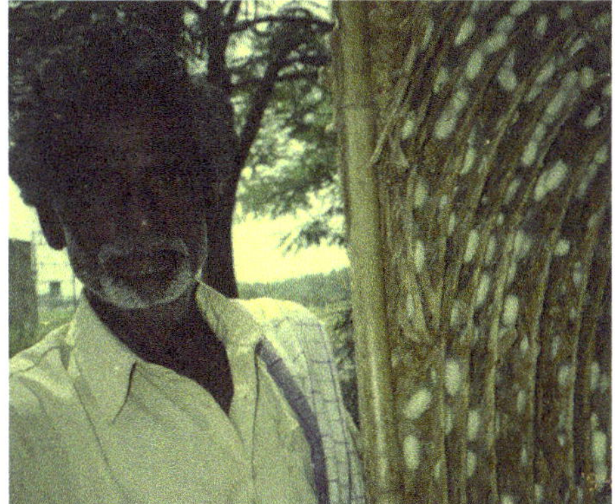

Farming silkworms

Being a bodybuilder at the time meant that Jordan needed to eat five times a day. He brought with him a huge container of protein powder that completely filled his backpack. A vegetarian diet can be the safest to follow, but all food is delicious and safe if chosen wisely. I am happy eating anywhere in India as long as the food comes hot off the stove. To Jordan the idea of vegetarian food wasn't acceptable and I couldn't control what he ate for the extra meals in between.

Staying in Bangalore in the middle of the night, I was awoken with a very sick Jordan wanting a doctor. He obviously had a bad case of food poisoning. I went down to the reception wanting to get the hotel doctor. That turned out to be impossible, with the reply that he would have to go to hospital. They offered to have the doorman, who was an old bloke sleeping in the reception area, take us to the nearest private hospital. So the three of us went off in the middle of the night in a tuktuk.

Entering this small hospital, the director came to greet us. He explained we would have to first go to the dispensary and buy supplies. He also suggested it would be best if we hired a private nurse. It seemed like a good idea. Jordan was installed in a room and put on a drip, as dehydration was the biggest problem. But it was explained that I would have to bring him food. They only had a kiosk downstairs that sold items for visitors that looked greasy and indigestible. So our hotel prepared broths that I could take via tuktuk to Jordan. He stayed several days and by that time, we had to fly to Hyderabad, our final destination to catch up with our other connections. We decided to have a day and night at Ramoji Film City and see what filming was going on. Outside our hotel there was a street scene being acted out, so we went to observe. It wasn't long before the actress decided she wanted to meet Jordan. Later that evening she phoned our room and wanted Jordan to go to the city with her. He actually declined, I can confirm. Hyderabad has many attractions and so the next day we went to Golconda Fort, visited the Bidri artisans and went out to the ICRISAT (International Crop Research for the Semi-Arid Tropics) campus, where Bob and I had spent so much time with his project.

We booked a special Christmas dinner at a luxury hotel and arrived. It wasn't long before we realised Jordan was not ready for such food. So back we went to our more humble accommodation and relaxed. Jordan was booked to go on to Europe that night at midnight, continuing his travels. Unfortunately it was longer before Jordan felt really well and Europe was freezing cold.

Jordan departed, but I had the excitement of awaiting the arrival of Jessie and Jenny the next day. We had a mother-daughters trip planned to Rajasthan, which is such a colourful part of India. It can be very difficult to find a block of time when all three of us could be available and free of responsibilities, so we grabbed it. Meanwhile back at home, Bob had gone with the men and smaller children to have a holiday at Mossy Point. I knew he would be fully occupied with fun activities, and I would not have to worry about him being lonely.

Jenny and Jessica were en route but when they got to Chennai, the flight to Hyderabad had been cancelled due to flooding and cyclone. All the passengers were put up in a hotel, but somehow, on the quiet, the girls were offered an opportunity to get on the next plane to Hyderabad that only had two seats available. Their luggage was taken out the back of the hotel secretly and the girls were told to just casually walk to the street as a vehicle was waiting for them. The hotel was full of people very anxious to get a flight and not in a happy mood at all.

In Hyderabad, one of our main activities was to spend a day with the Gajam's, my Master Weaver Govardhana's extended family. All the wives, daughters in-

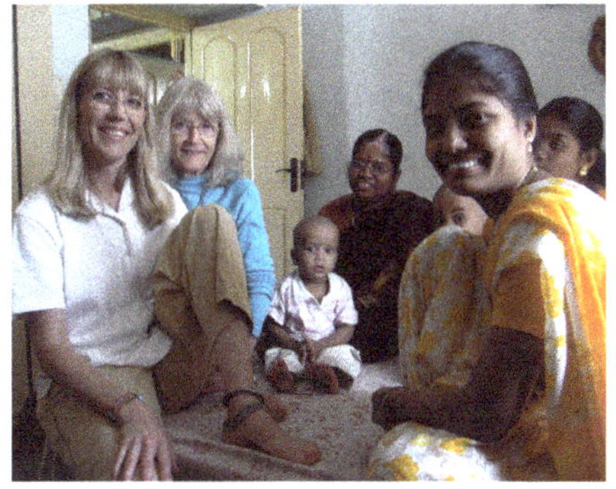

Trying on jewellery

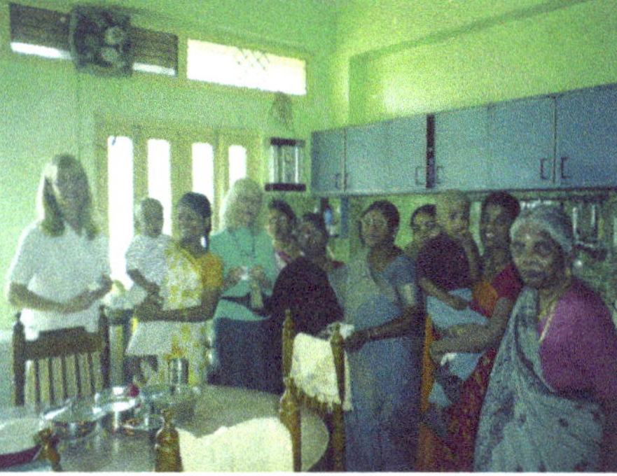

4 generations Gajam women

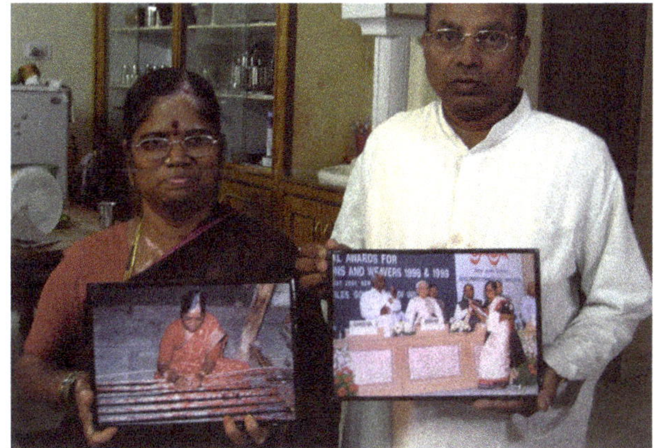

Rambiyamma receives government recognition with an award

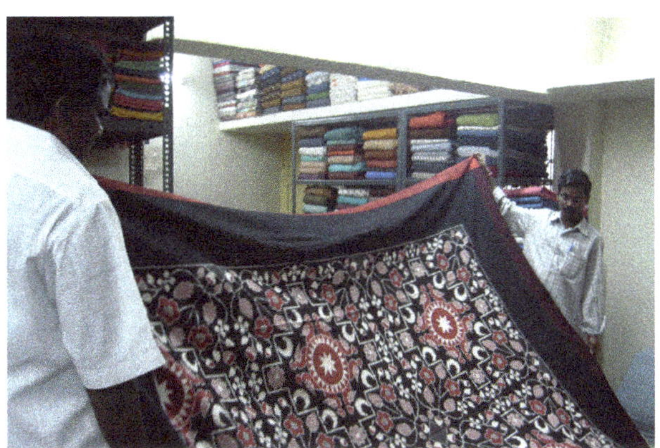

Govardhan's new product with design from my book

law and grandchildren were there and it seemed that my daughters were a big attraction. We were taken up to the apartment and to the bedroom where they brought out some of their heavy ankle jewellery for us to try on. We also had a delicious chicken curry meal and mango ice cream.

Since the last time I was in Hyderabad, Ramulu's wife Rambyiama had been awarded a certificate of Master Weaver. As in all weaving families, each member has the skills that support the main Master Weaver to enable him to achieve what he does. Now it was her chance for recognition. And we saw the new products that Govardhan had developed for the market in their Muralee Sari Emporium.

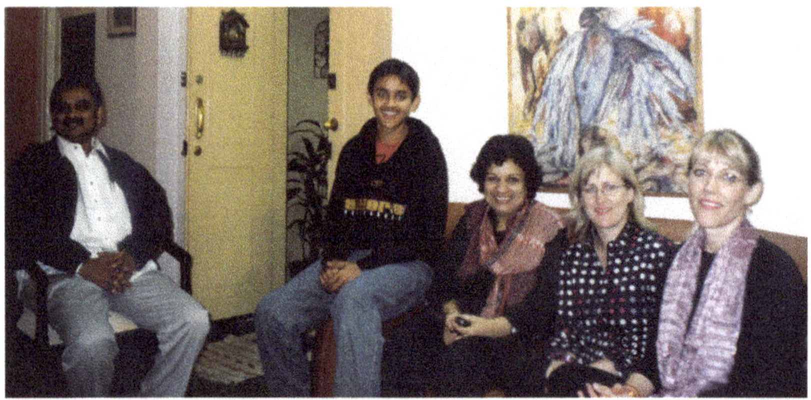

Spending the evening with Bina, Kesav and Mani

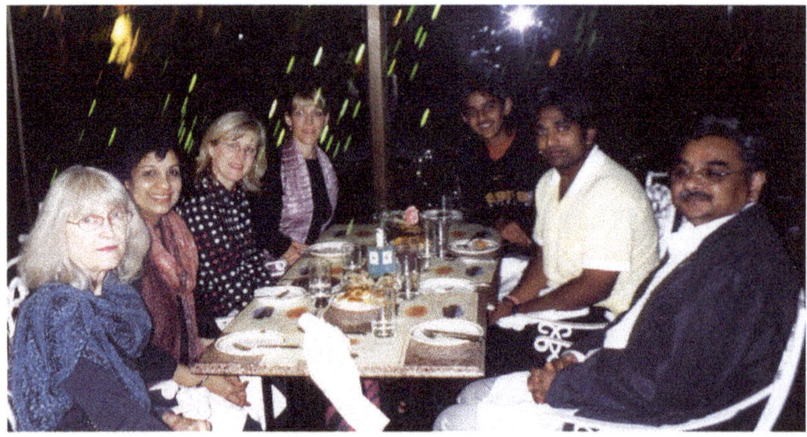

Having famous Hyderabadi Biriani at the Viceroy Hotel with Bina and family

It was lovely then to see Bina, Kesav and Mani again. They had been to Australia to teach at the Forum and Jenny had the opportunity to meet them there. It was always interesting to see the projects they were involved in. Bina had many village weavers producing products for her shop "Creative Bee".

Both Bina and Kesav had done degrees at Ahmedabad at the National Design Institute. Bina is basically a textile designer and Kesav's first talent is in painting, but has developed skills in printing and dyeing with natural dye stuffs. So he has requests to teach these skills at special textile events overseas.

We also planned a day out to the Banjara market, as the women of this tribal group have such colourful clothing and jewellery. They often can be seen on the roadside in construction gangs, still wearing their distinctive dress. There have been modern trends of changing the mirror decorations sewn to the clothing from small round mirrors to larger rectangular ones. However the basic headpiece, bodice and skirt have not changed much. But recently there are areas where the Banjara women are starting to wear saris, perhaps to fit into society. It seems a shame.

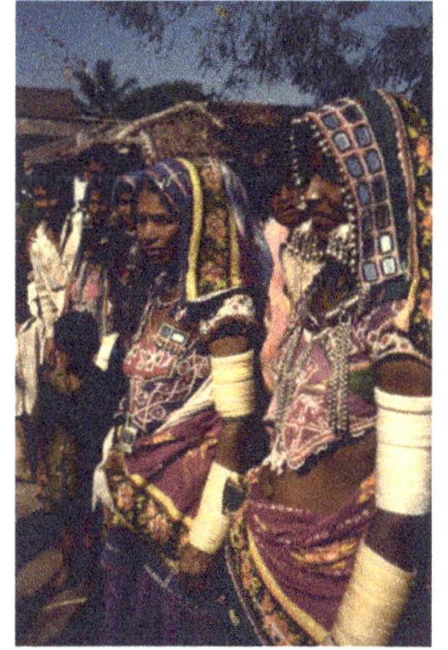

Banjara women

The next day, Rama Rao took us to the airport to start our Rajasthan adventure. We flew to Delhi as a starting point, just wanting to visit the National Craft Museum. I told the tour operator that it is my main interest and he told me it doesn't exist. We explained the location and he said there is only a motor show at that address. Well we were booked on

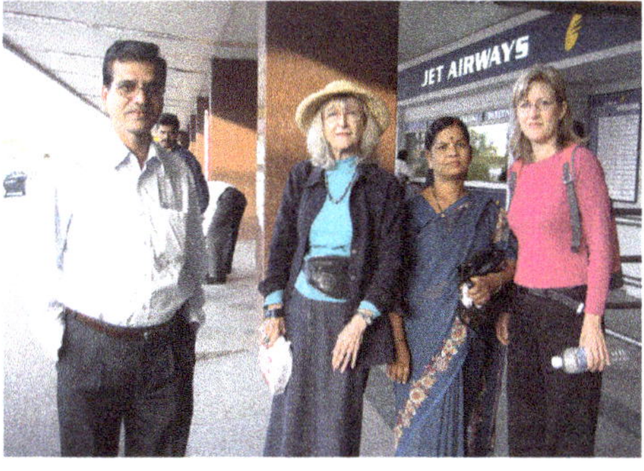

Rama Rao and Janaka take us to the airport

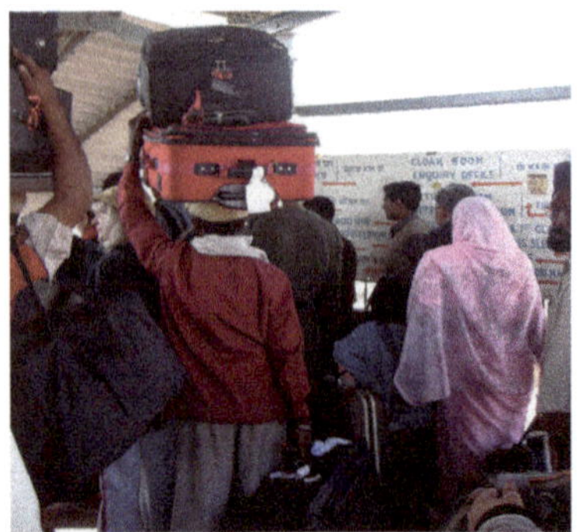

Porters get us to the train

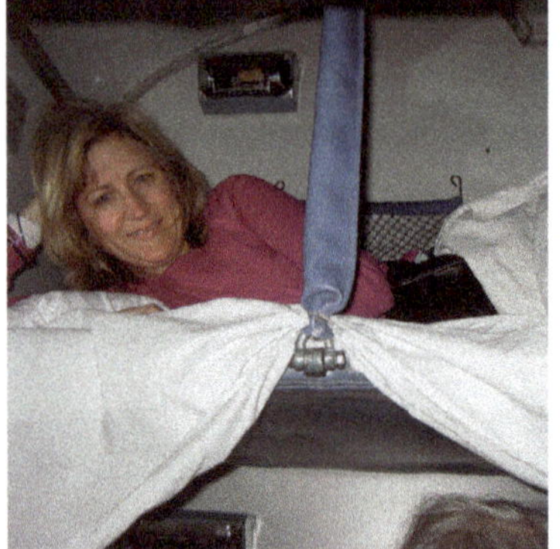

Comfortable bunks

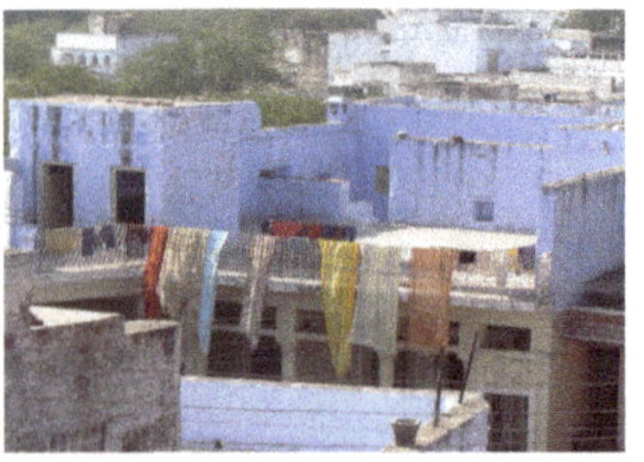

Blue city

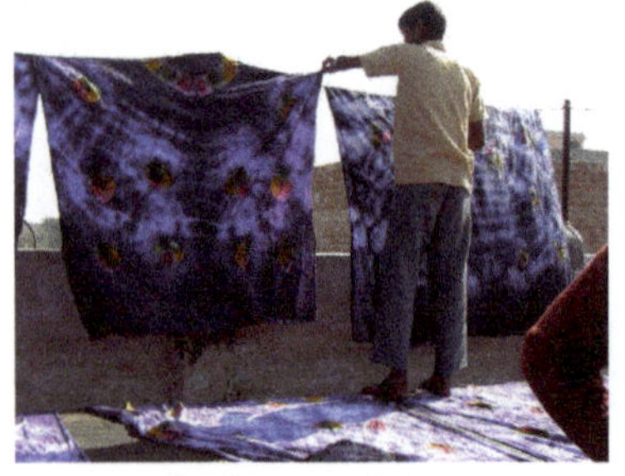

Roof-top workshops

the overnight train headed across Rajasthan to Jodhpur, and were planning to have more time in Delhi at the end of our trip, so hoped to have the Craft Museum sorted by then.

Somehow we loved the rhythm of the train movement and arrived the next day in Jodhpur at noon well rested. It was New Years Eve and our hotel had planned special entertainment. There was dancing and singing, but at some point the compere asked for people in the audience to participate. A woman came to our table and asked me to come dance with her. It was only when I returned to our table that the girls told me I was dancing with a female impersonator.

Jodpur is called the Blue City as many buildings are painted a light shade of blue. Driving along I could see some building that had textiles hanging from the building and we convinced the driver to stop and let us investigate. We visited Mehrangarh Fort and found someone to decorate our hands with Mehindi. Sardar Market was great for jewellery shopping.

It was time to be off to Jaisalmer to start our anticipated camel camping trip in the desert. In Hyderabad, the girls found out that I had hurt my back and it was doubtful that I could spend several days riding a camel. So we agreed that it could be possible if I was given a cart that could be pulled by the camel and the organiser arranged for that. We were excited to have this adventure and learned that we had been given one of the best camel men in Rajasthan for the trip.

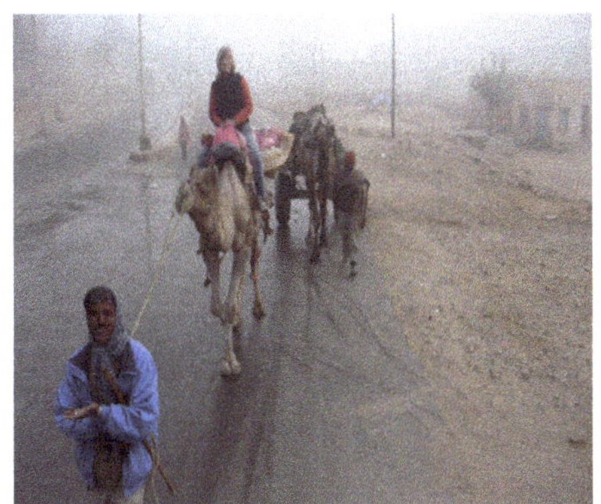

Early morning start

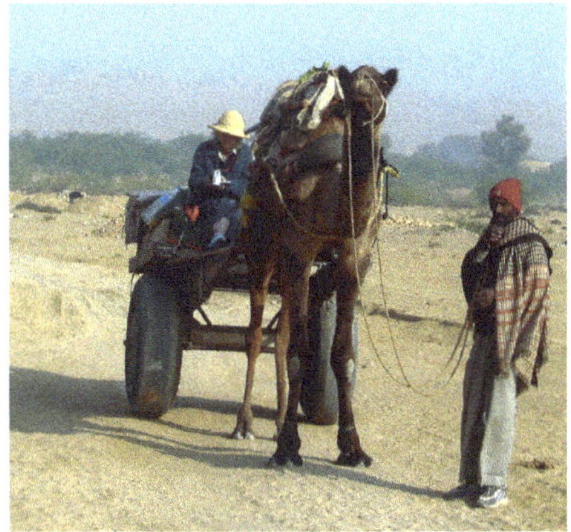

My camel cart

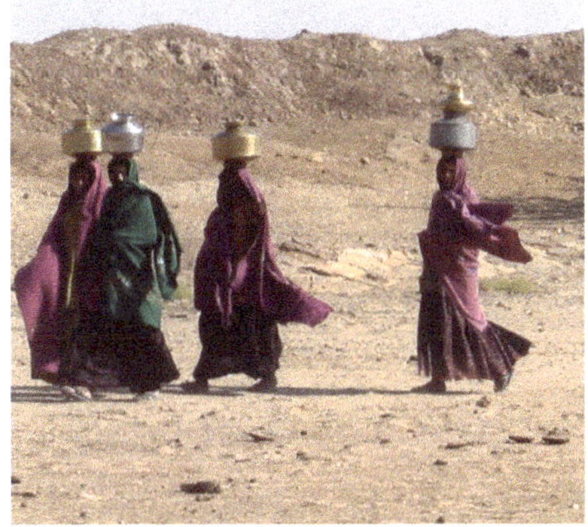

Graceful women carrying water

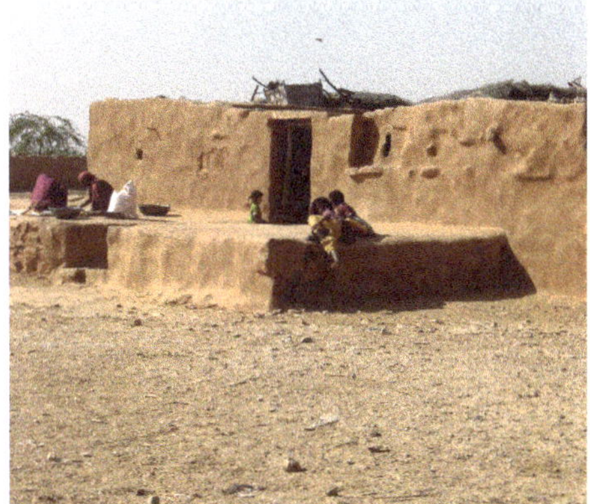

Desert homes

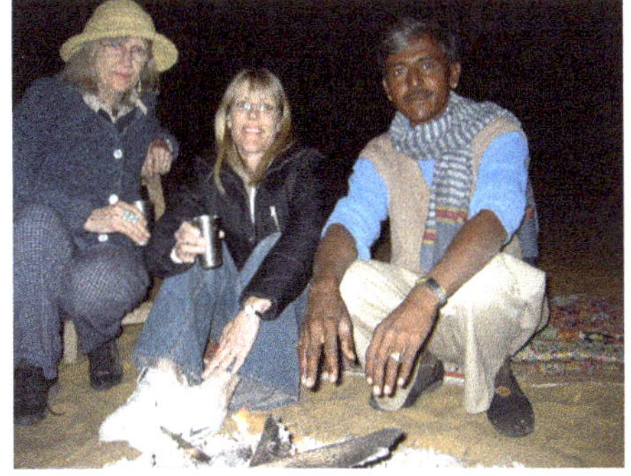

Camping with the camel men

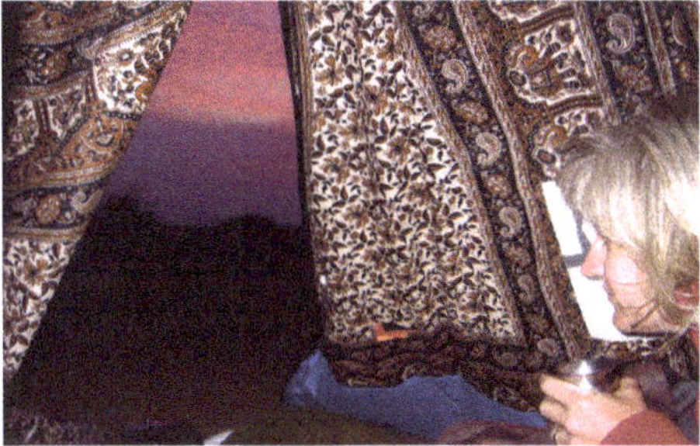

Daybreak

A special event was a visit to Bikanner for the Camel Festival. Bikanner was originally on the silk and spice route, so much commerce passed through the city. Many rich businessmen had Havelis there, but when the trading routes changed, these mansions of red sandstone had been abandoned. The Camel Festival had entertainment with Gypsy dancers and singers. There were competitions for decorated camels created by carving the fur on their backs in lovely designs. It was a colourful and exciting day.

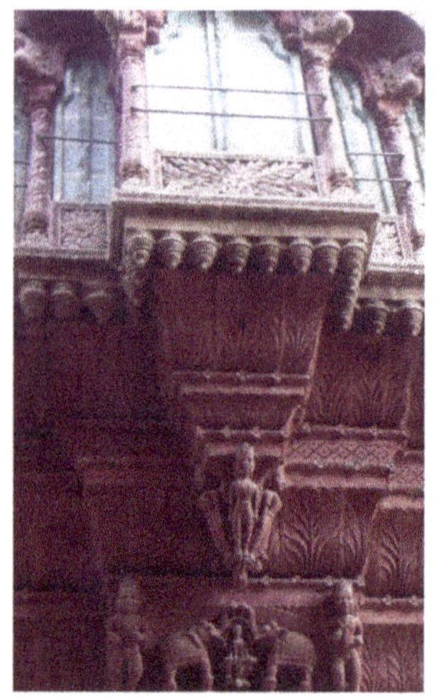

Haveli detail

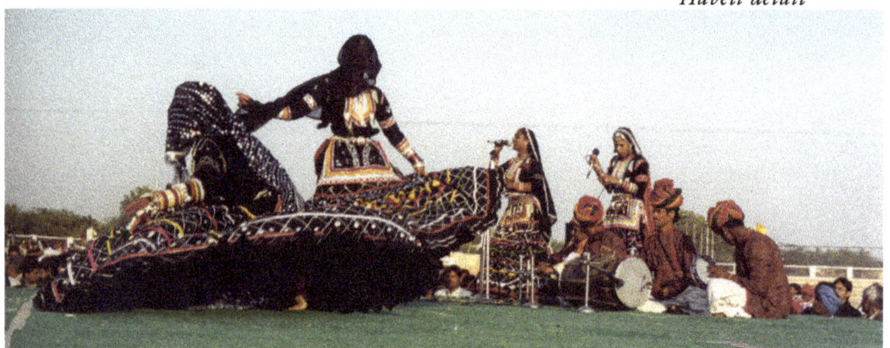

Camel Festival entertainment with Gypsy dancers

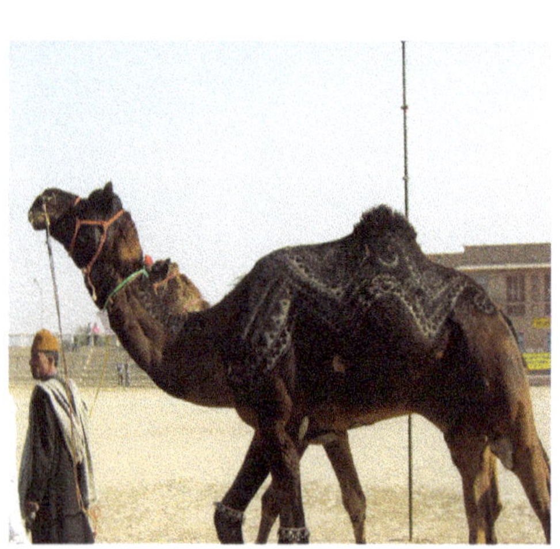

Camel fur clipped in design

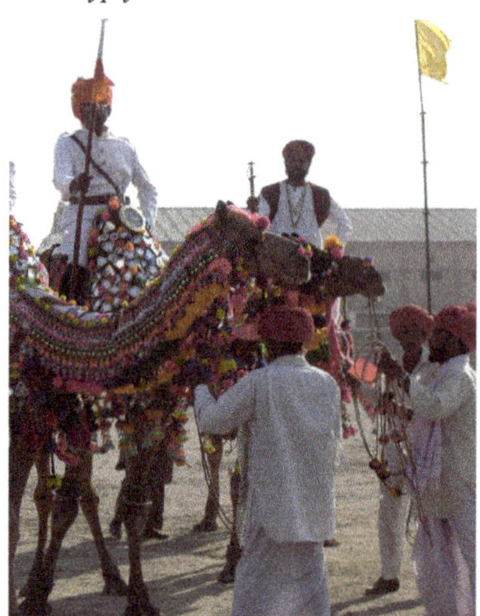

Camel decoration colourful

Then it was on through the rest of our itinerary to Mandawa, Bundi and Udaipur. We loved it all. Back in Delhi for the last day before returning to Australia, it was time to see the usual offerings, but the tour company could see I

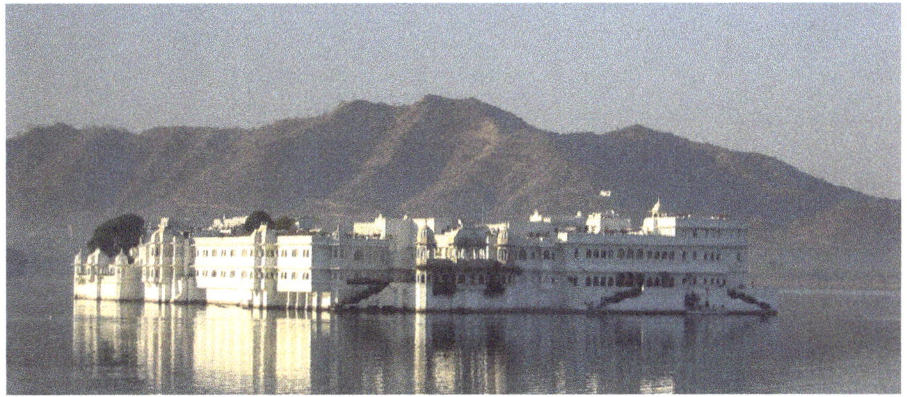

Udaipur Palace, now a hotel in middle of lake

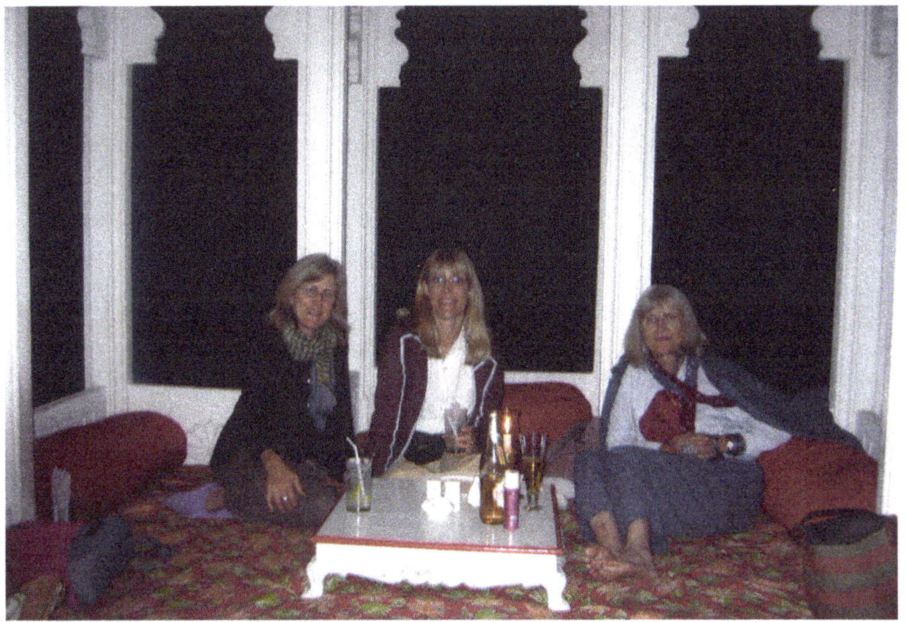

Udaipur relaxation at end of trip

was not happy to have missed the Craft Museum. So they took me to the area to show how wrong I was.

But driving along what did we see but a building with a big sign, Craft Museum. It was well worth the effort. We arrived when a group of dancers and musicians from Orissa were performing in the courtyard. Inside the museum is set up so beautifully, I think it is the best in all of India. We flew off the next day happy.

Jenny wrote these words of her feelings of the trip: *"And so the day, and our fabulous Indian adventure, ended as it began, and as it had remained throughout - exciting, wondrous, fun-filled, intimate, vibrant, and forever engraved in our memories and our consciousness."*

I received a surprising email before I left for India in 2003 to announce that Winchester Thurston, my high school, was holding it's annual alumni reunion in 2004 and it was the 50th for my class. I was asked to be the Distinguished Alumni of the Year". It seemed hard to believe as our class had contained so many

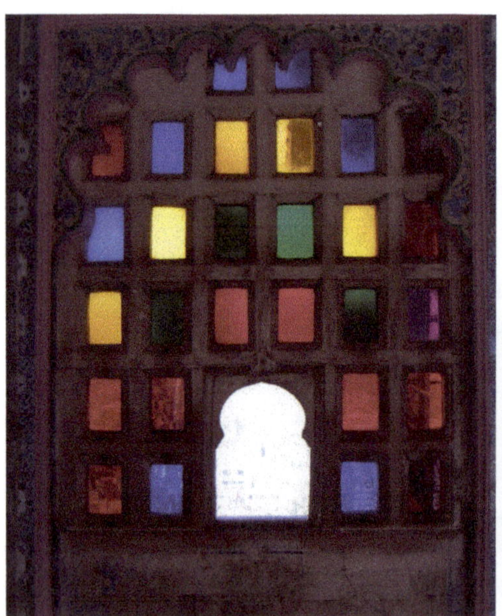

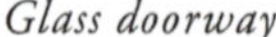

Glass doorway

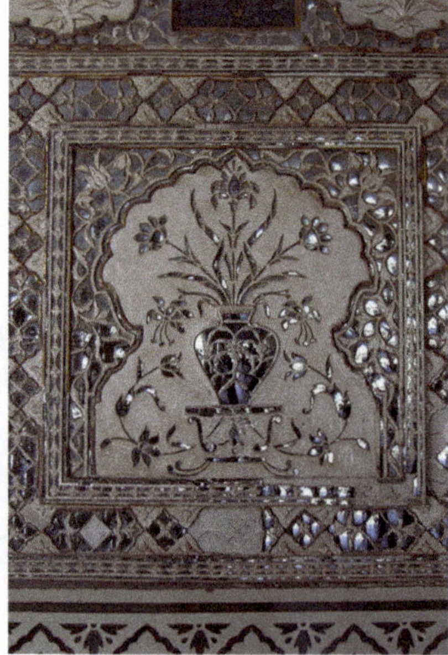

Mosaic detail

brilliant students. I was sure they had made their mark in important fields. But it turned out that this particular year, the school was honoring the Arts. As I had recently finished my Master's Degree after researching the Telia Rumal, South Indian ikat and had been a practicing textile artist for nearly 40 years, they thought I had something to contribute. I asked what the responsibilities would be and was told that talking to students at both campuses would be a way to pass something on. Back when I attended school, there was only one campus catering from kindergarten through to grade 12. Now there was a 'Lower School' in a different part of the city and also the school had become co-ed and greatly expanded.

2004 DISTINGUISHED ALUMNA

Dana Spicer McCown '54

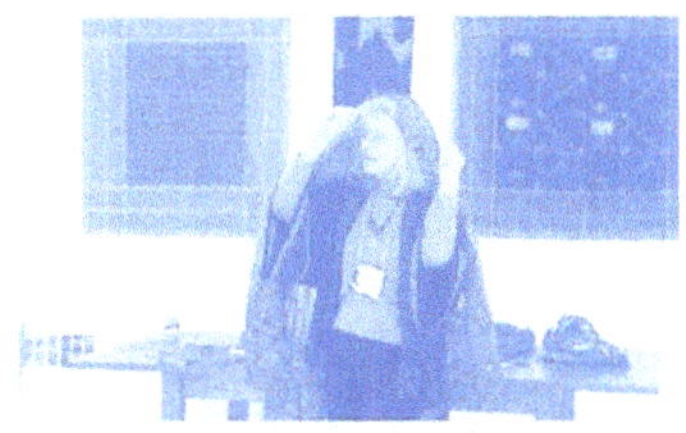

ana Spicer McCown '54 was honored as a Distinguished Alumna during the week of her 50th reunion.

While majoring in Art Education at the University of Wisconsin, Dana chose jewelry as her primary medium. In 1965, her husband Bob's work took them to Australia for what was supposed to be a three-year stint. They have lived down under for nearly 40 years, with periodic opportunities to live in other interesting countries such as India and Ethiopia.

Upon her first visit to India in 1969, Dana became interested in ethnic traditional techniques of weaving, in particular the Ikat technique. In 1995, when Dana and her husband began spending two to three months a year in India, her concentrated research in obscure and endangered weaving techniques began.

Dana's skills as a weaver combined with her talents as an educator led to the creation of an exhibition of *The Telia Rumal.*

Thistle article

We arrived in Pittsburgh to stay with Bob's parents. It seemed that Bob never mentioned to his folks about my role in the weekend. It was only because a newspaper phoned wanting to talk to me about my award when I wasn't there, that Grammie learned about it. Somehow Bob was always quiet about any honours that he received as well.

The week-end had many social activities. There were other 'years' having their reunion as well, but special activities for our group gave us the chance to catch up with old friends. Unfortunately some of my closest friends could not attend. Sue Marshall had apologised as her husband was seriously ill. It was nice to catch up with Louise, Betsy, Sarah, Kiki, Mary, Dotsie, Brenda and Alice among others. I did spend week-days talking to the students. I had taken along some of my interesting Indian textiles and talked about culture and identity. Lifelong learning was also something I felt was important to pass on. The school had an art exhibition with items from all the alumni who would contribute. I did take some of my work for that exhibition. I also had a display of my Telia Rumal project. And it was nice to meet Alison Wolfson, Alumni Co-ordinator who made the week a special time for me.

While in Pittsburgh, Betty, my mother-in-law told me about a woman who had written a genealogy of the McCowin clan. Bob and I had been doing a great deal of research and were anxious to make contact with this person. We had a phone call with Marge Simard out in Utah, who then sent a copy of the publication her mother had produced. It started a long correspondence and an eventual visit to Australia, along with her sister-in-law Bernice and niece Marcia McCowin. It was wonderful getting to know these delightful distant relatives. Our branch had dropped the i in McCowin generations ago.

JAPANESE PROJECT STARTS

In 2004, I had been asked to host a Japanese textile artist, Tomie Nagano, visiting Toowoomba. Her main medium was quilting using antique traditional Japanese textiles. Her aim in coming to Toowoomba was to attend a quilting event held during the annual Festival of Flowers. But she wanted to hold an exhibition of her own work in Australia and felt the Toowoomba Regional Art Gallery would be perfect. I helped her get an appointment to meet with the Toowoomba Mayor who was very enthused by the idea and did support her project with the gallery staff. Then it was up to Tomie to formally apply to the gallery.

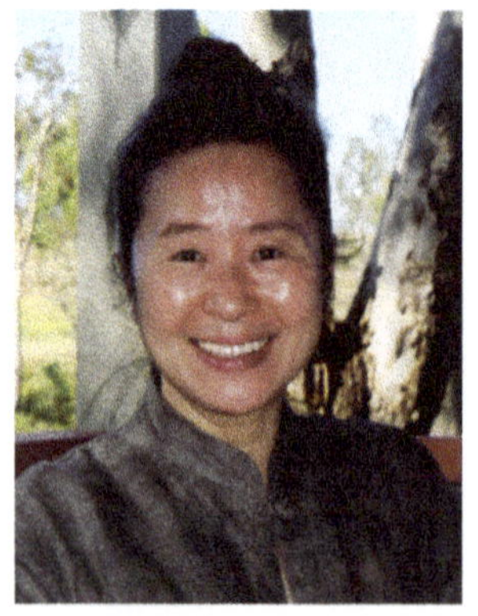

Tomie Nagano

Eventually the gallery decided to give her gallery space and I was contacted and offered a contract to curate the exhibition. The conditions did not cover the expense for going to Japan to work on the project. It was suggested I could apply for a grant to the Regional Art Fund to take such a trip. My application was successful and I went to Japan and

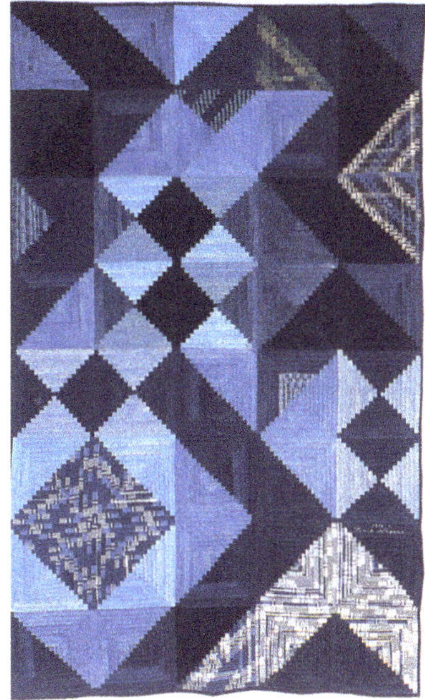

North Ground

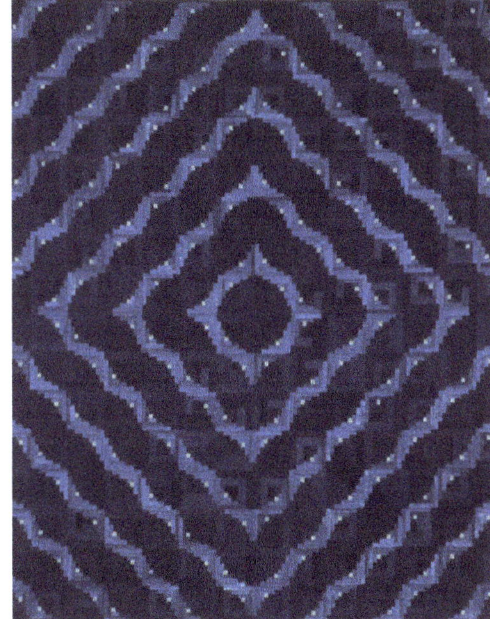

Okhotski Blue 1

was met by Tomie in Sapporo, the capital of Hokkaido. We visited the Ainu Cultural Center and then travelled across the island by car to Shari Town where she lived. The island had beautiful scenery of forests, lakes and long coastal shoreline. The ocean actually freezes over along her shoreline in winter, which is reflected in the design of several of her quilts.

Her studio is built as an addition to her grandparents home. They became pioneers in Hokkaido when the government wanted to build up the population so that Russia did not eye this island as a place of empty spaces to invade. When her grandparents garments were given to her by her mother, she was so moved by the beauty of the simple cloth and dyes that she got the idea of making quilts with this fabric. She travelled to antique shows for two years collecting 4000 garments to use. I had the opportunity to select the quilts to travel to Toowoomba. I brought my video equipment, as I wanted to create a DVD documenting her workspace and capturing her philosophy. We chose the quilts to represent the different fabrics and techniques used in the grandparents clothing.

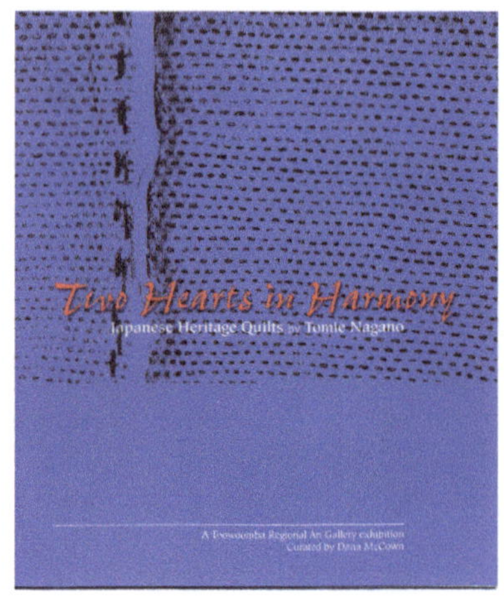

Catalogue from exhibition

The exhibition was entitled, "Two Hearts in Harmony: Japanese Heritage Quilts". I wrote the text and essay for the catalogue to accompany the exhibition as it travelled around Australia and Tomie wrote a lovely introduction entitled "My quilts - My Dream". Diane Thorley, the Mayor of Toowoomba wrote the Foreward. I wanted to include items from her grandparents, possessions such as grandfather's Yogi Futon, shaped as a kimono that could be displayed at floor level as it would be used. Her grandmother's quilted bags, made to carry rice as a present and her tobacco pouch, pieced from colourful fabric, showed how quilting and piecing small fabrics had a long tradition in Japan. The exhibition looked wonderful, with 16 large quilts on the walls and a large fine hemp quilt top displayed so one could see the back with the textured piecing contrasting to the smooth front and creating an almost transparent floating wall. The exhibition was well received with people coming from a distance to see it.

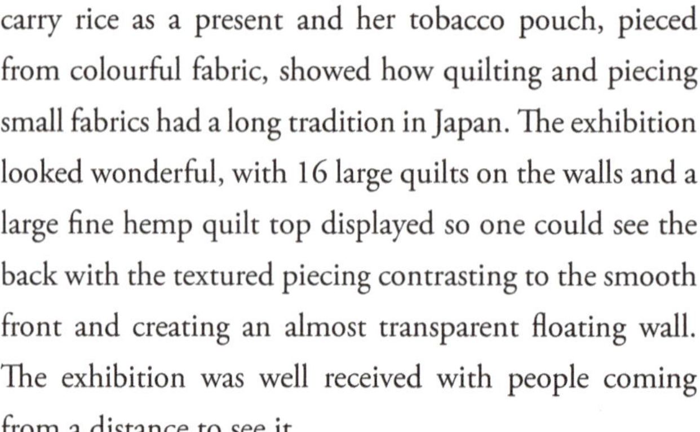

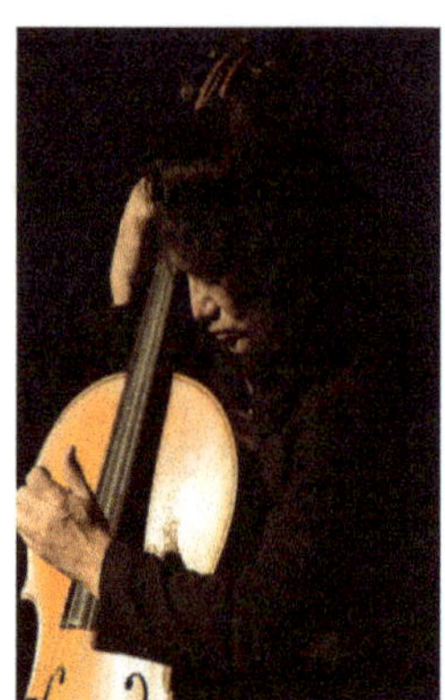

Yoshi

To enhance the opening ceremonies, Tomie had arranged for a Japanese jazz cellist to come from Japan and play at the opening. Yoshi Kikkawa came with his manager and wanted to play at more events if possible. I was able to arrange for him to play at the Toowoomba Jazz Club for a great night. Then the Uniting

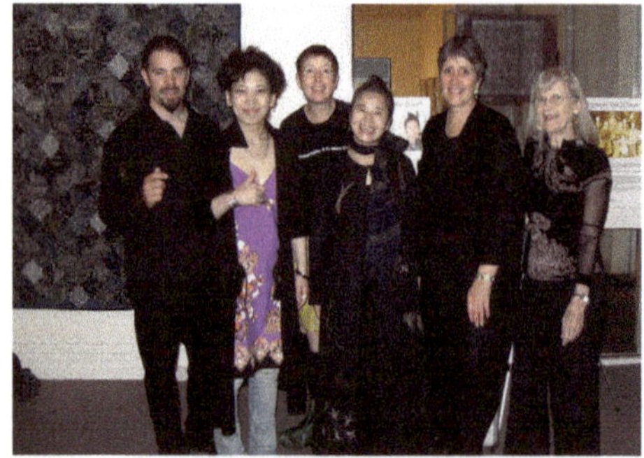

Setting up team in Albury Wodonga

Church in the city gave him the opportunity to have a concert in the church sanctuary, as the minister Peter Banney was always eager to promote the arts within the church. And Yoshi played at a dinner party I had the night before the opening. Then he was able to play after leaving Toowoomba at the Brisbane Jazz Club. He was a remarkably talented musician and we all felt fortunate to have heard him. The exhibition did travel to other locations during that year. Tomie came back from Japan and invited me to accompany her to Albury Wodonga when it was on display there. At that opening she brought a young Japanese jazz pianist to play at the opening.

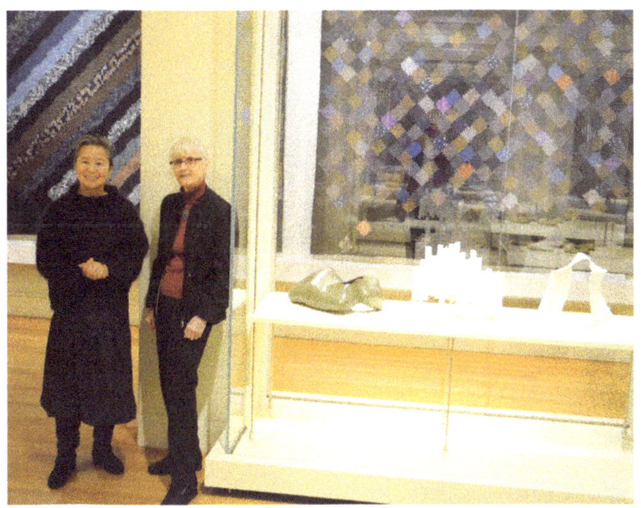

Visiting Tomie in Boston for the opening of the exhibition

Bob had a conference to attend in Baltimore and I went with him again. Afterward he had plans to travel to Colorado with Peter Carberry, his colleague and friend. I had just received an email from Tomie who had moved to Boston, where the Boston Museum of Fine Art acquired her collection of quilts from "Two Hearts in Harmony". They were having an exhibition featuring a selection of those quilts together with fine Asian basketry and glass art. The opening was happening in a few days. I was able to fly up from Baltimore for the opening and stayed at her home, while Bob had his plans. Sometimes there are lucky opportunities.

ANOTHER GRANDCHILD ADVENTURE

Sam was turning 21 years old in 2006 and was anxious for us to plan his trip to India. I had taken note of Mani's wonderful boss, Faith Pandian, who actually

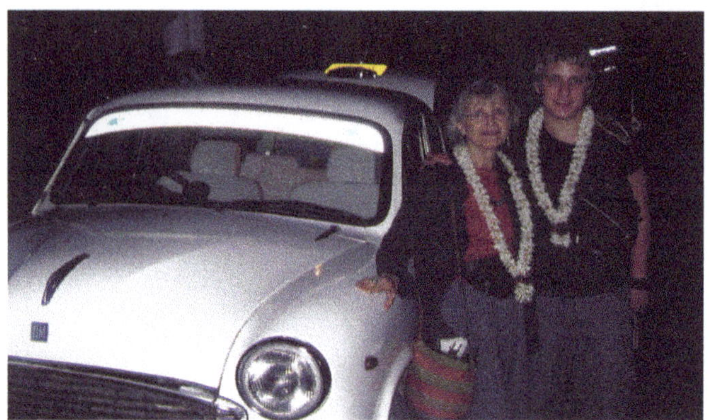

Welcome flowers

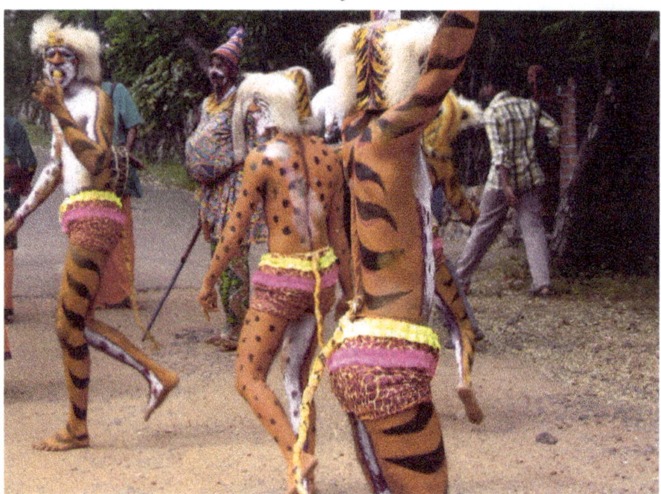

Tribal dancers

was from New Zealand but had worked as a nurse in Melbourne and contacted her again. We created quite a different itinerary so he would have stories and memories mostly different to Jordan. We started out in Chennai, where Faith had

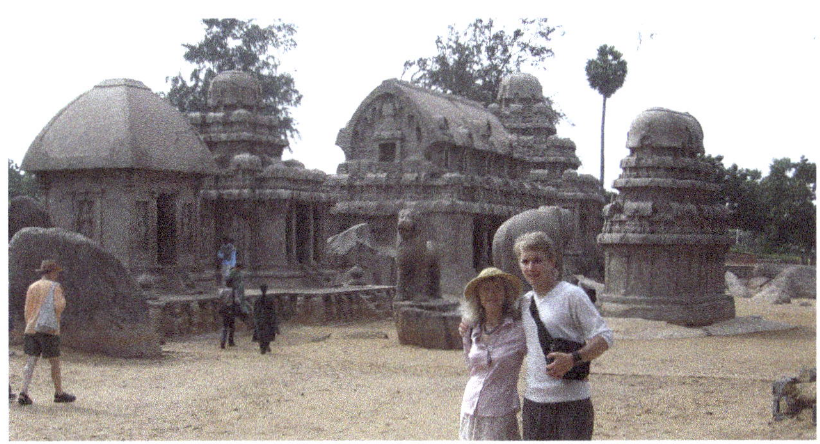

At the 5 Ratha's Mamallapuram, TN

provided a driver named Gandhi and a vehicle. It is always lovely to be welcomed with a festoon of flowers. We headed south toward Mamallapuram, stopping along the way at Dakshinachitra, a unique cultural museum with a village with traditional homes from around India. We no sooner pulled our vehicle off the road before a group of tribal dancers, looking like tigers, came and met us dancing and beckoning us to follow. It was an interesting stop and also a place to have a tradition meal.

Along the way we also saw Marina Beach, where the 2004 tsunami happened, killing many people. Most had never heard of a tsunami and didn't know that when the water suddenly pulls out to sea, that it will then reverse and come in covering the land. So they just stood and watched instead of running away.

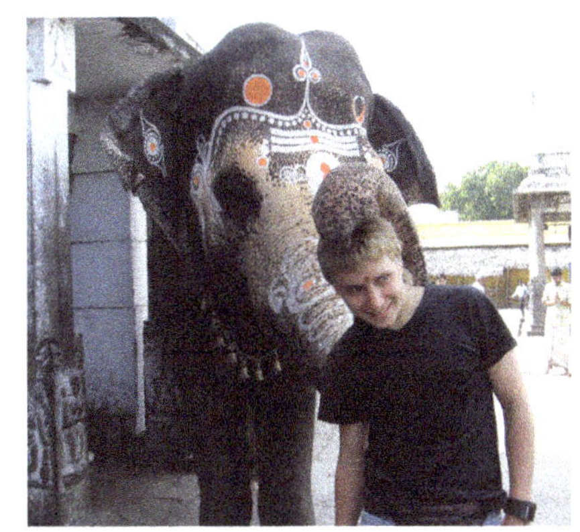

Blessings

We wanted to get to Mamallapuram to see the wonderful monolithic sculpture. But it was also the time of the annual dance festival held with the background setting of a large stone wall of bas-relief. We were getting a full range of cultural events all at once. We did get further south to Pondecherry which was a French territory and still has that influence. Then back up to Kanchipuram where there are 1000 Hindu temples, where we were given a blessing by a temple elephant. The town is also known for the finest quality silk saris.

It seemed to be a time of pilgrimage as there was a group of men dressed in green getting into the holy water of the temple tank. We saw large groups of women, all dressed alike getting on a bus to go further on pilgrimage to another holy place. And we saw men who were devotees of Lord Ayyappa in black garb going on pilgrimage to Kerala after fasting and wearing no leather for many days.

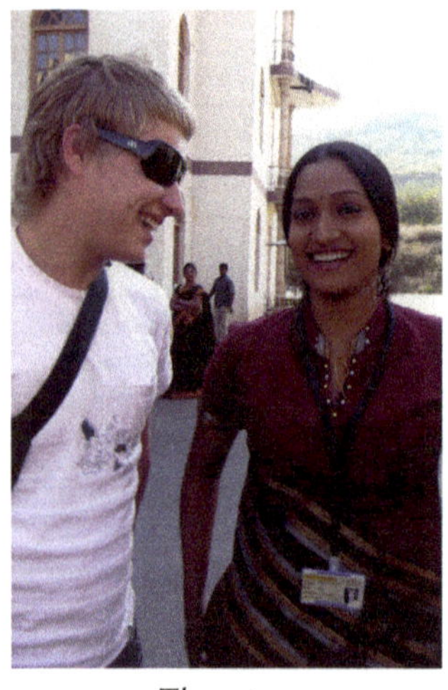

The actress

We returned to Andhra Pradesh and had plans to stay at Ramaji Film City to see some movie making. There are two hotels within the ground, many settings for various filming and studios. There are bus tours one can take around the grounds. However much filming is done throughout the complex along the streets. We did find several scenes set up outside our hotel and cameras rolling. It didn't take long for one of the actresses to come wanting to meet Sam. Why was I not surprised?

When we were staying at ICRISAT during the late 1990s, some of the staff wives were signed up to come to Film City and be extras. They did make some money that way and also had fun. I had found during the earlier years, before Ramoji Film City was established, that many studios negotiated to come to the ICRISAT gated campus to film. There would be no hoards of street people wanting to come and watch, getting in the way. There were lovely lakes and green vegetation. I was out birdwatching one day and had taken my video camera to film a large group of weaver birds building their nests. As I walked along toward the lake, a man approached me and said the film director wanted to speak to me.

He was sitting back lounging in his "Director's Chair" and asked if I could play in a scene. All very impromptu. I was to act as a tourist with my video camera. Then a man would come and say he would take a picture of me on the camera and I was to do a swirl around. Then he ran off and stole my video camera and I chased him. I wonder if that footage ever saw the light of day? Another time in a museum I was asked to take a smaller role yet. One time I had been out early on a Sunday morning birdwatching. When I came back across the fields, suddenly I saw that there must have been 100 toilet pedestals sitting spaced out nicely among the crops. Later I learned it was for an advertisement. All that has stopped, but it was fun at the time.

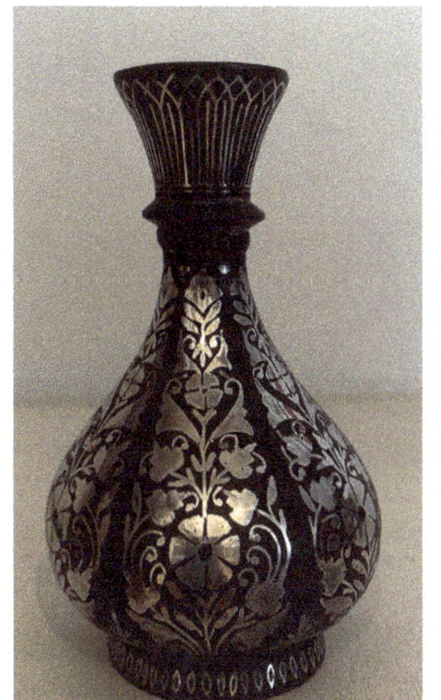

Bidriware

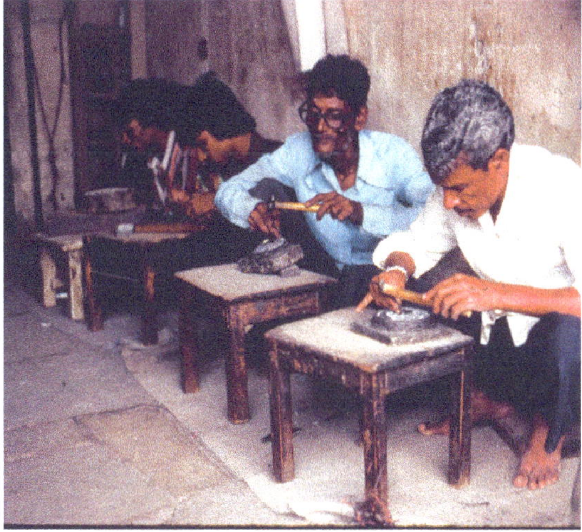

Bidriware workroom

Sam and I planned to stay in Hyderabad for a time, as it is such an interesting place. There is a special craft called Bidriware that I used to visit when in town, making metal objects cast in sand and then inlayed with pure silver designs. Then when the base metal is treated with the soil from the Bidar Fort, it turns black. All the steps are very interesting from making the mold, watching the metal melted down and then the finishing and embellishment. The workshop was a simple hole-in-the-wall with about six men doing various steps with an office at the end.

Sam made a little video of the process and remarked that they wouldn't pass the Oz health and safety regulations as the artisans all had bare feet.

Another big attraction for us was visiting the impressive Golconda Fort, which was the capital of the Qutb Shahi dynasty. The famous Koh-i-Noor diamond came from the vicinity and was kept there at one time. It had ingenious features of air-cooling and acoustics. We climbed up and saw all of the massive structure. In 1687, the Mughal Emperor Aurangzeb attacked the Golconda Fort with an intention to seize Hyderabad, looted and destroyed the fort and left it in a heap of ruins.

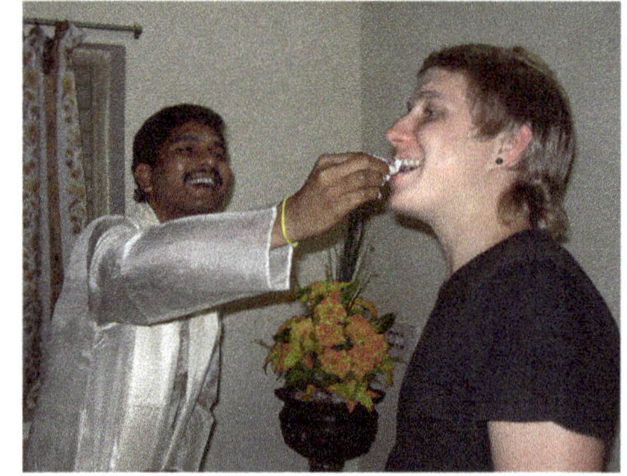

Anil's birthday party

It happened to be Rama Rao's son Anil's 30th birthday and they were having a party that we were invited to attend at their home. Anil was dressed in white silk and enjoying the attention. I had met Rama Rao's daughter Anita before and now she was there with children and husband. Several aunties and friends made up the group. Rama Rao had recently upgraded his home, adding on another floor, which is often the option in the way houses are built with reinforcing rods

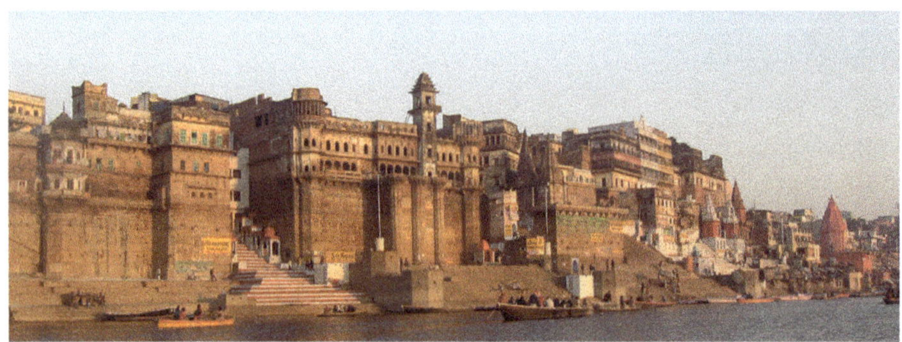

Varanasi

still sticking out the roof, ready for some time in the future to expand. He had also relined the flooring with a lovely white marble in large panels.

Sam and I took a train to Varanasi on the Ganges. Visitors will always be confronted with the bodies being cremated on the banks of the river while worshippers are entering the holy water along the ghats. At night, while the priests are conducting rites on the riverbank, we went out in a boat so that we could look back and take in all the elaborate ceremony. We participated in a ceremony with a small floating floral offering.

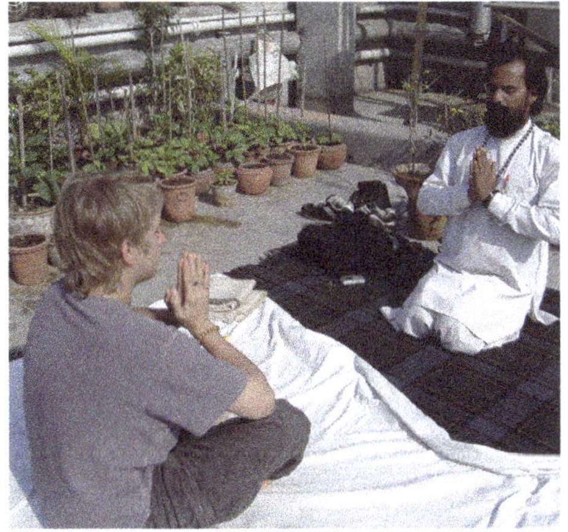

Rooftop yoga

Wanting to have some different experiences, we hired an expert yogi to give us some training in yoga on the roof of our hotel. However, he was far too expert for us to achieve any real experience ourselves, but

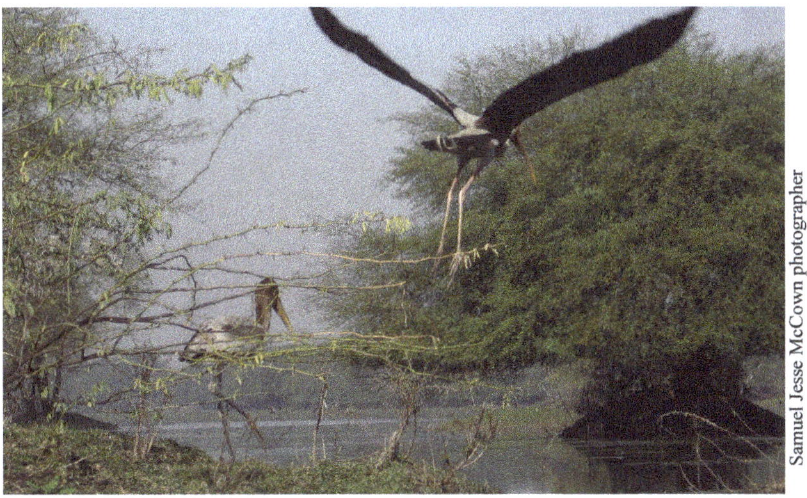

Samuel Jesse McCown photographer

Storks at Bharatpur

watching what contortions he put his body through was worth seeing. Then we hired a palm reader to come to our room and tell us what our hands could reveal.

We travelled to Bharatpur where there is a famous bird sanctuary and hired a guide to spend the day with us. He was an expert on all the birds and told us the story how he used to be a buffalo herder. Salim Ali, the famous father of Ornithology in India, asked him to come and work in this sanctuary he had established, recognising his vast knowledge. We actually had Salim Ali's bird book with us on the trip.

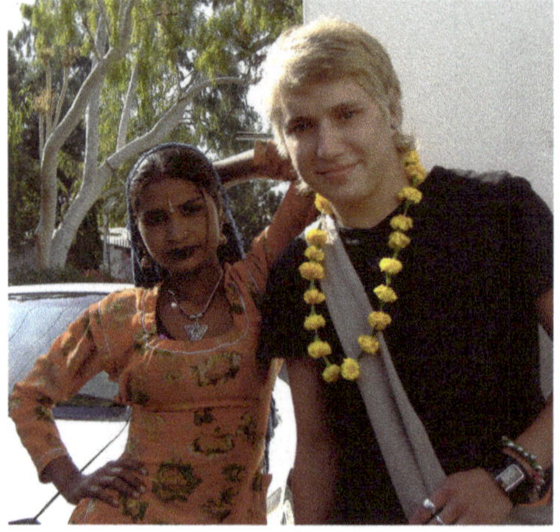

Gypsy friend

Previously I had travelled close to Pushkar, but hadn't actually time to divert. Pushkar is famous for its camel races and

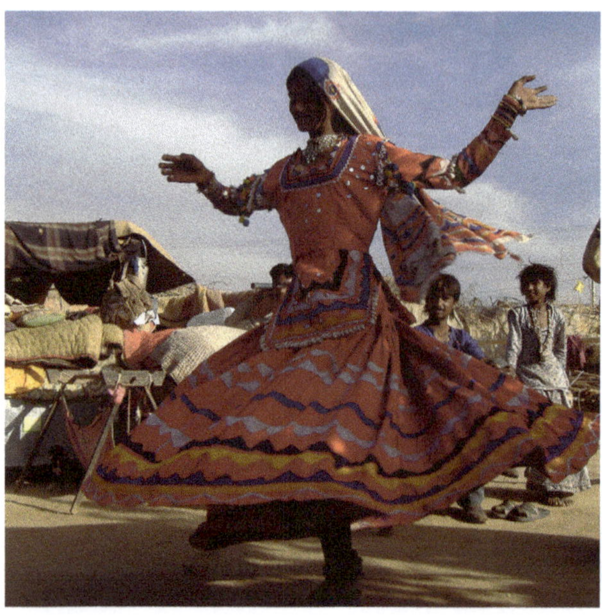

Gypsies dancing for us after they cooked us a tasty meal

festival, but this was not the time of year. What was most interesting was the large group of gypsies living there and trying to make a living from the tourists. Sam was discovered very quickly by the gypsy girls who took him to their compound. I am very fond of having a henna tattoo, called Mehndi. So I hired one of these girls to come and give me a design on my hand. Then I was invited to have a meal with them and watch some gypsy dancing in their compound. We were told about one of their group who actually married a young German fellow and went to live in Germany. I think that was what these young girls hoped for themselves.

We did get to Agra to see the most iconic Indian landmark, the Taj Mahal. Sam and I visited Jaipur and saw the Jandar Mantar, a UNESCO World Heritage site of astronomical instruments constructed in 1734 by the king of Jaipur. The brilliant design of instruments giving precise measurements using the sun caught Sam's imagination.

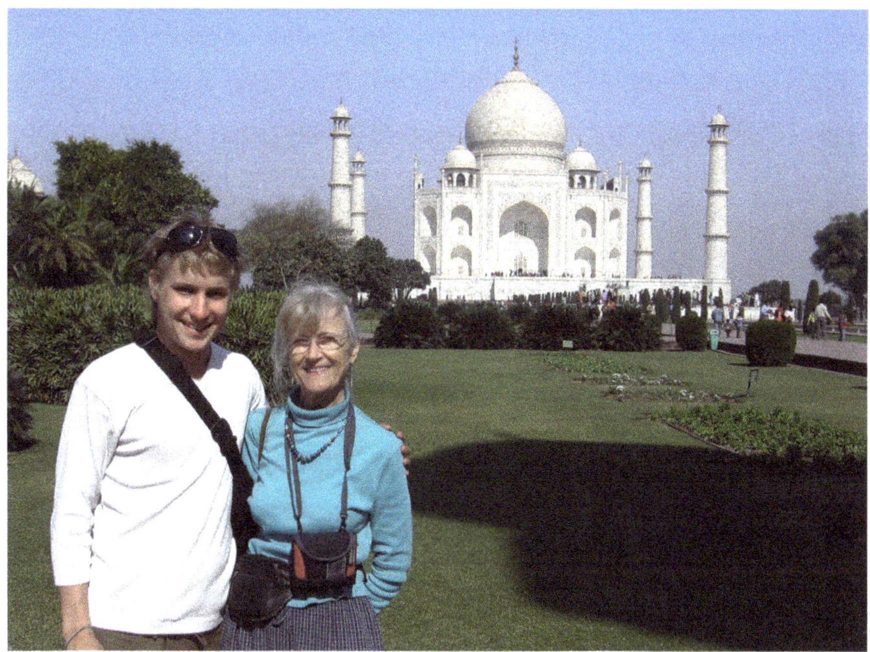

Well worth visiting even if it isn't in moonlight

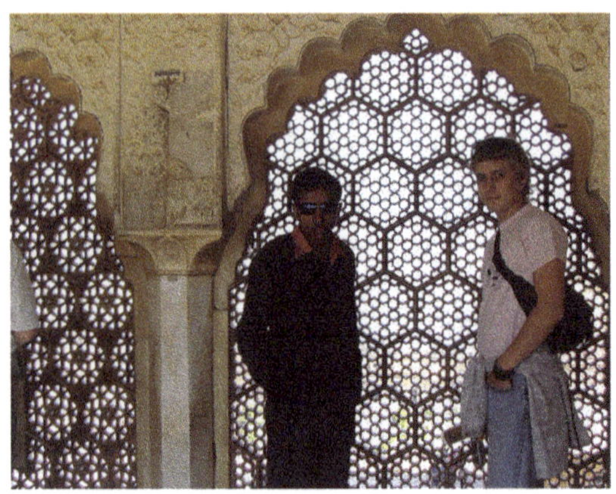

Sam with a friendly guide

We had a guide while in the city and I wasn't surprised later in the day to hear that he was going to take Sam on his motorcycle for more adventures that evening. Everywhere we went, Sam met locals that became friends and gave him opportunities to see some of the local life away from the tourist attractions.

HYDERABAD -THE NATURAL DYE SYMPOSIUM

Later in 2006, a special event was planned for Hyderabad of a Natural Dye Symposium with people attending from all over the world. I decided to design and plan a tour to take people to see wonderful traditional textiles around South India before the Symposium, with an additional add-on to the north at the end. Again, I had Faith work out prices for various numbers, depending on how many wanted to come. I joined forces with Barbara Skye who had been taking tours to Thailand for years as she had a vast list of clients.

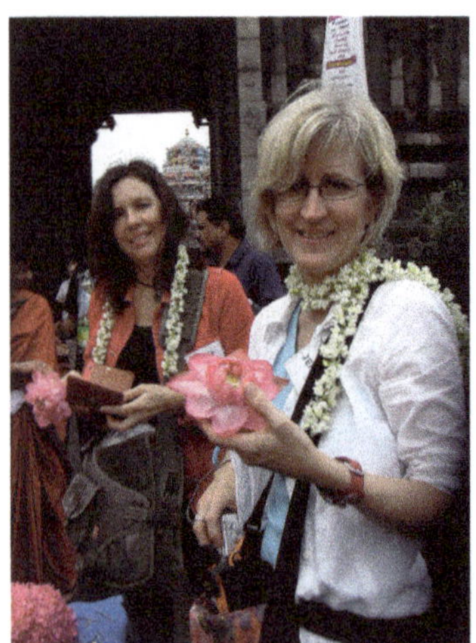

Lotus and Jasmine of course

Daughter Jenny decided to come and asked Rose to come, too. We arrived in Chennai and travelled south about an hour or so to Mamallapuram, where world famous monolithic sculptures were discovered. Along the shore is a series of cave temples. We stayed in a small resort on the shoreline with simple fishing boats going out early each morning.

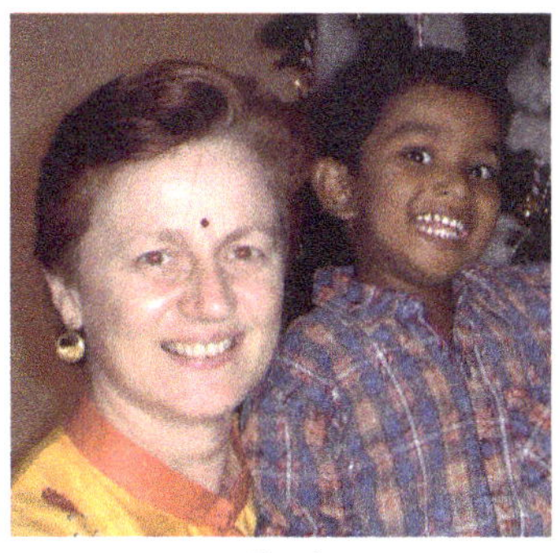

Faith

Later, there was much activity along the beach sorting fish and mending nets.

Faith came and joined us, bringing her young son along, driving up from Tiruchchirappalli where she lived and had her main office. In the evening we all came together for "happy hour" to talk and share what we had seen. I asked Faith to tell us her story of how she got to be running a business in India. She told us she had travelled to India to help in the south at an orphanage. Needing to have a source of some income, she started taking friends and others from home on some tours five or six times a year, as she was getting to know the country. One of the craft establishment where she always took her guests had a man working there, who was very knowledgeable and explained things to customers well. She ended up marrying him. Her business was mainly in the south and had a fleet of vehicles with drivers. She expanded to have offices in a number of cities. She could arrange any travel throughout the country and work out accommodation to suit any budget. So I was finally happy to meet Faith in person.

I had researched textile experts to visit along the way to Hyderabad for the Natural Dye Symposium. Our bus was quite new and comfortable, but we had some long distances to cover. So several of the tour members were organised to

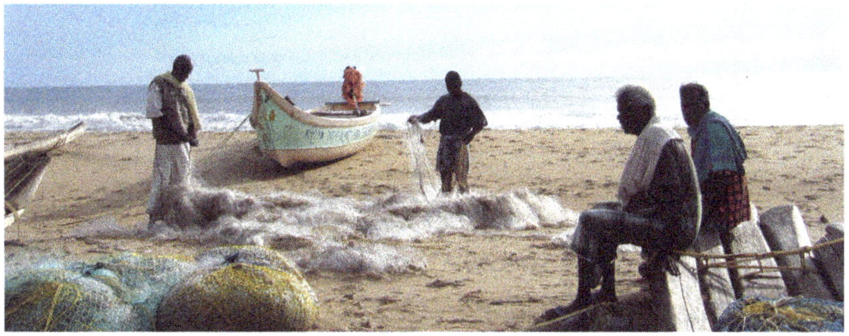

The beach in front of the Sea Breeze Hotel where we stayed

give us all mini workshops on the bus. We made beautiful felt flowers and enjoyed the process. Another day we wove small bags that could be used for mobile phones or other small items. Cardboard looms had been handed out with cotton yarn to make a warp. The weaving was done with strips of fabric. They turned out so well, many of us wore them around our necks for the rest of the trip.

Arriving in Vijawada, we then wanted to go to Masuliputnam to see the Kalamkari printers using natural dyes. There had been a monsoon depression recently and we started to get into water rising along the side of the narrow road. A member of the group came quietly from back of the bus and suggested we needed to turn around. I already had that plan and was nervously needing to find a spot where we could do so. Luckily we came to small town and it had a hill that we drove up, as the lower part was under water already. But we had another hour or more drive back to our hotel at Vijawada and people needed to go to the toilet. The bus driver was looking around and prospects were limited. Half way up the hill was a rooming house and he asked the manager if we could use the facilities. The answer was no. So I asked him to find out the price of a room for the night. It was something like $15. Luckily they had a room to rent, but this room was on the second floor and there were 22 of us, one at least had limited mobility. We traipsed up the stairs and formed a line down the hallway. People in those rooms started opening up their door to see what was happening. It was a slow process. But it worked.

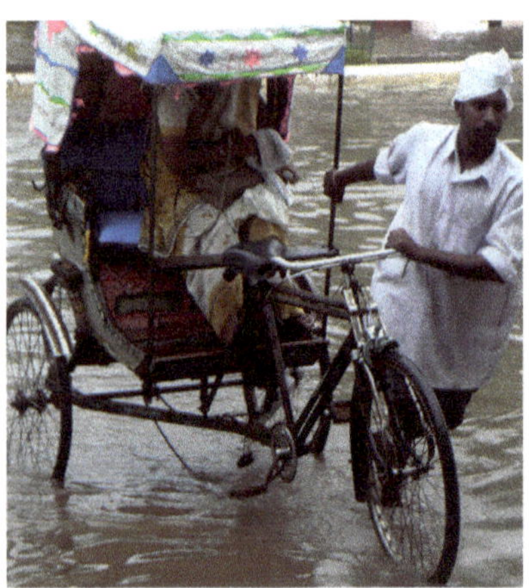
Wading through flood waters

We arrived back to our hotel eventually and had experienced a big adventure, but missed seeing the Kalamkari printing. What is even more interesting in Masuliputnam is watching the young boys taking the lengths of fabric to the canal, jumping in and washing it, ready for the next process with much splashing and exuberance. But there would have to be a next time for that.

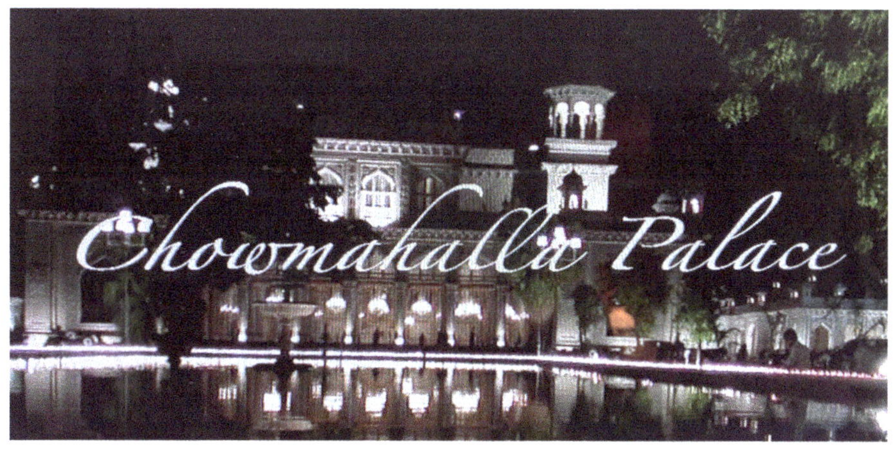

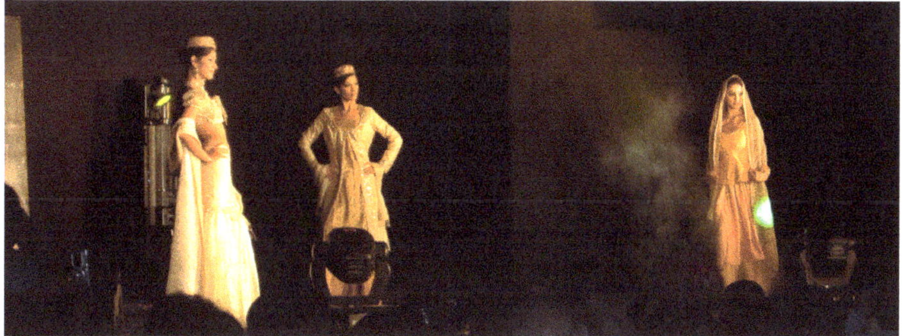
Fashion extravaganza

Arriving in Hyderabad, we found our hotel was not quite finished being built. In most instances, that wasn't too big a problem, but walking from your room, you wanted to be wide awake as the outside wall was not enclosed except for some plastic sheeting. The local conference committee had planned a rich program with many seminars, expert speakers, exhibitions, fashion parades and a special dinner at Chowmahalla Palace on the lawn. The waiters in pink turbans and white coats were elegant and efficient. The fashion parade had components

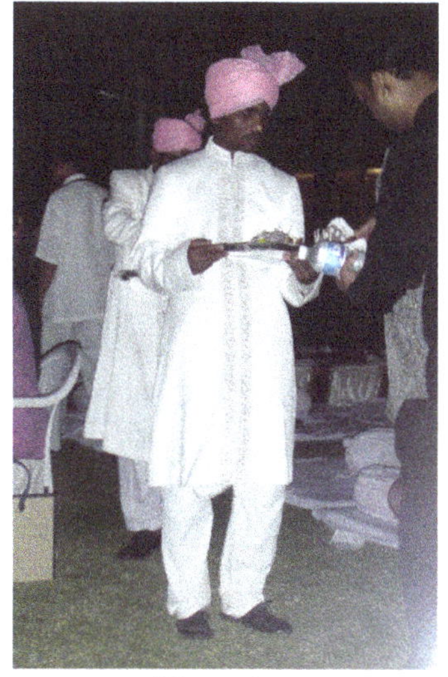
The waiters

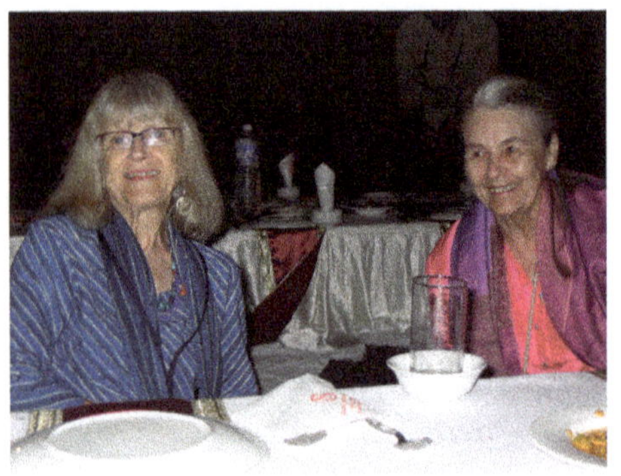
Dana and Jill at Chowmahalla Palace

from different countries, with the Indian segment being orchestrated by my friend Bina Rao.

While at the palace, we were invited in smaller groups to enter an area of the palace where the Nizam had his quarters and we were able to see his wardrobe. Needless to say the Nizam of Hyderabad no longer resided there, in fact he had gone to Australia and bought a sheep property in Western Australia. He also married a local woman there. At one time he was considered the wealthiest man in the world. A fascinating book has been written about him entitled "The Last Nizam".

Another day we visited the Salar Jung Museum, which usually is limited to European art, but they had an outstanding exhibition of the Nizam's Crown Jewels. Of course I arranged for the group to visit the Bidriware artisans, and Rama Rao provided vehicles for us to get around.

There was also a craft fair during the week at the conference, where the Gajam family and their weavers had a display. And then there were side trips to see indigo dyeing. It was a week so full of speakers, demonstrations, and special events. Even some of the delegates who came with us from Australia presented papers and posters about the dyestuffs from Australia.

After the Symposium was over, part of our group flew to Delhi especially to see the Taj Mahal. There was so much more to see and enjoy. In Delhi the Craft Museum is outstanding and not to be missed. But as we had discovered, many of the local guides don't even know of its existence. The Gandhi shrine was another inspiring place we visited.

From Delhi we went on what is called the golden triangle, next down to Agra to see the Taj Mahal and then across to Jaipur for block printing. In order for block printing to happen, first wooden blocks have to be created usually using hard Teak wood and carved with sharp tools to create designs. We went to see them being made and had the chance to buy finished blocks of all sizes and shapes. We had met some artisans from the Symposium whose special skill was Leharia, a Shibori technique all in natural dyes. So we visited one of them and saw him demonstrate techniques to create his lovely scarves. We saw hand-made paper being created in a factory using only rag cotton cloth. Many steps were going on and the manager kindly explained it all. In the final area lovely products were made such as covered boxes, shopping bags, writing paper, and many more. We all took away our share. Along the way were numerous historical sites and always the unexpected happens. So everyone was happy that it had all been interesting. Some of the travellers said, *"Can we come on your next trip to India?"*

COUSINS TRIP

In early 2008, my plan was to design and take textile tours further than South India eventually, but I thought that I would start with a cousins trip to Rajasthan and Gujarat. So I contacted Faith and mapped out a tour with dates and timing. We talked about what sort of accommodation I preferred. I did a great deal of research and selected hotels. She was able to work out affordable pricing for us. My two cousins, Lisa and Sandy, originally from Milwaukee came, my two daughters Jessie and Jenny came, and also our cousin Charlotte from Sweden. Charlotte brought a friend to travel with. So it was a small group of seven. We had a great time and it helped me do some fine-tuning for the next tour with 15 textile enthusiasts who were coming later in the year. For the Gujarati section of the trip we had the wonderful Judy Frater, author

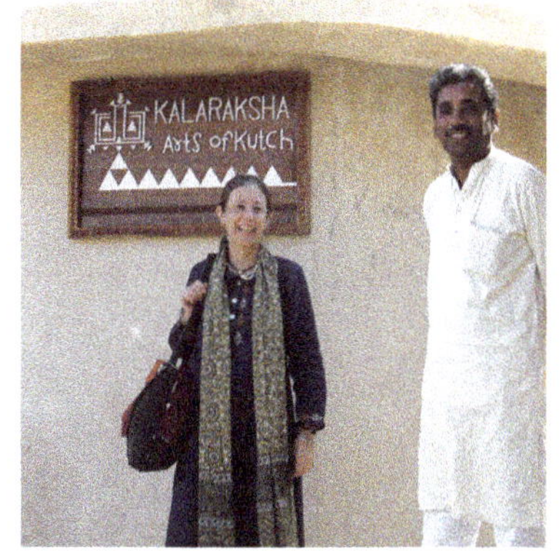

Judy at the museum

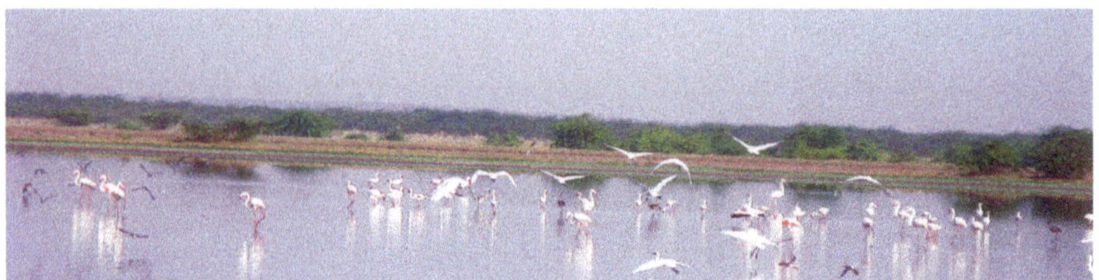

Flamingos

and expert on tribal migrations and embroideries, guiding us. Judy originally traveled to Gujarat to study the people and ended up staying and helping them set up a textile organisation with museum, design school and sales outlets. After Rajasthan, we started at Ahmedabad, the capitol of Gujarat, which is home to the famous Calico Museum. Then travelling west to Bhuj, across the Rann of Kutch salt flats with flamingos and wild ass, one sees a variety of tribal groups, each with their own distinctive style.

We visited the SOS Children's Village which was initiated after the 2001 devastating earthquake which hit Bhuj, killing 20,000 people. Many children were left without parents or homes. The design of the village caters for a number of small family groups with a "mother" who generally is a widow. In the Indian society, widows have a hard time in life and this employment with SOS benefits both woman and children.

The block printers of Ajrakh were also badly hit by the earthquake and had to

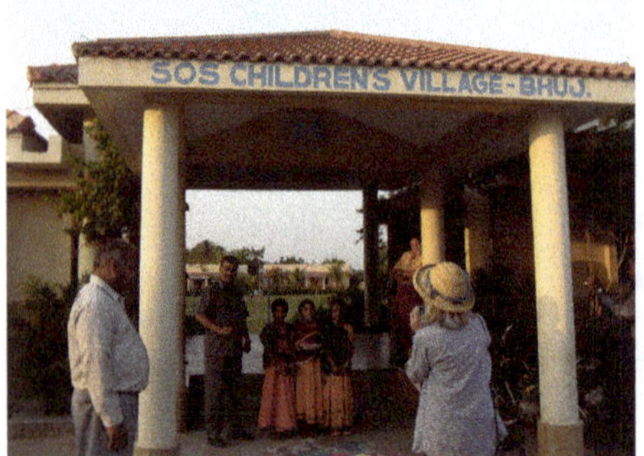

I enter the village

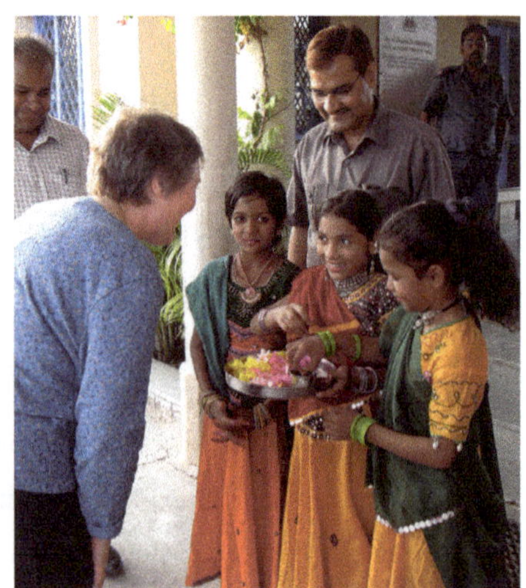

Sandy receives a warm welcome

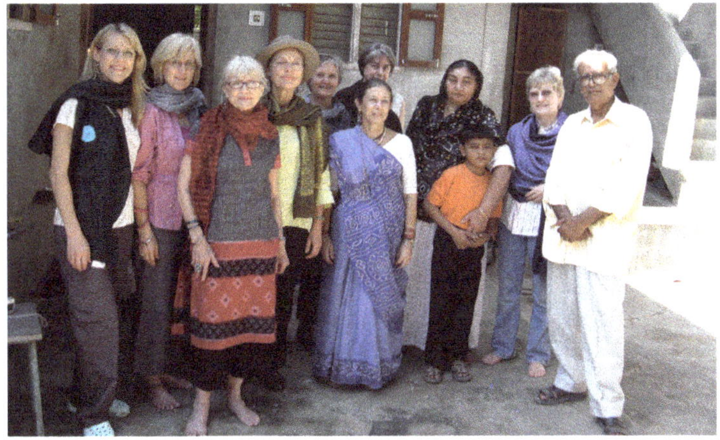

Our group with Judy in the middle and Ali Mo with family

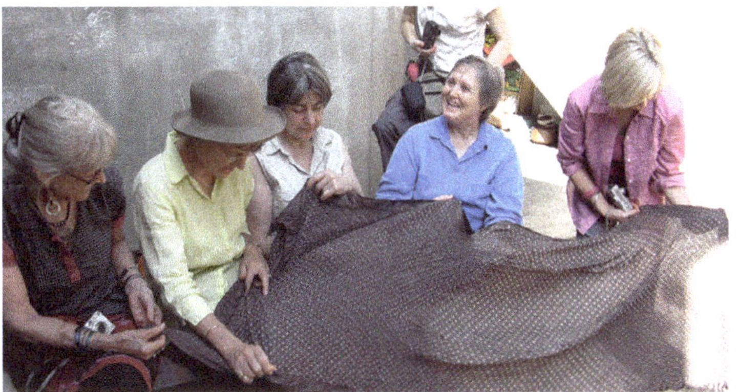

Inspecting the bandhani technique

find a new location to re-establish their village. Their fabric has distinctive designs in red and blue natural dyes, but are increasingly adding to the colour pallet. Another wonderful textile in Bhuj is Bandhani, a form of Shibori. We visited the expert, Ali Mo Isha Khatri, to see his work. He has travelled to Australia and worldwide to put on workshops at events.

For part of the time, we stayed in an eco-village made in traditional style called Shaam e Sarhad. It was a special time in that we saw wonderful textiles and interesting people, but it was a rare time to spend time with cousins, some

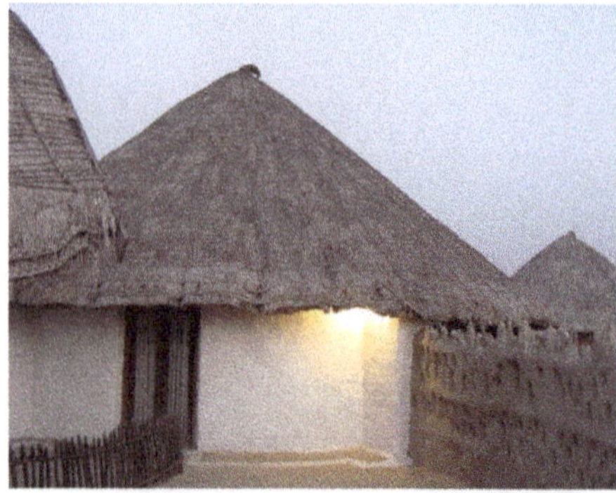

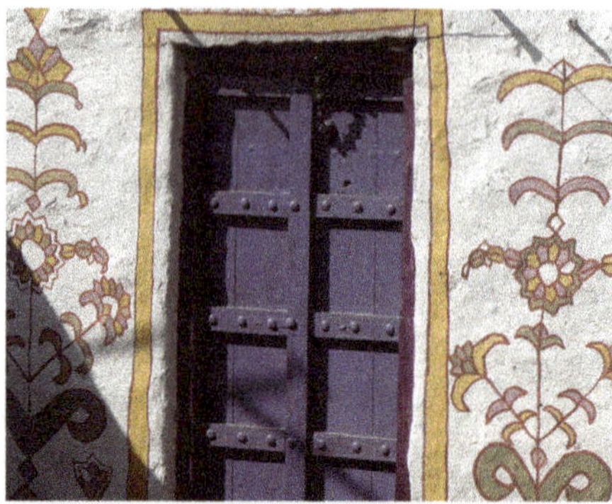

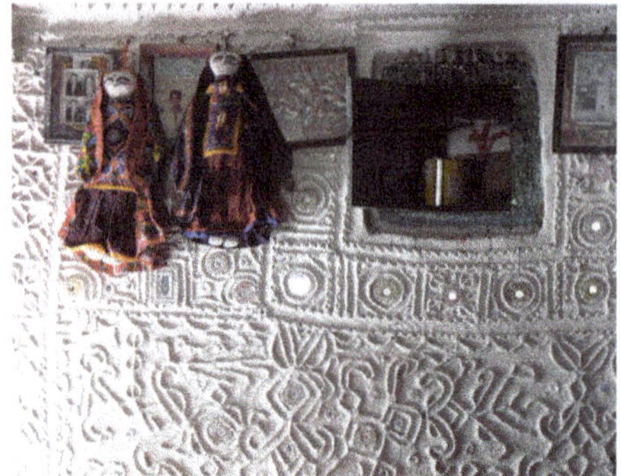

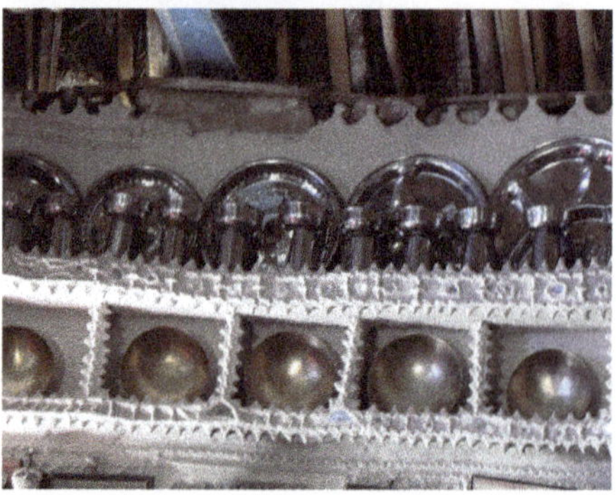

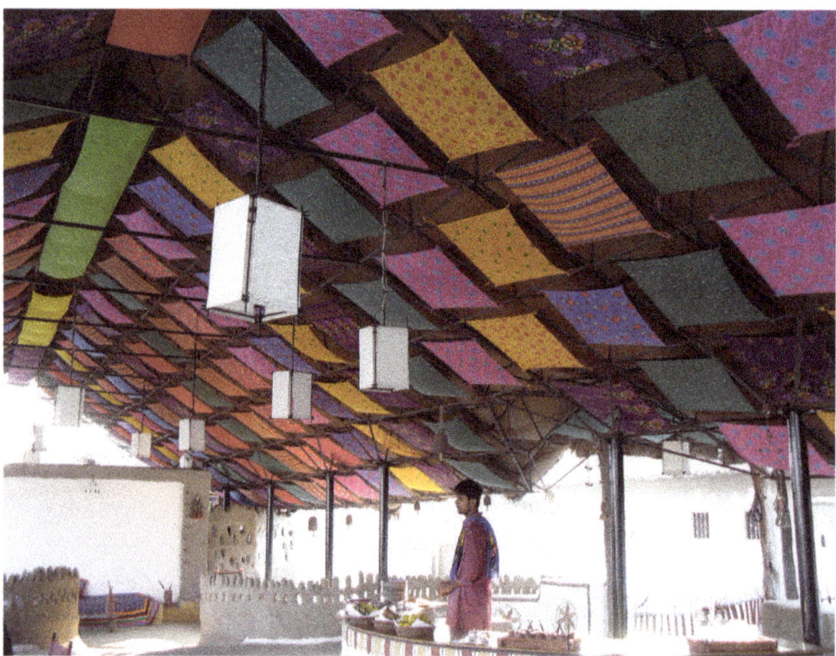

Shaam e Sarhad eco-village resort details

of whom had never met before, but had a background of common stories and ancestors. And it created bonds despite the distances we all live from one another.

Within months, my second group of 16 people would be coming on the Rajasthan/Gujarat trip. We were doing this slightly in reverse, starting in Bombay and flying directly to Bhuj. At the airport we were met by Judy Frater and learned that the bus to pick us all up had not arrived. I learned that Faith was no longer living in India and had taken her son to be educated in New Zealand. But her secretary at Indian Panorama had ordered a bus from another state and it was stuck at the border with a big backlog of buses and trucks trying to get through a check-point. In the meantime Judy contacted some friends and arranged for a few vehicles to take us to our accommodation. It actually took another day for the bus to get through. We did have an amazing time in Kutch and when travelling east toward Ahmedabad, stayed at a heritage mansion called a havelli with a Maharaja.

Then further north in Gujarat we stayed at the palace of another Maharaja. But the next morning I was embarrassed to learn we had depleted all their water tanks with long luxurious showers. Having lived only on rainwater in Australia for years, I knew how precious water is.

Two very special events happened there in Poshina. The first night we were invited to attend the local temple for a ceremony that only happens once a year. Special terracotta plaques of their special god are renewed or replaced with young men going to collect them from the potters village, quite a distance away. Originally they had to walk carrying them on their head, but now they go by Jeep. We arrived and found a large open ground with hundreds of worshipers in two circles holding hands, dancing and singing in response. The men were in the outside ring and women the inner ring. Each circle was moving in a different direction. But the Maharaja came and asked if I had gone into the temple yet. It

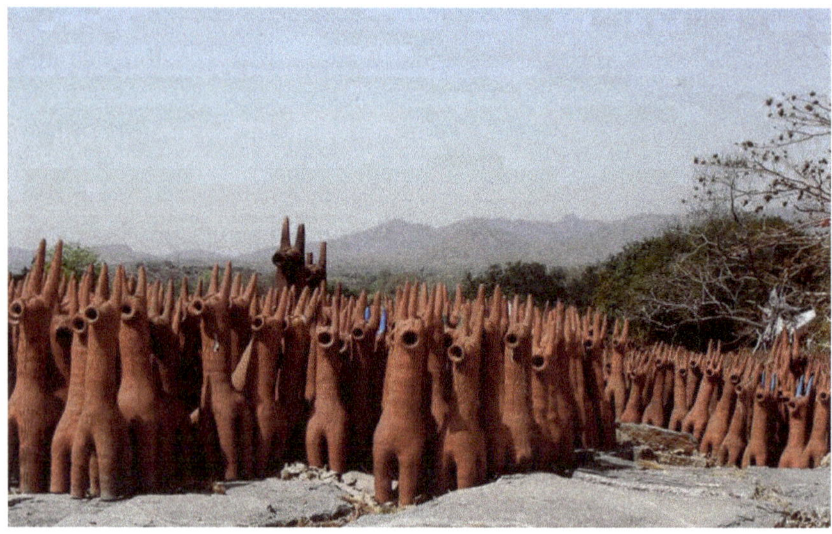

Votive terracotta horses in Poshina, Gujarat

was a small unassuming structure. Inside the priest was going into trance. Again we saw this fascinating occurrence of trance.

The next day we were given the opportunity to partake in a ceremony for our group offering a terracotta votive horse in an area with thousands of these horses of all sizes. This is a custom among the Adivasi community. We went to the potter and each bought a horse. The Maharaja then acquired some flowers and other items and we each had our own little ceremony. The offering is usually made with a request hoping to be filled. It was an uplifting experience.

SOBERING NEWS

I came home from India about the time Bob returned from the USA having gone for his stepmother Betty's funeral. Betty had been a lovely friend to me, but there was no way I could attend, as my group of 16 people were arriving in India for my tour. Bob stayed on with his brother Dan and his wife Nancy, helping to sort and pack Betty's things, which would be kept in Dan's barn. Bob had been doing a lot of lifting which resulted in his complaining about sciatica. At home, he tried to stretch out his leg to relieve the pain. Eventually he went to the back specialist and returned home to tell me he had cancer in his spine. Radiation combined with chemo was successful in fixing that spinal area, but the problem was that the cells had originated in the lungs. Nothing was found in the lung, but we were warned that it could send out other dangerous cells. It was explained that most people with the problem would have a life expectancy of 18 months. So we went away very much sobered.

But Bob started to feel like his old self and we got back to normal life. Although he had previously been required to retire when the magic number of 65 came up, CSIRO gave him an Honorary Research Fellowship, which meant he could continue doing the work he loved (without pay) and retain his office and computer. Well he had told me through the years that if they hadn't paid him to do the job, he would have paid them to be able to do it. So now, that was the situation, almost.

PARTY TIME

The girls had started early to think about organising a party for our 50th wedding anniversary because of Bob's bad health prognosis. Our real timing for the party should have been June 2010, but it seemed improbable to wait that long. Sam was recruited to design the invitation, and they were cleverly calling it a celebration of "50 Years in Love". It was going to be a chance to bring so many friends together from many walks of life.

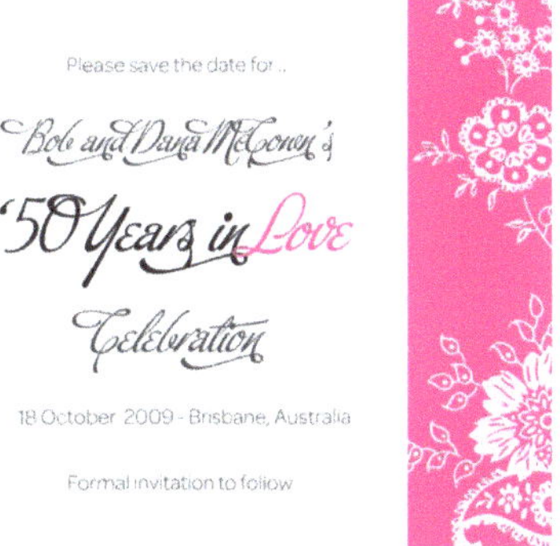

Date claimer invite

We had been to Sydney visiting Kathy and Brad Bitner and family as Brad was here from the USA doing a PhD. Kathy is cousin Ruth Ann's daughter and we have known her since she was small. A few days before our 50th celebration, they made the trip up to be here and have the chance to visit our homes, seeing a bit of Queensland. We decided to have a day with the children at Lone Pine Koala Sanctuary with Jess and Jenny, who had come up from Canberra. We were waiting in the ticket line and Bob got tapped on the shoulder with someone trying to get his attention. He turned around and was stunned to see his old college roommate standing there with his wife. Sam and Bev Minor had arrived and the girls arranged to have a surprise greeting there at the Koala park. We were really thrilled that they would come all the way from Pennsylvania for this occasion. It was a great reunion and eventually Sam told us about a time-share holiday unit in New Zealand they were then going to stay at. He invited us to share the holiday with them. It was all such a surprise and happy time. But in the meantime the party would be happening in a few days.

Paris was organised to entertain the Bitner boys during the party, as it could seem long with speeches for the three little ones who ranged in age from about three to five. She had a great collection of toys that were great for entertaining little boys. She did have some help from Conor, too.

The girls had outdone themselves, creating a party to remember as a happy time, full of laughter.

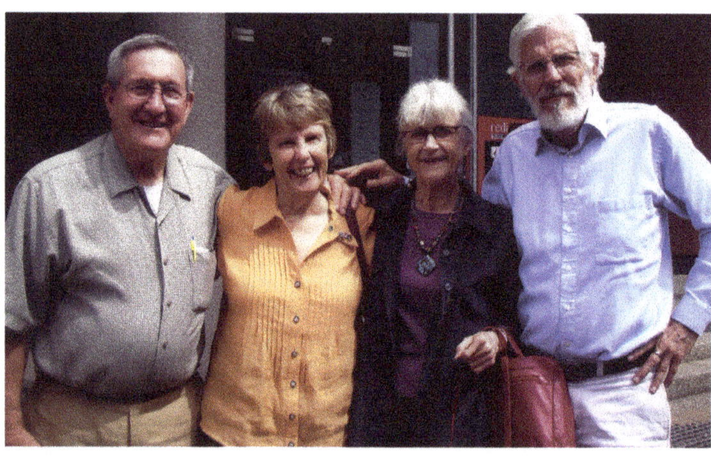

Sam, Bev, Dana and Bob

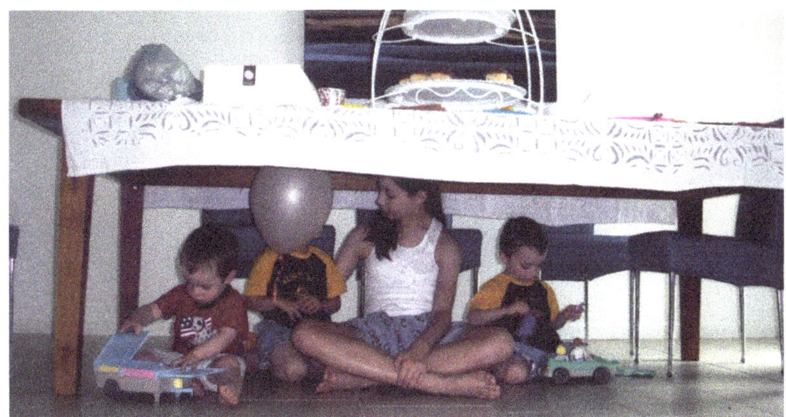

Paris with the Bitner kids

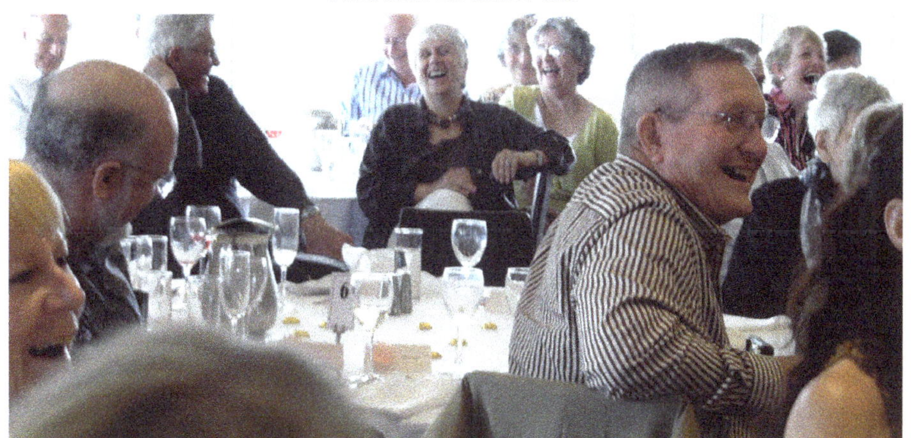

Laughter

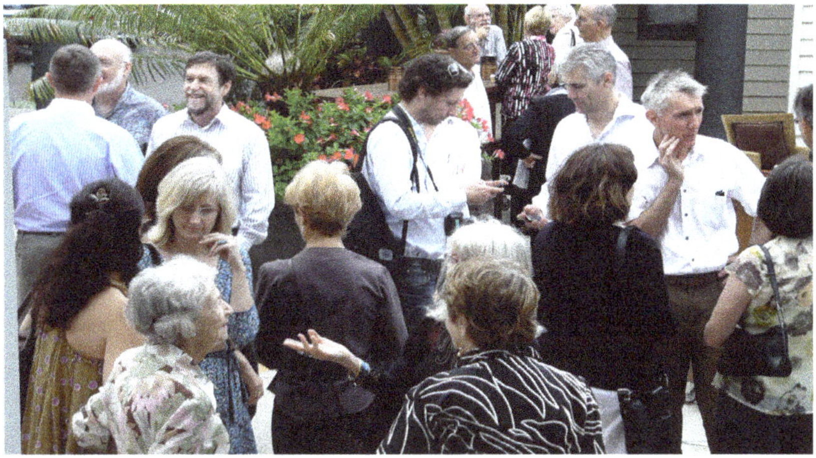

People had come from Townsville and much further

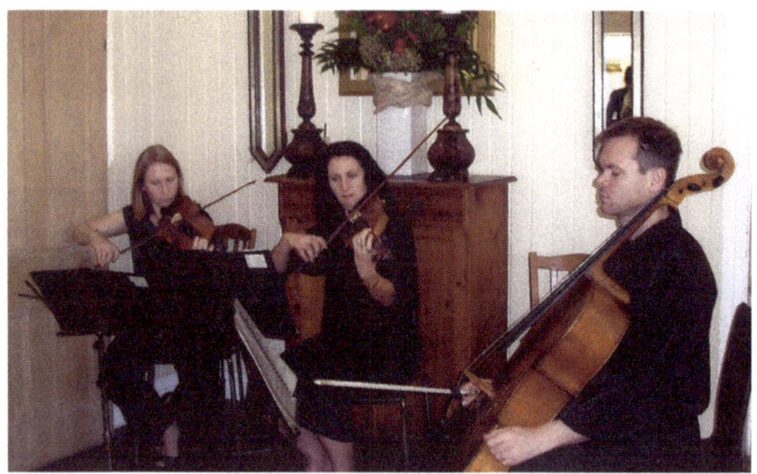

Musicians at "50 Years in Love"

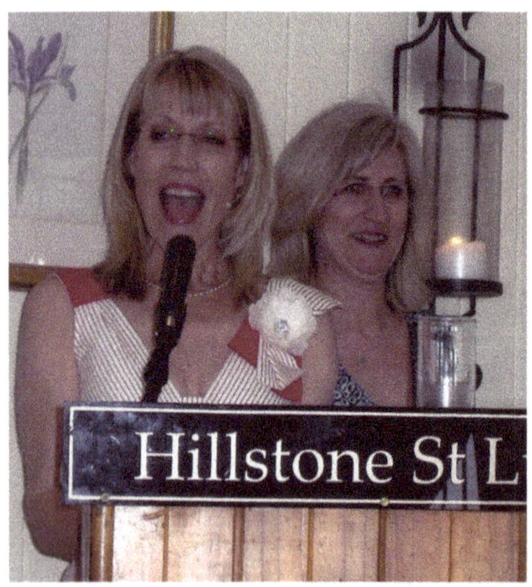

The daughters are telling stories on us

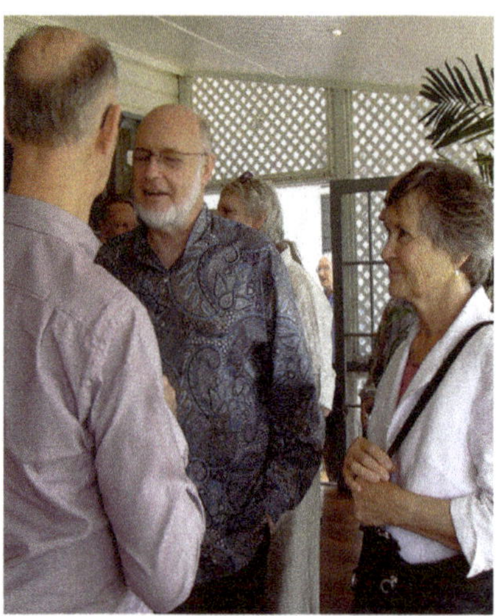

Paul, John and Ruth

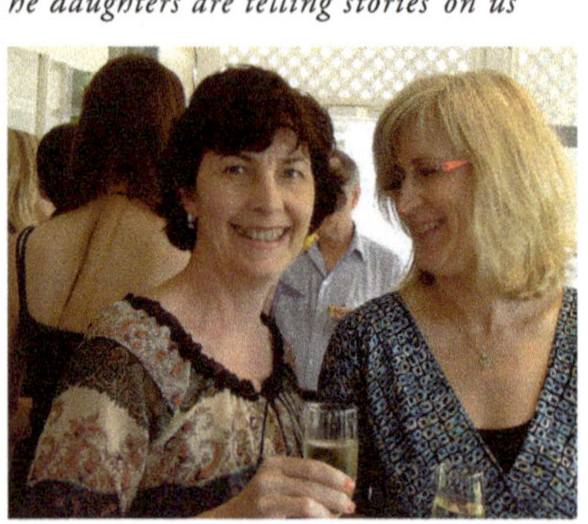

Nonie and Jenny

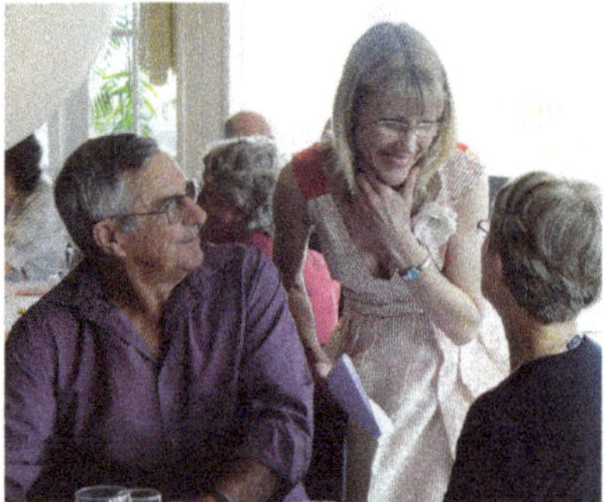

Jess with the Murthas

NEW ZEALAND WITH THE MINORS

Our trip to New Zealand came a few days after the party. We were based at Lake Taupo on the North Island which was central, enabling us to have day trips. We started off attending a Sunday morning church service and sat next to someone we talked to after the service. The man turned out to be a dairy farmer. Well, what could be more interesting for both Sam and Bob, who had been dairy majors at university. Although New Zealand is known as lamb country, in recent years dairy has taken over and produced an excellent income for those in the industry. We were invited to visit the dairy farm and home of our new friends and learned more of the special markets they have developed.

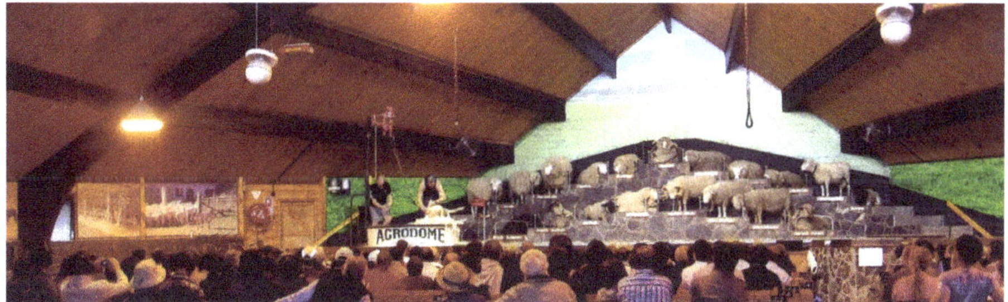

The Sheep Pavillion at Agrodome

We did enjoy a show featuring sheep in a special event facility. But we found it was almost impossible to find a lamb roast dinner on a menu of any restaurant.

When visiting New Zealand, there is the opportunity to visit the film sites where the "Hobbits" series of movies were filmed. We climbed up the hill and went into the house. Here is one actual film set prop that we saw.

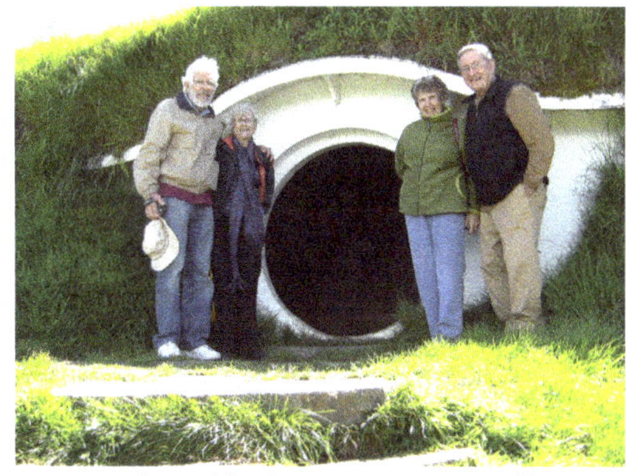

The Hobbit house was pretty small

The county is green and lush with beautiful vistas. This reminded me of the first trip taken to New Zealand in January 1978 when Bob's parents, Betty and Willard McCown, met us there for a holiday before they then came to Australia. We were there for 14 days and it rained for 12 of those days. We were feeling cold and damp, in spite of it being the middle of summer. But this holiday with the Minors had the perfect weather and plenty of time for the guys to reminisce.

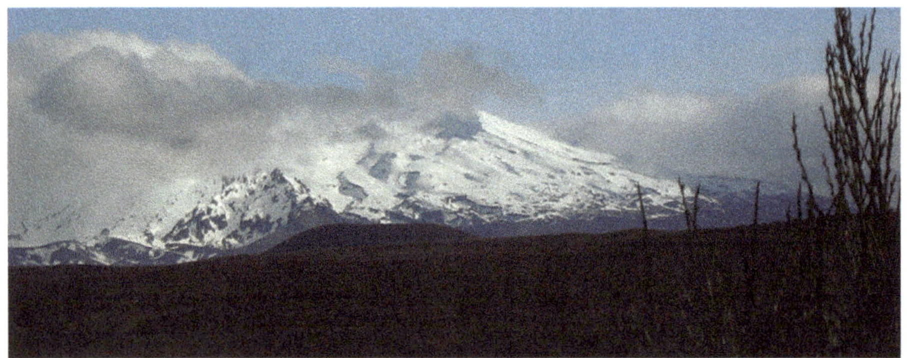

Scenic beauty as we drove along

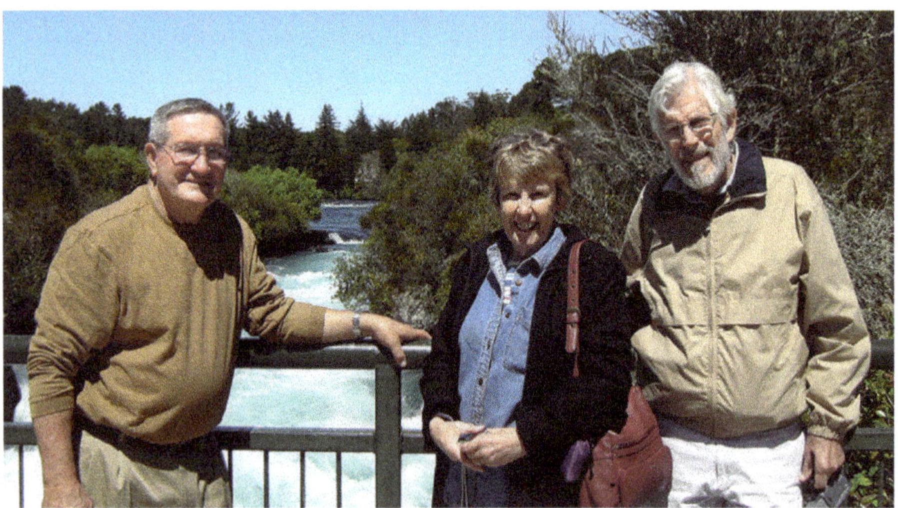

Enjoying the beauty of New Zealand

ASIAN ADVENTURES

Our grandson Sam had moved to China in 2010 and set up a design business there in Beijing and invited us to visit. Bob and I went with Jenny and her family and found a traditional courtyard home to rent in the Hutong district. The visit had been great, seeing the art districts, parks with groups of people exercising, antique markets, monuments and wonderful restaurants. And most of all, we had special time with Sam and could see how he lived and worked. I had remembered all the bicycles on the roads in 1987 when I first visited China and was surprised that they had been replaced by cars in large numbers.

We decided to take the train and go further out to see Xian and the Terracotta Army. And I did get my bicycle ride in Xian, riding around on top of the city wall.

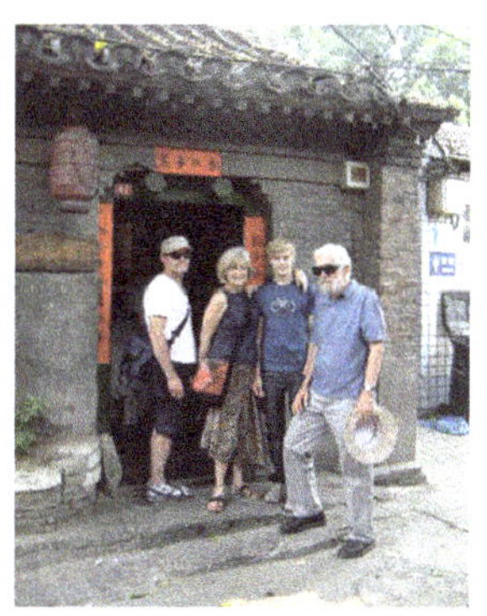

Hutong doorway

Jordan started asking us when we were going to visit him in Japan, as he had taken his business there. We thought we had better do so, and enlarged the group to include, Jess, David, Paris, Maddie and Sam. We found a date when all could go and booked

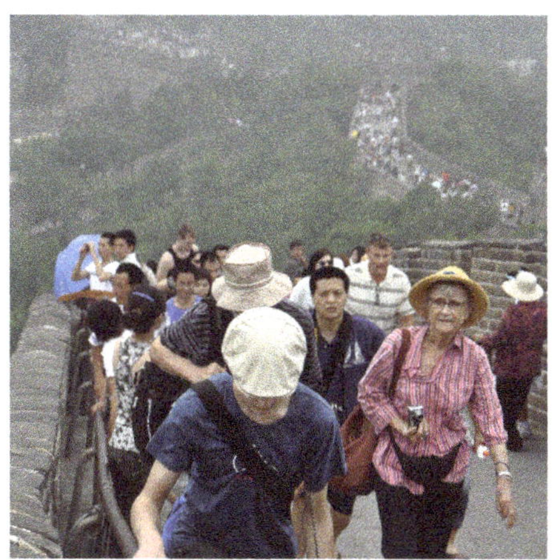

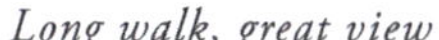

Long walk, great view

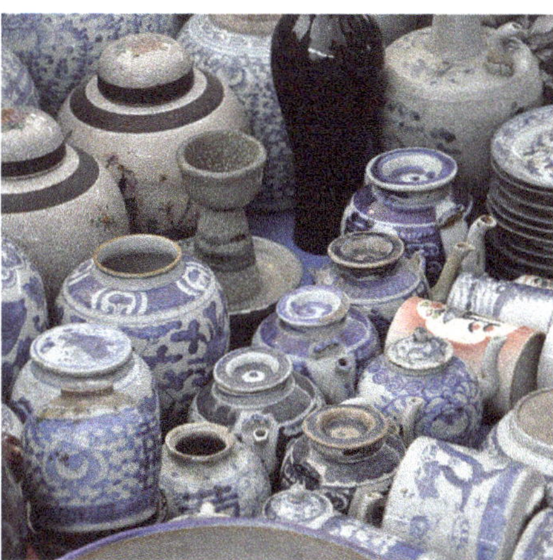

Antique porcelain

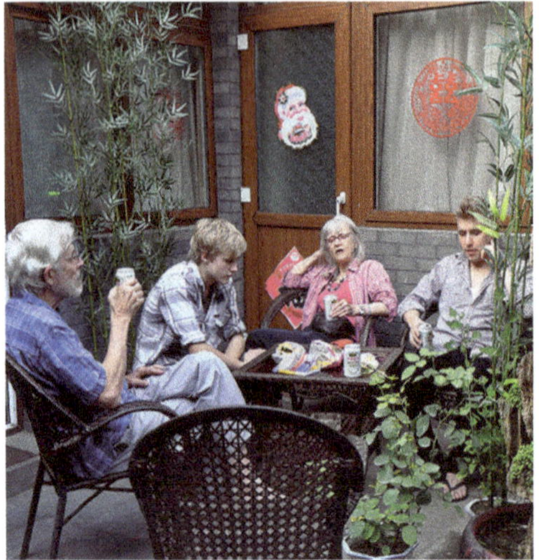

All tired from the long walk

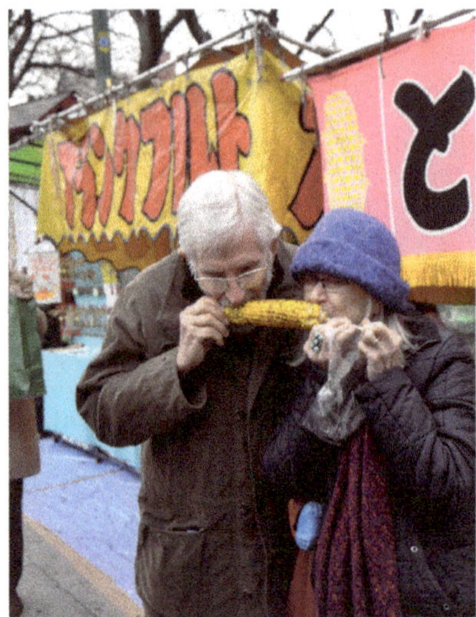

Sharing an ear of corn

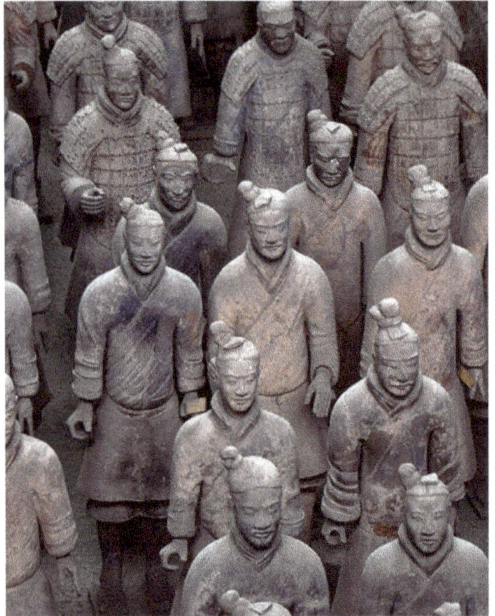

Xian and the Terracotta Army

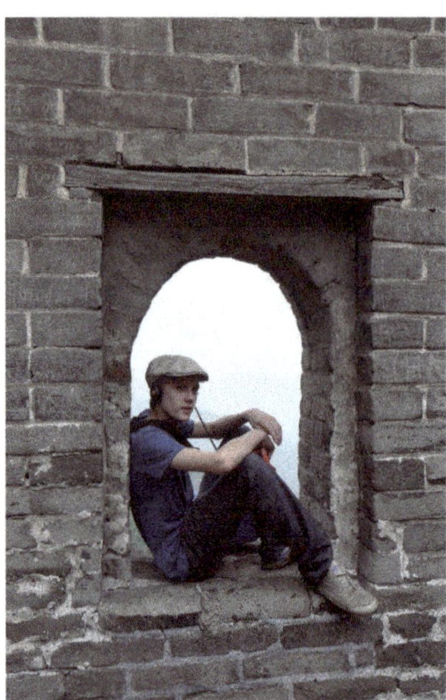

Conor found a great lookout

the trip. We would spend time in Tokyo where Jordan lived but also take the fast train out to Kyoto, which I loved because of all the textiles, but it also had much to offer of historic interest. This all took time to work out details and find a time when all were available. We touched base again with Jordan giving arrival dates and other information. He got back with us quickly and said he had taken a job at the Gold Coast, Queensland and would not be there. He couldn't understand how we wouldn't want to go to Japan anyway and have a great trip. Well we did go and did have a great trip. But I took our group picture at the Golden Temple and photo-shopped him into the picture for a coffee mug I had printed when we got home.

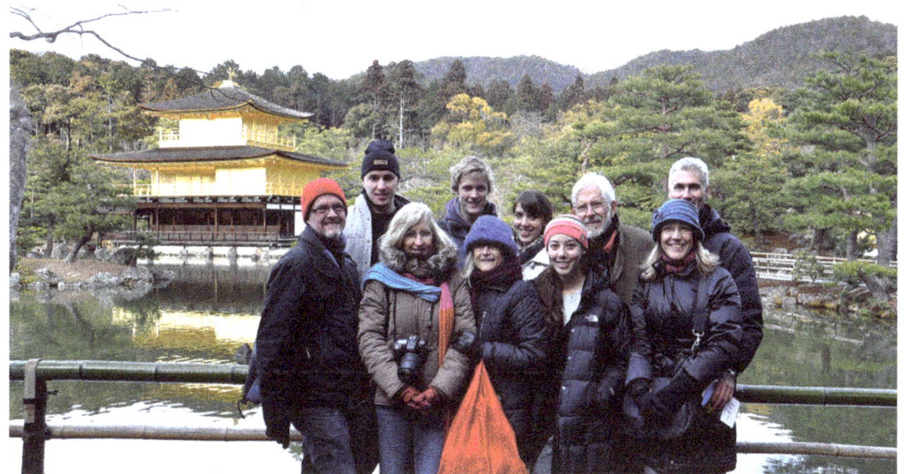

The Golden Temple, Kyoto

On the morning that we were to fly to Japan from Brisbane, there was a big flood starting in Toowoomba, coming down the range, washing out houses in the Grantham district and joining with a large volume of water from the Wivenhoe Dam to do a lot of damage along the way. I had a hair appointment in Toowoomba that Monday morning, but our creek had started to rise Sunday and we were afraid we wouldn't be able to get out for our flight. So we went to Brisbane on the Sunday night. As it turned out my hairdresser shop, Shim Sharee, got floodwater coming in the back door, pushing furniture to the front window, and water coming from the front pushing in so that the front door couldn't be opened. Help had to come to let them out. People did lose their life in Toowoomba and down the range.

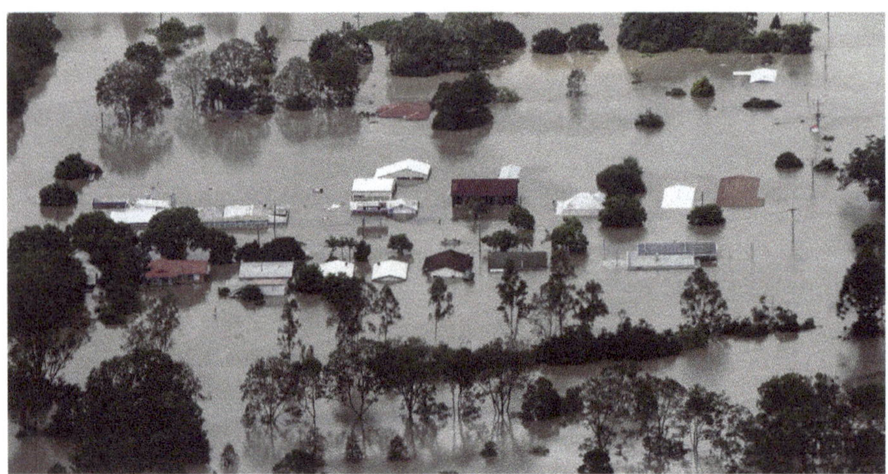

Photo compliments Chinchilla News

When we arrived in Tokyo, we watched the news of Brisbane in flood on the television.

A highlight was going to a Sumo wrestling event, and learning more about the rules and strategies. Although we missed the fish auction which is an exciting event, we did attend the melon auction and discovered how very expensive melons are. We got a hint afterward from the judge how we could get a special melon at a

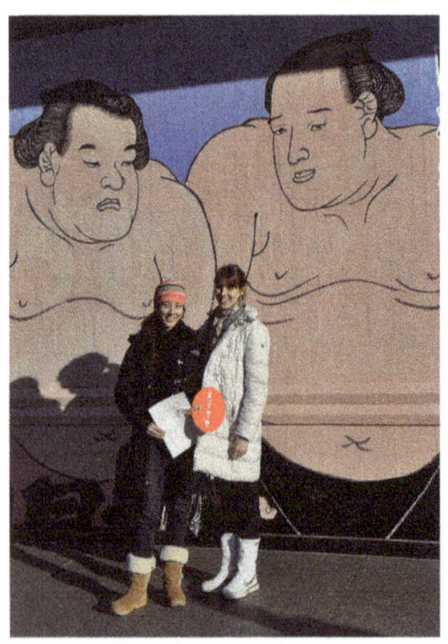

Ready to see the competition

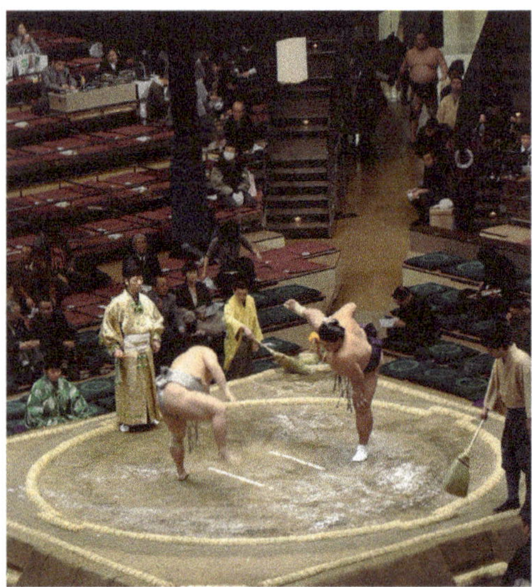

Sumo action

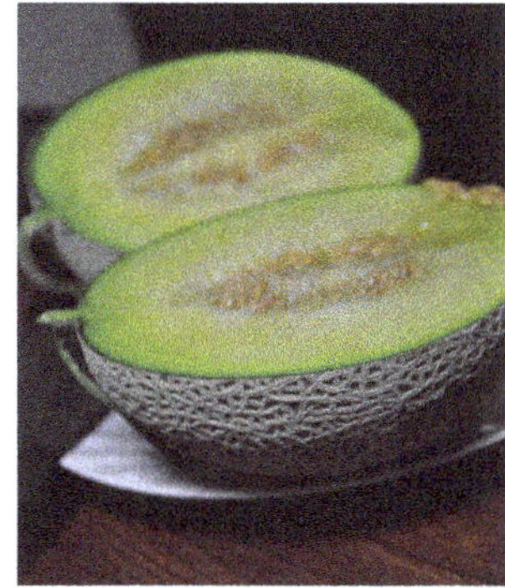

Superior taste

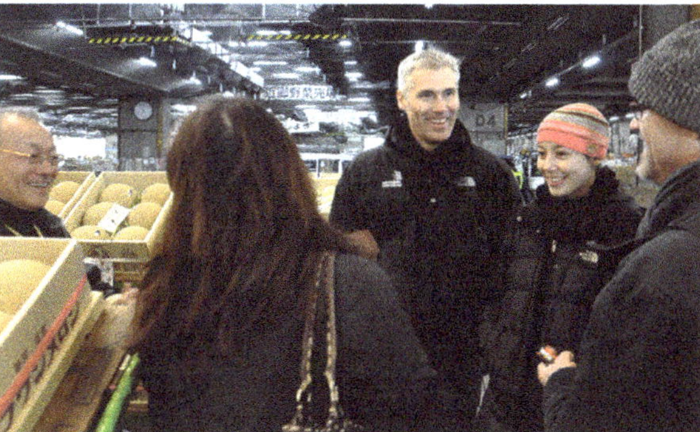

Talking to the expert judge

much reduced price. Appearance is everything, especially the webbing design on the outside. So we were directed to a fruit shop where the rejects could be found and all shared tasting the special melon and all agreed it was delicious. On the bullet train, headed to Kyoto, we passed Mt Fuji and could see the snow capped peak. We did indulge in some textile experience, and everyone thought it was interesting. Visiting a park, we found a large display of ice sculpture. Considering the outside temperature, they were going to be long-lasting.

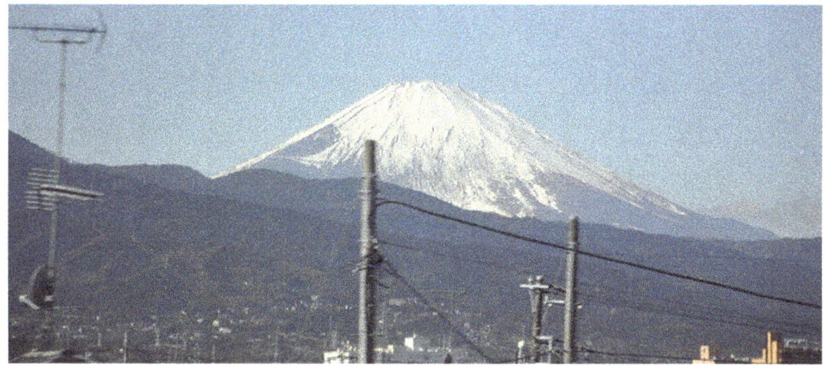

From the Bullet train

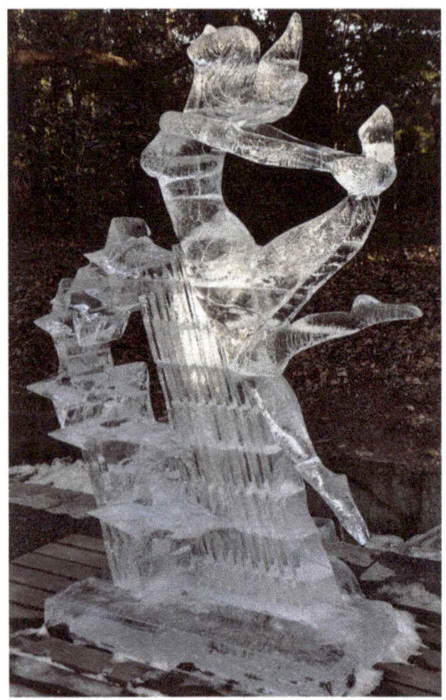

Ice sculpture park

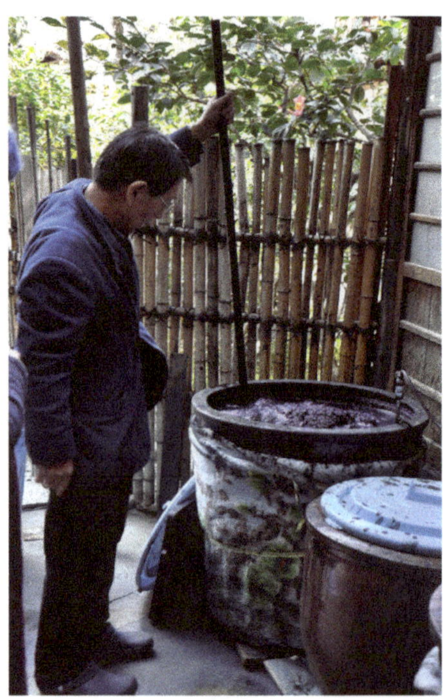

Indigo dyer, Kyoto

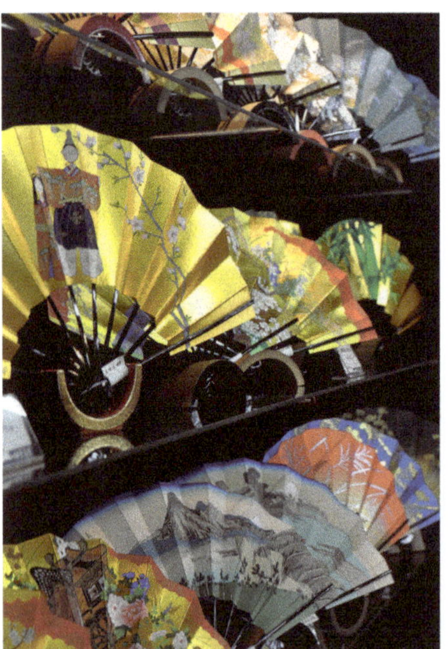

Exquisite Japanese fans

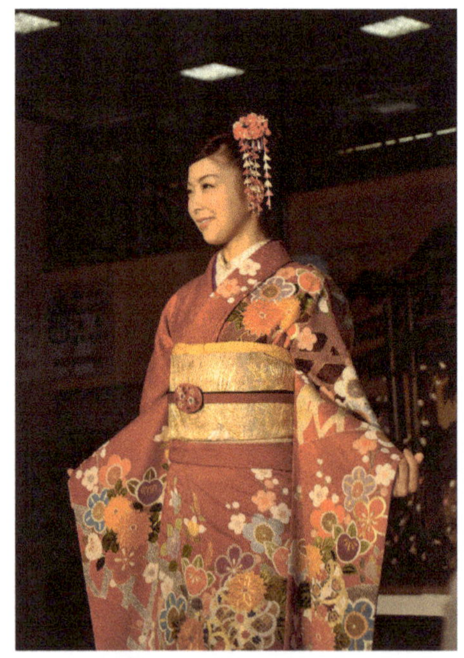

Kimono fashion parade

07

It's Time

TIME FOR NEW DIRECTIONS IN 2011

Returning home from Japan in 2011, we could see that our creek banks had been damaged with slippage from so much water. We had previously, after moving in, started a large regeneration project with native plants appropriate for the area to hold the creek banks as there had been some slippage. We put in dripper lines and thousands of small tube stock, with the help of Jim, our handy gardener and handy man. Bob woke up one morning and rolled over and said to me, "I think it's time - time to move to Brisbane." He felt he could not face tackling the natural phenomenon of our environmental problem. Besides that, the girls had been suggesting to us for years we should move and be closer to them and also closer to Bob's medical team. Although Bob had received a bad prognosis, all further testing had indicated he was in remission and he was living his life free of problems.

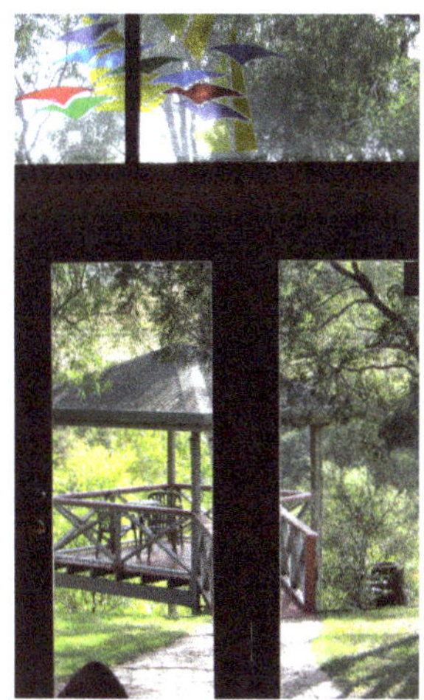

View out to gazebo

I had reservations about leaving our lovely home that we had renovated to include special features we loved. But realistically I knew it was the right decision and would have many benefits. Within days we went on an exploratory trip to Brisbane investigating the market. An apartment or town house seemed like a good way to go, limiting upkeep. I did find a house that all the furniture would fit in well, but the rest of the family vetoed it because of a pool and upkeep. So then I looked at new West End apartments and found them so small without many walls to hang paintings. Driving back to East Brisbane where the girls lived, I passed a sign, "Kangaroo Point," and thought another time I would look there. And back we went to Toowoomba.

As I was a member of Arts Council Toowoomba as their treasurer, our committee was brainstorming about a significant project we would organise to address what the flood had done in Toowoomba. After looking at the idea of sculptures on the footpaths and finding out all the legal rulings and restrictions, I received a photo from cousin Marcia McCowin showing mosaic work done in San Francisco where she lived. The possibility of using mosaic seemed ideal and had limited dangerous elements to consider. In the end, 10 businesses were invited to become involved and receive a mosaic panel near their entrance relating to the experience they had with the flood. And ten artists were chosen after doing workshops with an expert to design a panel for a specific business.

Someone then came up with the idea of videoing the stories to have on our website which I was managing at the time, both from the artists point of view and from the shopkeepers. To incorporate this into the mosaic panel, QR codes were baked on tiles to be part of the work. A person could come along and use a smart phone by scanning the QR code, to listen to the stories while standing in the street facing the store. I will always remember the great gals that worked on these projects with creative ideas like Jennifer Summers, Kim Beasley and Mary-Kate Thompson, in whose

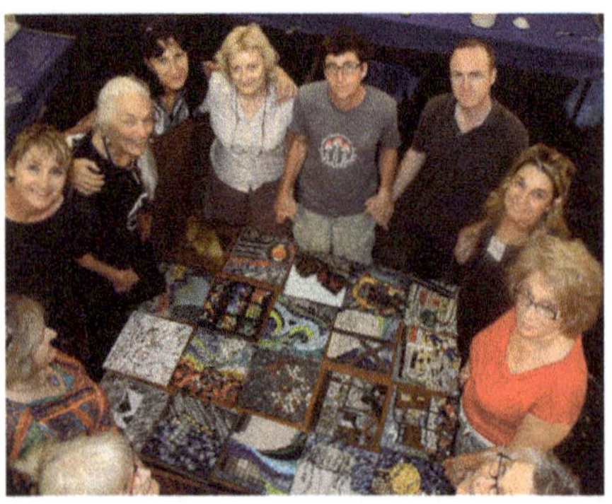

Workshop sample tiles

home we met and planned. I would miss the good times. When I had to farewell the ACT group, I was surprised by being given an award called "The First Inaugral ACTer's Award". It has pride of place in my office.

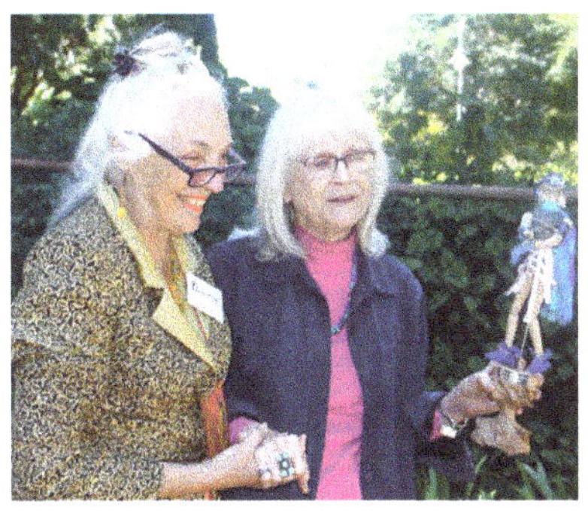

Jennifer Summers presents the award

Meanwhile Jenny called me up one morning while we are having breakfast and said we had to come today to see an apartment in Kangaroo Point. I said we were coming on Saturday and had many things on at home to address. She didn't like that, but we persisted and did wait until Saturday. Jessie and Jenny had done their homework, trying to check out road traffic sound, by sitting around in spots at peak hour time, listening morning and evening. They had a list of six open houses they wanted us to see. In actual fact, we were just trying to get a feel for the market and were not ready to commit to anything. We had made no attempt to get our Toowoomba home ready for sale. We started looking at a town house, which had stairs as it had two floors. Bob was much against that as he said, *"Dana will break her neck on these stairs, as she runs everywhere."* So we worked our way down the list. Some apartments had no view or a bad view.

The last apartment on the list was at Bridgewater River Terraces. The layout from the front door was not ideal, but we went on out through the lounge area and sat on the balcony looking at the river framed by Jacaranda trees. We could see the gardens and yards below, as this apartment was one level up. Coming up to the entrance we had seen extensive gardens that went along to a lagoon pool and gym. We sat there and Bob said to me, "*Let's take it.*" I was shocked, as I didn't

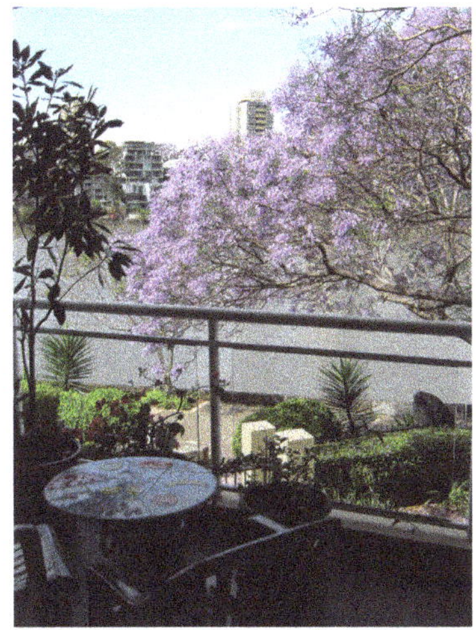

The view which sold us the unit

think we were anywhere near ready to move ahead. But, yes we signed a contract with three months settlement as we hoped it would give us time to sell our home. We didn't even look at the basement garage because we were so stunned with the view from the balcony. Later we learned the garage had filled up to within one foot of the ceiling with water during the flood. What entered the garage was storm water back-flowing from the river up the pipes.

Back in Toowoomba there was painting to do and downsizing of so much stuff that wouldn't fit in the three-bedroom apartment with limited storage. I had a cleaning team of three women who came in once a fortnight and were out again within the hour. Those women took a truckload of furniture away. Bob's ute came in handy as I took a ute load of books to the Middle Ridge Uniting Church book sale and a ute load of yarns to Spinner and Weavers and a quilting frame to the Quilters Group. Bob had the biggest job of disposal yet, as he still had about 10 or 12 horsedrawn vehicles to find homes for. And then it was his blacksmith shop and wheelwright gear. He had spent years gathering this collections and it must have been sad for him to see it disperse. He even had a collection of cabinet timber for restoration of vehicles. In earlier years when his parents and Mary Irene and Ed McCown, his aunt and uncle, came to visit they all had to bring some hickory spokes for restoring wheels for the horsedrawn vehicles. Usually the airlines from USA allowed two bags a person. The spokes had been ordered and made by Amish craftsmen for work during the winter when farming was in abeyance. So there were still many of the spokes that had not been used yet. Luckily Bob had a friend who was a skilled craftsman and doing similar work who benefited by receiving some of the gear.

Selling of our beautiful property took longer that we expected. Open houses were held with no one attending. One day two families arrived at the same time, both with young boys who ran out to the gazebo that sat on the edge of the ravine. One boy noticed a large boa constrictor type of snake curled up around the rafters and ceiling fan of the gazebo and thought this was wonderful. The real estate woman was scared and backed away, trying to get the families to come inside to see the home. She had a hard time tearing them away from the attraction of some wildlife. Both families were interested and one bought, finalizing just before our date to purchase the apartment arrived, thanks to the snake.

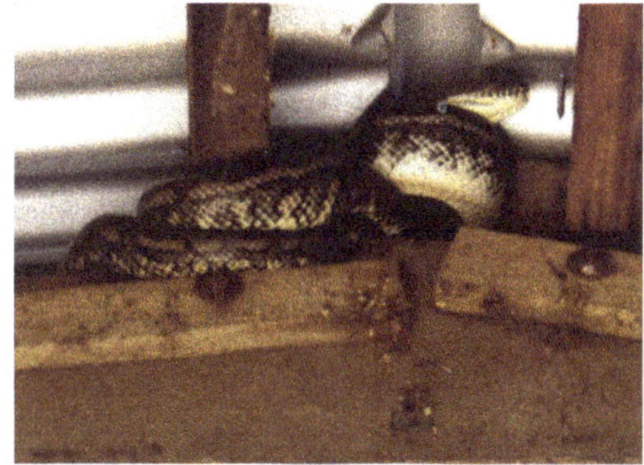

That little snake

Before we actually took possession of our new Brisbane home, Bob's cousin Ruth Ann and husband John came to visit along with daughters Jenny Mansell, Kathy Bitner, and family. We could bring them to see the apartment complex.

Moving day was exciting, seeing how things looked in their new setting. Some items just wouldn't fit and so David Butt loaded them on Bob's ute and delivered them to the local community thrift shop. It wasn't long before I was contacted and asked to attend a Body Corporate meeting. I had always like committee work and being a part of our complex seemed a good way of knowing what was going on.

There was a BBQ coming up for the committees of those buildings. That is how I met Kay and David Rees. Kay told me about an organisation she had joined when coming from overseas as a new resident. She said that she instantly had 60 new friends many of them having lived overseas. It seems like something I could be interested in joining. Her group, Brisbane Ionians, is a women friendship group for new people to an area, to make friends and join in activities. The main monthly meeting involves a lunch and meeting, followed by a speaker. Then there are activities through the month of interest groups. So I did join and eventually became a committee member. And Bob joined the group called Mates (husbands of Ionians), that had a lunch meeting the same day we women were meeting. And those men who offered him rides in the carpool were kind and caring when Bob needed extra help due to his health problems.

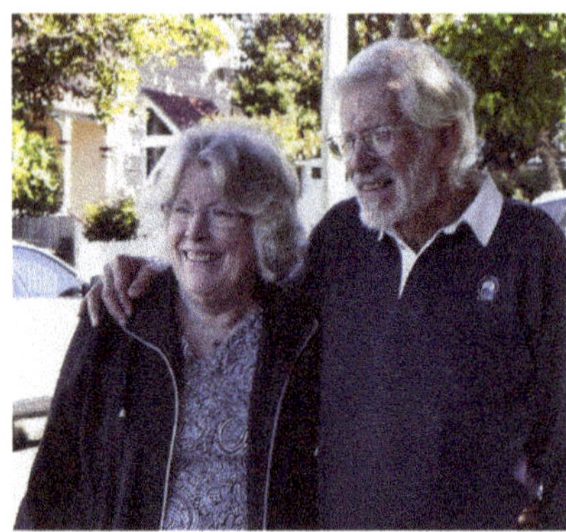

Ruth Ann Mansell and Bob

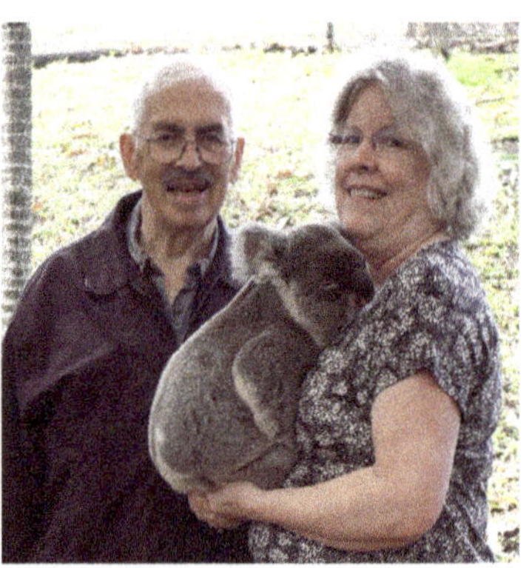

John and Ruth Ann at Lone Pine

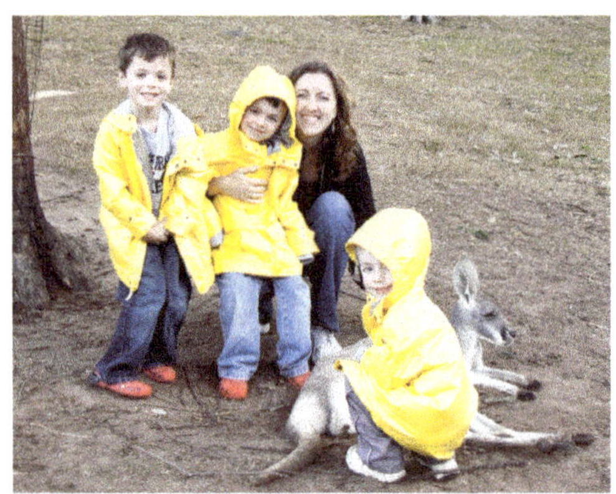

Jenni Mansell and the Bitner boys

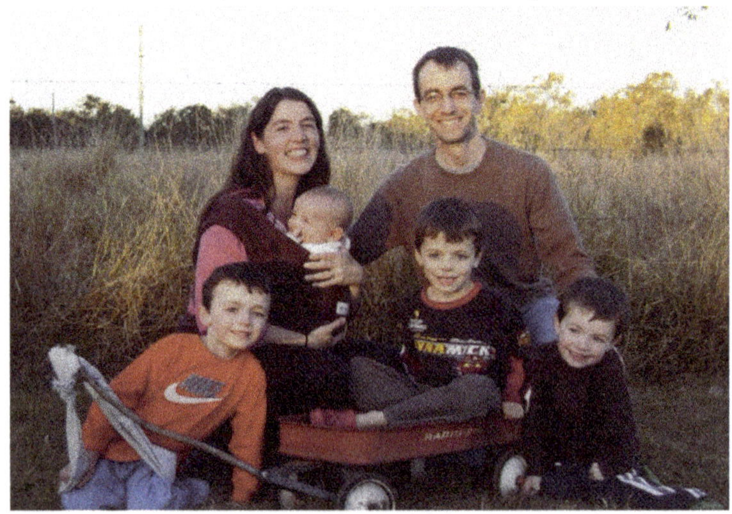

The Bitner Family

A SET-BACK

Meanwhile I had my activities with the Queensland Spinners and Weavers attending their Experimental Dye Group. I had shipped various Indian dye stuffs from Hyderabad when Bob withdrew from project work. I had been selling these to textile people and was down in the garage weighing up some product. When I came upstairs Bob said someone had called and he told them I was in the basement doing Bonsai. I thought this was rather strange. He continued to say some things that were not usual the next day and I suggested he should see the doctor. To make a long story short, an x-ray was suggested and Bob was found to have a brain tumour. Needless to say, we were directed to a specialist brain surgeon and Bob underwent the knife, but then month-long full-brain radiation was scheduled without much opportunity to take a different path. At times following, I regretted that had happened, but writing this I still wonder in amazement at the great trips and experiences we were able to have in spite of his balance problems and am thankful.

We set up our apartment with an office for each of us, which meant we really didn't have a guest room. Bob's office had many filing cabinets, a desk that had been David Hoey's as a student and many bookshelves. One of the precious books Bob unwrapped to show me was a civil war diary written by his great uncle Robert Smiley Dunnan. It was written in pencil. We started to take time to copy the text, some of which was smudged and hard to read. Bob took it over one day to show Jenny's family and David Butt said he would help transcribe it, so Bob left it with him. Before long he contacted Bob saying, *"I think I've got a book here"*. He had started adding footnotes and bringing in the history of the times. So the book had the diary pages together with stories surrounding it. Many pictures were searched in archives.

I had decided to set up a publishing company called "StoryBridge Press" using a digital on-demand printing company to produce hard copies. We had started being interested in publishing when our friend John Tothill had a stroke. He had

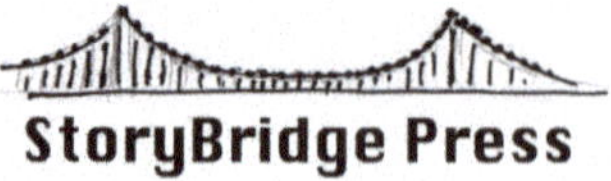

been trying to get his uncle's Tottie book republished. The original book was out of print and the publishing house in England had been bombed during the war, losing all the files. Then John's aunt combined those stories with her version of events. But the typing was done on oilskin paper with an ancient typewriter of defective keys. It was impossible to scan it to recapture a digital file. Therefore Bob bought the software, "Dragon, Speaking Naturally", and read the entire book into his computer. I then did editing and we were able to get it printed and available in a hard cover version before John died. The new version also included paintings by John's uncle that I had photographed, as he was a talented artist as well as being a medical doctor.

David's book was published and went online with Amazon, in 2013. Sam did the finishing touches by creating a great design for the cover. Bob was interested in doing some further work on a video, replicating the actual trip taken by Robert Dunnan when he joined the army, showing animated trains moving across a map with photos and other real footage from the museum at Gettysburg. He entitled it "Robert's Journey". We joined Apple's program called "One to One" and enjoyed taking the bus into the city which stopped right in from of the Apple store. We were able to book appointments with experts to help achieve the new ideas that Bob would think up. Although Bob lost many of the skills on the computer due to memory problem, he never lost his ability to think creatively. He would wake up at night having had another good idea. They said they always enjoyed the task of working through the challenging problems Bob brought them. Some weeks Bob wanted to go to "One to One" two or three times. How sad

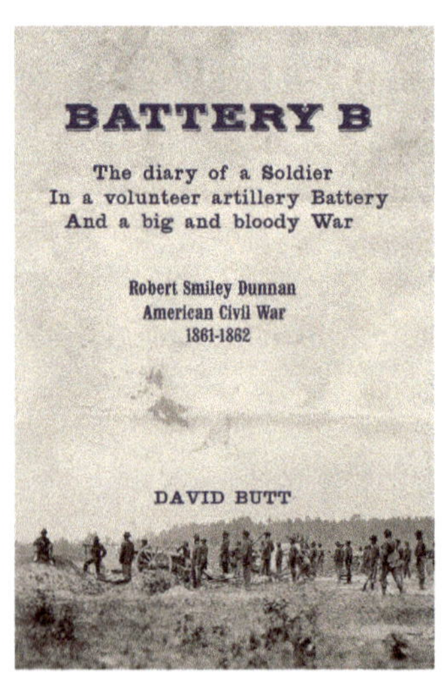

Book cover

when they finally discontinued the program. As a final touch we needed a voice-over for the diary and hired an actor from Hollywood through an online company called "Fiverr" which offered small tasks for $5. What a great find!

Bob decided he really wanted to take that trip that Robert made starting in Western Pennsylvania. His cousin Ruth Ann loved the idea, so she and husband John provided a car and joined us for the adventure. Part of the idea would be to actually do some marketing for David's book. We were successful in Western Pennsylvania at the Historical Society in New Castle, and we provided them with books. All the soldiers in the book which was entitled "Battery B: the diary of a soldier in a volunteer artillery Battery and a big and bloody War," came from the area, so it was a logical place to market it. However on our travels to Gettysburg and the Virginia battlefields, there were hundreds of books about the Civil War, so we had no luck getting the book into those venues. But we did get to the Glendale Military Cemetery and saw Robert's head stone. And we were graciously hosted in Spotsylvania by the Schuneman's, old friends of the Mansells at a location of the battle of Fredericksburg that happened down their street. We were living the adventure.

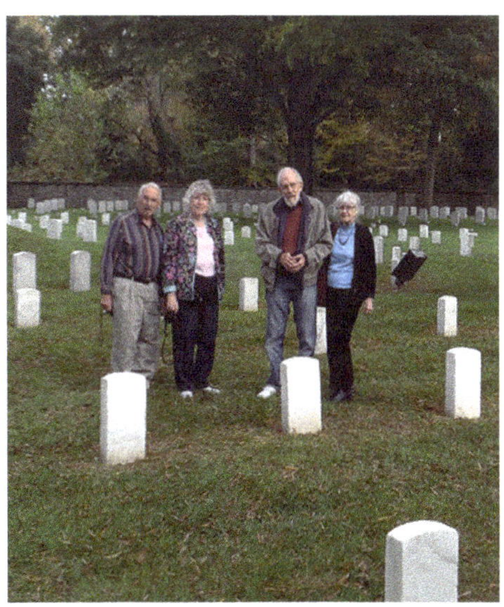

John, Ruth Ann, Bob and I at Glendale

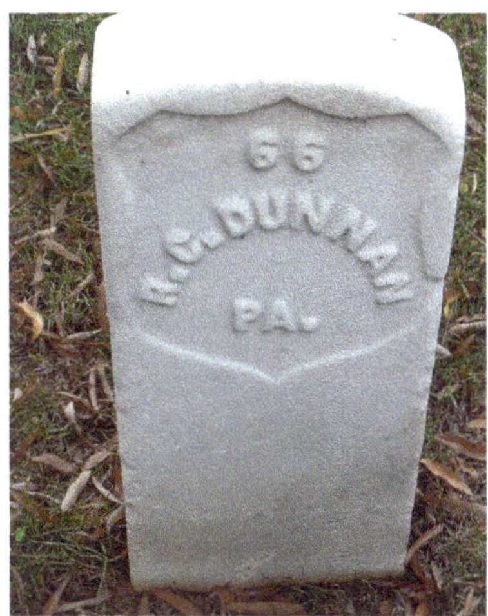

Robert's headstone with wrong middle initial

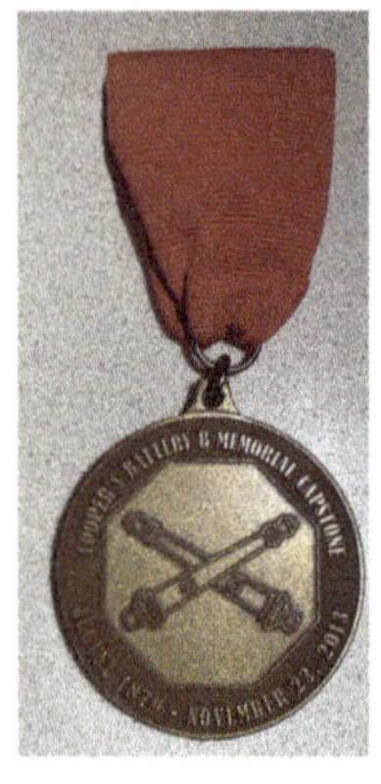

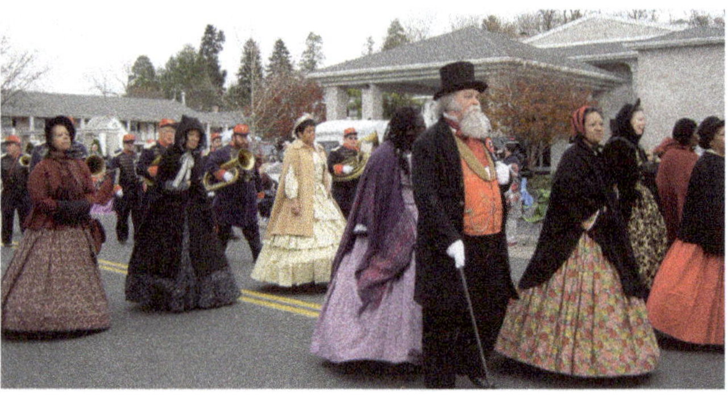

150th Anniversary Parade

GETTYSBURG

Bob and I decided to take an additional Civil War trip to the famous battle field of Gettysburg as it was the 150 year celebrations of the war ending. Dan and Nancy lent us a vehicle and off we went. We were able to meet up with Bob's cousin Jerry and his wife Erma Jean on one of the days. I don't think I had seen them since our wedding day over 50 years before. Their son John and family lived close by, so we met their family for the first time. We hired Gar Phillips, an expert guide and spent a full day being taken on the whole adventure.

But there was a special ceremony commemorating the placement of a new capstone on the monument in honor of Battery B, the unit which Bob's uncle had been in. Bob was given one of the commemorative medals marking the occasion. It was organised by the Western Pennsylvanian Battery B group and Judy Foster had an important role in the ceremony. On the way back to Dan's we stopped in Washingon, D.C. and the Smithsonian for more history.

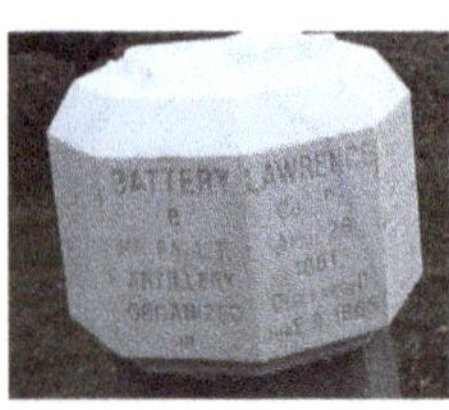

The new capstone

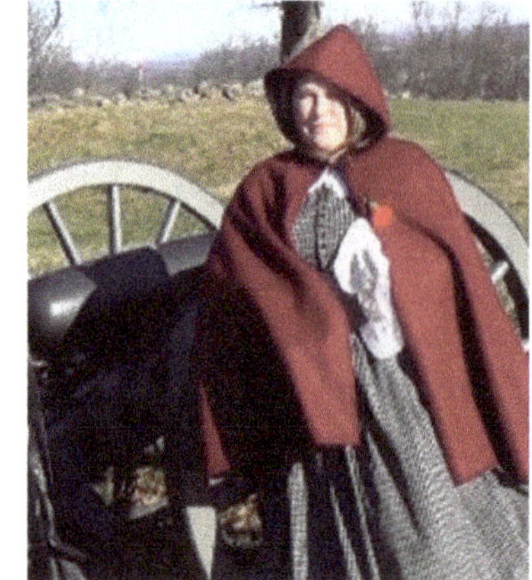

Judy Foster at the dedication ceremony

GRANDCHILDREN AND INDIA 2014

I started to think about the remaining grandchildren and the trip with me to India. Maddie had turned 21 year the previous year and had not had the time to get away. Thinking about Conor being younger and not turning 21 until I would be over 80, I started to think "*Who would want to go to India with their grandmother when she is in her 80s*"? So I thought that I had better wrap up the trip, taking all three of the grandchildren together. We left for a three-week trip to South India. For the first time, I did not organise all the details, but we selected an "Intrepid" trip with a small group of 12 total. My daughters thought that having other people with us could be a benefit, so everything would not depend on me. We did meet some fun people and there was a range of ages. Afterward we added on four days in Sri Lanka, seeing places our family had visited 45 years ago. It was an opportunity to have quality time together. Meanwhile Bob was holidaying at the Hoey's.

Jenny had worried about Conor and his severe nut allergy. Much cooking in India includes nuts. She had small cards printed in several Indian languages stating that Conor had a nut allergy. In addition she felt she had to send food for the trip. There are some nice products in single servings that she packed in his backpack. Part of the problem was going to be getting the food through security onto the plane. The initial problem started at Brisbane airport, but eventually it was allowed. Conor did show his card with allergy notice to eating-places and carried an EpiPen to be injected in emergency. We actually had several that could be used in

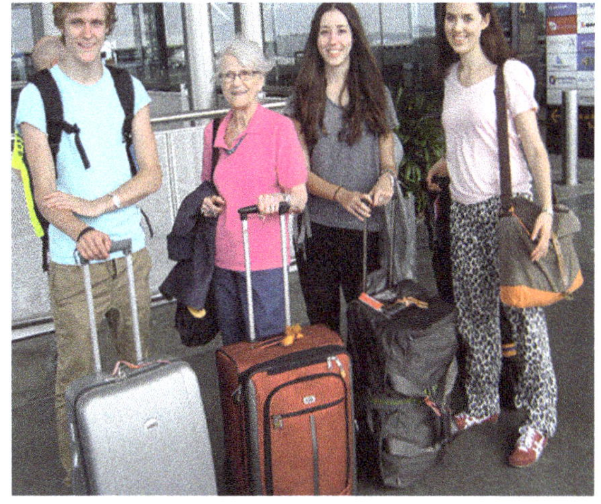

Ready for departure

case of an attack. In the end, the only time those food parcels were eaten was on a long train trip and we all shared Conor's supply.

Conor had just completed grade 12 and had attended "Schoolies" on the Gold Coast, a tradition of high school graduates. My friend Betty Tudberry belongs to an organization called "Red Frogs" who go as volunteers to "Schoolies" to try to keep it a safe environment for the young people, patrolling the beaches and visiting the hotel rooms to make sure people are ok. These young people are feeling liberated from study and celebrating and letting loose. So Conor had just come from that environment and was enjoying the freedom of meeting new people. But instead of Conor having a holiday with his grandmother and cousins, it was a bit like having a holiday with three grandmothers to begin with. It is true he did some smoking, which no one with asthma should attempt. And he did have a bottle of beer. But several years later on a visit to Dr Larsen, he was asked if he smoked. Conor replied, *"Not really, only with my grandmother." I*n the next few months, Conor would be starting at Queensland University studying business and marketing, Then all three of these grandchildren would be in Uni.

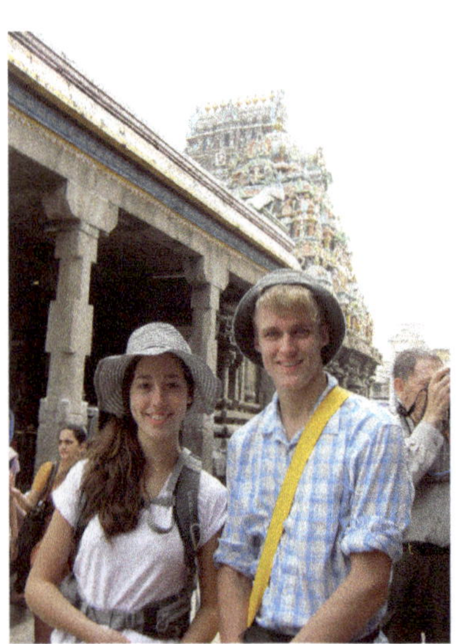

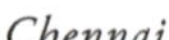

Chennai

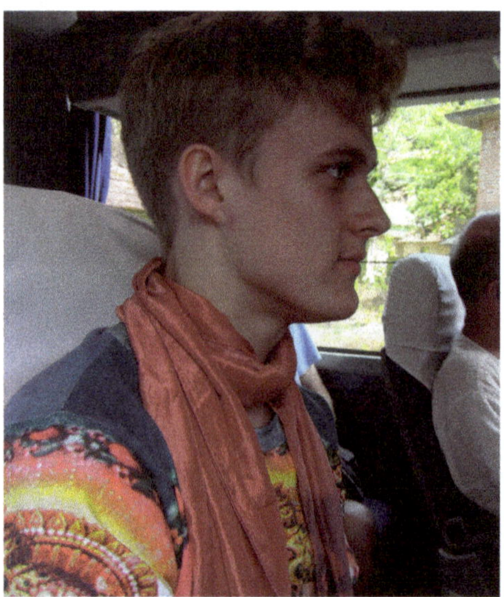

Conor and his Ganesh shirt

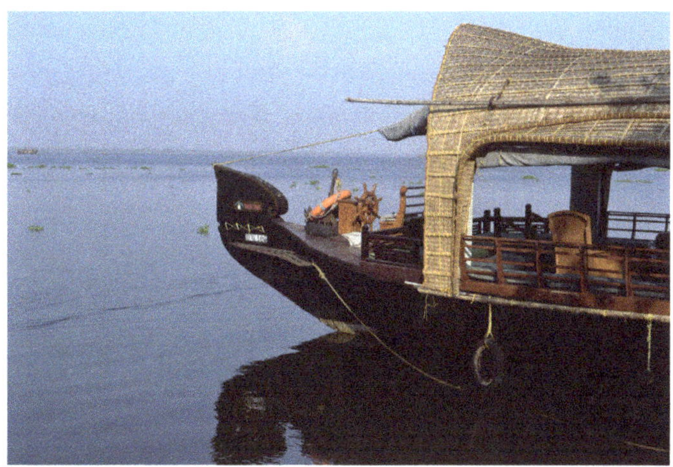

Our canal boat in Kerala

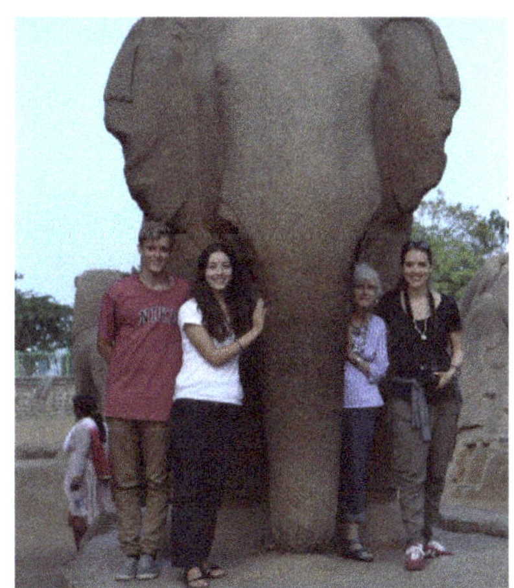

Mamallapurum monolithic elephant

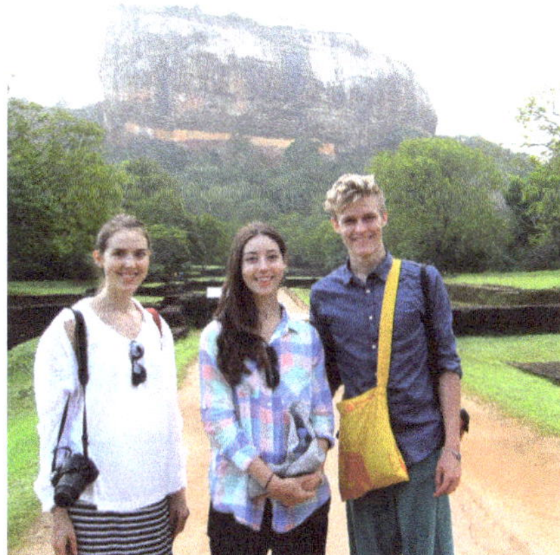

Sigiriya Fortress in the background

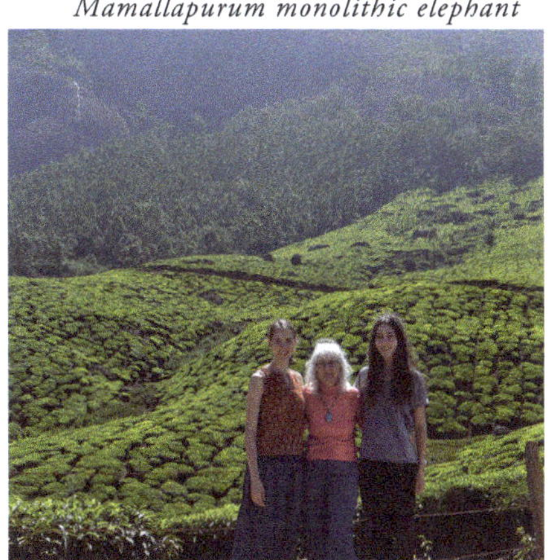

Lush tea plantations

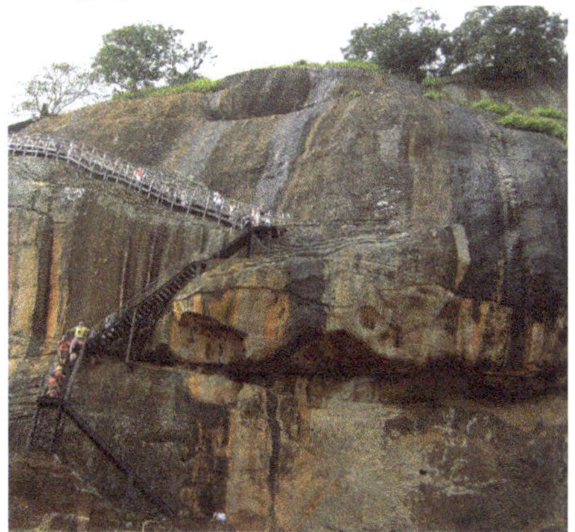

Climbing the 1300 steps

Maddie would soon be finishing her degree in Economics and would be looking for a job. Paris early on, had to make some important decisions. Both girls had started ballet early and enjoyed the physical challenges of achieving beautiful dance. There was the social camaraderie of the group of friends dancing and also performance. It demanded much practice and commitment. Paris achieved a high standard and was chosen to take leading parts in many of the performances that the Brisbane Youth Ballet Company put on. She was also selected to go to Melbourne for holiday workshops with the Australian Ballet Company. One time, Jess and David had been overseas, so I had the opportunity to go to Melbourne with Paris. We stayed in a serviced apartment close to the ballet headquarters. Once Paris was off in the morning for her day of tuition, I was free to explore the great art opportunities in Melbourne, which were all close together in the cultural hub. Then we all attended a performance of the Australian Ballet.

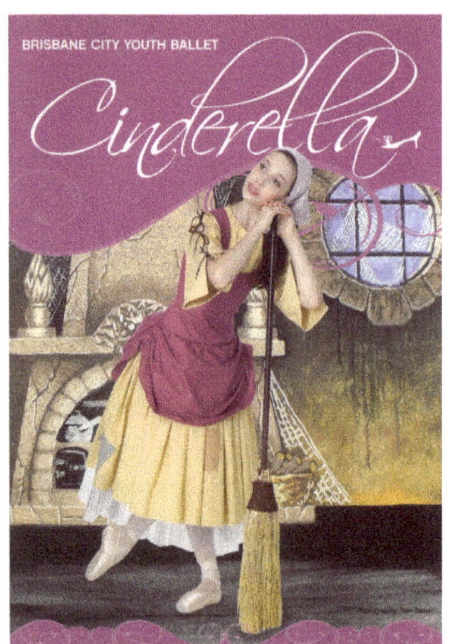

Paris is on the cover of the program

There came a time when Paris was about 15 years old that she had to decide her path of study. It seemed she could be travelling to Europe to audition for ballet companies, as this was the appropriate time. Or should she continue in high school and take the math and science subjects she would need, if she wanted to study medicine. In the end, continuing study won out, and she eventually entered James Cook University in Townsville as a medical student.

LONGREACH

When I returned from India with the grandchildren, Bob had wanted to go on a trip to Longreach to visit the Hall of Fame, but landed in the hospital for over three weeks, first with a broken hip and subsequentially with Aspirational Pneumonia that developed from inhaling regurgitated stomach contents. It is a serious illness that takes a long recovery time. The week after he got out of hospital we booked the 1300 km train trip to Longreach in Far Western Queensland. We had talked about this trip before the hospital incident and the delay meant that temperatures were expected in the 40's (105 °F +) in that part of Queensland in October. However, the train called "The Spirt of the Outback", was air-conditioned and we had a sleeper. At our destination, the museum and the motel were air-conditioned. A pleasant surprise was an unseasonal cool change in the weather that forced us to bundle up to keep warm! I had to buy Bob a sweater.

One of the items on Bob's bucket list has been to see the Abbott Buggy in the "Stockman's Hall of Fame" that was given to him by late friend, Harry Clark, a former grazier, shire chairman, and community leader. Bob wanted to restore the entire vehicle, but ran out of time and skill, but did manage to get the wheels reconstructed. In the end he did a deal that brought in an expert to complete the restoration job - Ian Stewart-Koster, a professional sign writer, who is arguably Australia's top horse-drawn vehicle painter and liner. The arrangement was that Ian complete the restoration in exchange for many of Bob's tools and gear, and Bob gave the buggy back to the family to be gifted to the Stockman's Hall of Fame and Outback Heritage Centre, in Longreach, Queensland, a unique museum in far-western Queensland.

While in Longreach we rented a car and drove up to Winton to see the dinosaur county and visit The Australian Age of Dinosaurs Museum of Natural History. We only missed going to the fields of discovery where much more dinosaur material is being retrieved because we would need a 4-wheel drive.

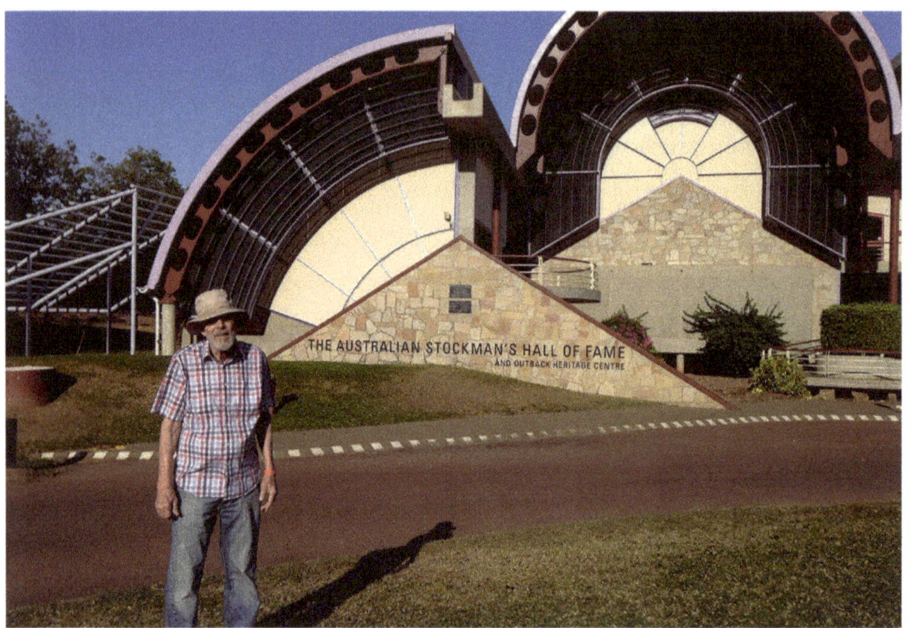

Bob's dream realised

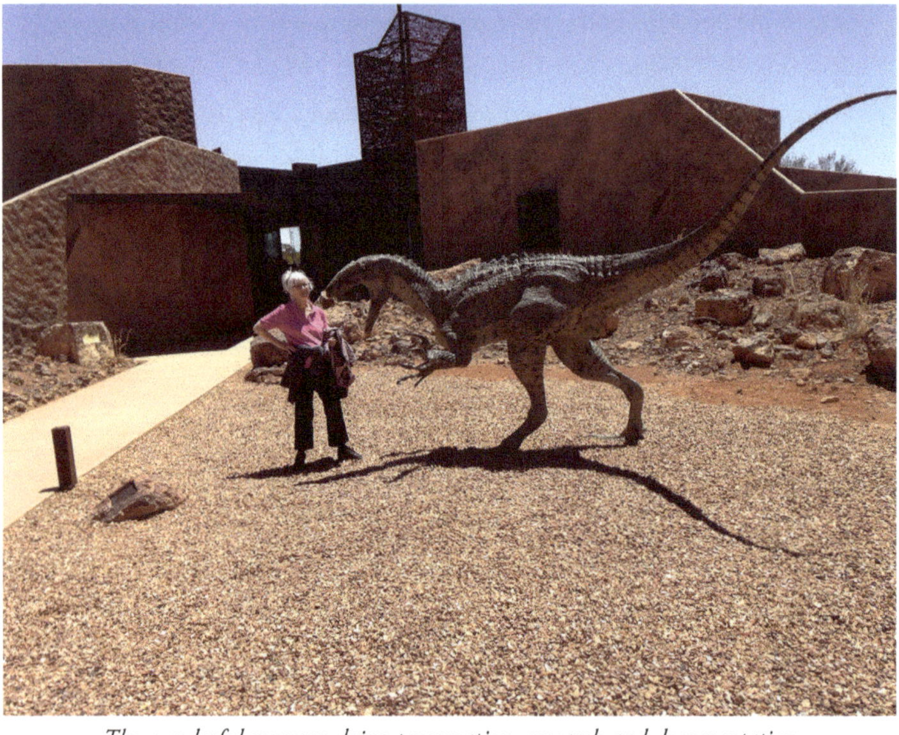

The wonderful museum doing preservation, research and documentation

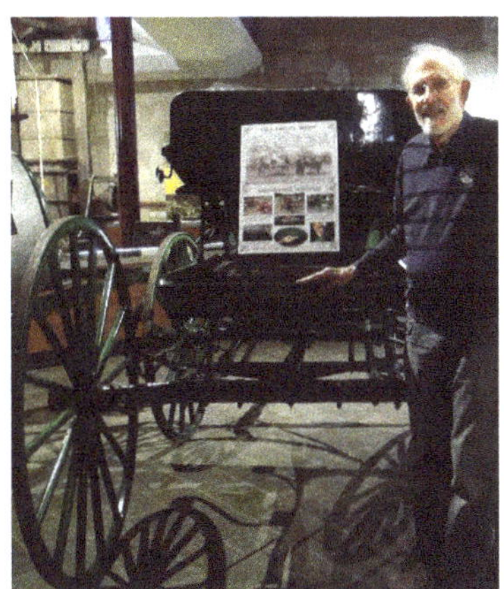

The Abbott Buggy

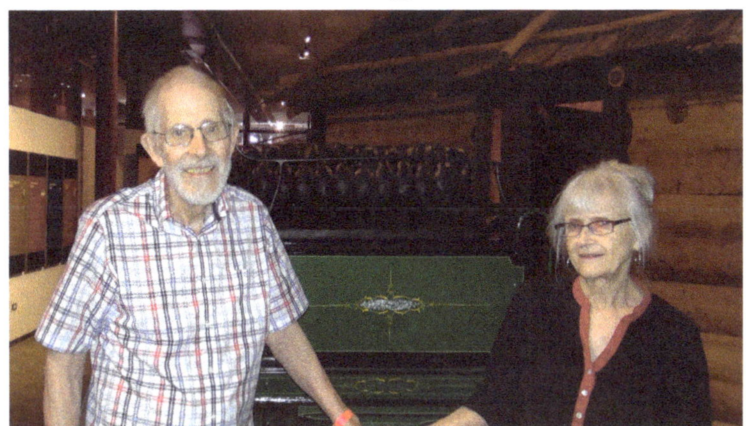

A big smile

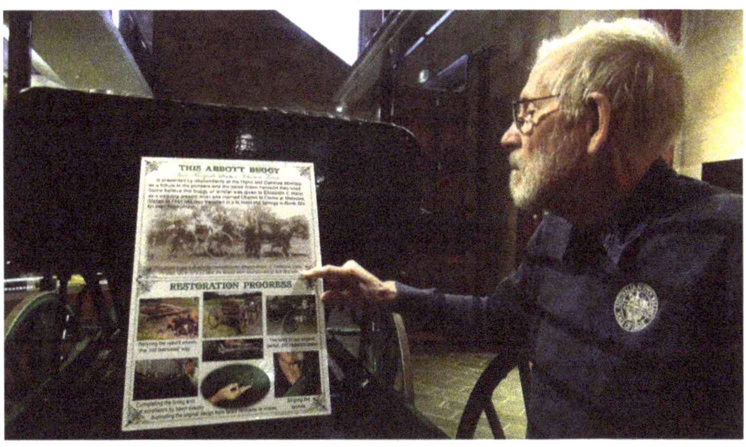

Documented nicely

INDIA 2015

After Bob's long standing involvement in India, being invited back to ICRISAT Research Institute by Bob's protégé, Peter Carberry, and wife Anne was too tempting not to accept. The first attempt in August was halted when Bob fell and broke his other hip three days before departure. But there is no holding back Bob when he has a plan of action and we rescheduled or trip as soon as Bob was out of hospital. Having had so many visits to India, Bob had never played tourist, being too busy in the office to take time for pleasure. So I was determined to start off the trip in South India with a visit to Mamallapuram seeing the UNESCO World Heritage temples, sculptures and ancient monoliths, which is one of my favourite places.

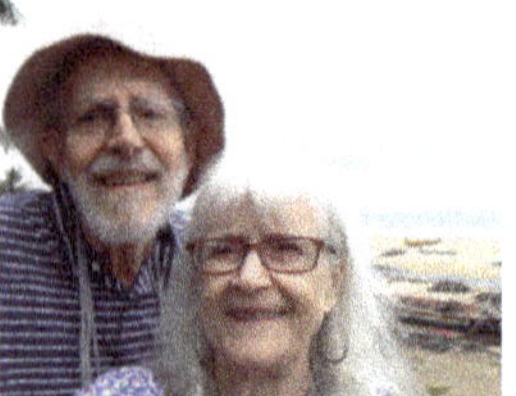
Beach at Sea Breeze Hotel

Although cancer appeared to be gone, Bob was left with a bad balance problem, which meant that he either walked with a walker or with a cane. In actual fact, more often than not, he held the cane above ground, being sure he didn't need it. It did mean some "interesting" devices to get him on and off planes. One involved a device similar to a forklift.

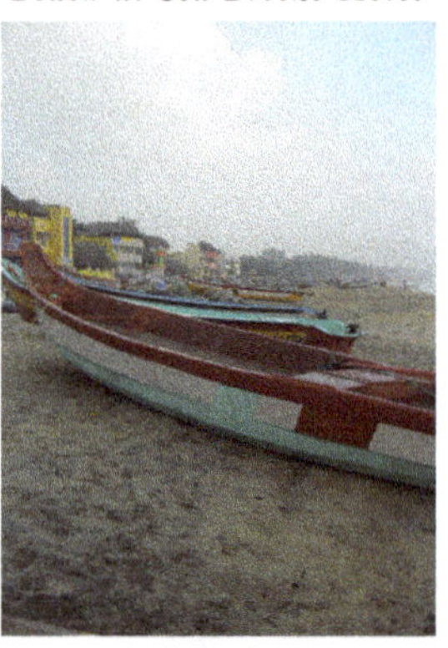
Fishing boats

It was rewarding to see how Peter had gone from one success to another since Bob first hired him after he acquired his PhD. Now he was Deputy Director and would before long become Director. It was wonderful to be on the research station again, after spending so many happy times there. It happened to be Diwali, the Festival of Lights, with celebrations of various kinds. There were activities on campus and also invitations in town. It seemed that Ann and Peter and friends still liked "Palace Heights" restaurant, a favourite of mine from 25 years ago, as we went with a group there for dinner one night.

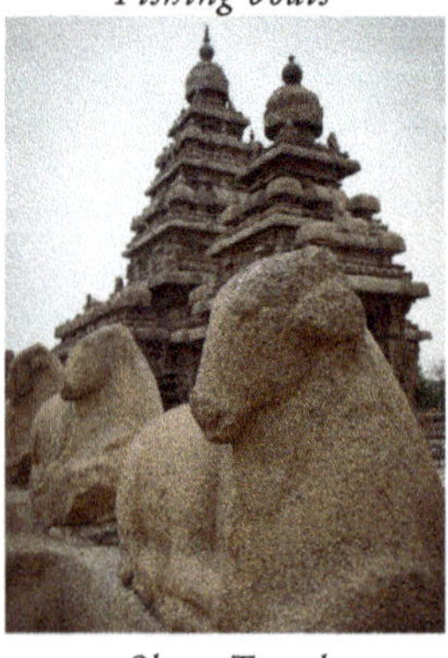
Shore Temple

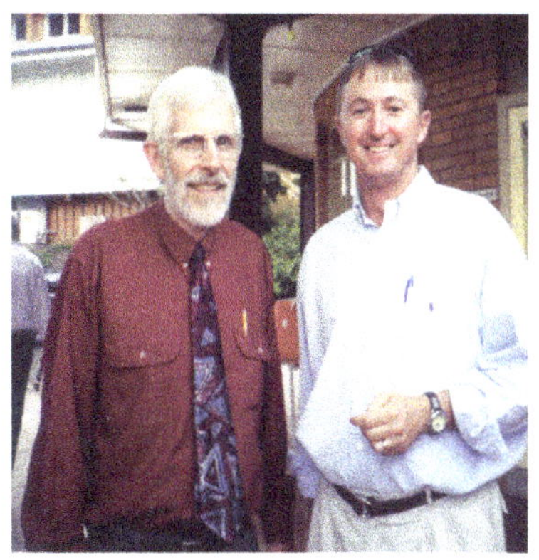

Bob and Peter

And we were invited to a party at a home, where I met a colleague of my Indian eye specialist working here in Brisbane.

I was very sad to learn that my old friend and driver Rama Rao had been crossing a street and had been hit by a motorcycle. He fell hitting his head and died shortly afterwards. His son, Anil, who has taken over the driving business came to visit us at the airport.

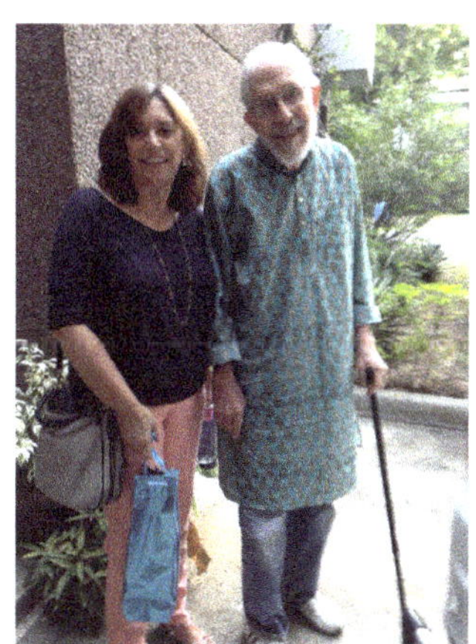

Ann and Bob

In Hyderabad we had the opportunity to also visit my old textile friends made during my research of the Telia Rumal, double ikat woven fabric. We spent several days talking to artisans and designers, looking at fabrics in successive shops and visiting weaving villages in the countryside. Bina Rao and Kesav took us out to lunch along with Ann Carberry. Govardhana showed us his 100 image Telia Rumal that he had woven to win the prestigious Sri Padma Award. He really wanted me to buy it. When visiting Suraiya Hasan Bose, she grabbed Bob by the hand and made sure he was stable. She is older than us and still running her school and business, with the help of brother Dominic. I previously acquired many of my textiles for my research project from her. It was always nice to take visitors to see her business as she is training widows to weave traditional special brocades and gold inlayed fabrics to keep these skills alive. In addition there is a multi-storied school she has built on her land and the widow's children can attend free of fees. Recently a large book has been written about her life called, "Suraiya Hasan Bose: Weaving a Legacy, by Radhika Singh".

We then had a week in Jaipur, Rajasthan, visiting the palaces, temples and museums. Seeing through a small paper factory, observing the carving of wooden blocks for block printing, dying of fabrics, pottery arts etc. made for a most interesting and enjoyable trip.

Faith had her brother Tim managing her interests in Indian Panorama. Tim was able to recommend accommodation for Bob that would have walk-in showers and limited steps to climb. So we were very happy with his bookings and drivers. Our fabulous heritage accommodation had a mezanine floor, alcoves and more.

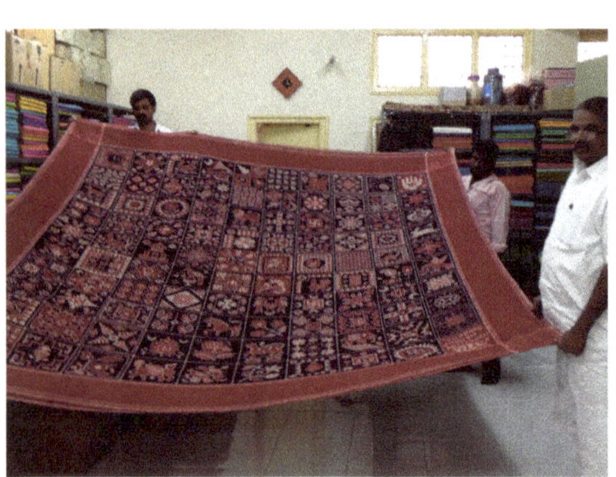

The 100 square Telia Rumal

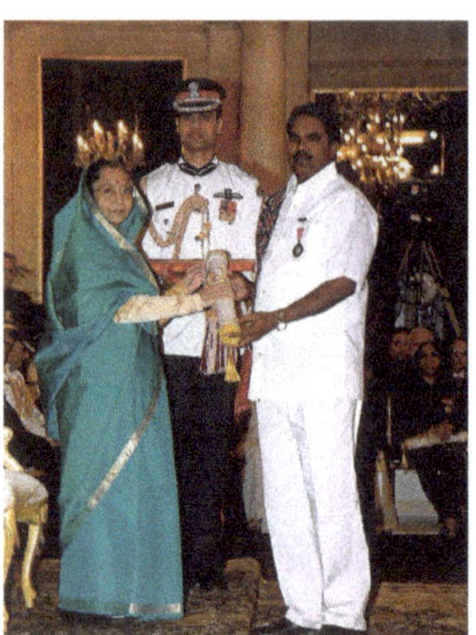

Receiving the award

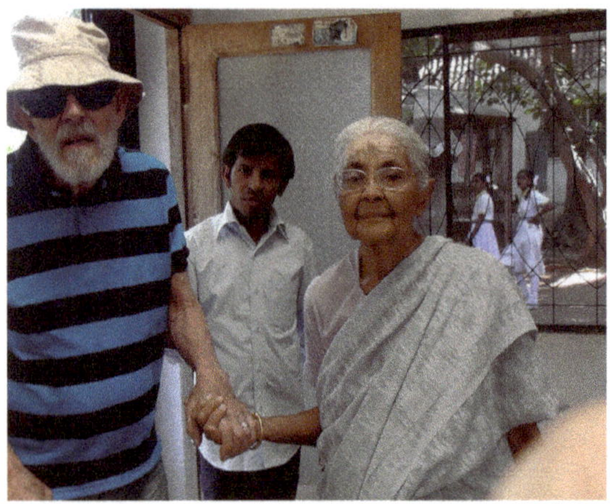

A helping hand

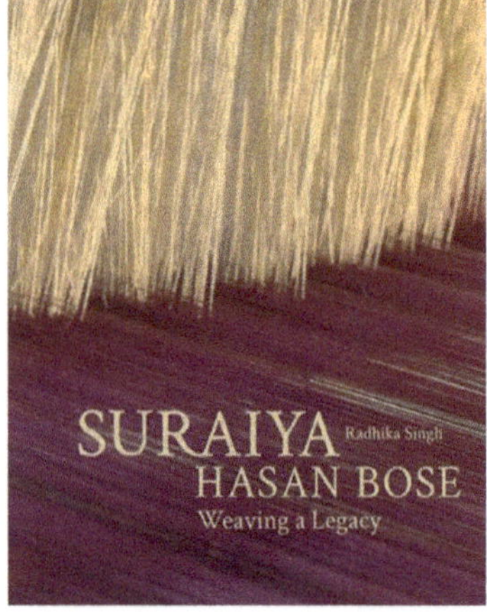

The lovely book

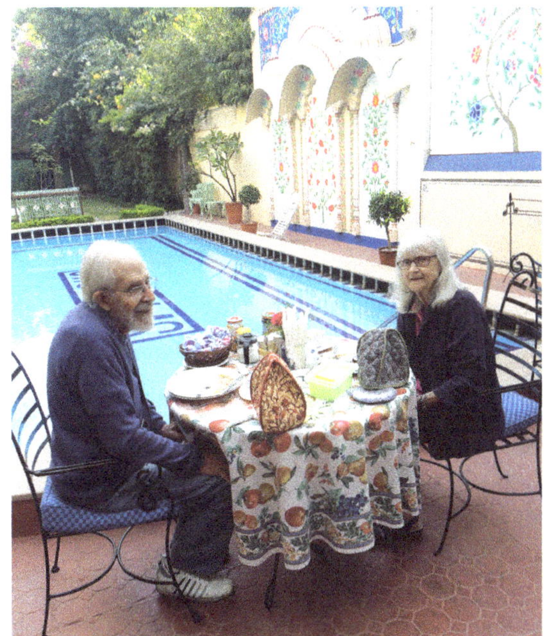

Breakfast setting

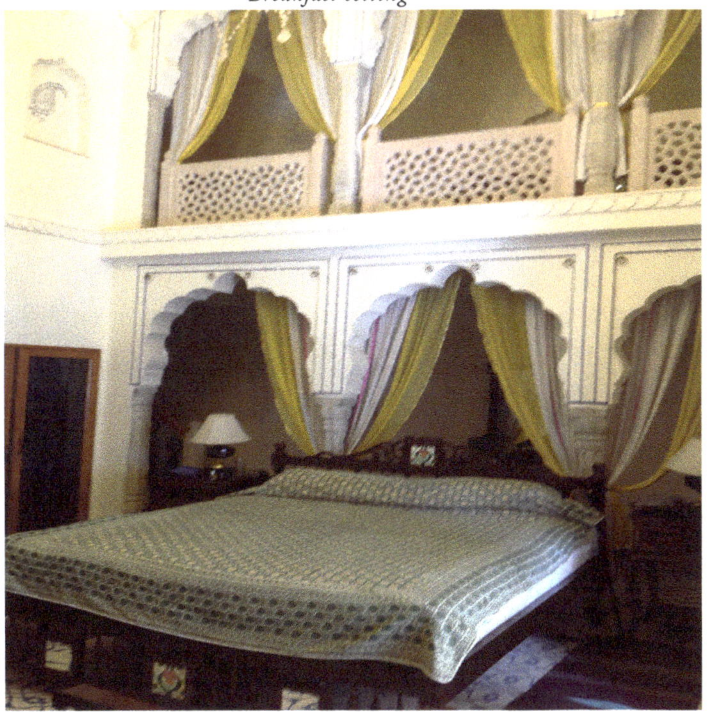

Old world charm

QUEENSLAND SPINNERS & WEAVERS

Now that I am living in Brisbane, I can take full advantage of the Queensland Spinners and Weavers. However even when living in Townsville, I did take the opportunity to come down to some workshops offered by the group. One in particular was for ikat. I had been fascinated by ikat since that visit with Dawn Faris, but now as a member of the Weaving group, I have to admit that I "talk the talk", but don't "walk the walk". As we moved into an apartment in Kangaroo Point, it was eventually necessary to sell my big loom, because it didn't fit. But I did borrow a table loom this year and participated in a project. It's nice to get some hands-on involvement. Back in Townsville and again in Toowoomba I had organised a project of weaving a Friendship coverlet. Twelve weavers each would weave squares measuring 15 x 15 inches. The weave structure was overshot with the possibility of many designs. Each weaver chose their own pattern, but was given instructions to follow to keep the squares the same size and firmness. Each could pick their own colour. We had a workday winding off enough balls of Swedish yarn for each person and then distributing them. After weaving the length, they were cut apart and handed out one to each of the other participants. Then they could join their 12 (or 15) squares in either crochet or adding woven stripes. Some of the Brisbane weavers joined in the project. It turned out that Joan Clarinbould, one of the Brisbane members did not get her squares put together and now at the age of 92, donated them to our weaving group to put together as a raffle prize for the club. Clare, Jill and Myrna participated and finally I did the joining. Joan had also joined the textile trip to China that I organised in 1987.

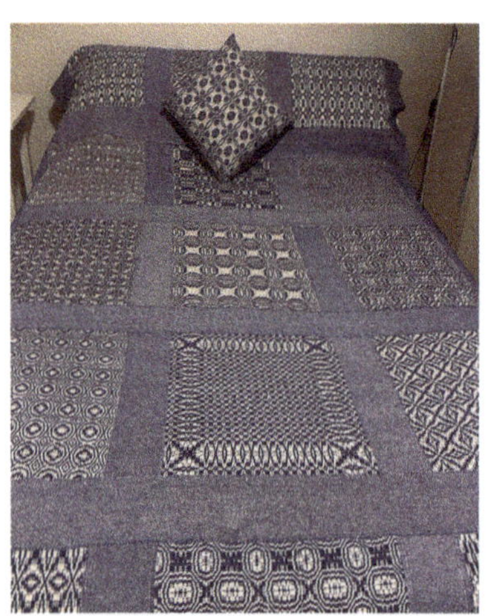

Coverlet for the raffle

It's great to belong to an organization where there are friends that can join in projects working together.

Because weaving is no longer a big part of my life, I seemed to fill up the days with all my other interests and continue to publish at least one book a year. I have examples in my list of published books of all size formats. Recently I have done more memoirs in the collection and have a large poetry collection coming up.

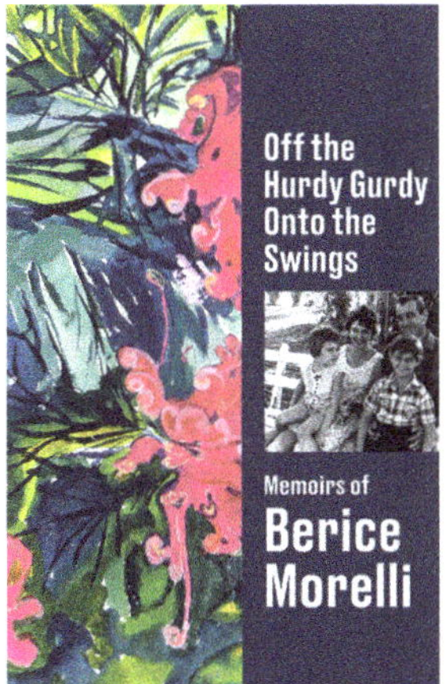

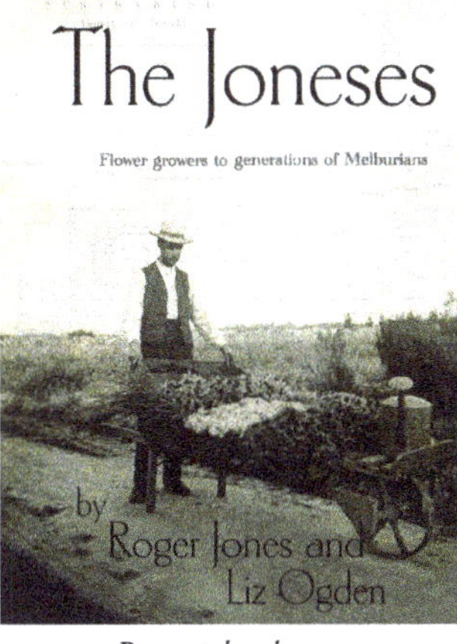

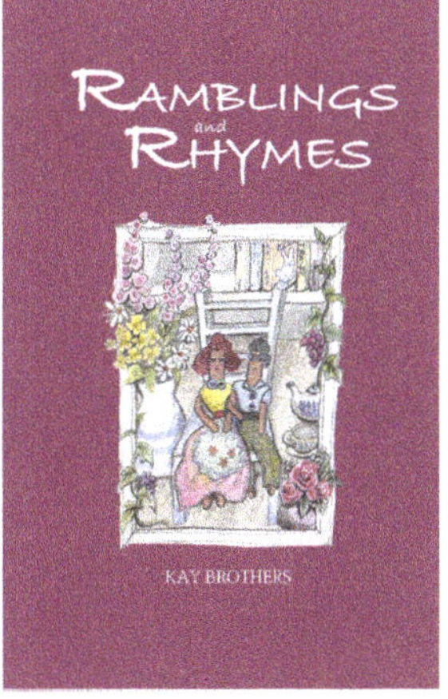

Recent books

My recent challenge was to create my first eBook, which is now on Amazon as a Kindle. It is always fun learning something new.

IONIANS

Many of my monthly activities are part of the offerings of the Ionian Club that Kay Rees invited me to join in 2012. An enjoyable interest group has been book club, meeting in members' homes. It's been easy getting to know this group of about 12 ladies through discussion. Another activity is a dining out group. The walking group has had varied places to walk and one month, I organised a walk through Kangeroo Point looking at the local public art.

One year the club organised a weekend away at the Jumpers and Jazz event in Warwick. The street trees were decorated with textile adornment and the gallery had interesting exhibitions, one by my friend Margaret Barnett called "Morning Glory" inspired by the unusual cloud formation in Northern Queensland.

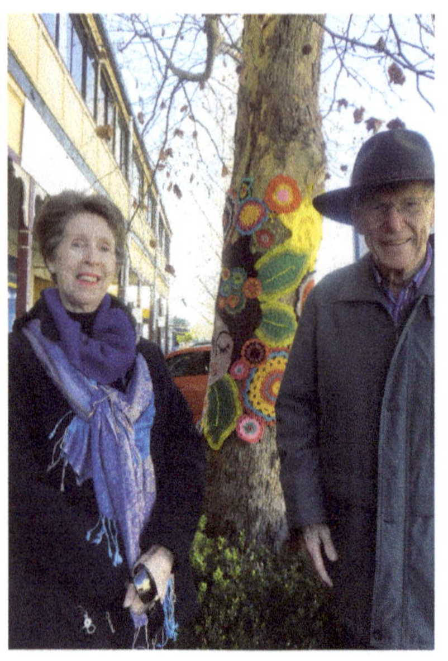

Kay and David Rees at Warwick

Margaret went in a glider, flying through this phenomonen.

In 2016 I decided to go on a four-day trip with the Ionians to Darwin visiting the Darwin Club birthday celebrations and combine it with sightseeing. Jordan agreed to stay with Bob and keep things going at home. It was a happy group of friends going to the National Park, riding on a river cruise to see crocodiles, and eating seafood at the beach. The actual birthday luncheon was our purpose for being there and keeping ties going between the two clubs. Some of our members already knew some of theirs from attending other functions around Australia. Every four years there has been a Convention held in different locations. Our Brisbane Club had organised and held the convention not long before I had joined. I attended Convention when it was held in Newcastle and had a great time.

In the middle of the night my mobile phone rang and it was Jordan telling me that Pa had fallen and was in hospital. The Doctor talked to me and it was clear this was a serious event. It was uncertain he would regain consciousness. He did but cancer had returned and he had several more tumours.

I organised my flight the next morning and returned to Brisbane. Again he was in Wesley Hospital, which was getting to feel very familiar. I can't remember much of that time in hospital except that suddenly we were told that we would have to make other arrangements for Bob within two days as his insurance would run out. That was quite a shock. Bob's condition had declined and we needed to find a nursing home that had facilities he required with little time to do it. We somehow found a broker who sourced the right place for clients needs. But time was the problem. Some people have their name put on a waiting list hoping to find something in a year or so. Our broker managed to find a bed at a place in Nundah, north of our area only about a 20-minute trip. I knew there were facilities in the next suburb to home, but was told no places were available. I had looked into having Bob come home, but the hospital explained that finding the required home help was virtually impossible.

Zion Lutheran Home turned out to be our only choice, but a very good choice. The girls and I alternated to be there to share meals with Bob at lunch and dinner. On occasion, the girls and I took him down the road in his wheelcair to a Thai restaurant. He had some nice visits from friends such as Roger Jones, Sue Byth, Margaret Myers and of course the family. John Williams came up several times from Canberra and had quality time with Bob. Bob's personal trainer, David Fernandez came and gave him some exercises to do. Bob never gave up working to regain his mobility, but his balance was not going to make it possible. David had worked with Bob ever since we came to Kangaroo Point, helping him stay active. One thing he gave Bob training in was how to fall and protect himself. Unfortunately that lesson didn't sink-in properly.

A special event to celebrate the retirement of Brian Keating was happening at the University and Peter Carberry, back from India came to organize for Bob to

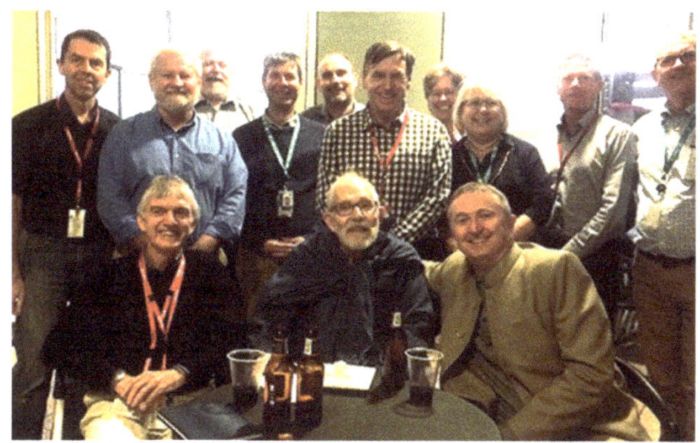

Brian's retirement seminar

attend, going in a maxi-taxi and wheelchair. Bob saw about 50 people there that he had been influential in their work, according to Brian.

For Christmas we were able to use the special Regency reclining type of cot to have Bob visit with family over Christmas at the Hoey home, by transport with maxi-taxi. There is nothing he enjoyed more that being with all the grandchildren. Sam and Zippora came back from Shanghai and Bob had been so pleased to be told that they were expecting our first great-grandchild.

Bob lost his valiant fight against cancer on the 6th of January 2017. He had been at Zion Lutheran Home for only two and a half months where the dedicated loving care was more than we could have imagined. We have such appreciation for the fine staff we got to know there.

All the grandchildren were able to return to Brisbane for the funeral service that was conducted by Bob's dear friend John Williams. John's wife Ruth played the organ beautifully. Other dear friends like Peter Gillard, who came up from Tasmania also spoke and gave tributes. We were so pleased that Peter Carberry could be there from India. The family created a wonderful slideshow that was part of the service. The girls took a great deal of time to pick music that was just right. Bob's wishes were to be cremated and to have a headstone in Western Pennsylvania at the McCown family plot. The ashes will eventually end up there as well.

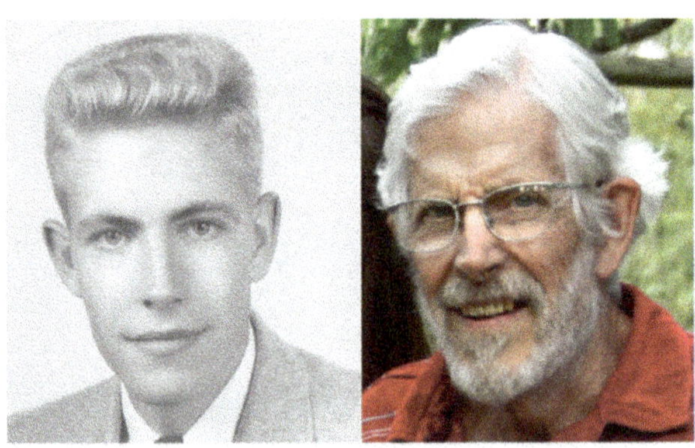

September 17, 1937 - January 6, 2017

My friend Jill Loughnan recommended I get out and do things every day, so that is what I have done. And when opportunities have arisen, I have taken them. Jessica invited me to accompany her to NYC where she was attending a short photography course. It had been awhile since I had been there, so I was delighted I could share some time with her doing interesting things. She introduced me to the Tenement Museum, which I visited several times. A visit to Harlem and the Abyssinian Gospel Church for Sunday service with their amazing choir is something I will never forget. Afterward I had "Soul Food" down the road at a restaurant that also had a live jazz group entertaining.

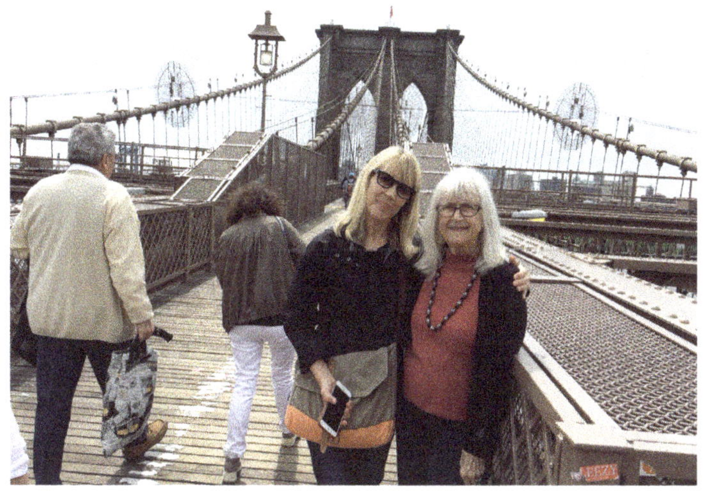

Walking the Brooklyn Bridge

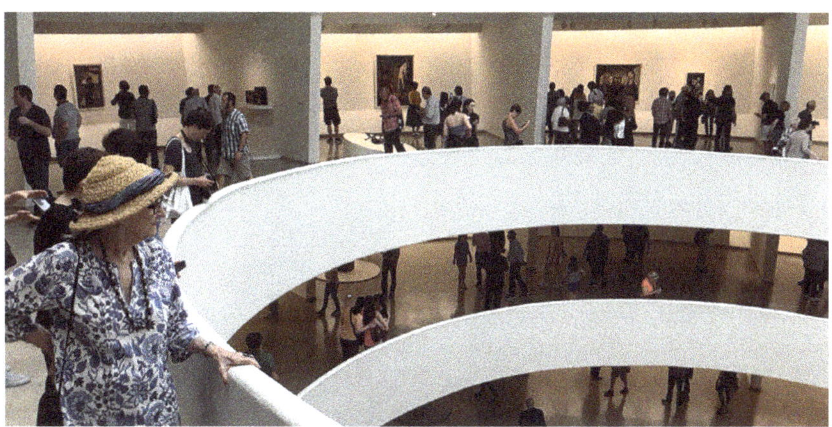

Looking down the spiral, I can see many galleries

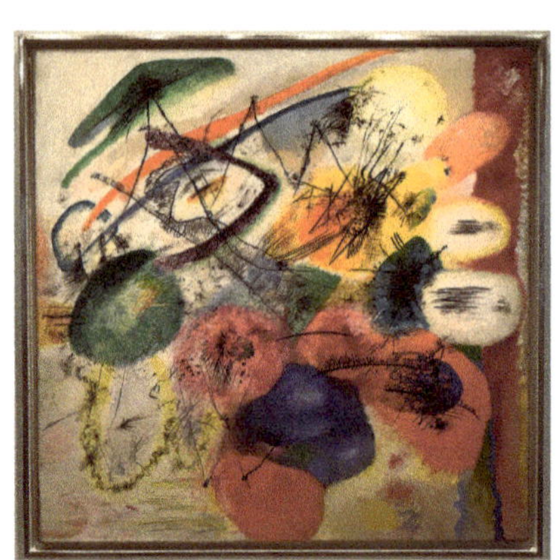

Black lines by Kandinsky

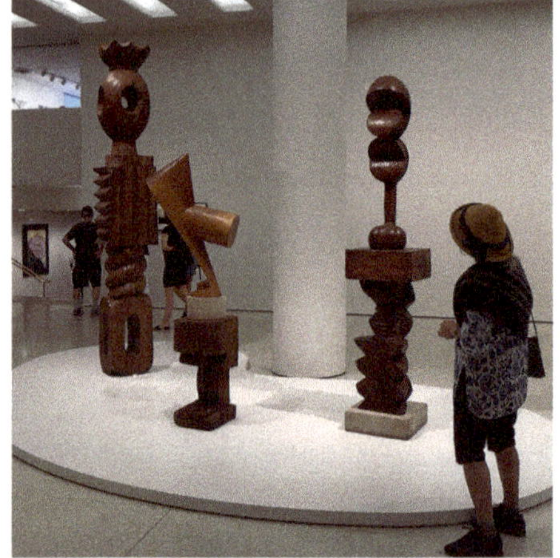

Adam and Eve by Brancusi

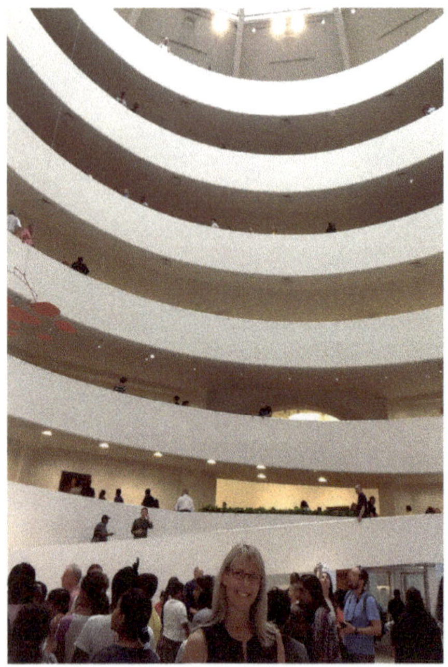

Frank Lloyd Wright's beautiful design

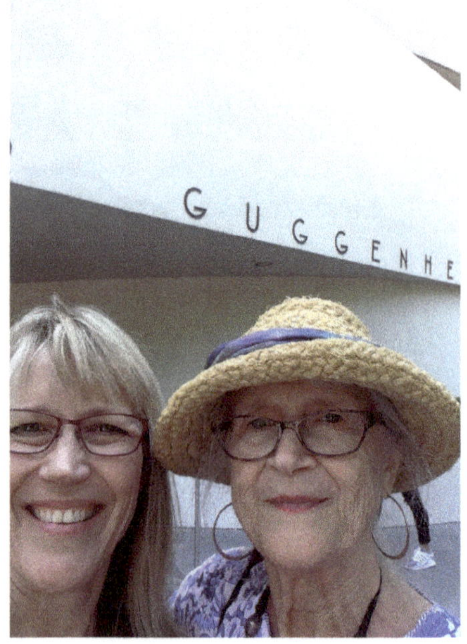

The Guggenheim Museum

NEW LIFE - A NEW GENERATION

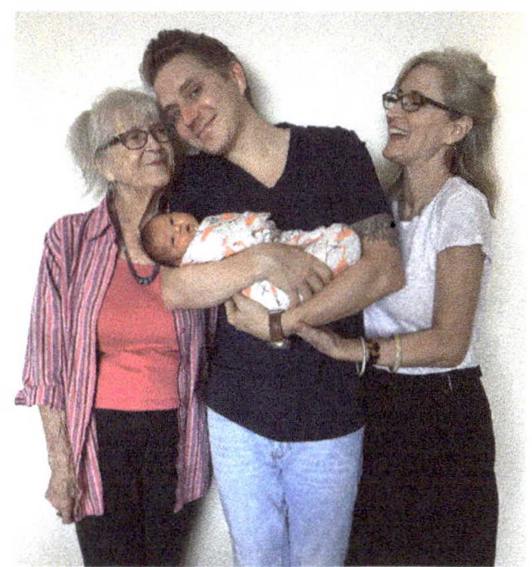

Four generations

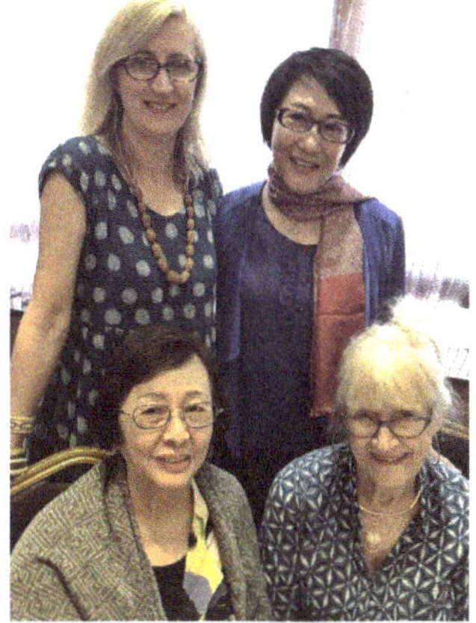

Siane and Helen with us

Jenny and I went to Hong Kong to welcome the newest family member into the world. Sam and his wife Zippora now have daughter Azaiah, born Aug 2nd 2017, who delights us all. Most often this little great granddaughter is called ZaiZai. Bob was very happy learning at his last Christmas that a new life was coming. Although Sam and Zippora live in Shanghai, they wanted the birth in Hong Kong so that ZaiZai would have a Hong Kong passport. Zippora's father, Willy also lives in Hong Kong part of the time, as his mother Siane, and sister Helen are there. It was a special time getting to know them all well and feeling like one big family. The big bonus was that the birth came on the exact day of Paris' and Willy's birthday. Now I am happy to finally have become a great grandmother.

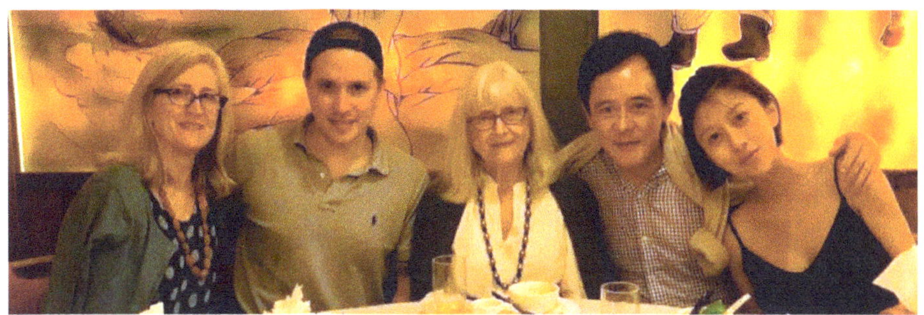

Dining out with Willy, Zippora's father

Other opportunities arose and I happily accepted an invitation to visit the Playnes in Melbourne. Moira had mapped out a full week of art activities seeing the Van Gogh exhibition and visiting the Australian Tapestry workshop. At the Victorian National Art Gallery we saw a wonderful Aboriginal exhibition of three-dimensional work. Martin drove us down the Mornington Peninsula to visit a stunning outdoor sculpture garden. Martin and Moira would have needed a week to recover after I left.

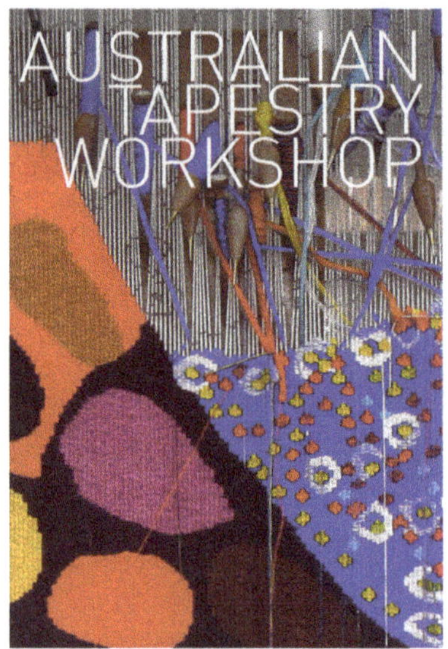

Australian Tapestry Workshop

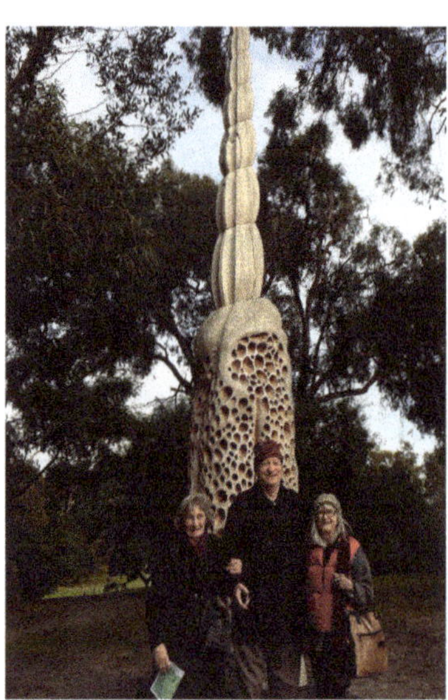

Sculpture Park, Mornington

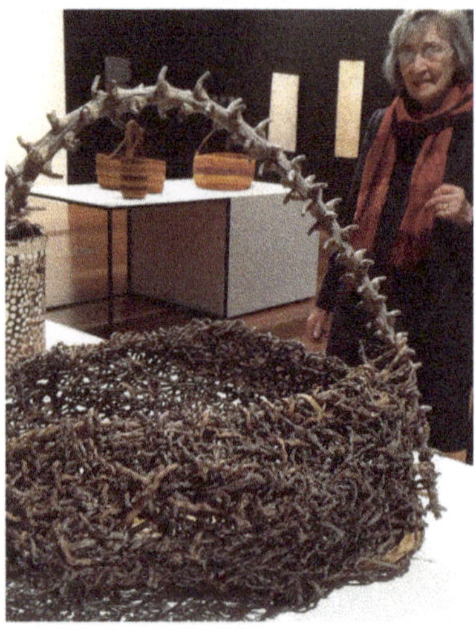

Moira and basket

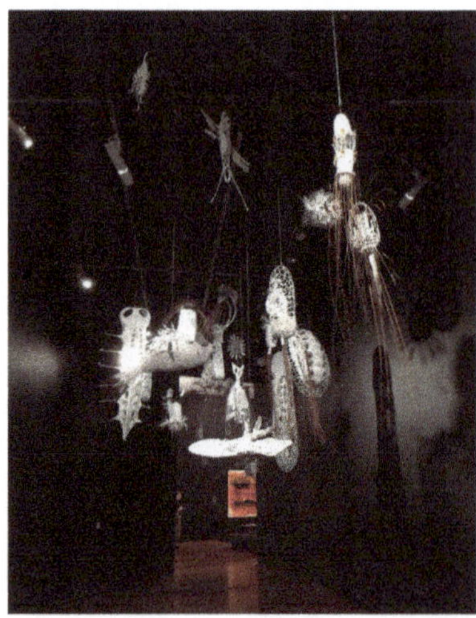

Sea Country Spirits by Jenny Compton

A visit to Morocco was something I had dreamed of doing someday. I had taken some of Bob's books to CSIRO where Zvi Hockman met me and took me for some morning tea. He started telling me about his cousin Lisa who also takes groups on textile trips over seas. He suggested I look at her website called, "Dyed and Gone to Heaven". Going to her website, I saw a wonderful textile trip to Morocco coming up, so I felt the timing was right and I went. Visiting a family living comfortably in a cave was a highlight there in spite of all the fabulous tile and mosaic work seen throughout. We did have a special opportunity to have a meal in a home and a workshop in special button making. And we all enjoyed a cooking course, learning to make Tagine Chicken, a traditional dish.

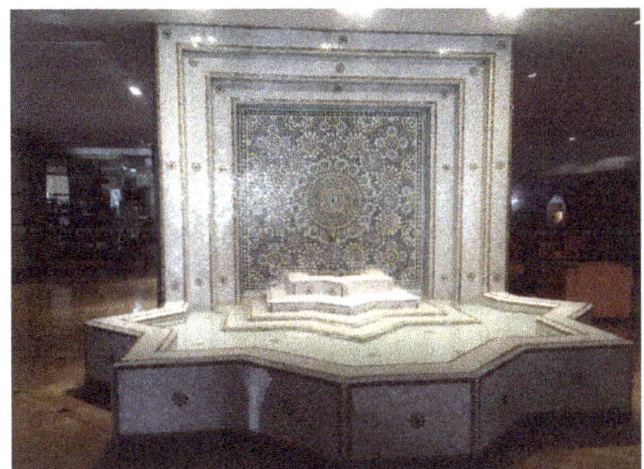

Tiles and mosaic everywhere

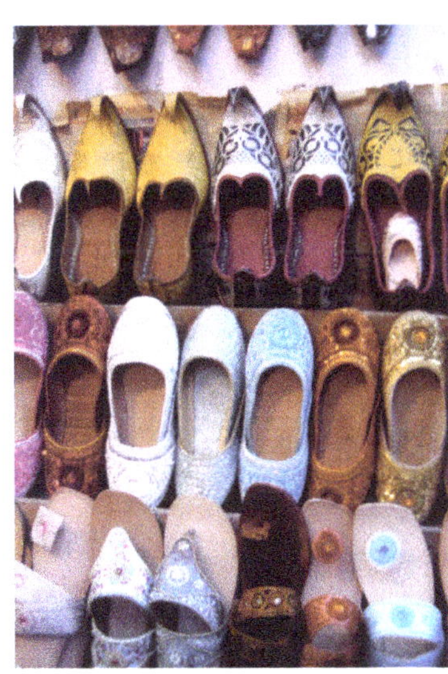

Leather shoe display

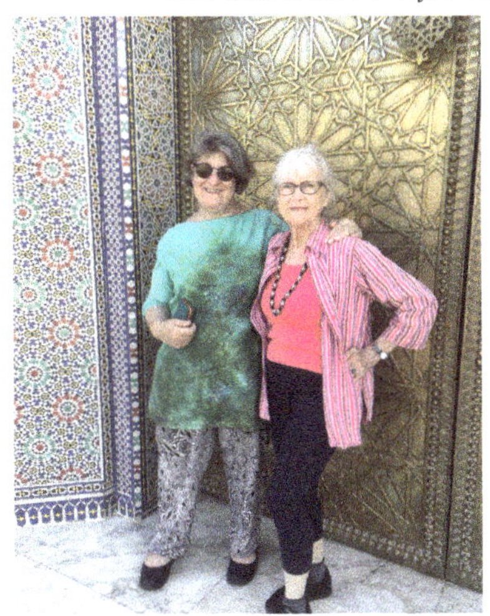

Lisa Walton, our tour leader

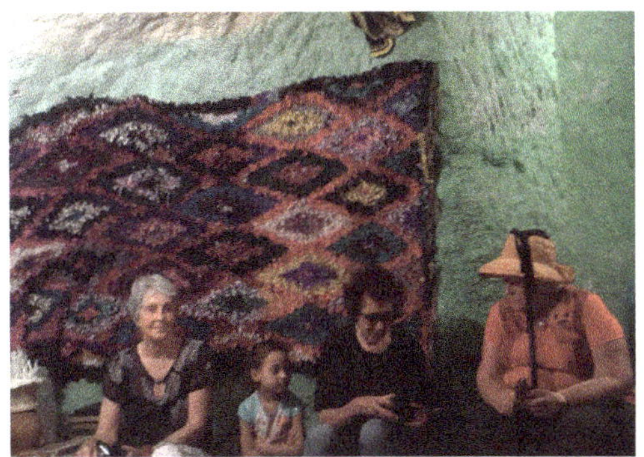

Cave living with silver service Morrocan tea

HORNBILL FESTIVAL - DECEMBER 2017

When my Indian art curator friend, Minhazz Majunder from Delhi, offered an opportunity to visit the North Eastern Territories of India, what could I say but yes! Helen Ward, my friend in so many of my activities, was supposed to go with me on the trip incorporating visiting her brother-in-law in Tamil Nadu, but Helen became ill in Italy with a pulmonary embolism and wasn't able to travel. Having been to the Spinners and Weavers recently, I thought about asking Jill Lynch to go with me. I was surprised to hear she had a close friend, who was a Jesuit priest living in India and she wanted to see him, as his health was failing. So yes, Jill would like to come and we tailored our trip to include a visit to Patna, in Bihar, to see him. We stayed in the residence of retired priests whom we enjoyed getting to know. For the North Eastern Territory tour, my Ionian friends Di and Brian Nielsen came as well. In addition, Di's sister Chris and brother-in-law Sandy from England, joined us. Minhazz's friend, Madhu made up the numbers to just eight of us travelling together. Again it was an outstanding visit, highlighted by seeing a tiger in the wild having a confrontation with a buffalo. The Hornbill Festival in

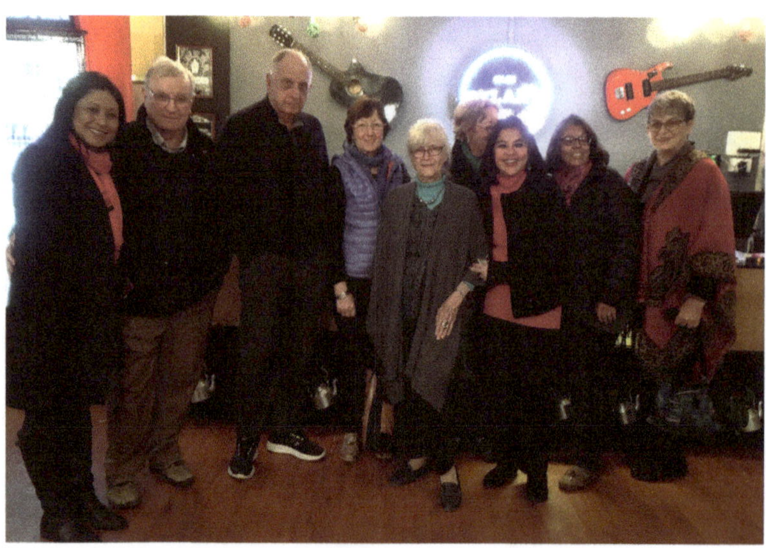

Our speaker on the left with our group. Minhazz is beside me.

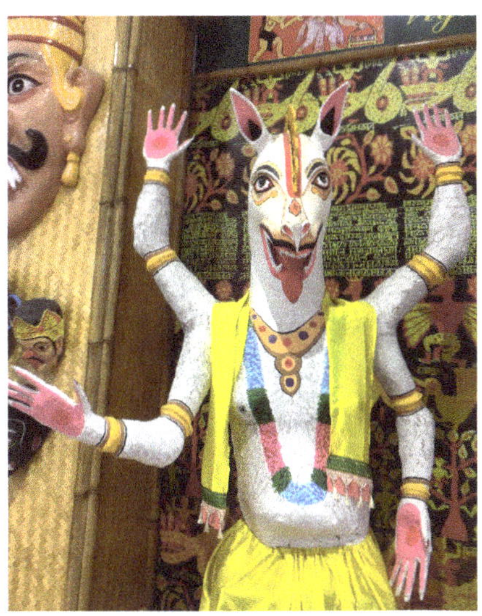

Airport Assam greeting

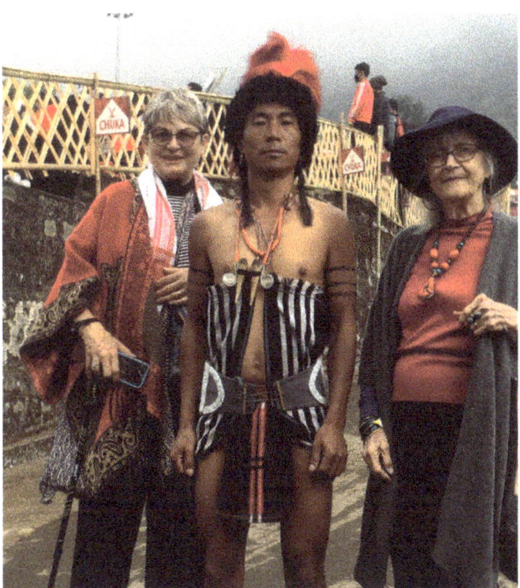

Naga tribal dance performer

Nagaland was our destination, but only one of many treats. We had guest speakers in places, usually on a social issue.

Jill and I did get to meet Helen's brother-in-law, Josh, in Tamal Nadu, who gave us a private tour of his great river restoration project in Chennai called Adyar Eco-Park. Besides the restored natural landscape, it was created as an art experience as well. In addition, we visitied Hyderbad of course to see the ikat weaving, as Jill

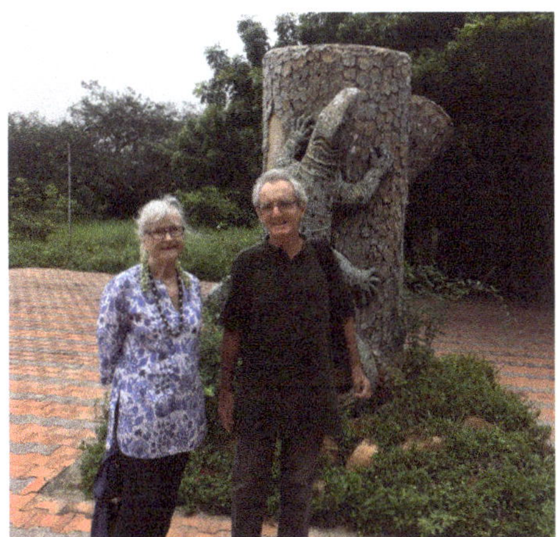

Meeting Josh Brooks in Chennai

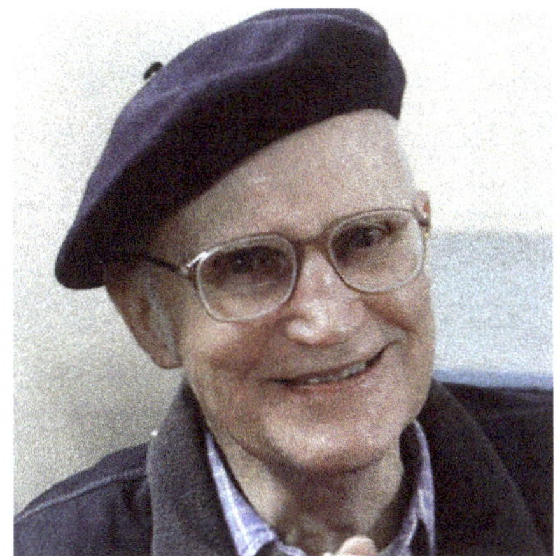

Paul Jackson SJ

has been a weaver as long as I have. Govardhan had arranged for his cousin to demonstrate the entire Telia Rumal experience for us at Puttapaka village.

2018 The year did have trips again, first of all back to Townsville for dear friend, June Tonnoir's 90th birthday party.

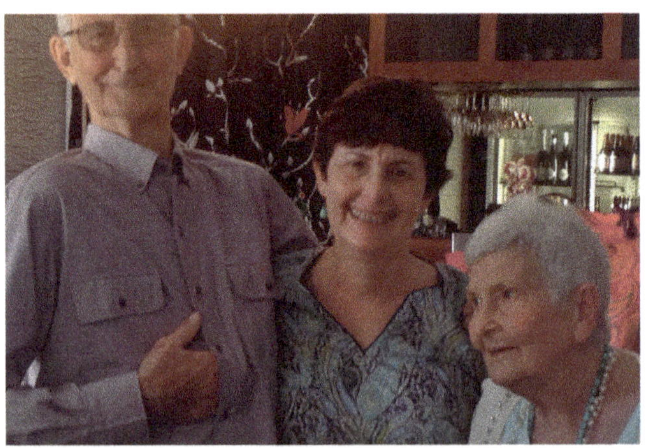

Paul, Nonie and June at the party

I stayed with Berice and Serge. Berice had brain surgery, which has affected her swallowing and balance, but with Serge's help was managing well at home. We did some final photography in preparation for my publishing her memoirs. The Morelli's took Jenny and me up to visit their son Ricky's place at the Black River. It was wonderful seeing his achievements since the early days when he worked in our nursery. He and his wife have started an additional business to the nursery of providing a venue for "County Weddings" and have won awards for their facility. It was fun for Jenny and Rick to see each other after all these years.

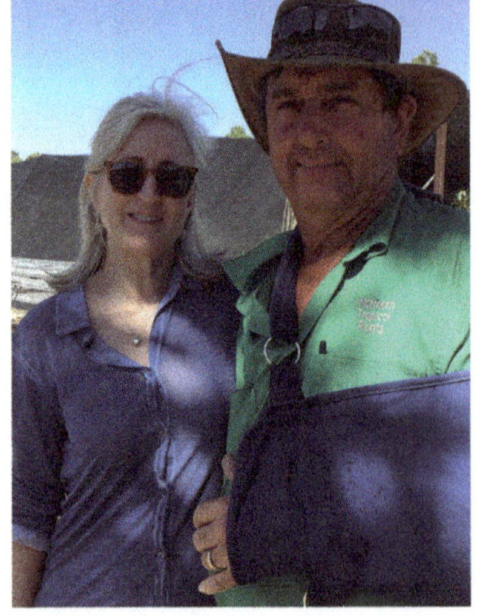

Jenny and Rick meet again

SHANGHAI CALLS

Then Jenny and I went to Shanghai for ZaiZai's first birthday in July. Jenny adores being a grandmother and has been able to watch all the developments of Zaizai from afar thanks to WeChat, the Chinese social media app. Sam posts photos and videos, but also invites us to WeChat meetings. What wonderful technology for friends and family living at a distance. It was wonderful sharing in Sam's life, staying in their new home and seeing his work environment. Zippora was so welcoming. We had lovely visits with her family, Virginia and Alan, who kindly gave me a beautiful framed silk embroidery, which has pride of place back here in Kangaroo Point. Virginia's artist friend, Lan took Jenny and me out to a resort for lunch along side a lake. Another day, Sam took us on a fascinating tour of the Jewish getto in Shanghai, with all its history. And we had a night out in town for dinner and then jazz, where I met a drummer from Squirel Hill, in Pittsburgh. So we had a fun-filled time.

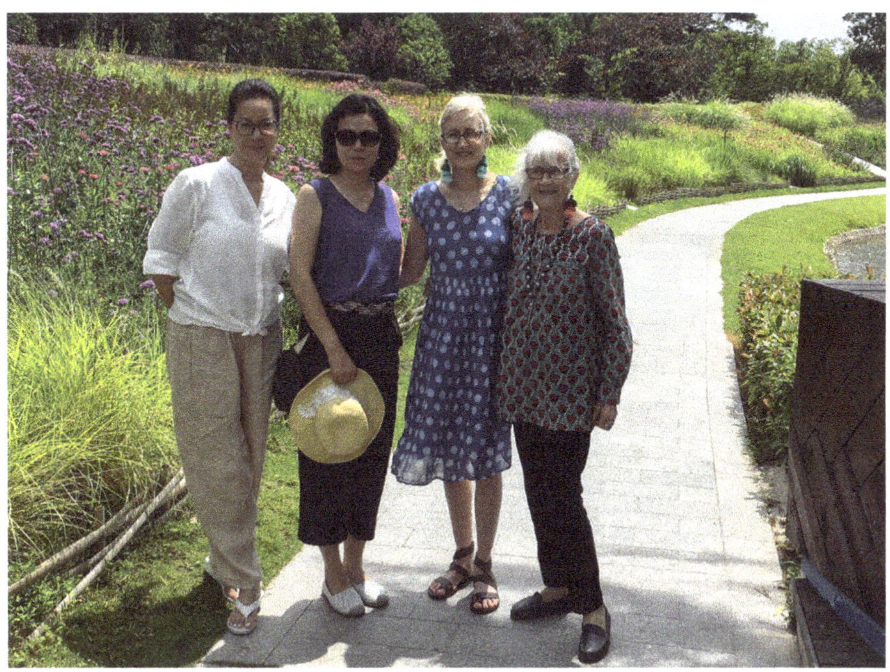

Virginia, Lan, Jenny and I were at the resort

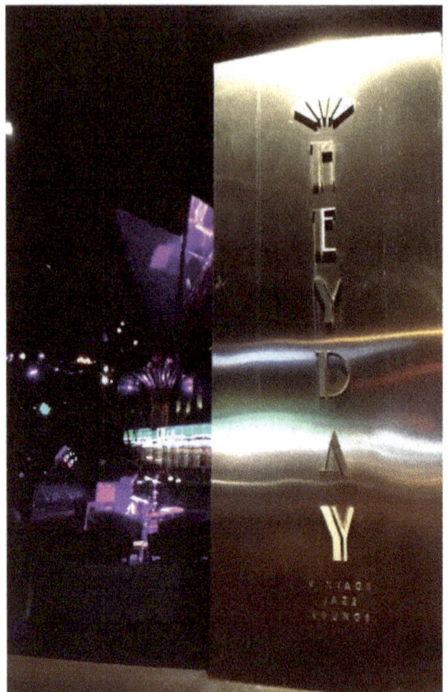

Jazz

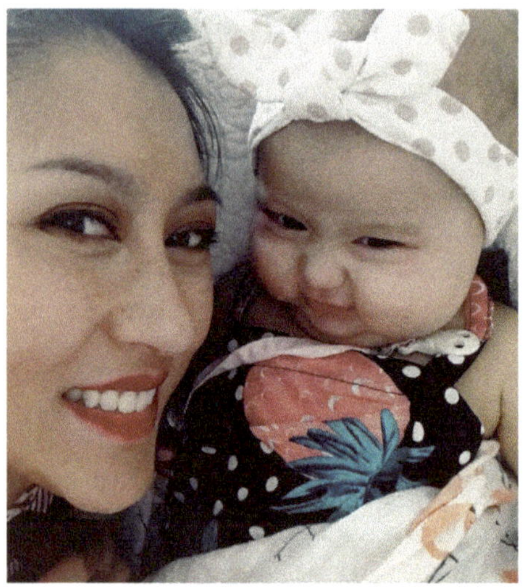

Zippora and Zaizai

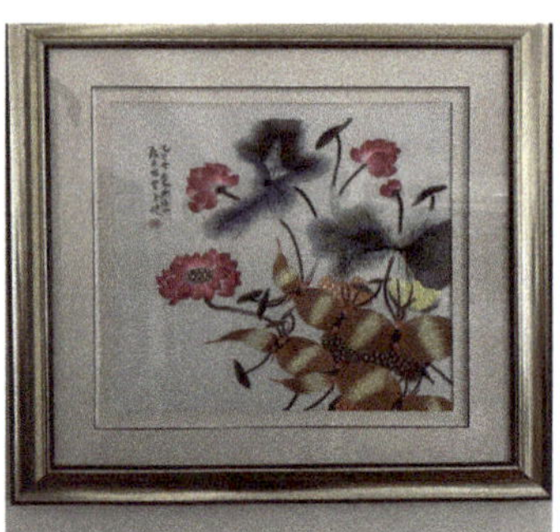

Silk embriodery from Virginia and Alan

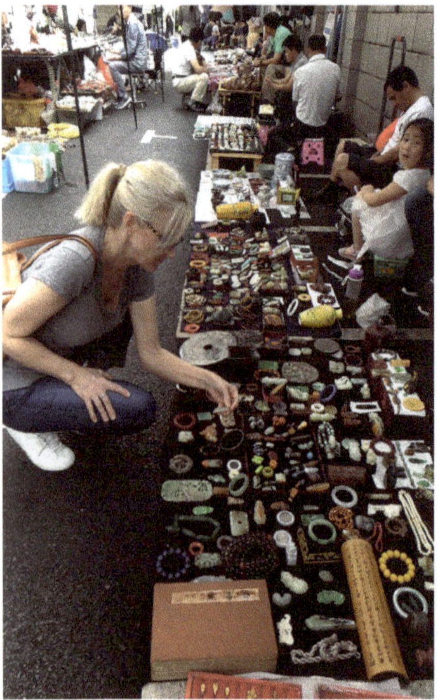

Jenny loving antique markets

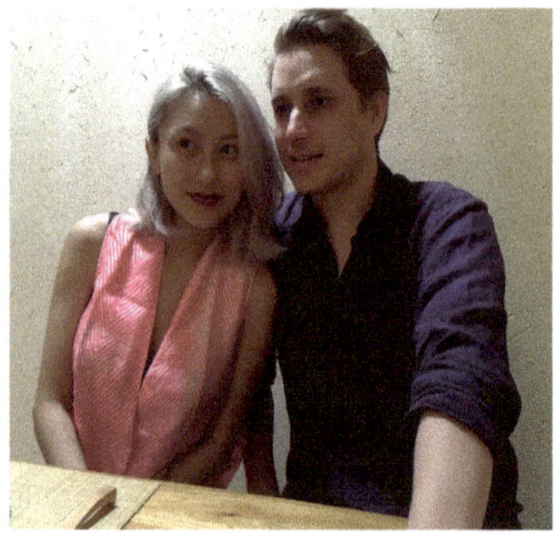

Zippora and Sam - a night out

TAASA

When my friend Joyce Barnard introduced me to The Asia Art Society of Australia (TAASA), I was living in Toowoomba area and not able to take part in their activities, as their meetings were in Sydney and Melbourne. But their quarterly journal was well worth being a member to receive. A branch group in Brisbane was attempted, but until James MacKean took over the leadership role, not much happened. Since then there has been a good calendar of events, both in the Textile group and the Ceramic group. I have enjoyed both areas of study, which relate well to my research in India and general interests. I have been able to present some activities for the textile group, like Kalamkari and most recently organizing indigo dyeing with resist techniques to create design.

FAMILY OPPORTUNITIES

Although I took my children halfway around the world from my parents, I can understand so much better how hard that was for them, once my own children starting having a life of their own. I now am living almost next door to Jenny and down the road from Jessie and can only feel blessed to share in their lives in so many ways. But some of the grandchildren have not stayed too close to home. It is wonderful to know that both Jenny and Jess have life activities that give them satisfaction and creative rewards.

Jordan has had several periods of working overseas with his own businesses. After Japan, he did return to Oz and eventually came back to Kangaroo Point. He had met a young Japanese woman who was on a working holiday here in Australia and eventually we got to know her. They went to New Zealand while Jordan was developing an online application for businesses. We loved seeing the photos they sent of their leisure activities of fishing. Uta seemed to have the golden touch.

Jenny had been painting for a number of years, and decided to have her first solo exhibition in Brisbane at Wild Canary. So she had been building up a collection. She had a previous outlet that had worked well, but no longer existed. The exhibition was scheduled for a date in August, but Jenny went shopping and had a fall, breaking her hip. Well hospital happened. In the end, she was out of hospital and there for the opening on crutches. It's been a long struggle to regain proper walking and attempt to be free of pain. Of course the diagnosis was Osteoporosis and she is now trying to build up better bone density. She was able to travel to Shanghai again to celebrate ZaiZai's second birthday, travelling with her crutches, but later than first planned.

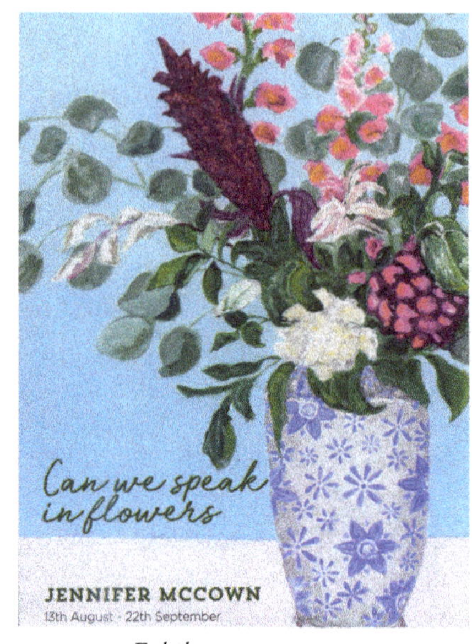

Exhibition invitation

Jessica completed a two-year course in photography, which gave her many new skills. Having good equipment and a great space with lighting, she has set up a studio in her home. Her business is limited to newborn babies and maternity. However she does accept the families as they grow older and want to capture more moments in the children's lives. Some of the work I have seen she has done with twins and triplets is fantastic. On

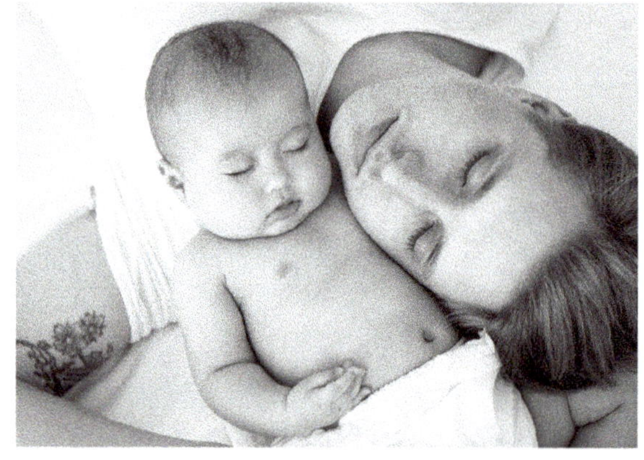
Zaizai and Sam: photo Jessica Hoey

occasion she does some photography for me that I need for my publications. Her work is exceptional.

Conor had been studying at Queensland University, and was also doing some parttime modelling, which led to him being offered a contract to go to Milan, Italy for one term as a model. This sounded like a fantastic opportunity to see some of Europe and experience the centre of the fashion world. In order to do this, he had to take a deferment from his course. He did have a great time in Italy, but came home and resumed his study. But he was anxious to start earning, so took a full-time IT job. His study was most often done by watching the lectures online. His work situation was going well and he had some great opportunities such as going down to Sydney for workshops with Google. He was very keen to save money towards an overseas trip when he finished his university degree in 2019 and took additional work as a waiter at night. He succeeded in graduating after that marathon time schedule and took off with his mates to have a European holiday. In Belgium, he had the opportunity to stay with Seble, Jenny's Ethiopian friend, who lives there.

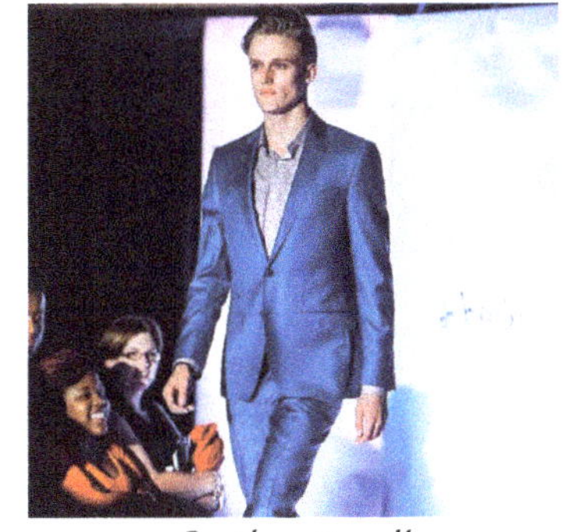

On the cat walk

Then Conor went to London and needed to get a job as his money was running out. It proved easy to get a job in hospitality as he had such good experience in Brisbane. He chose a job at an Ottolinghi restaurant over other offers as our family had been using the Ottolinghi cookbooks for years. Eventually he decided to get a job in his field of marketing. So his plans were all working out. But the pandemic hit and London was not the best place to be. He was fortunate to get out before flights shut down and was able to go into lockdown at home for two weeks. As an IT worker, he could carry on at Jenny's home, online. Meanwhile he had applied for a job in the Netherlands and was successful. They are allowing him to work from Brisbane. What a crazy world we live in!

Maddie was successful in having job offers and chose to start with KPMG. She has worked hard and became a manager. She has had various projects, one being for the Queensland Government and their transport network. They seem to have liked her work and offered her a place working for them. So it is rewarding seeing all the young people succeeding in their work and having opportunities come along.

Paris meanwhile was successful in acquiring a position at the Royal Hospital here in Brisbane and so we see lots of her at family events. In fact she and Maddie came and took me walking yesterday afternoon, and then for wine and cheese. How lucky am I? It does take some encouraging to get me out exercising recently, as I am trying to complete this book before Christmas.

FUTURE PLANNING

Thinking about the future and looking back at Bob's difficult decisions to make about the collection he had worked so hard to build up, I felt I needed to make plans for my Telia Rumal collection. In actual fact I also had a large collection of textiles from around the world that did not fit in our apartment. Eventually I had an exhibition at Gallery 159 owned by Fibre Forum and run by director Janet de Boer and her husband Peter. I must have had about 200 items which all sold with the help of Janet taking the leftovers to some Forum events.

However I still retained the Telia Rumal travelling exhibition collection all rolled up on padded tubes, under my bed. This collection contained items that would not be available ever again and needed to be preserved. Previously I had been to Canberra to the National Gallery and spent time with the conservator, Wendy Dodd and learned some techniques of conservation for some of the small pieces. I felt it would be a shame to let this collection disperse.

My hope was to have it acquired by a state gallery as part of its collection. It would have professional staff and storage facilities to care for items safely

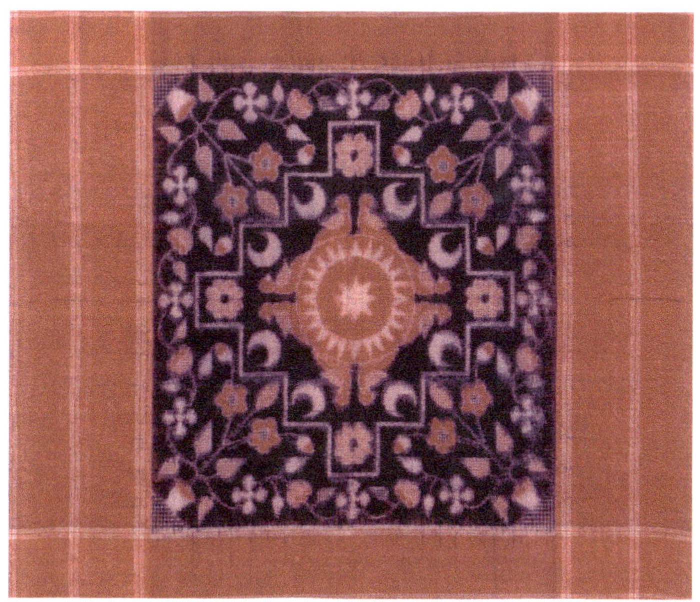

My first and favourite Telia Rumal woven by Gunti Bhaskar Rao

when they are not on display. In the TAASA organisation, one of our members is Tarun Nagash, a curator of Asian Art at the Queensland Art Gallery/Gallery of Modern Art (QAGOMA). Tarun was able to explain the procedure to follow in attempting to have my collection accepted. Many items are offered to galleries around the world, but only those that fit the collection framework of the particular gallery are accepted. Because QAGOMA holds the Asia Pacific Triennial event, it seemed to me, it would be the appropriate home. It was a long process of providing quality images of each item and documenting the works with supporting information. It was good that my initial submission could be checked over to provide me a list of what more was needed. And finally in January when the Acquisition Committee met, they gave approval of work to be accepted into the gallery. It included the 100 square Rumal which Govardhan wove to win the Sri Padma Award. It has now been delivered and entered into the database of gallery artwork. I feel very happy that it has found a good home. Recently I met with the conservator and gave him additional information about the work. The gallery has a journal sent out four times a year telling about the exhibitions on show and other opportunities for lectures, book club, floor talks, and movies available. There was a two page article about my donation to the gallery in the Issue 2/3 2020 of Artlines.

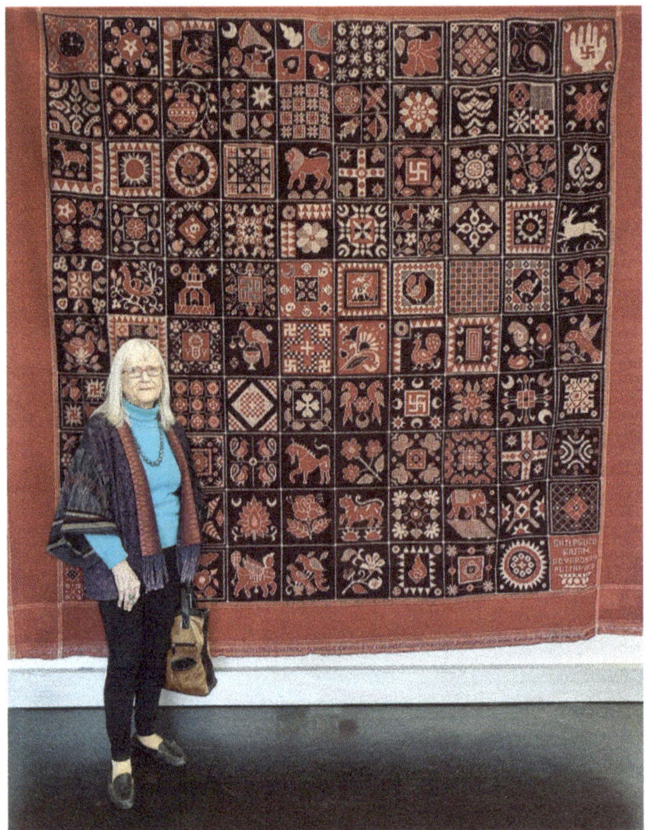

Inspecting the 100 square Telia Rumal at GOMA

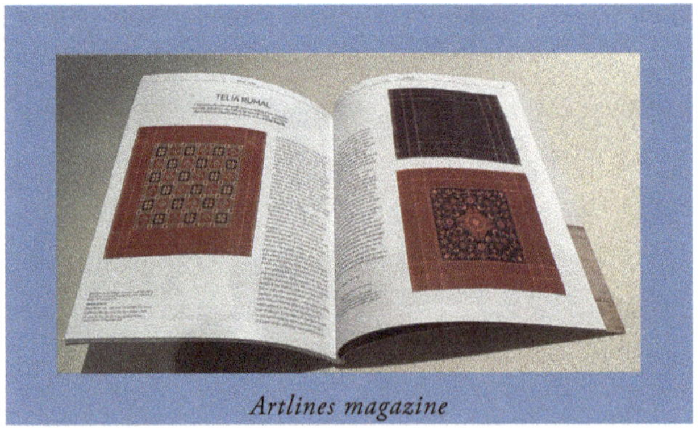

Artlines magazine

JAZZ CLUB

Living in Kangaroo Point, nearly in the shadow of the Story Bridge, when going for a walk, I always pass the Brisbane Jazz Club. It sits on Brisbane's best real estate, on the Brisbane River looking over at the CBD. Bob and I would always say yes, we must come along one night. Somehow we just never got around to it. But now that I am on my own, I have become a member and feel lucky to have this facility nearly in my backyard. I have friends from Ionians who are only visiting Australia from near Washington, DC for part of each year and are great jazz fans. Marj and Dan Druckman are always good for an evening out either for jazz or folk music. I'm always sorry when their visit comes to an end. Other good friends who like sharing an evening at the club are Jill and Tony Lynch. And then there is my family who is harder to get there, but all came along to celebrate my birthday.

During break time it is always nice to go out on the deck for some fresth air and breathtaking views along the river, When it it high tide, the water is nearly lapping onto the platform. During the 2011 flood, much damage was done to the building.

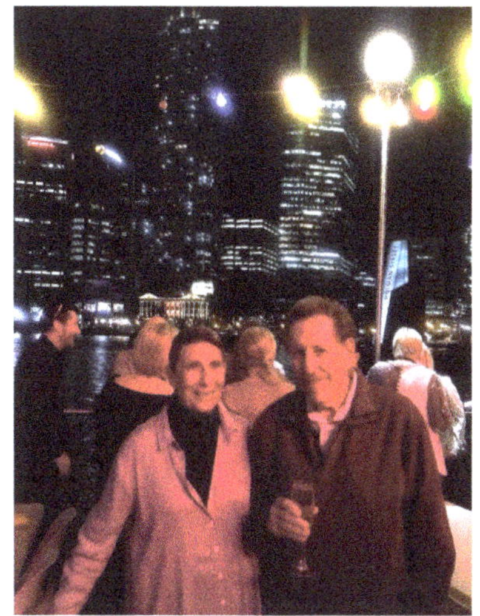

Marj and Dan

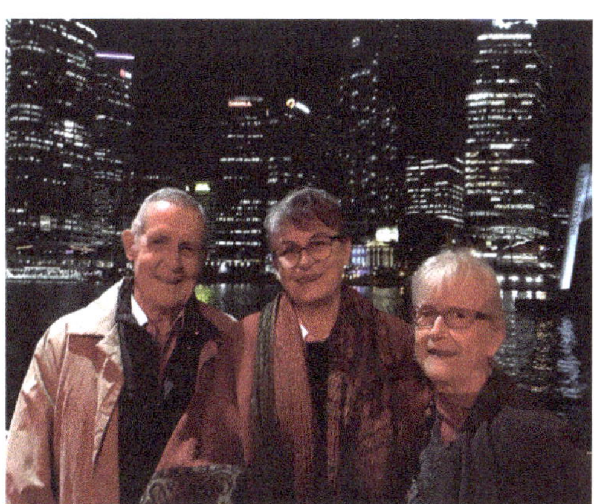

Tony, Jill and I enjoy the view

TRAVELLING FEET

In 2019 my son-in-law, David Hoey had his big WorldSkills International project happening in Russia. These "Olympics" of trade skill events are held every two years, with countries vying to hold them. There are 85 countries around the world that participate in the competitions sending delegates who have won their playoffs in their own countries. David has been CEO of this organisation for 15 years now, making sure that each country has the infrastructure to get the event off the ground. He also negotiates with more governments to join WorldSkills with the aim of working together with youth, educators and industries to help prepare the workforce and talent of today for the jobs of the future.

As it happens every two years, there is always the next event to follow needing supervision. This means that David is travelling over 100 days a year. Jess loves travel too, and when an event is coming up, always goes with David. But she likes to incorporate the WorldSkills event with some side trips. She invests time in planning logical itineraries that work in with the main destination.

The Russian event was held in Kazan, the capital of Tatarstan. This time, I was fortunate to be invited to go with them. This was going to be the trip of a lifetime for me. David had gone ahead to Russia, making sure that all would be ready. Jessica and I were arriving in time for the event, but as we had to go through London to get to Russia, we planned to overnight there and catch up with Conor. We knew he would be working, and would catch up after his shift. Just before leaving on the trip, Sue Byth-Smith mentioned to me that Kew Gardens had a wonderful exhibition of glass sculpture, by artist Dale Chihuly. The installation was entitled, "Reflections on Nature". So we planned to spend the day there before meeting up with Conor. There was also work in the Victorian domed glasshouse. Even without the glass, the gardens were beautiful. We dined at the restaurant where Conor worked and had some gallery time with him. Jess and I went to see the popular musical, "Hamilton" at the theatre but I fell asleep.

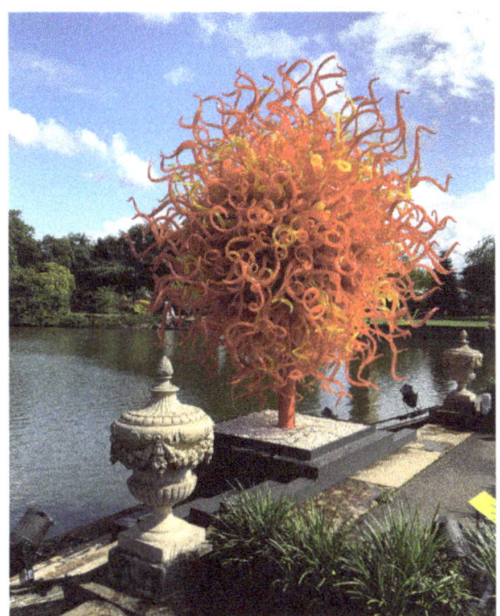

Kew Gardens, Chihuly glass

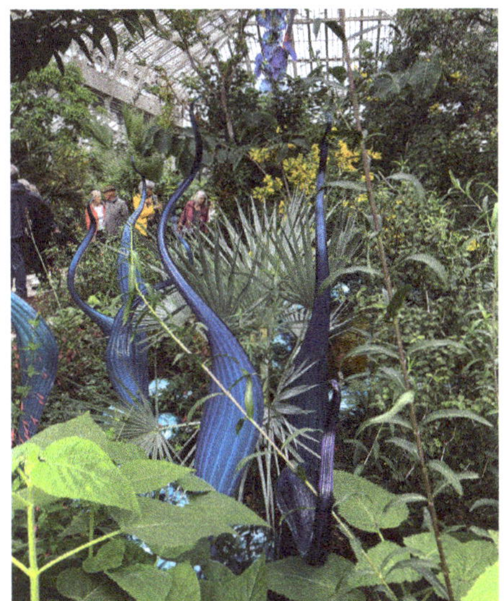

In the glasshouse

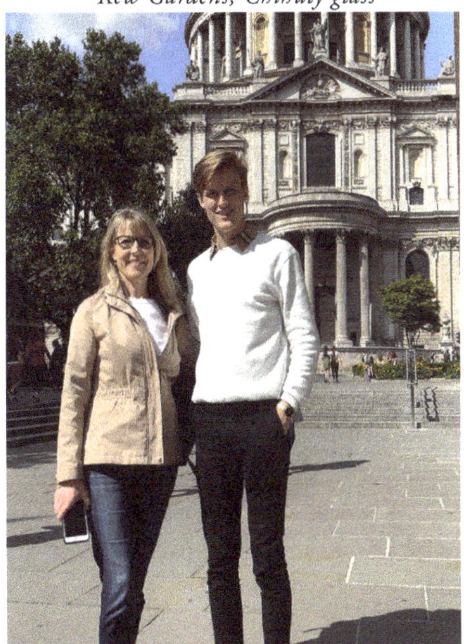

Tate Modern Gallery outing with Conor

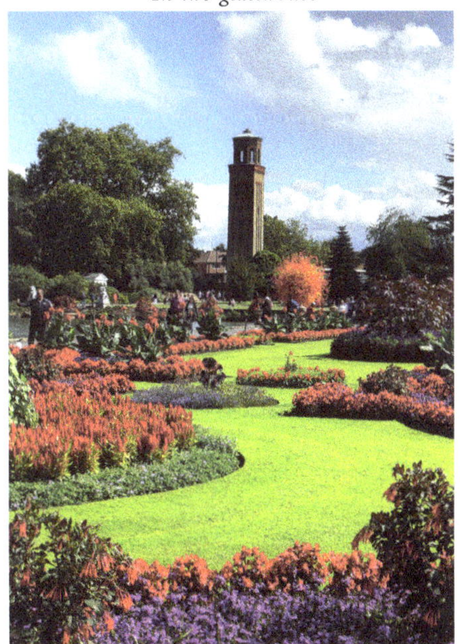

Burst of colour at Kew

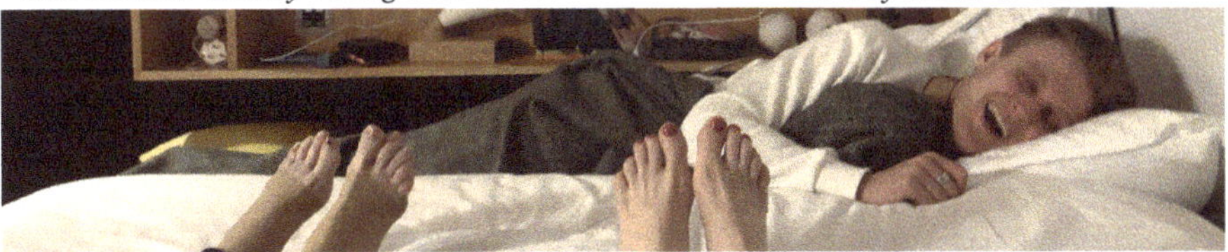

Conor had a sleepover with us

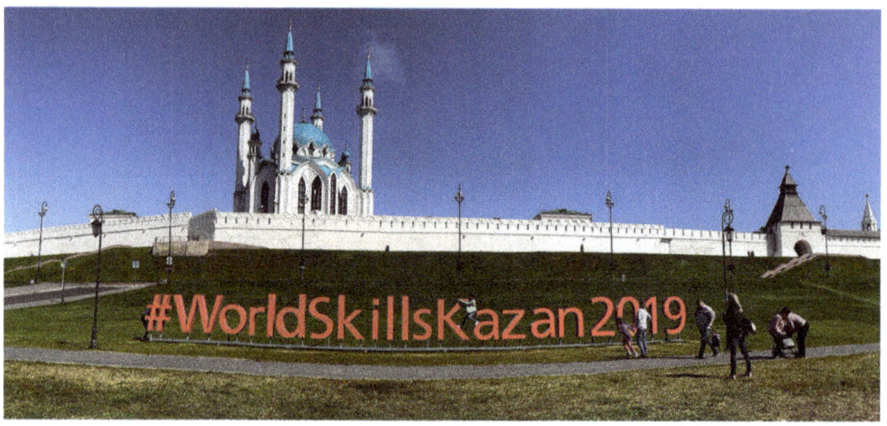

Looking up at the Blue-domed Kremlin

We were going to attend the ceremonies and competitions, but also had the opportunity to be involved in some of the competitions. For Fine Dining, Jess and I along with two other friends, had a table for four. The waitress assigned to us from Indonesia was tested by a panel of experts on how she performed. We sat down and I was surprised to see so many glasses, starting with a shot glass. I didn't know I would be having my first ever shot of vodka before lunch. It didn't go down too badly in the end. We did have a very nice lunch and it was fun to be actually participating in the competition.

Later we walked around seeing various skills being tested. I was interested in the jewellery exercise set for the competitors. It was quite complex and required ability

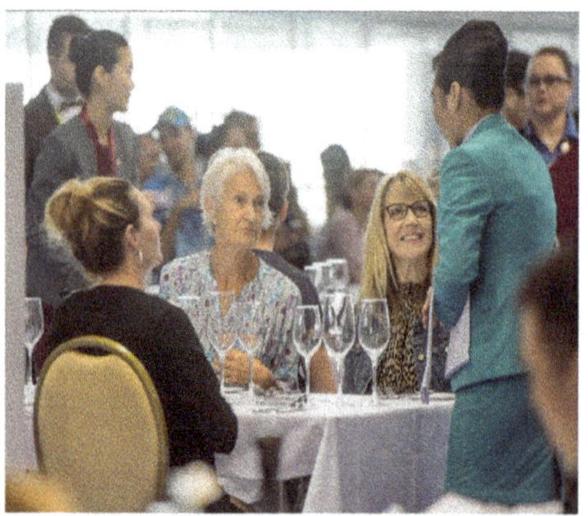

Mary and Jessica with our competitor

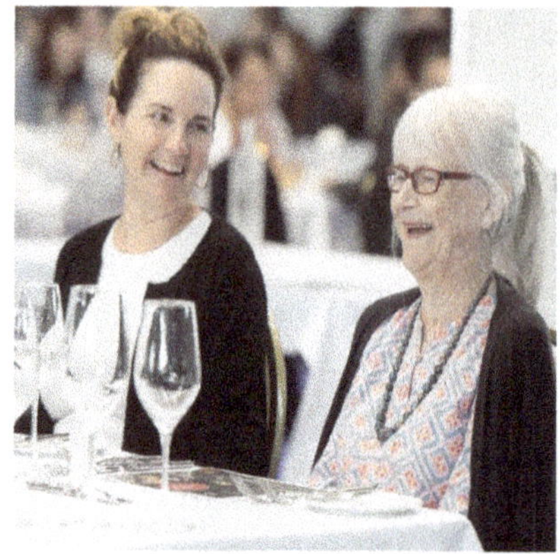

Anouschka and Dana

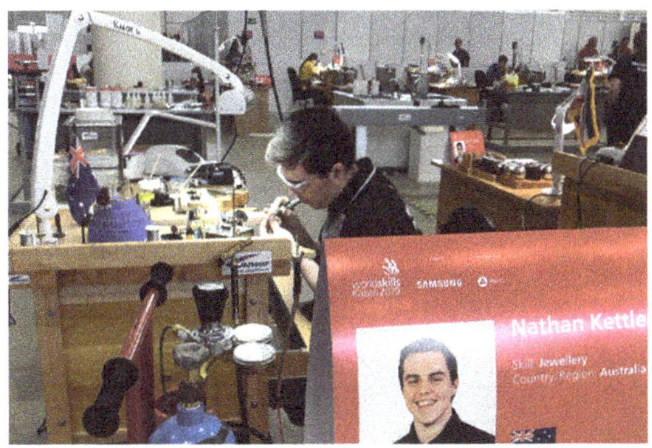

Australian competitor in the jewellery section

in many skills and processes. There were 56 different skills tested, 1500 competitors, and 63 countries involved.

It was interesting to see many groups of high school and technical students being bussed in to get a good look at what trade skills can offer. You could see groups following a guide with a flag to give them the chance to get a good cross-section of activities. And each host country gets to see the quality of work being taught in some of the other countries, often giving them the impetus to improve their own training facilities. The opening ceremony had been held in the arena with an audience of 40,000 people. The competitors filed in following a flag for their county just like the athletic Olympics. The entertainment was world class.

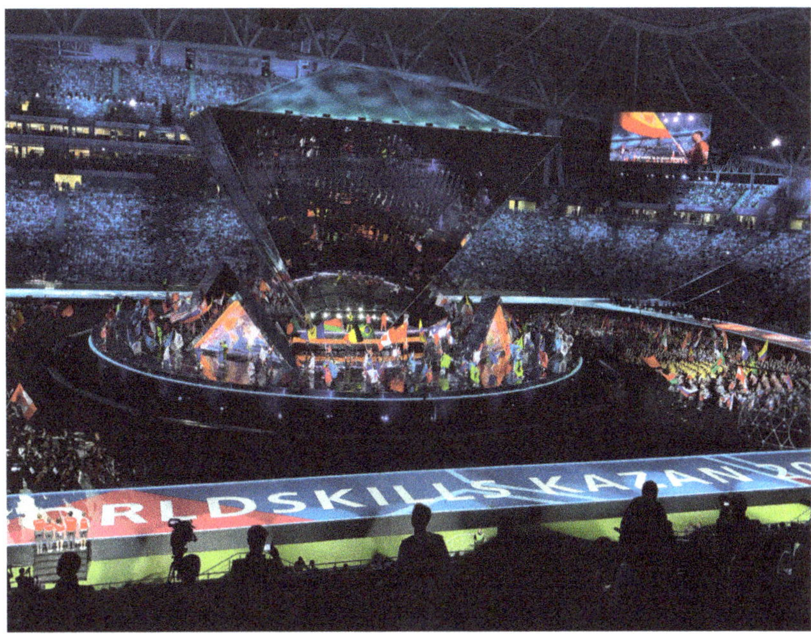

Opening Ceremony at Kazan

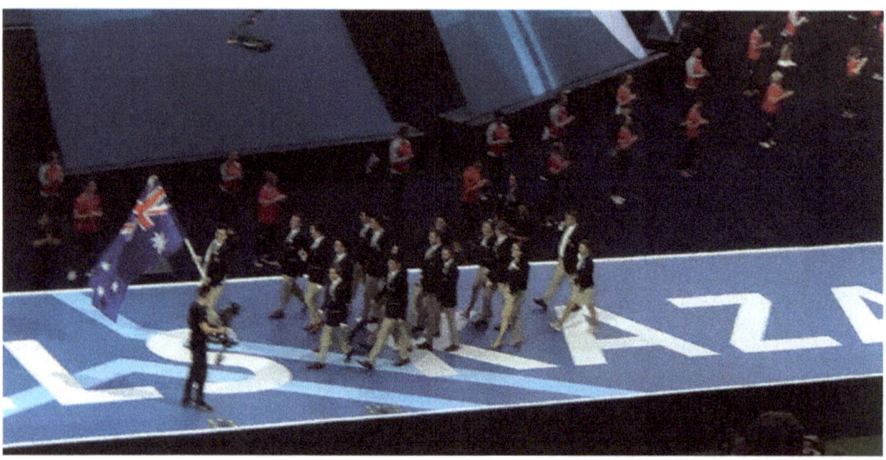

Australian team entering the arena behind the flag

The Closing Ceremony involved the prize-giving and there was obviously strong competition between Russia and China, the host for 2021. It was neck and neck for awhile, but in the end China had the most gold medals. And Putin did attend and spoke at the closing ceremony. Afterward he met with David and some of his staff. I thought I would be going into that reception, but the bodyguards had other thoughts. After hearing about these WorldSkills events for years, until I was actually there, I could not imagine how big an event it all was. As China is the next country to hold the WorldSkills Competition, they put on a banquet for everyone and we attended. The location of the competition will be Shanghai.

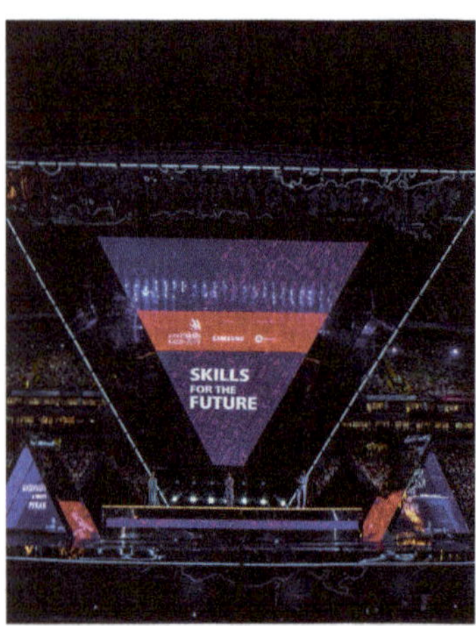

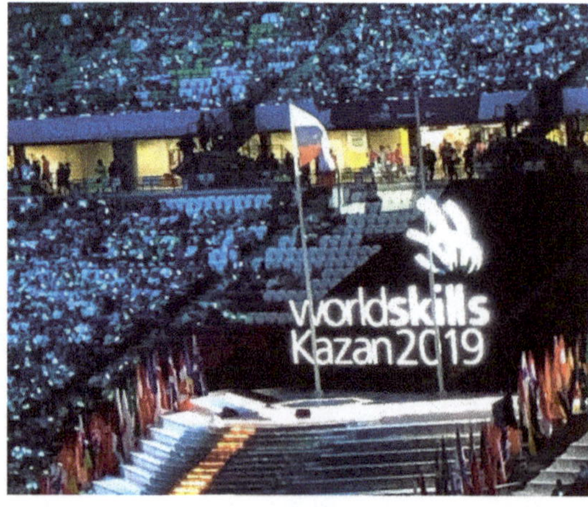

Photos: courtesy of WorldSkills International *Arena*

Jess and I did have some days where we could go around Kazan and other days where we could take side trips. We went to an island where a monastery had been turned into a prison for the priests during the days of religious oppression. Political prisoners had also been kept there. The sculputure imbedded in the outside wall was a reminder of the oppression. But now we saw Orthodox cathedrals and Moslem mosques side-by-side and active in the city of Kazan, known for its tolerance. Quite fascinating was The Temple of All Religions, representing a peaciful harmony of different cultures. It is privately developed.

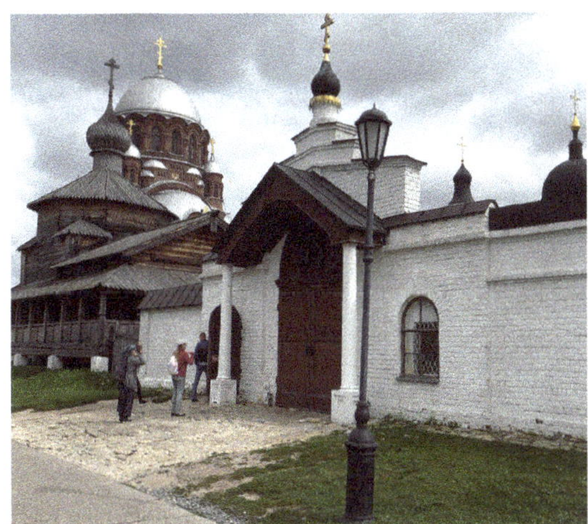

Assumption Monastery

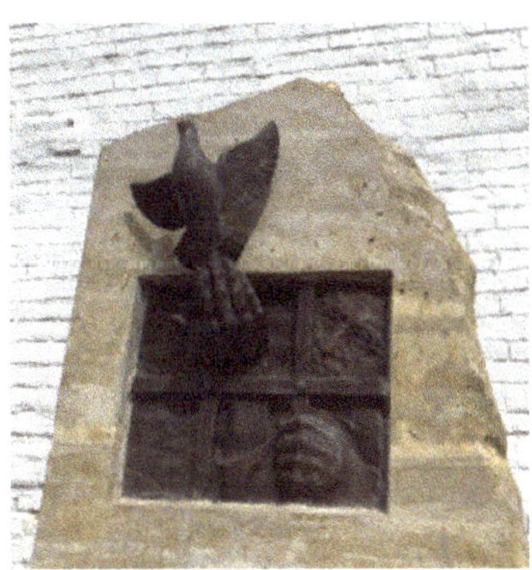

Symbol of the past oppression

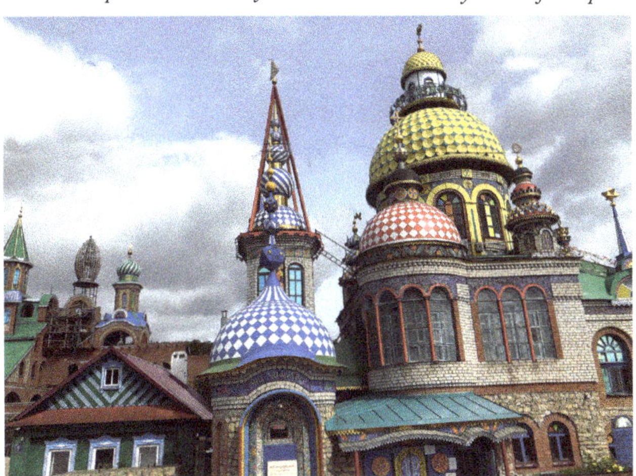

The Temple of All Religions is still being expanded

After Kazan we had travel plans to see more of Russia together with Jess and David's good friends Jos and Anouschka de Goey. First we had to go to St Petersburg and visit the Hermitage without a doubt. We saw works there by the world's best artists that I had never seen duplicated in any book. It was a feast for the eyes. There were whole rooms of Rembrandts, Matisses and Renoirs and much more.

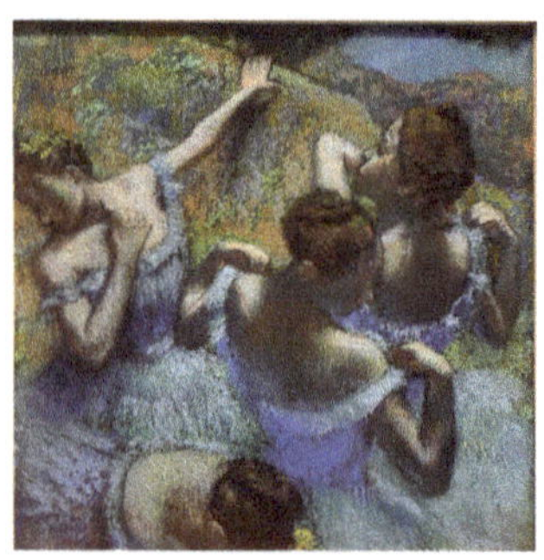

Dancers in Blue by Degas

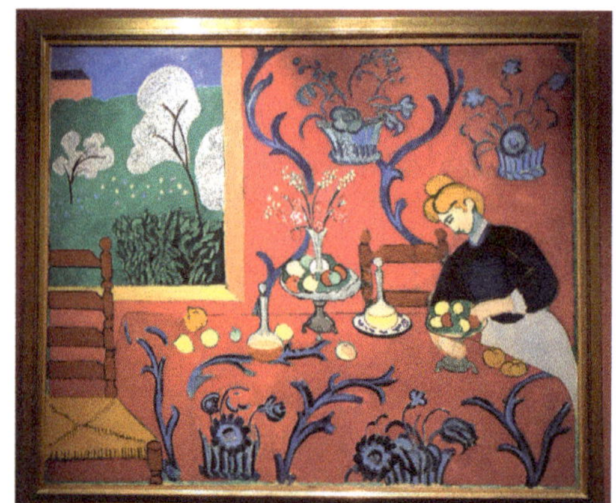

The Red Room by Matisse

There was a fascinating exhibition of porcelain from the famous Meissen Porcelain Manufactory of "Forbidden Fruit". It might have been my favourite. This exhibition was a collaboration with American ceramic artist Chris Andemann, who had been headhunted by Meissen to produce a collection based on their heritage figurines to have a new viewpoint of related and exciting contemporary works. The theme based on the Garden of Eden showed an impressively grand porcelain structure. It combined the Temple of Love idea also with

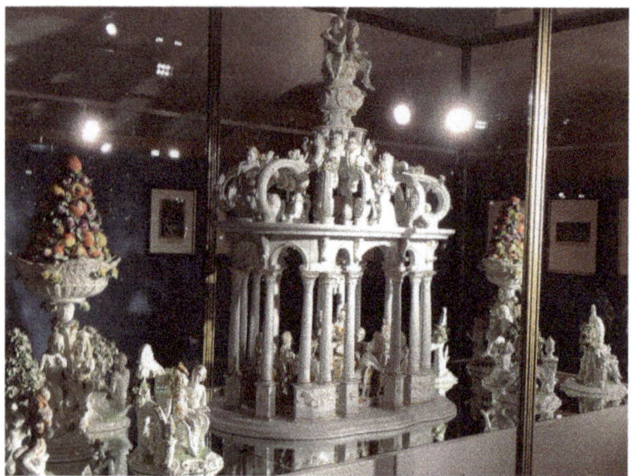

Forbidden Fruit by Chris Andemann

vignettes of seduction. In this interpretation, the women are dressed, but the men are often naked.

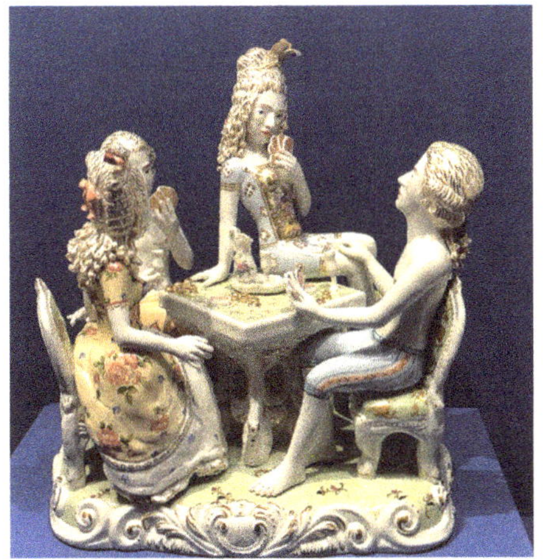

The card game

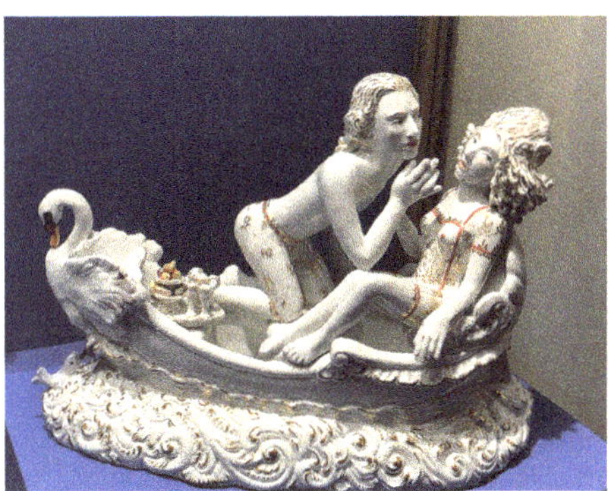

Amour in the swan boat

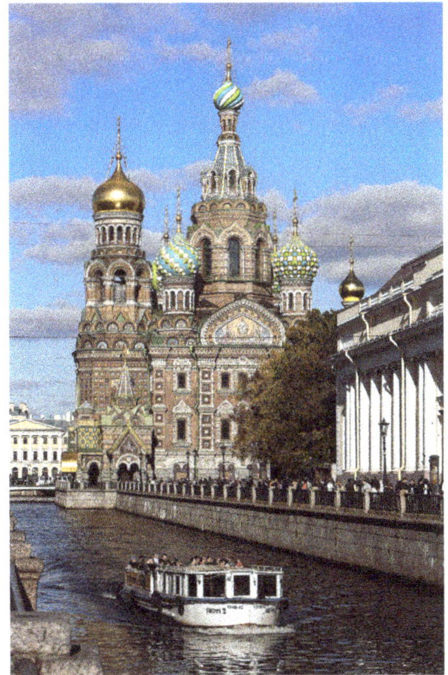

Perfect site for the Church of Spilled Blood

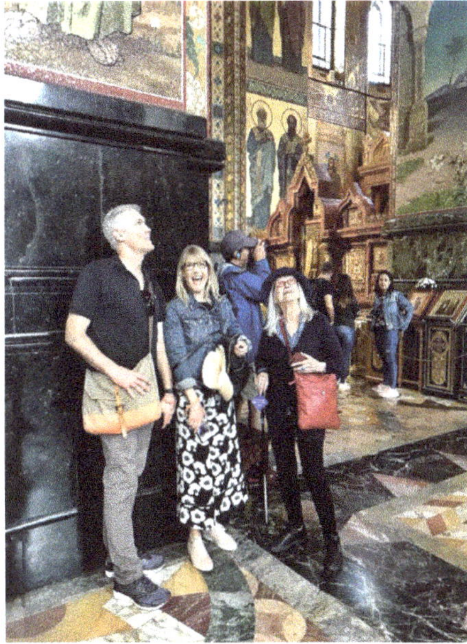

Interior of Church

We visited the Church of Spilled Blood and marvelled at the architecture and the art within. Icons were of interest to me especially as I have two cousins who became icon artists, studying with Russian teachers. I do own an icon by Judy Kaestner of Arch Angel Michael. I was sad to learn that Judy had passed away this past year after a long illness with Multiple Sclerosis. Recently I received an image of an icon by Sandra Lillydahl of the Trinity, which has an interesting twist. All seem to be women.

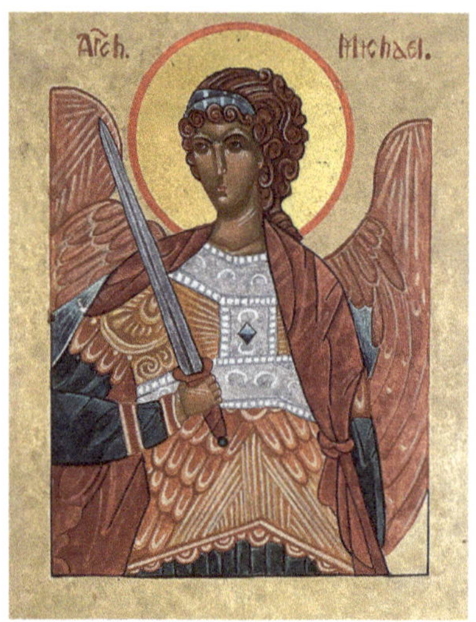

Archangel Michael by Judy Kaestner

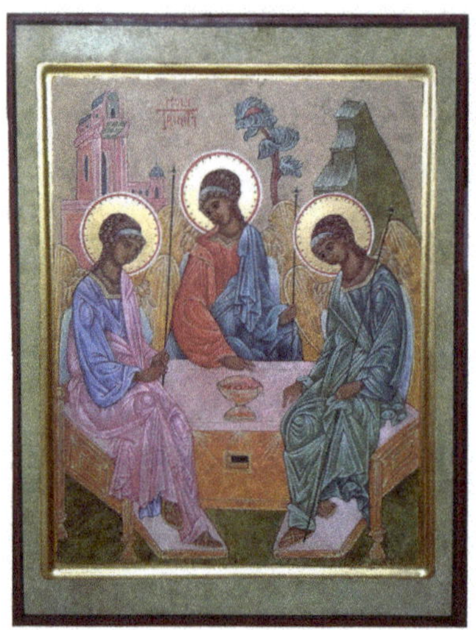

Trinity by Sandy Lillydahl

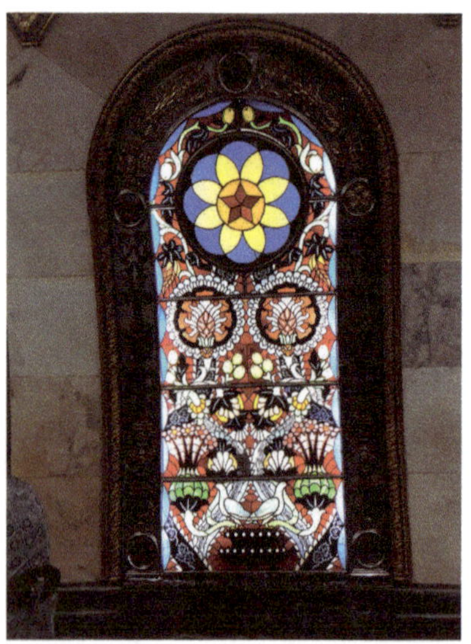

A whole station full of stained glass

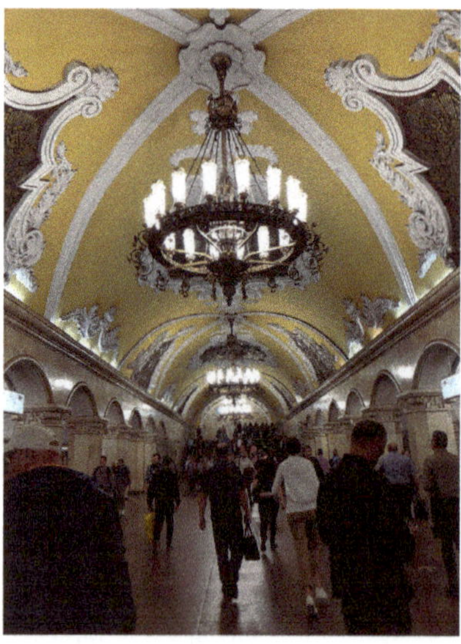

A station of chandeliers

Our last stop in Russia was Moscow. It was a priority to see the underground Metro stations that in actual fact are Art Galleries in their own right. It was interesting that each station along the line had entirely different types of art.

As part of Ionians, I belong to a book club. One book on our list was "A Gentleman in Moscow", quite a popular book presently. Count Rostov lived at the Metropol Hotel under house arrest, unable to go out the door. I desperately wanted to stay at the Metropol after reading and enjoying this award-winning book. However as we would be travelling with Jess and David's friends it was best to let them help in the decision-making. David gave them a choice of several hotels for Moscow and when they picked the Metropol, I was very happy. The location was perfect being close to Red Square and St Basil's Cathedral. The Bolshoi Ballet Theatre was across the road, but unfortunately the company was performing away.

Besides having the freedom to roam around the hotel, we did a lot of walking to take in the sights and Jos gave us a running tally of how many steps we did each day. The best or most demanding day was 22,000 steps. We thought it was a good attempt to stay active and healthy.

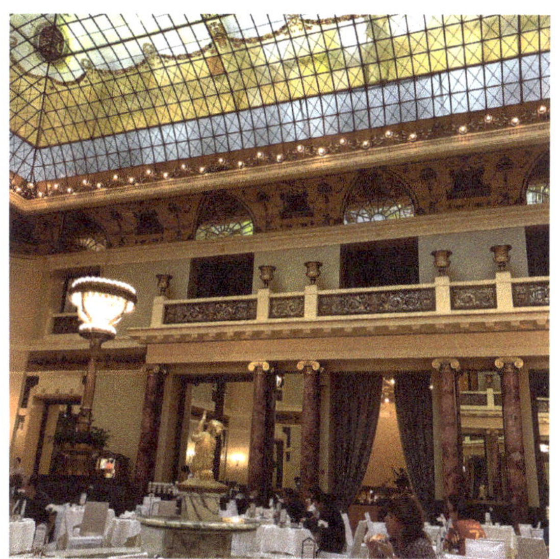

The Metropol Atrium Dining

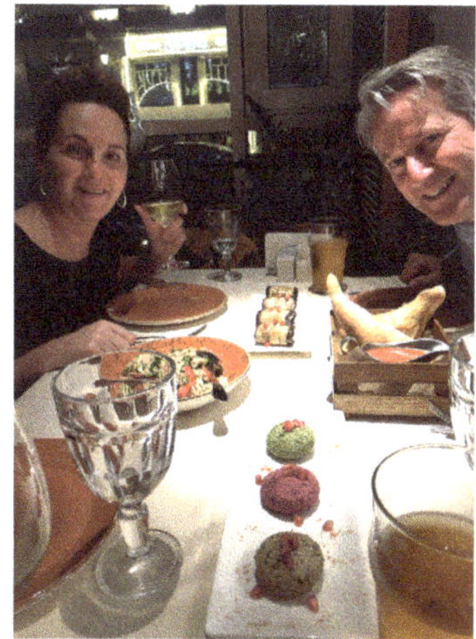

Anouschka and Jos

Cathedrals had been closed and used in different ways due to the atheistic government. The UNESCO World Heritage site, St Basil's at Red Square, was taken over by the government in 1928 and made into a museum. Its history dates back to 1555-61 when it was first built. It was shaped like the flames of a bonfire pointing upward. Since the breaking up of the Soviet Union, services are now held.

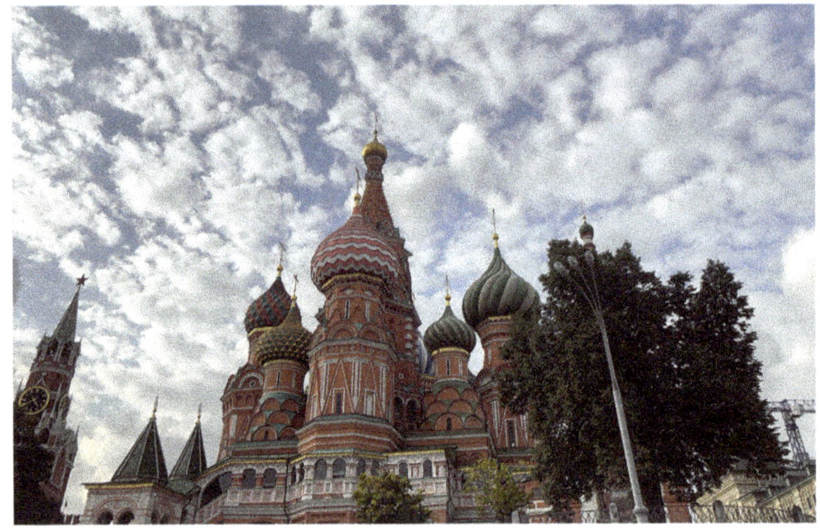

St. Basil's

The Cathedral of Christ the Saviour had an unfortunate demolition as the government eyed the large amount of gold in the domes. Dynamite was used to blast it apart on orders of Stalin. For many years it was the site of a large pool.

Rebuilding by the Orthodox Church started in 1995 and finished in 2000.

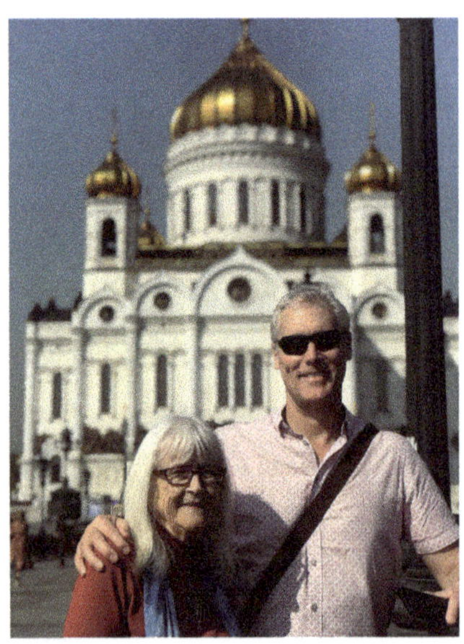

Christ the Saviour Cathedral

PARIS CALLS

We farewelled the de Goeys and departed for our next adventure. Jessica was having her birthday and had organised that we would be in Paris to overlap with her special day. Besides picnicking at the Eiffel Tower, visiting the Rodin Museum, seeing the damage at Notre Dame, we found that there was a special Luminaire show of Van Gogh at Atelier des Lumieres and it was an outstanding immersive experience in the round. And we had a great Airbnb.

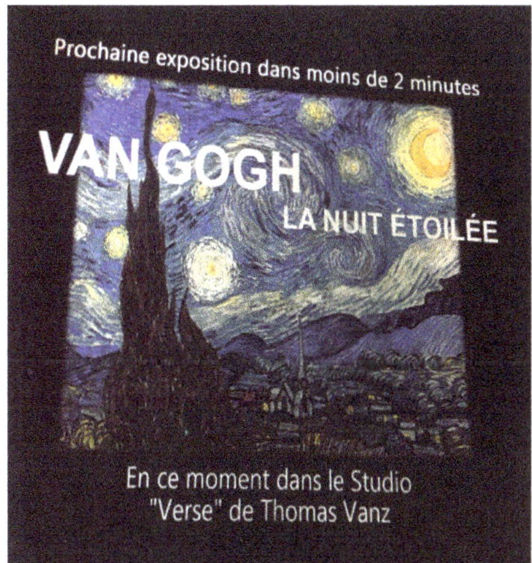

Atelier des Lumieres

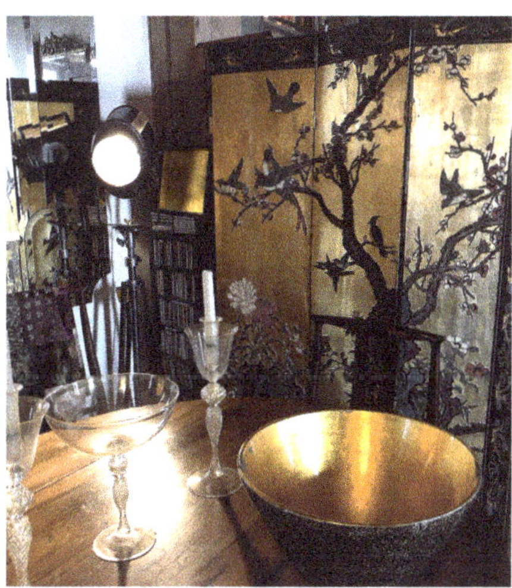

Airbnb

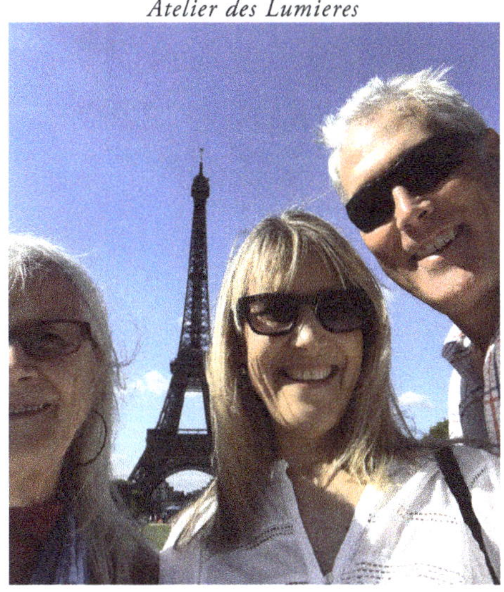

At the Eiffel Tower

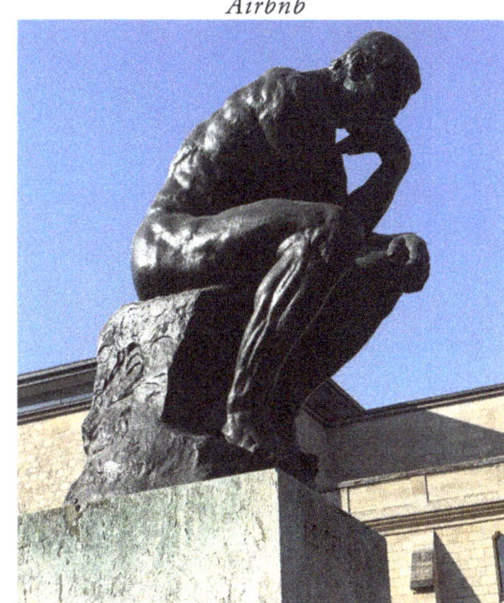

Rodin, The Thinker

Our next adventure was in Croatia having a cruise of a different kind. Our vessel, The Agape Rose, had a total capacity of 40 passengers, however we only had 34. The week-long trip took us north along the coastline from Dubrovnik stopping between the Dalmatian Islands and the towns along the way. We had walking tours every day, getting to see historic sights and scenic natural beauty. It was planned that we would have either our lunch or dinner off the boat, in small cafes and restaurants trying the local fare. The trip had been recommended to Jess and David by friends who had done it the year before. A couple on the boat had done the cruise the year before and like it so much they came again. And we met such nice travelling companions.

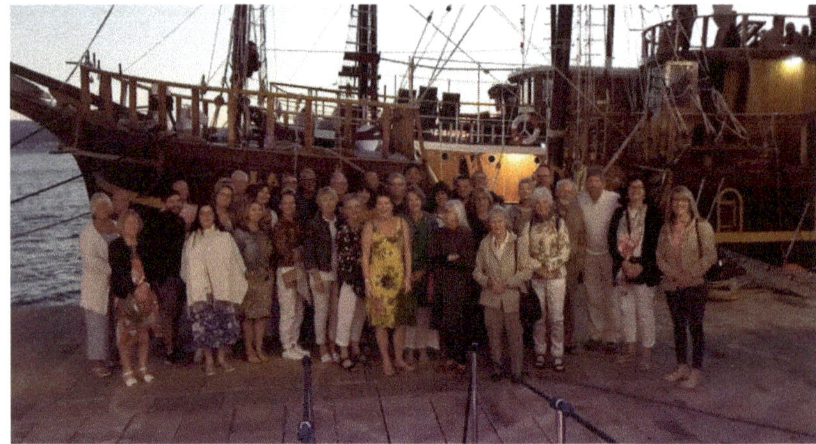

Our group

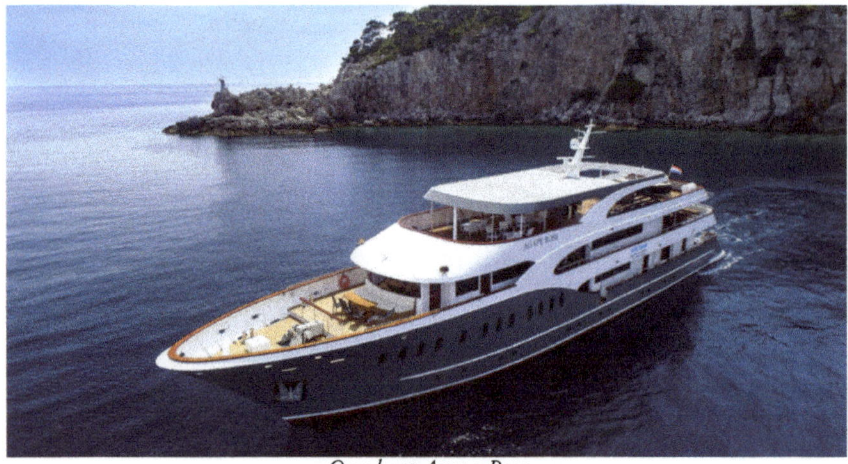

Our boat Agape Rose

One of the most fun activities was swimming off the end of the ship in the Adriatic Sea. I hadn't taken swimmers along, as I had no intention of getting in water. But I couldn't resist and bought bikinis in town after dinner, so I wouldn't miss out the next day.

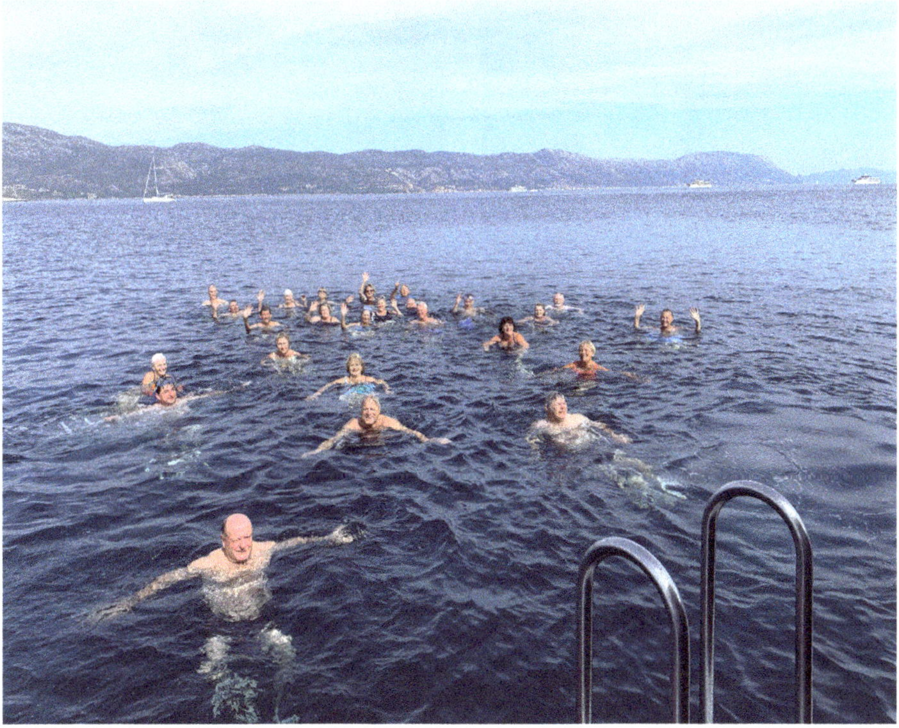

There I am, way in the back

Croatia is a beautiful country with much history and ancient buildings even from the Roman times. Our walking tours were educational and fun. We learned that the church brought in Benedictine nuns that taught the art of lacemaking giving women a way to earn an income, using fine

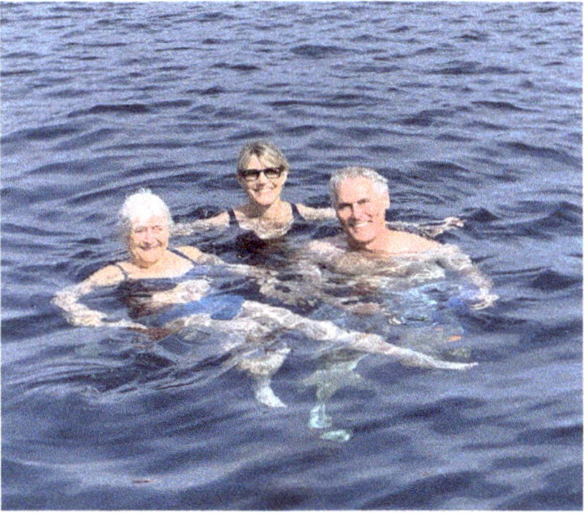

The three of us

agave plant fibre, hundreds of years ago. Traditionally there was embroidery done with different designs for folk costumes of each community group. The museum had good displays of local dress. There was a labyrinth of narrow lanes.

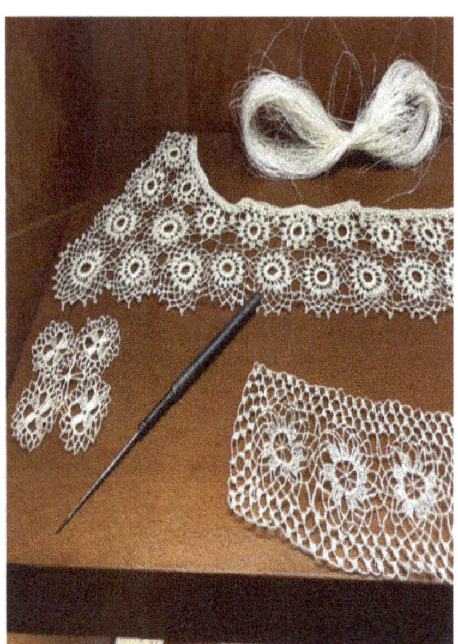

Agave lace making

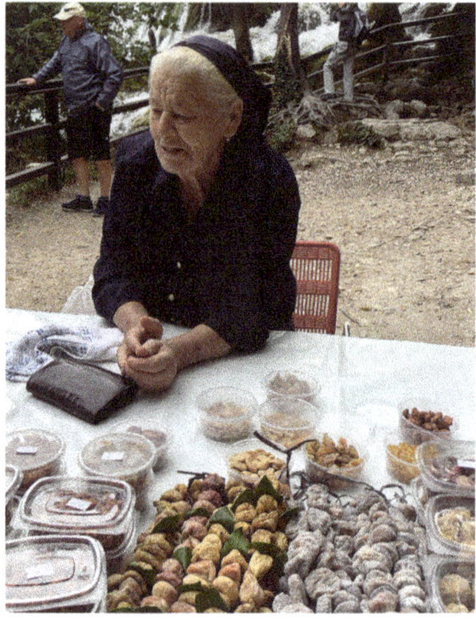

Fig and nut season

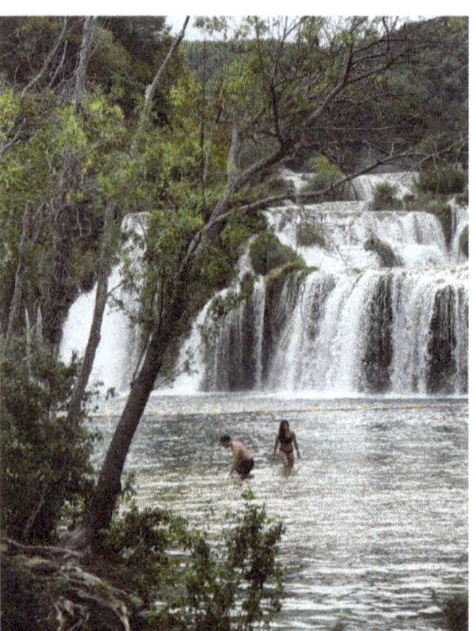

Abundance of water

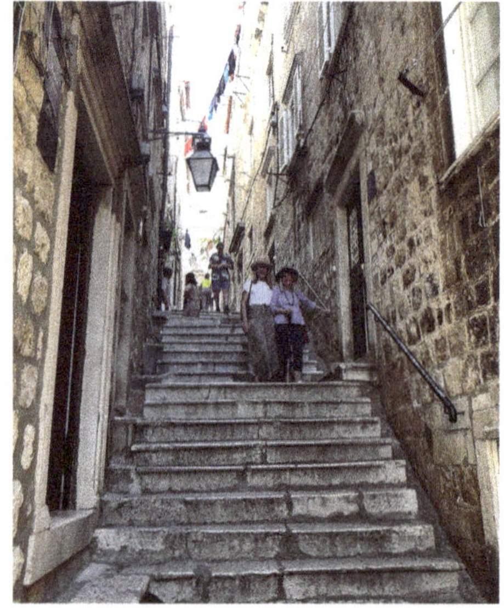

Small lanes and stairways everywhere

All good things come to an end and it was time to leave Croatia, but we had to fly to London to get our return flight to Oz. So this gave us the opportunity to catch up again with grandson Conor, who had been working in London during the year. It was very rewarding to see that he could start off on an overseas holiday with friends and end up getting a job without too much effort. All that work experience he got both in hospitality and then IT, while obtaining his degree, paid off.

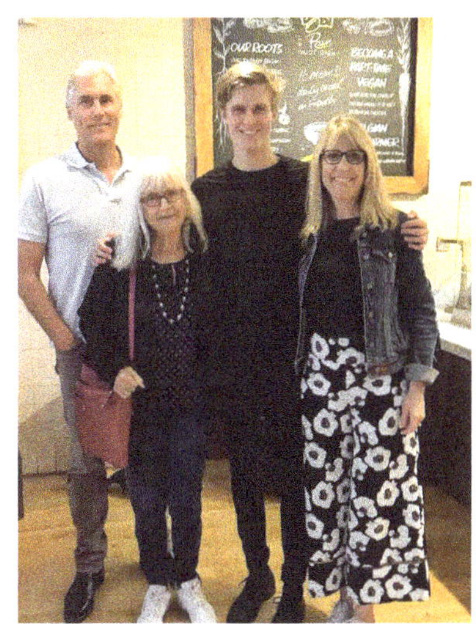

Quick lunch with Conor

There are times when good opportunities all come at once. Having had this exceptional trip to Russia, I must have been in the mood to keep in the swing of things. So I signed up to go on a trip to Taiwan with my Ionian Club for February 2020 to be there for the Lantern Festival. The group consisted of people I like and so knew it would be fun. Then Jessica and David invited me to travel to Vietnam with them and also granddaughter Paris in January. But I said I couldn't possible go, as the trip to Taiwan was already paid for. Of course they thought that was no excuse at all, considering all the travel they do. So I went. They knew I had wanted to go to Vietnam for a long time, but could not interest Bob in doing so. I did want to see some of the after-effects of the Vietnam War, and heard how beautiful the country is.

We took an Intrepid tour for a change to take the entire heavy planning away and just enjoy the experience. We started in the north and worked our way down the coast. It included overnight train travel, bus, and overnight boat on the Halong Bay where we did cave exploring, mountain climbing, and kayaking. Luckily that came early on, as I became ill with food poisoning and was in hospital in Hue. The hospital was international, but few staff spoke English and it did make for some problems. At least it was an experience, but I have to apologize to Jess and

David. I had been resisting use of the gel hand sanitizer that they always carry. Bob had been dead set against it and thought we all needed a bit of dirt. Needless to say, I regret giving them the inconvenience, but the tour leader from Intrepid was fabulous and helpful. I have now reformed.

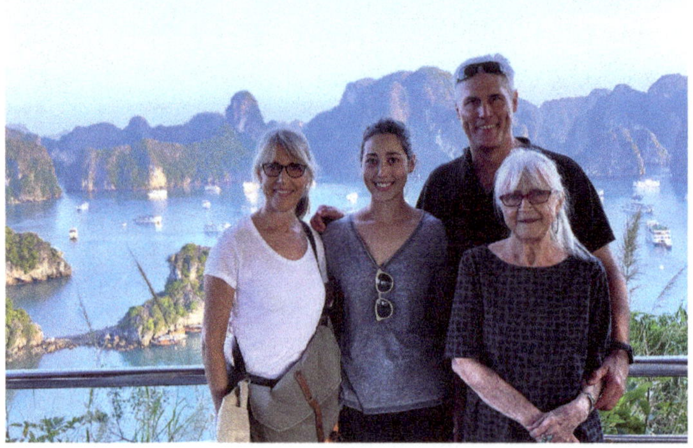

Lovely view of Halong Bay

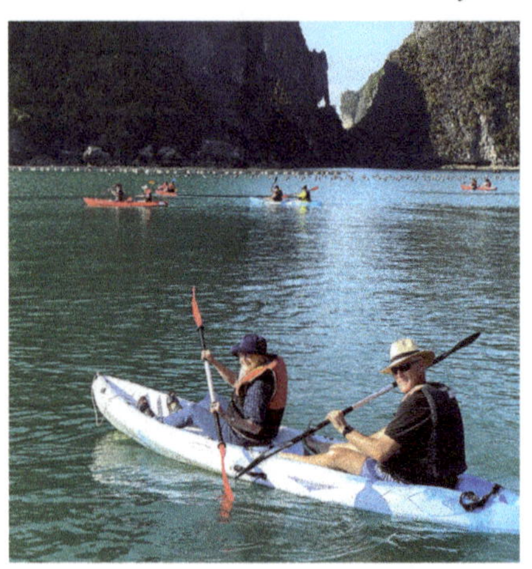

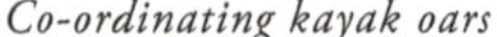

Co-ordinating kayak oars

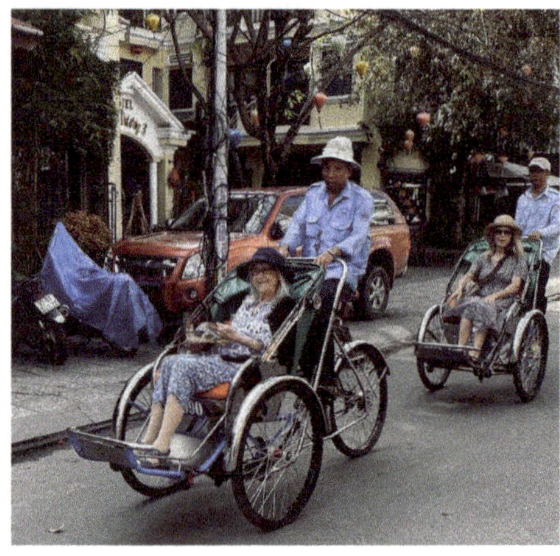

Transport best for me after hospital

So home again and getting ready for the trip to Taiwan for the Lantern Festival, suddenly the Corona virus appeared out of nowhere. Well - actually out of China. At our morning coffee group, some friends going on the trip started worrying and thinking of dropping out of the trip, but were told no refund would be give through travel insurance. Masks were discussed and my granddaughter, Maddie provided me with a selection. It was early days with the virus, so not much was known. But conflicting advice was being made by government and medical staff.

We did go and all precautions were already in place in Taiwan. We had our temperature taken each time going into a restaurant or museum. Getting back into our bus, the leader came around and sprayed our hands with an alcohol mixture. And a new mask was handed out each day. Our tour guide requested we wear our masks when out of the bus in public places. We had a great time and saw everything as planned. Especially wonderful were the treasures in the museum.

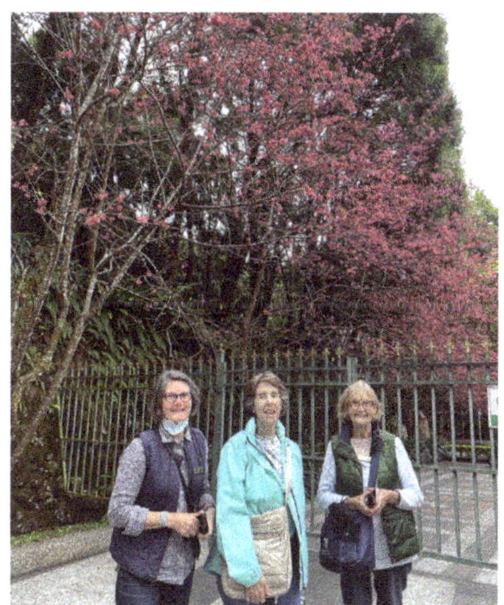

Cherry blossom season

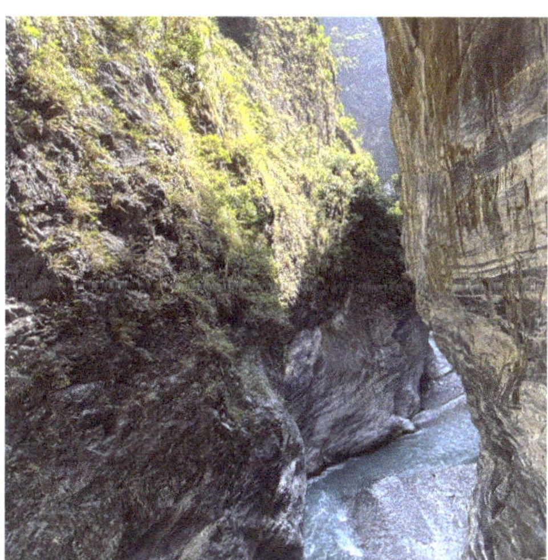

19 km long marble gorge

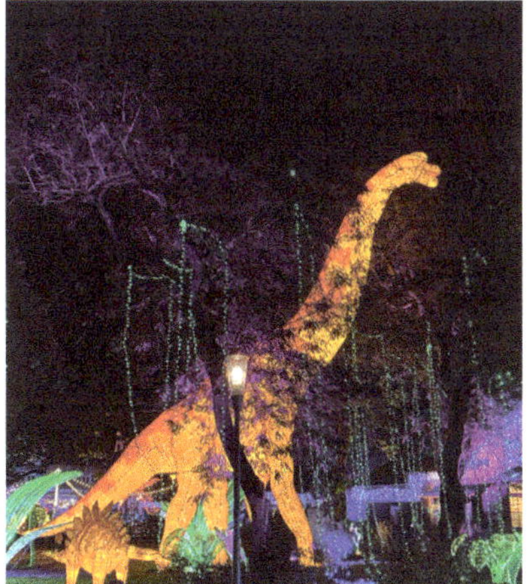

Illuninations of all sizes

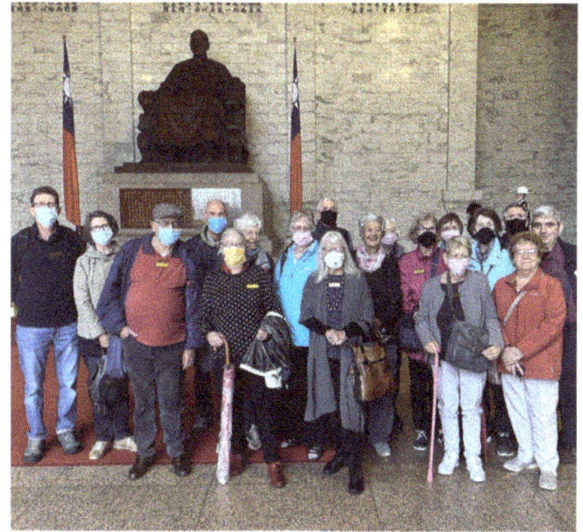

At the National Art Museum of Taiwan

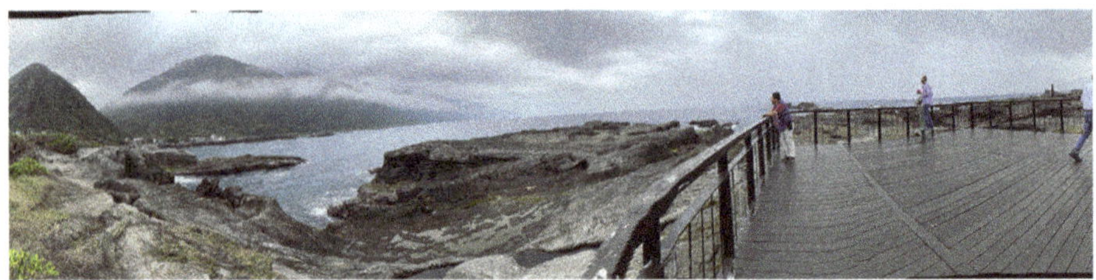

Taiwan coastline

When we arrived back home, we learned that Taiwan is one of the star countries dealing with the virus. It was the safest place we could have been. In Australia we are following isolation and lockdown rules that are working very well. Our biggest problems have come from cruise ships offloading passengers carrying the virus. But it is sobering to think about other infections in the world that are still killing millions each year, such as malaria and TB.

ROSE'S RHAPSODY 2020

Through the years since living in Townsville I had run many indigo dye workshops, as it is still fascinating and magical to me after all this time. I have put them on for Spinners and Weaver groups, Ionians Third Thursday events, TAASA and most recently at "Rose's Rhapsody" in Tenterfield. Rose was approaching her 60th birthday and wanted to create a week-long event to celebrate. Rose has been in our lives since that time she and Jenny were roommates at St Peters. She and her mother June have had a special place in our hearts. So it was always going to

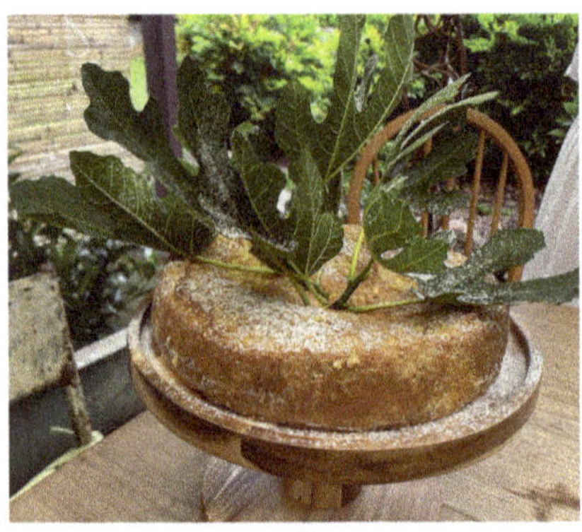

Fig infusion cake

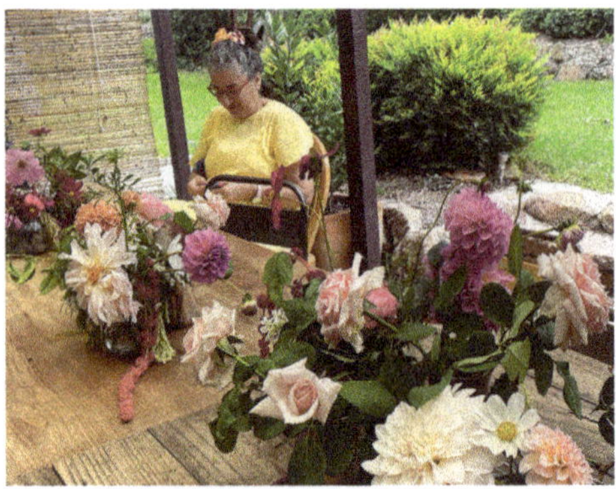

Simple but beautiful arrangements

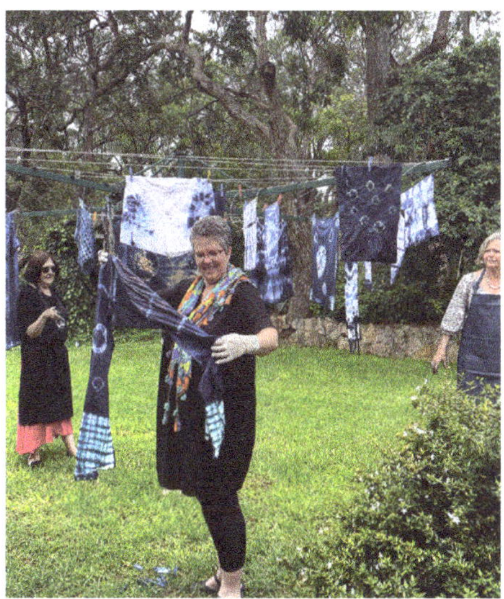
Finella hangs her dyeing

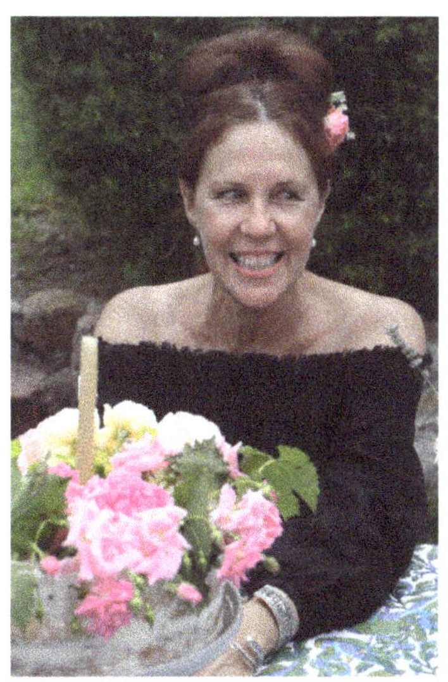
The Birthday girl

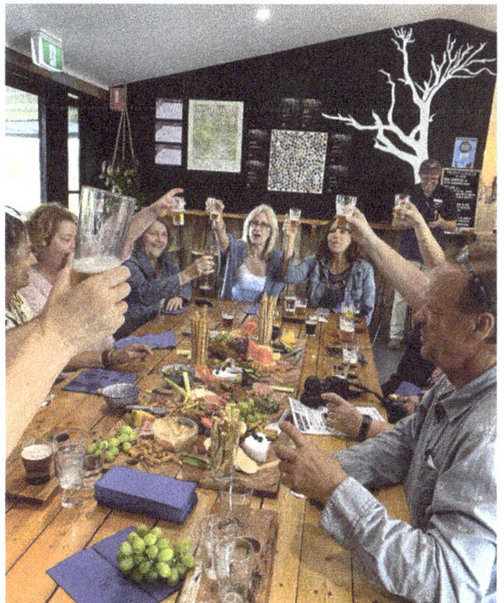
Boutique beer sampling

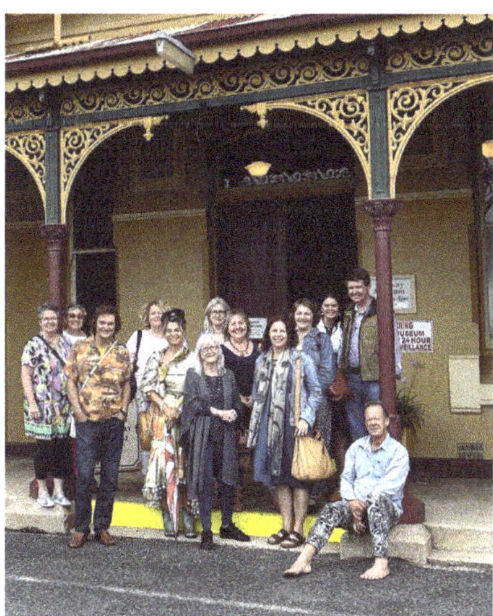
The historic train station

be a priority for me to get to Tenterfield to run a workshop. Luckily the lockdown wouldn't start for another week. There was to be a flower arranging workshop, a yoga session run by Rose, cake making demonstration, historical bus tour, visit to brewery, a garden birthday lunch for 60 people and an indigo dye workshop run by me. Oh yes, there was a jam night of music and dancing, but I missed it as I had to go home for another party. And I missed the Birthday lunch which was put on by Rose's son, Tom who is a chef. But I drove back to Brisbane in time for the special birthday of friend, Kay Brothers, and there I decided to offer her a birthday present of publishing a book of her wonderful poems. Kay is part of the Kangaroo Point Neighbourhood Watch Group that I have a "cuppa" with every Saturday morning at a local cafe. There is a monthly meeting and as the treasurer, I make out the financial report. Our claim to fame this year was updating the Heritage Walk booklet to now include stories of the people who lived in these heritage buildings.

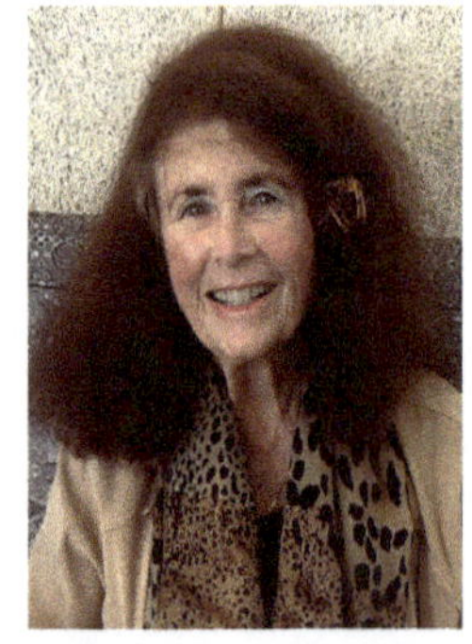

Kay

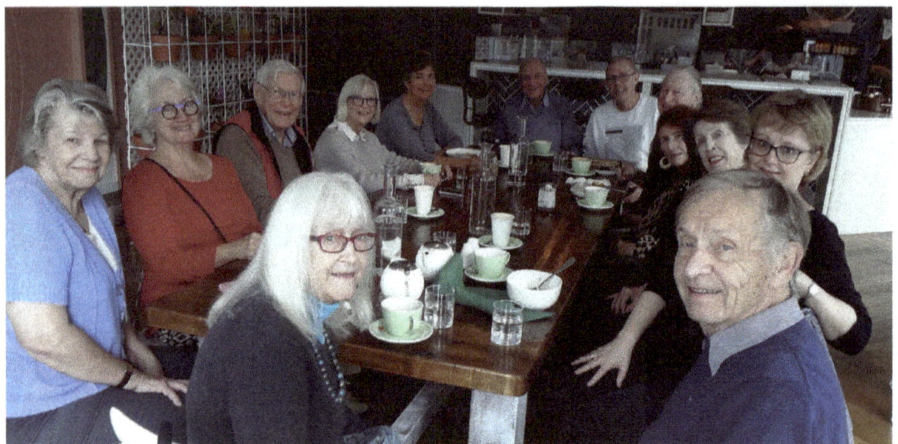

Kangaroo Point Neighbourhood Watch Coffee Group

Recently I have been keeping an indigo dyebath active in my garage, as Jessie, Jenny and Uta, Jordan's wife like to do some dyeing. Sometimes it's clothing and most recently Jenny dyed a tablecloth for me for Mother's Day complete with napkins. This has been another good activity, when I was limited to what the family would let me do in the pandemic, as I am considered to be in the age group of higher risk.

Soon our gyms will be opening again. It has been too easy to lapse into bad habits, so I will need to get fit again. Going out on a walk along the river, I feel that I am so fortunate living here and enjoying the beautiful sunny days near family and friends. But I have to acknowledge what a difference it made, having Facebook and other digital means of having contact with friends and loved ones each day. I have not felt isolated, but given an opportunity to use the time of isolation to sit at my computer and write this story, with little distraction. And I must acknowledge that grandson Jordan and his wife Uta have been staying with me. They go out and stock up on groceries at supermarkets and get my needs from the chemist. Not only that, they prepared the most delicious meals in the evening. And it is no wonder I have put on weight, with such great cooking going on. Uta is shown in this photo with her feast of handmade rice paper wraps, Korean pancake, seafood laksa and sauce. Jordan did BBQs but also created handmade black squid noodles (as shown), lasagna, tiramisu and more.

Now I've put the last words in my story. But at the age of 84, I feel I still have time to have many more adventures and experiences in life, to write some new chapters in my book for a second edition. Each day is an opportunity and a gift and I intend to use it.

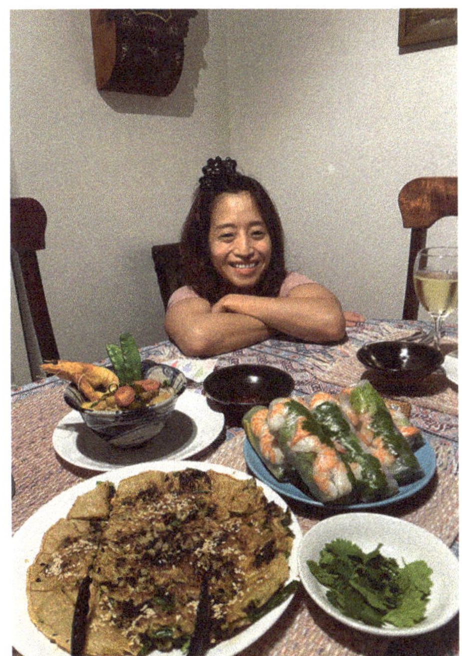

Uta and her feast

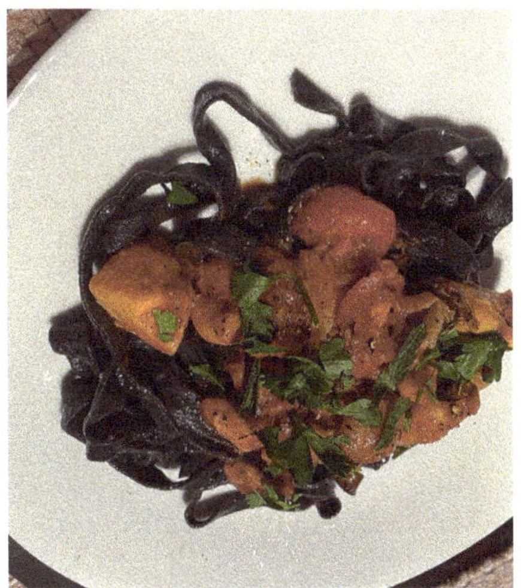

Jordan's squid noodles

ACKNOWLEDGEMENTS

Many thanks to family members for digging out photographs that I couldn't find. Special thanks for all the proof reading that was done by Jenny McCown and the entire Hoey Family. David Hoey did extra duty with proofing. Sam McCown needs credit for pushing me past my comfort zone into using Adobe InDesign for this book and being a backup support when I got into trouble. I had owned it for years and used it for graphics, but never attempted a large book project. Sam also came to the party with cover design, his special skill as an artist. So hopefully the family now know more about our family background and me, during the time before they came into being. And special thanks and all my love to the family for being my support in everyday life.

Epilogue

Last year our Sudanese friend, Paduol Ater, who Bob helped become a pilot, grabbed at a new opportunity. He was assured of a job flying in the Sudan, if he travelled to Nairobi and passed the aviation regulations in East Africa and trained on the planes they were using. He successfully achieved all the credentials. Meanwhile while doing the training, he became engaged to a young woman. He then started flying in Sudan, building up his hours. Much of the work was delivering supplies for the United Nations. He was in a team of three, as the first officer. The pilot was from Malawi, I believe. This little airline is actually a

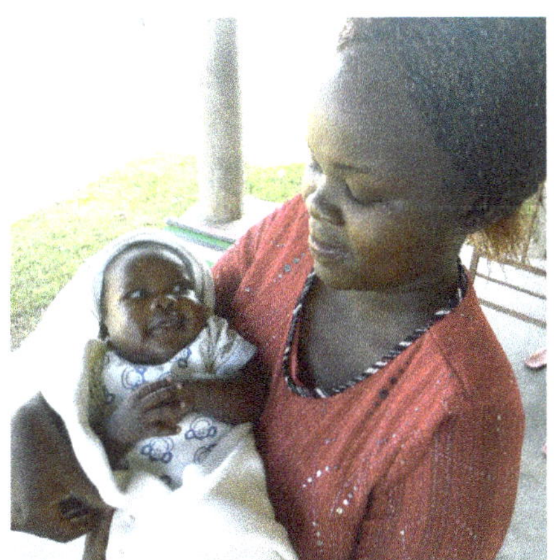

Baby Kucbeny with Ajok

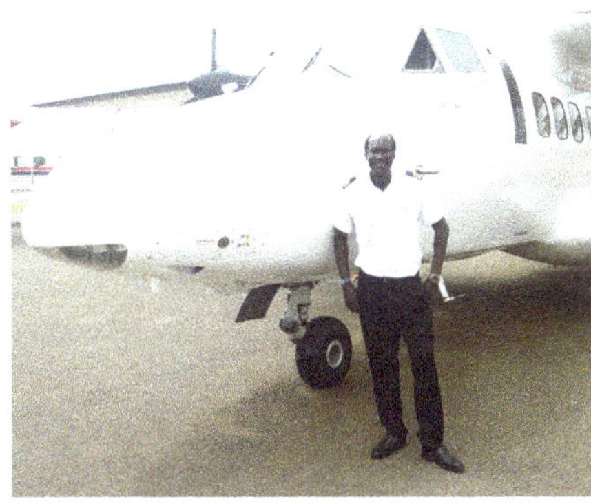

Paduol with the plane

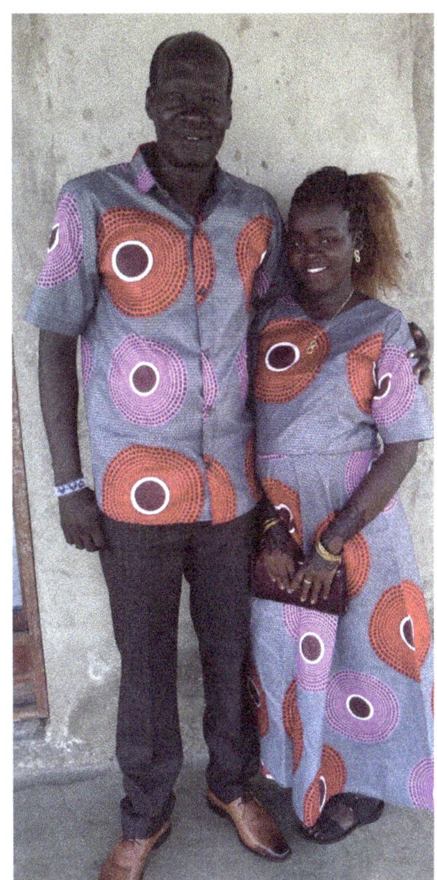

Paduol with wife Ajok

Philippine company that only has three planes. Paduol has related the story of what happened several months ago when trying to deliver UN supplies. They were hit by a wind sheer and came down, clipping a school building and landing heavily, damaging the plane. The area was controlled by rebels who took them as hostage for eight days, demanding money for the school. Finally when the airline management arrived from Kenya, they were released and sent to hospital to check for injury. Paduol was ok, but had come down with malaria and typhoid due to bad conditions in the area. Now he is recovering, but the plane is not fixed and it is a waiting situation. Luckily South Sudan is not having big numbers of coronavirus cases. But there is some good news in that Paduol became a father this year of a baby boy named Kucbeny. Bob would have been happy for Paduol.

After spending such wonderful times with David and Jess's good friend and collegue, Jos, and his wife Anouschka, last year, it was a great shock to learn that Jos, in the prime of his life, recently died of a heart attack. During the two weeks in Kazan and also as we travelled through Russia together, Jos kept track of our walking steps each day, keeping our fitness up. I feel priviliged to have known him for a short time and know he will be missed greatly by many.

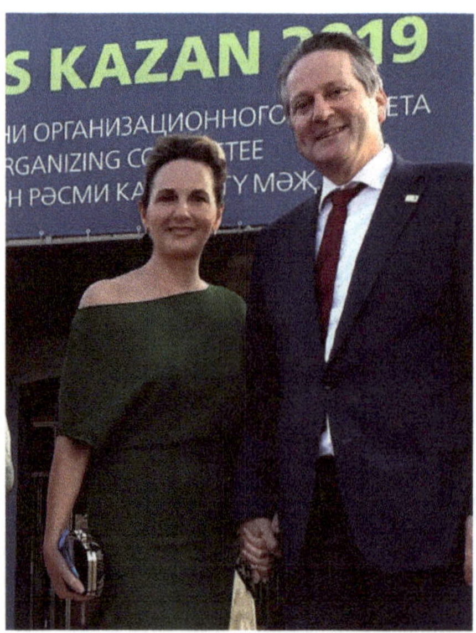

Anouschka and Jos de Goey

A NEW INTEREST

When Bob found he could not continue with his Honorary Research Fellowship, he suddenly approached me with the news that he wanted to learn cooking. He had never had the slightest interest before, so I was quite surprised. Although Bob can follow instructions of recipes, he had no basic understanding what some of the processes listed meant. For instance the instruction to cream the butter and sugar didn't make sense to him. So he had a few things to learn. Surprisingly he had an interest in baking and could make a delicious banana bread. He more or less stuck to a small range of recipes, mainly things he enjoyed eating. One of his favourties was a South Indian fish curry, which the family also grew to love. Nothing is more satisfying to a cook than having your efforts appreciated. Stuffed capsicums was another of his favourites.

Back in 2005, I had produced a cookbook, after various family members wanted to have a collection of the family favourites that the kids all grew up with. That edition, I printed myself using up all the ink in numerous sets of ink. I also took time to make many recipes and photograph the results for the book. Now that Bob was becoming a cook, I thought it time for a new edition with his recipes and recognising this was an important activity to him. And I also included some of other family members recipes. Now that I have a little publishing company, the edition is commercially printed. Bob and I did have some fun with cooking. Now family see the cover of the cookbook and can remember the good times eating some of Bob's favourite cooking.

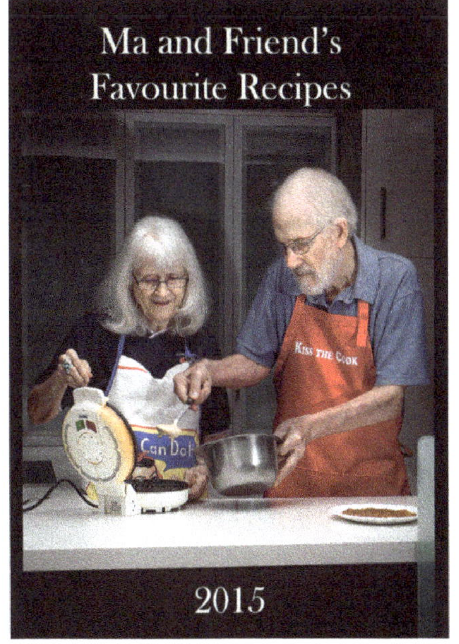

SOME OF THE FAMILY AND FRIENDS

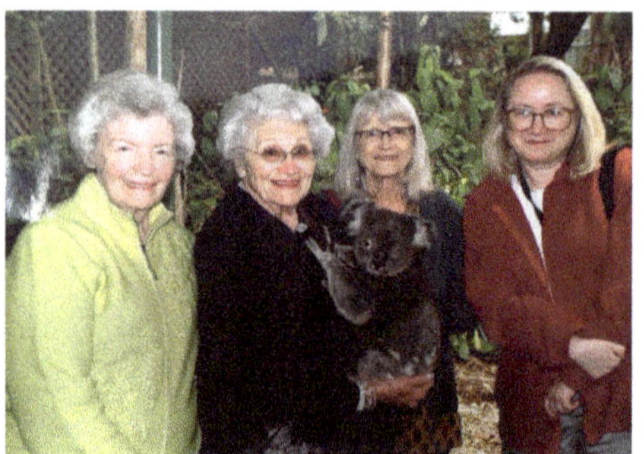
L-R Bernice, Marge, and Marcia McCowin

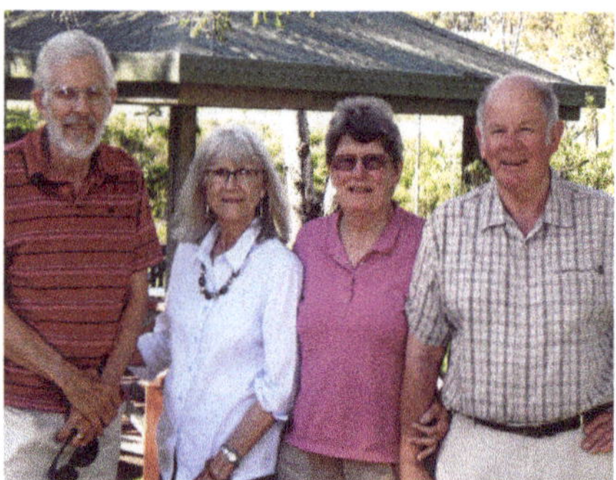
L-R Maureen and Peter Gillard

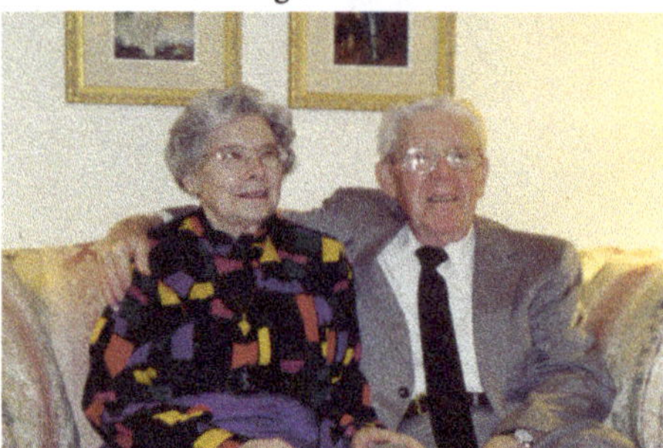
Betty and Willard McCown

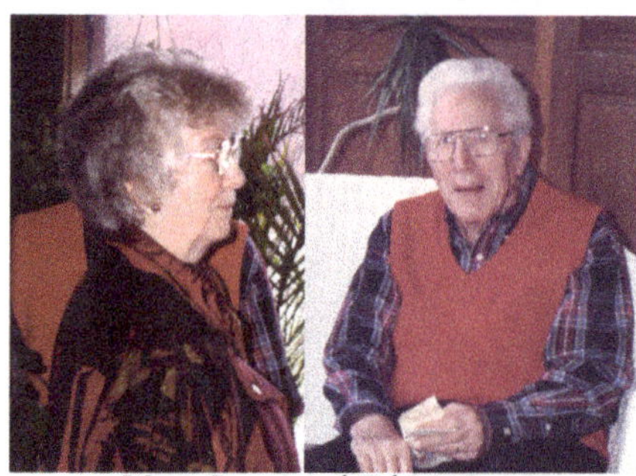
Mary Irene and Ed McCown

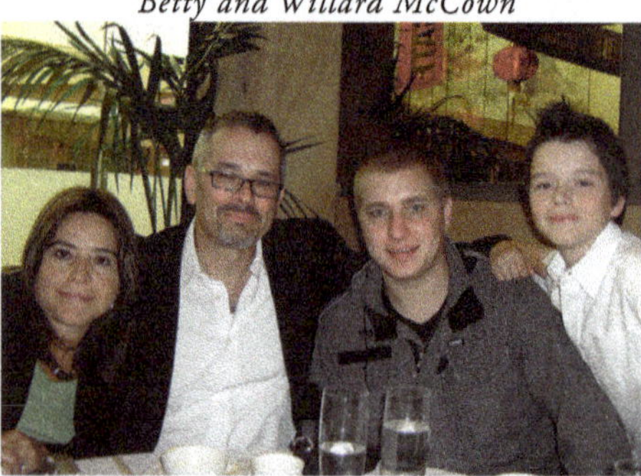
L-R Maria, JP, Sam (grandson) and Dani

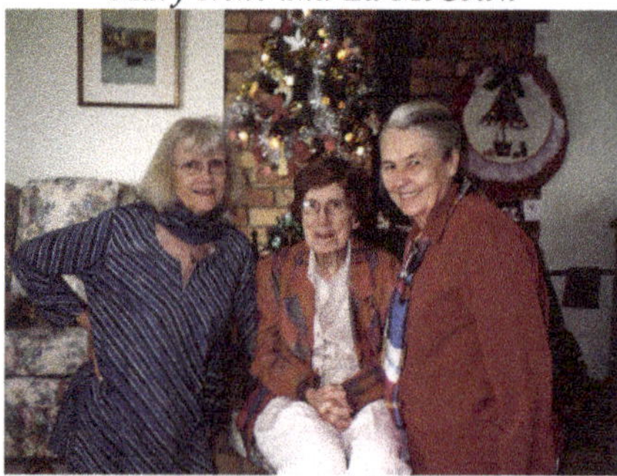
L-R Amy Casey and Jill Loughnan

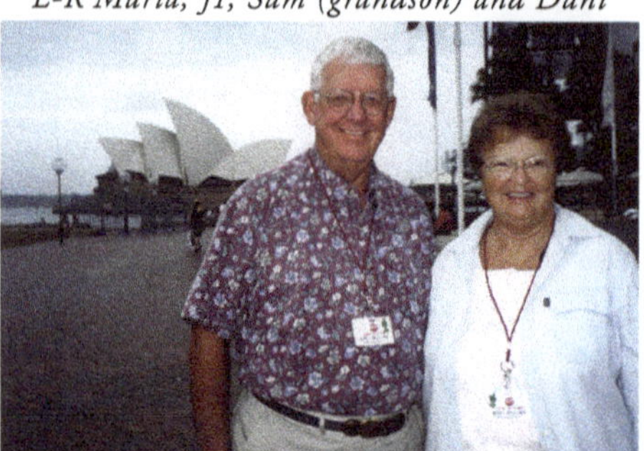
Gregg and Mary Mullins

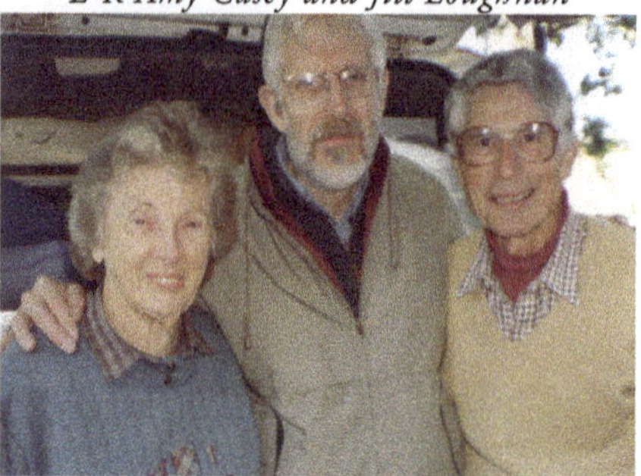
Maida and Wally Stern

WHO CAME TO VISIT

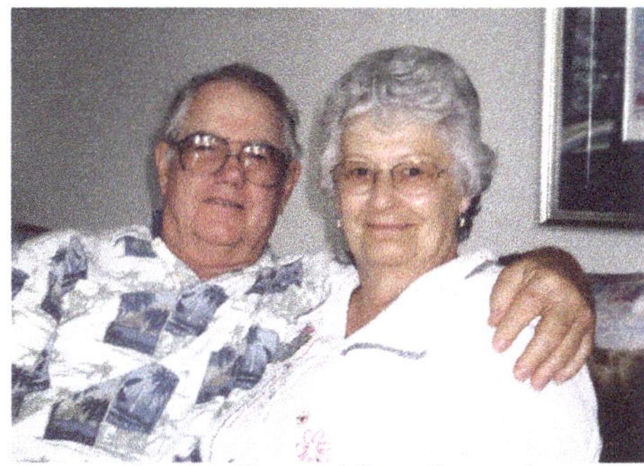
Cousins Bev and Don Fourcade

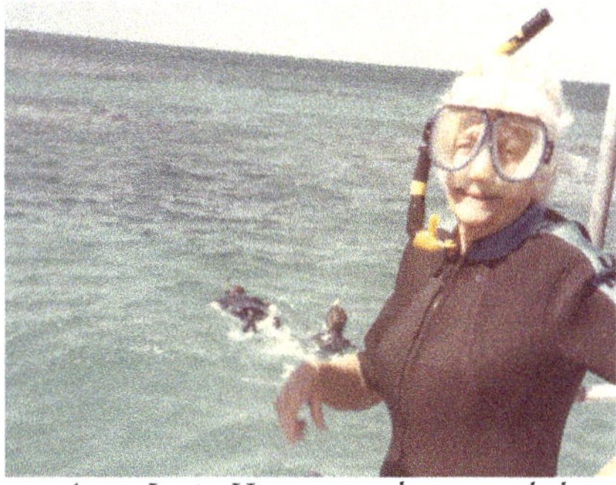
Aunt Jessie Hopper ready to snorkel

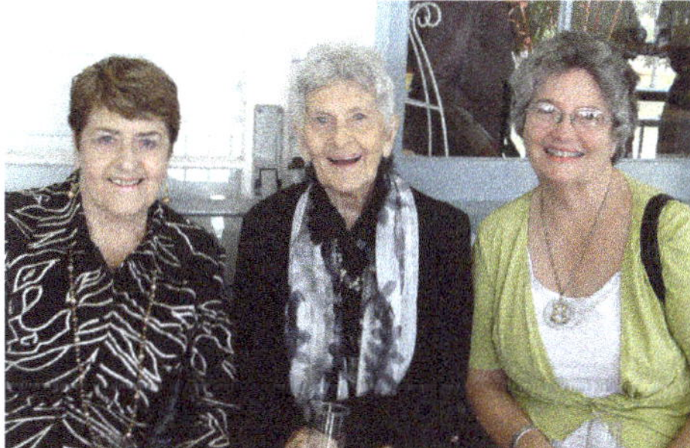
Berice, June and Judith

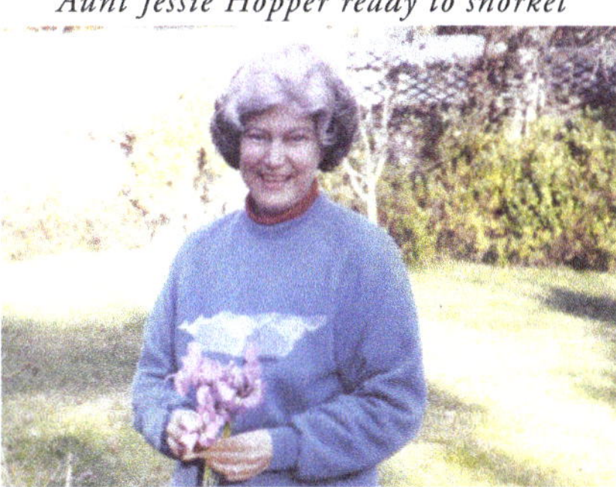
Joy Williams in Canberra

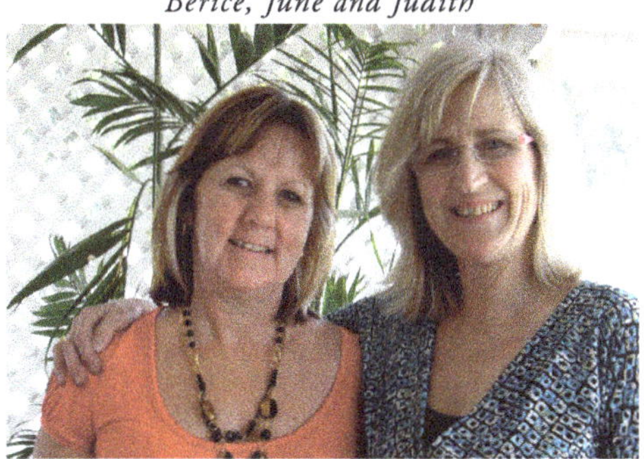
Barbara Crimston and Jenny

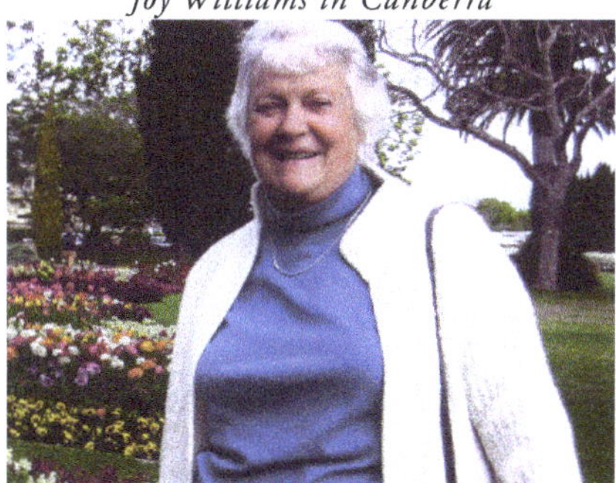
Sue Marshall from Pittsburgh

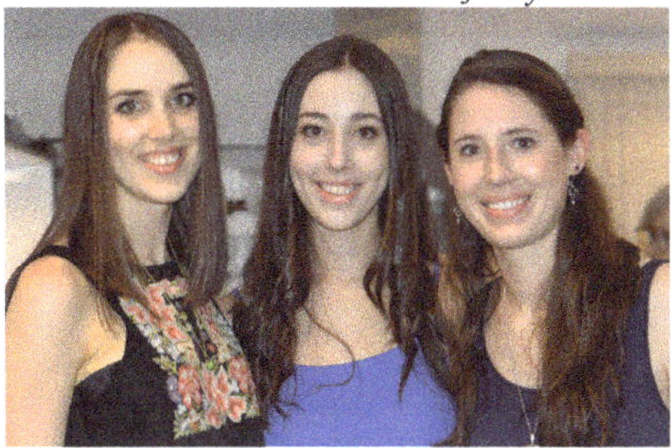
Maddie and Paris Hoey with Angela Parsons

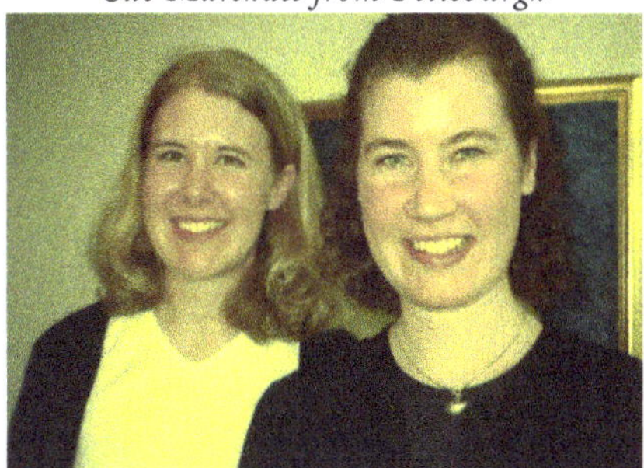
Karen and Lisen from Sweden

SOME FAVOURITES

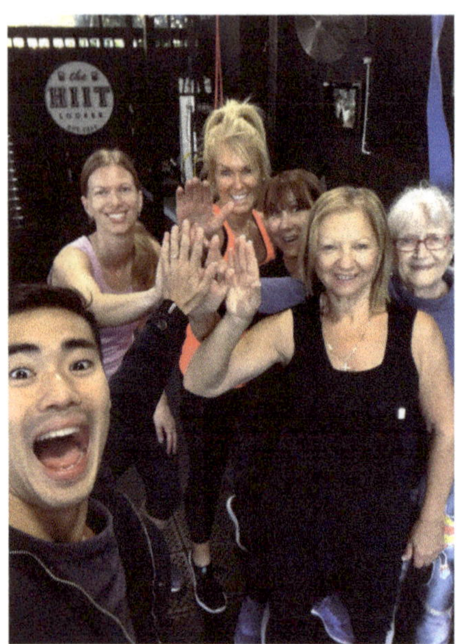

Good times at the gym with Zac

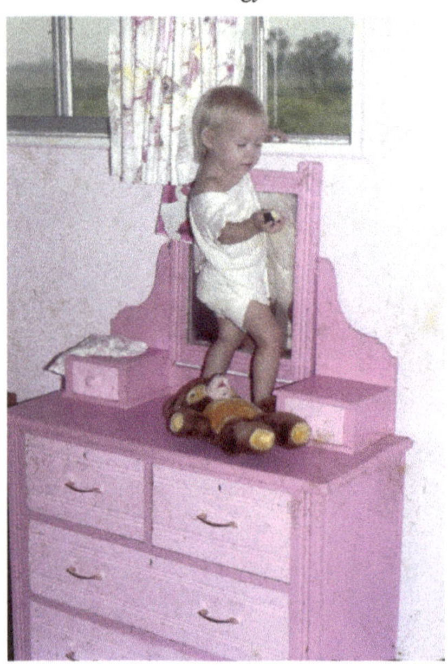

Jess still climbing

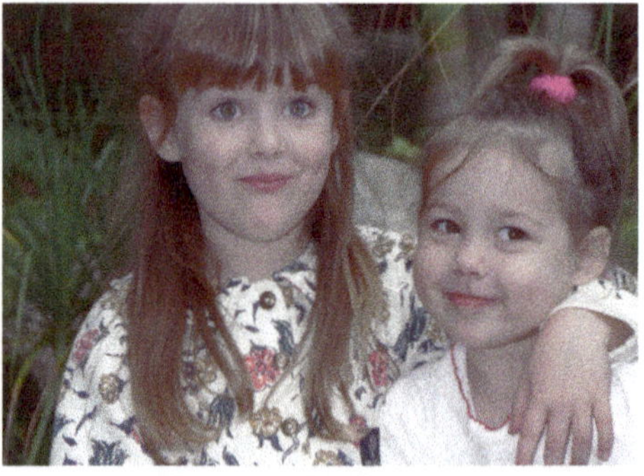

Little cuties Maddie and Paris

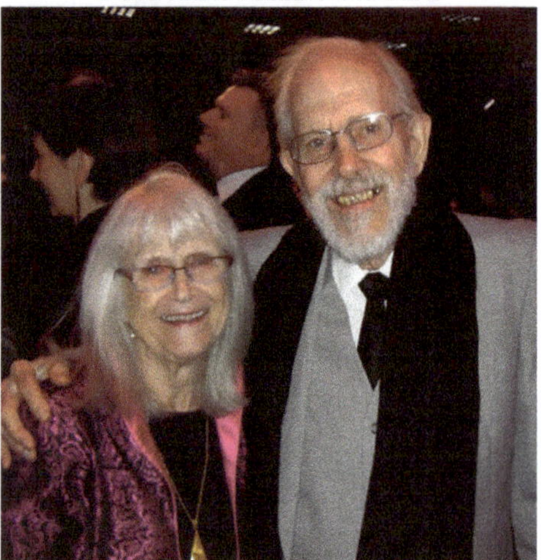

We attended the Romeo and Juliette Gala

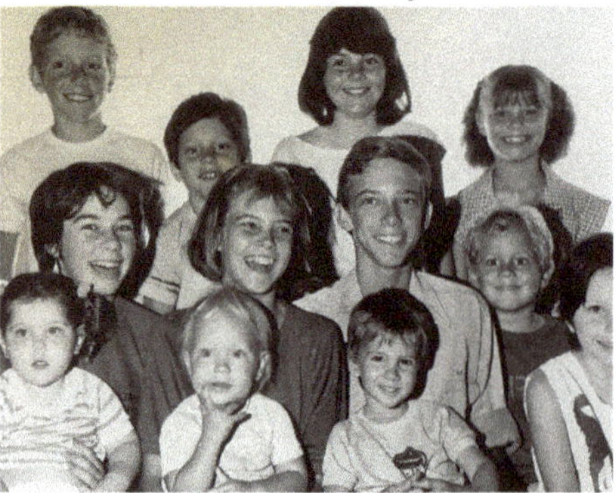

Framara Street Gang

MORE FAVOURITES

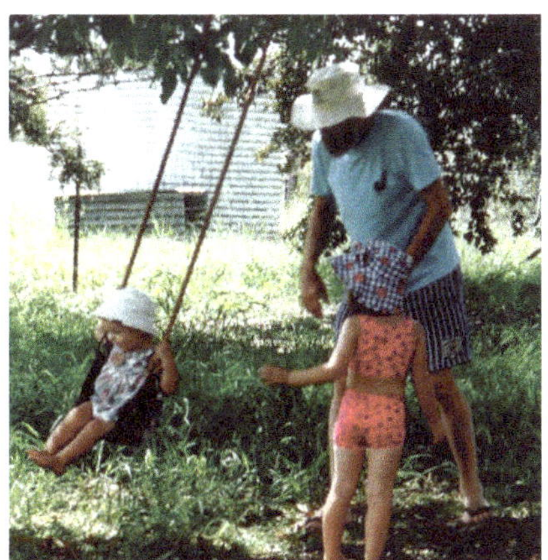

Swing time

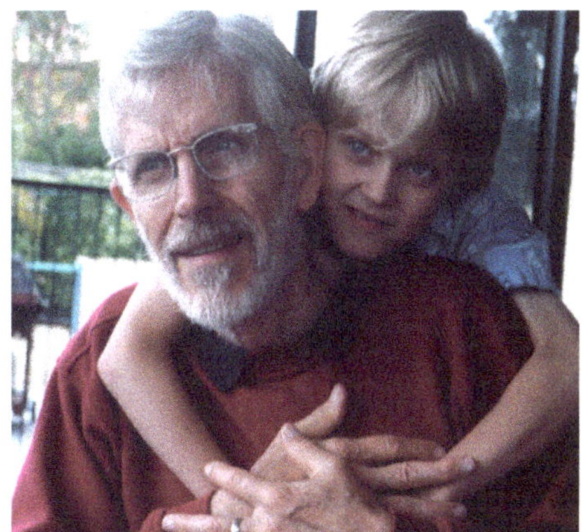

Conor giving Pa a hug

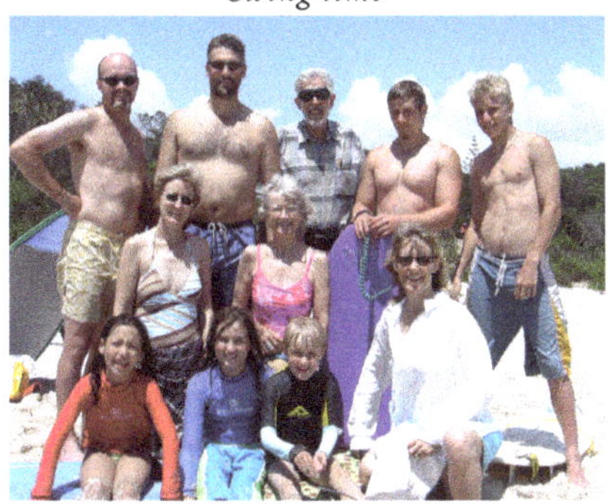

Byron Bay Christmas

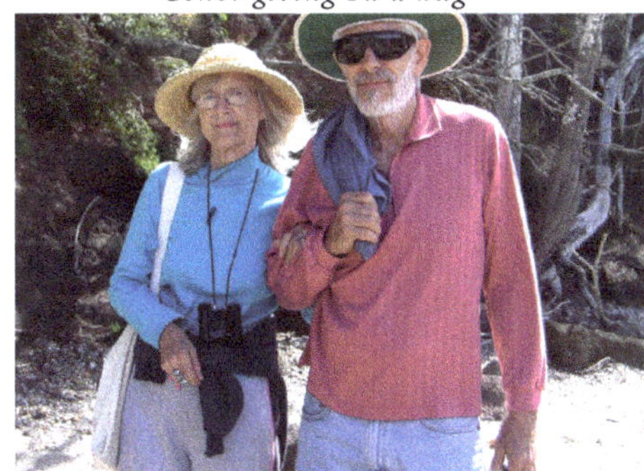

Mossy Point beach stroll

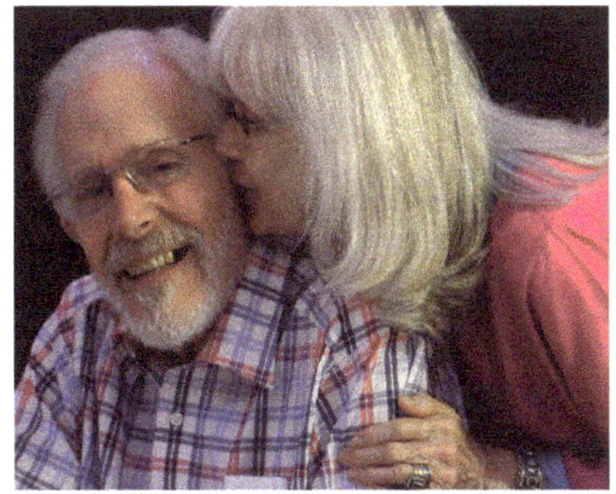

A little snuggle

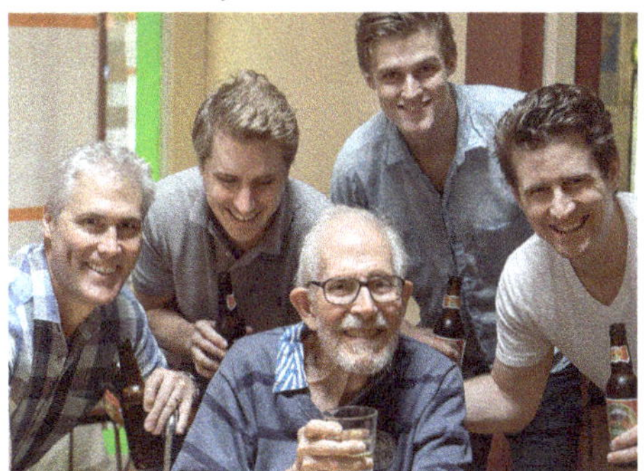

Bob's birthday outing with the guys

THE END

www.ingramcontent.com/pod-product-compliance
Lightning Source LLC
LaVergne TN
LVHW060932110826
845147LV00029B/749

9780648657941